PATTERNS
OF ENTREPRENE

SECOND EDITION

Jack M. Kaplan
Columbia Business School

Anthony C. Warren
Penn State University

WILEY John Wiley & Sons, Inc.

ASSOCIATE PUBLISHER	Judith Joseph
SENIOR ACQUISITIONS EDITOR	Jayme Heffler
ASSOCIATE EDITOR	Jennifer Conklin
EDITORIAL ASSISTANT	Carissa Marker
SENIOR PRODUCTION EDITOR	William A. Murray
MARKETING MANAGER	Frank Lyman
SENIOR DESIGNER	Kevin Murphy
COVER ART	©M. Kulka/zefa/Corbis
ILLUSTRATION COORDINATOR	Mary Alma
MEDIA EDITOR	Allison Morris

This book was set in Times New Roman by TechBooks and printed and bound by Von Hoffmann Press, Inc. The cover was printed by Von Hoffmann Press, Inc.

This book is printed on acid free paper. ∞

To order books or for customer service, please call 1-800-CALL WILEY (225-5945).

Library of Congress Cataloging in Publication Data:
Kaplan, Jack M.
      Patterns of entrepreneurship. – 2nd ed. / Jack M. Kaplan, Anthony C. Warren.
p. cm.
Includes bibliographical references and index.
ISBN-13   978-0-471-73750-6 (pbk.)
ISBN-10   0-471-73750-X (pbk.)
1. Entrepreneurship. I. Warren, Anthony C.   II. Title.
HB615.K366 2007
658.1′1—dc22

2006003342

Printed in the United States of America

10 9 8 7 6 5 4 3 2 1

PREFACE

Working in a corporation, or even a smaller business, does not prepare you for the challenges, long hours, social sacrifices, and financial commitment involved in being an entrepreneur. If you know that your future goal is to become an entrepreneur, how can you truly understand the rewards and pitfalls of this choice? How do you acquire the information and skills needed to support you in realizing your goal? This book hopes to provide just that—the necessary information you need to get you started as an entrepreneur, even in today's ultracompetitive and hostile business environment.

We have had the privilege of teaching entrepreneurship courses for over five years—Kaplan at Columbia Business School in New York and Warren at Penn State. During this time, students, alumni, investors, small companies, and business colleagues have sought our advice regarding the topic of entrepreneurship. Both of us, being entrepreneurs ourselves, have also had the opportunity to gain extensive experience. Professor Kaplan served as president of Datamark Technologies, a technology marketing company engaged in loyalty and electronic gift card programs, and Professor Warren was a founder of several companies and is now a venture capitalist. Thus, not only are we both in touch with the most recent academic research findings and best practices regarding entrepreneurship, but we have firsthand experience in starting and building companies and in advising other businesspeople on the concerns and trials facing entrepreneurs today. We hope to impart this experience, knowledge, and counsel directly to you through this book and its associated Web resources.

WHY THIS BOOK ON ENTREPRENEURSHIP

Patterns of Entrepreneurship, Second Edition supports an interactive learning experience that addresses the challenges, issues, and rewards faced by entrepreneurs in starting and growing a venture. The authors have spent many years both as entrepreneurs and teachers and passionately believe that entrepreneurial skills can only be acquired by actually confronting the problems that challenge every entrepreneur. This text, therefore, differs from others in that it challenges students with real situations and examples on which they can practice the broad range of skills required to start and build a company in today's complex world. Throughout this book you will find tips on how to become a successful entrepreneur, as well as issues to avoid. At the end of Chapter 1, you will have an opportunity to test your understanding of the chapter material by completing and answering a Personal Entrepreneurial Assessment on the Web site. The assessment is based on the roles and functions that entrepreneurs perform during the startup stage and on how capable you believe you are in performing each task. In addition, the Web projects and cases that accompany this book focus on the successes and failures of entrepreneurs and offer valuable business plan examples and assessment tools. Other outstanding features that the book offers are as follows:

1. *Focus on Real Entrepreneurs*. Throughout the text, we relate the material to real entrepreneurs, helping you understand how entrepreneurs position their companies to meet the various marketing, financial, and technological challenges.

2. *Finance Paths*. Every entrepreneur at some time needs to raise funds to grow their company. Many make fatal mistakes early on because they haven't clearly thought through the personal implications imposed by the source of these funds. The issues of control, lifestyle, risk tolerance, and ambition all determine this choice. This book is the first to delineate funding sources between closely held private businesses and high-growth equity funded companies and these are dealt with in two chapters on financing. Understanding these two mutually exclusive routes for their companies can save a lot of heartache for entrepreneurs and their supporters.

3. *Roadmap Actions*. Each chapter begins with a list of "roadmap" actions that lay out the practical tasks you will accomplish in the chapter.

4. *Case Studies*. Most chapters include a case study that looks at a potential entrepreneurial opportunity. Answering the Case Study Questions allows you to think critically about the various aspects of launching a business. Several case studies touch on important aspects of business such as setting up the management team, financing for early and growth ventures, and marketing ideas into viable business opportunities. Longer cases are housed on the Web site, which provides additional interactive cases.

5. *From Idea to Opportunity. Patterns of Entrepreneurship* is not merely a concept-oriented textbook. Through powerful examples, cases, and exercises students explore important "soft" issues such as how to continuously innovate, design sustainable business models, and create a culture in their companies that will increase their chances of success as they launch a new enterprise.

6. *Innovation and Technology Venture Framework. Patterns of Entrepreneurship* stresses the importance of innovation and technology. Throughout the book are sections devoted to creating a framework for screening ideas, thinking about strategy and business models, determining the capital and resources required, attracting management talent, and preparing the plan to ensure that practices are accepted and implemented effectively.

ORGANIZATION OF THE BOOK

This book is divided into four "roadmap" phases of entrepreneurship. Each chapter has been written to help you learn specific tasks that you need to complete and the deliverables that you need to produce. You can use the roadmaps located before each chapter to check off the tasks and deliverables as you perform them. Part One, "Starting the Venture," includes four chapters that establish the foundation for starting a venture, from developing ideas and business opportunities to preparing a winning business plan and setting up the company. The introductory Chapter 1 emphasizes the entrepreneurial process and the steps in becoming an entrepreneur and discusses why people become entrepreneurs and develop what is sometimes called the "entrepreneurial mindset." Chapter 2 discusses developing ideas and business opportunities in the early venture stage and conducting market research. Here you will also learn why innovation is important and techniques for you to become creative in developing new business ideas. Chapter 3 shows you how to analyze your market and potential customers and how to conduct a competitive analysis and create a marketing plan for the venture. Chapter 4 shows you how to set up and start the business with your first outline plan. You will also explore the various forms ventures may take and learn about name and company registration.

Part Two, "Sources of Financing," describes the many ways startup companies can access the resources they need, including funding at different stages of growth. Chapter 5 examines the methods entrepreneurs use to raise early-stage funding when their plan is to retain control of the company and remain a "lifestyle" business. These techniques, referred to as bootstrapping, are also important for entrepreneurs who later choose to grow a larger organization. Sources include friends, family, government grants, partners, and banks. Chapter 6 explains growth funding sources from "angel" investors and venture capitalists whereby the entrepreneur sells shares in his or her company where ultimate wealth may be traded with loss of control.

Part Three, "Implementation," concentrates on managing intellectual properties and developing business models for growth as the company matures. Chapter 7 explores the value of intellectual property and how to file patents, trademarks, and copyrights to build a competitive advantage in the marketplace. Chapter 8 describes how entrepreneurs continuously develop their business model for achieving rapid growth and maintaining high profits. This is accomplished through leadership to create an entrepreneurial culture.

Part Four, "Patterns of Entrepreneurship: Building and Exiting," examines the different alternatives for entrepreneurial businesses and exit strategies. Chapter 9 details the plan for managing money and the financial operations of the business, including preparing the annual budget, cash activity, breakeven analysis, and financial statements. Chapter 10 describes the exit strategies entrepreneurs may wish to consider, including selling the business, going public, or being acquired. Chapter 11 focuses on the business plan, which pulls together all of the concepts covered earlier in the book, and finally Chapter 12 will equip you with the skills you need to communicate your opportunity to different audiences whether customers, investors, bankers, or employees. No entrepreneur can be successful without the ability to communicate passion and drive to those who can help them reach their goals.

SUPPLEMENTS

For instructors, the Web site provides access to a test bank, a computerized test bank, PowerPoint presentations, sample cases and business plans, answers to end-of-chapter questions and financial and legal templates you will need to set up a business. The Web site can be accessed at www.wiley.com/college/kaplan.

The Web site gives students access to a variety of resources:

1. Additional case studies that allow students to review key entrepreneurial concepts.
2. Audiovisual presentations by entrepreneurs, venture capitalists, and successful students.
3. Sample business plans. These plans are divided according to market and stage of development. Downloadable plans are available for students.
4. Case summary reviews.

5. Downloadable legal documents. Students can download sample legal agreements, including stock and shareholder agreements, consulting contracts, and employee option plans, among others.

ABOUT THE AUTHORS

Jack M. Kaplan is an adjunct professor of Entrepreneurial Studies at Columbia Business School. He has taught the entrepreneurial courses for Launching New Ventures, The Business Plan, and The Entrepreneurial Manager. During his career, Mr. Kaplan started and managed three successful companies concentrating in smart card technology, health care information systems, and loyalty marketing programs. He is president of Datamark Technologies, Inc., an entrepreneurial business venture engaged in electronic gift card and loyalty marketing programs. Ceridian, a Fortune 500 company, acquired the company in November 2005.

Mr. Kaplan is the author of *Getting Started in Entrepreneurship* published by John Wiley & Sons in January 2001. His previous book, *Smart Cards: The Global Information Passport,* and articles have appeared in *Technology News* and *Crain's of New York.*

His professional seminar experience includes conducting courses for Fortune 500 companies. The list includes MIT Enterprise Forum, Aetna Insurance Company, Panasonic Global Sales Group, and Johnson & Johnson in New Product Strategies. He is judge for the Ernst & Young Entrepreneur of the Year® Award Program in New York, and has appeared on A&E Biographies, CNN, and CNBC. He is a graduate of the University of Colorado and received his MBA from the City University of New York.

Dr. Anthony C. Warren is the Farrell Professor of Entrepreneurship at the Smeal College of Business, Penn State University, named "the hottest school for entrepreneurship" by *Newsweek* magazine, and the recipient of the NASDAQ Center for Entrepreneurial Excellence Award in 2005. He leads educational programs in entrepreneurship at the undergraduate, graduate, and executive levels. Under grants from the Kauffman Foundation, Dr. Warren created unique courses in entrepreneurship based on problem-based learning, which have been recognized as being at the forefront of teaching methods by several national organizations. These courses are being introduced into colleges and high schools across the country.

Prior to joining Penn State, Dr. Warren started and grew several companies and is currently a venture partner in Adams Capital Management, a venture capital firm managing over $720 million. He consults regularly with both small and large companies on innovation management. A regular speaker at national conferences, Dr. Warren is often quoted in the press on innovation and entrepreneurship. He has authored several patents and research papers on technical and business issues and has contributed to many books. He has a B.Sc. and Ph.D. from the University of Birmingham.

ACKNOWLEDGMENTS

It has been a privilege for us to work with many inspiring colleagues and entrepreneurs to collect material for this book. We relied on the contributions of many people in the preparation of this book to discuss trends and ideas in the exciting field of entrepreneurship.

A number of entrepreneurs and executives have spoken to our classes about their experiences; their insights have helped shape this book. We would like to thank Tim and Nina Zagat, chairman and president of Zagat Surveys LLC, Liz Elting, president and CEO of Transperfect Translations, Paul Silvis, head coach of Restek Inc., Ted Graef, founder of Intuitive Controls, Bill Frezza, partner at Adams Capital Management, Thad Will, small-business loan officer with M&T Bank, Chris Hastings, head of the Private Equity Placements Group at Bear, Stearns & Co. Inc., Ed Marflak, CEO of Schoolwires, Inc., Rajeev Sharma, CEO of Advanced Interfaces Inc., and Craig Bandes, CEO of Global Secure Corporation.

Special thanks are due to Jeffery Barach, EMBA student at Columbia University, Murray Low, executive director of Eugene M. Lang Center for Entrepreneurship at Columbia Business School, Michael Farrell for his generous gifts and personal support for the entrepreneurship programs at Penn State, and the Kauffman Foundation for its continuing interest and funding of pedagogy research in entrepreneurship. We are indebted to the staff at John Wiley & Sons for their support including Susan J. Elbe, executive editor, Higher Education Division, Jayme Heffler, senior acquisitions editor, Marketing and Management, and Jennifer Conklin.

We would also like to thank the following colleagues and practitioners for helping to add a real-world perspective to this project:

Tom Byers	Stanford University
Robert F. Chelle	University of Dayton
Alex DeNoble	San Diego State University
Sanford B. Ehrlich	San Diego State University
Dr. Raghu Garud	Penn State University
Ralph Hanke	Bowling Green University
Liz Kisenwether	Penn State University
Rita McGrath	Columbia University
Dr. Paul Magelli	University of Illinois
Robert Myers, Ph.D.	Fairfield Resource International
Clifford Schorer	Columbia University
Dr. Michael Treat	Columbia University

Our personal thanks also go to the diligent research and support of many of our students. Particular mention is due to Anupam Jaiswal and Supreet Saini at Penn State and to Anna Mary Loope, administrative assistant at the Farrell Center, PSU, who managed to keep us all on track.

LIST OF CASES

CHAPTER	NAME	ROADMAP TOPICS
2	Greif Packaging	Listening to Customers, Services around Products
2	Blyth Candles	Incremental Innovation
2	SmartPak, Inc	Opportunity Recognition, Market Analysis
2	NetFlix, Inc.	"Points of Pain," Disruptive Innovation
2	SuperFast Pizza	Thinking Big, Analysis of Existing Companies' Weaknesses
2	Intuitive Controls	Opportunity Recognition, Perseverance
2	Starion Instruments	Opportunity Recognition, Market Analysis, Competitive Position
3	Smart Card LLC	Market Assessment, Technology Evaluation
4	D-Marc Technologies	Assessment of the Organizational Structure, Management Team, Products and Services
5	Dyson	Bootstrapping, Perseverance, Corporate Innovation
5	Chasteen	Bootstrapping and Contingent Litigation
5	Intrasphere	Friends and Family Financing
5	hIDe: Protecting Consumer Privacy	Early Stage Funding, Market and Team Assessment
6	CoreTek Inc.	SBIR and VC financing
7	Datamark, Inc.	Patent Claims
8	Dell, Inc.	Business Models, Supply Chain
8	DBI Services Corp.	Service Innovation
8	General Fasteners	Services and Customer Lock-In
8	ChemStation, Inc.	Data and Innovation, Franchising

CONTENTS

PART ONE

STARTING THE VENTURE

Part One, "Starting the Venture," includes four chapters that establish the foundations of entrepreneurship, from developing ideas and business opportunities to setting up the company. Chapter 1 describes the initial process of planning, organizing, operating, and assuming the risk of an entrepreneurial venture. Chapter 2 introduces the art of innovation for developing ideas and business opportunities in the early venture stage. It also discusses how to conduct market research. Chapter 3 discusses how to analyze the market and customers and how to create a competitive analysis and marketing plan for the venture. Chapter 4 explores how to set up the venture, including name and company registration, employee agreements, and stock option and incentive plans.

CHAPTER 1

THE ENTREPRENEURIAL PROCESS

"Education is not filling a bucket, but lighting a fire."

WILLIAM KEATS

OBJECTIVES

- Describe the five stages in the entrepreneurial process from opportunity analysis to scaling the venture.
- Understand why persons become entrepreneurs.
- Identify the different types of entrepreneurs.
- Define the growth issues for entrepreneurial companies.
- Understand the entrepreneurial mindset and commonly shared characteristics.
- Explore your own style.

CHAPTER OUTLINE

INTRODUCTION

No sector of the economy is as vital, dynamic, and creative as entrepreneurship. For the past 30 years, the impact of entrepreneurs and small-business owners in the creation of new ventures has been felt in every sector of the United States and in virtually all the world's mature economies. The startling growth of entrepreneurial ventures forms the heart of our changing economic system, as more employees work for these owners than any other sector of the economy. In the United States today, the number of employees in small and entrepreneurial ventures is growing faster than in any other sector of the labor force, and there is no sign of a reversal in this trend. The Global Entrepreneurship Monitor states that as much as one-third of the differences in economic growth among nations may be due to differences in entrepreneurial activity. A key factor affecting the U.S. economy is the annual creation of 600,000 to 800,000 new companies, which produces many new jobs.[1]

Entrepreneurship—the process of planning, organizing, operating, and assuming the risk of a business venture—is now a mainstream activity. Starting a business is never easy; it requires a special blend of courage, self-confidence, and skills, all of which determine the success or failure of an enterprise. However, a world of resources is now available to individuals who wish to launch ventures. The Internet provides access to up-to-date market and technology information and offers would-be entrepreneurs many useful support networks. In addition, business schools even *teach* the fundamentals of entrepreneurship, which were not even part of the curriculum until the 1990s.[2]

Although all entrepreneurs start new businesses, not all new startups are entrepreneurial. In this chapter, you'll learn to appreciate entrepreneurship as a process, understand the distinctions between starting a small business and being entrepreneurial, and meet some entrepreneurial role models that you may wish to emulate as you develop your own path to success. As you'll learn in this chapter, the path you take will depend on many factors. The economic climate, events in your personal life, your choice of lifestyle, ambition, luck, and accumulated experience gained through working for someone else are all factors that come to play in the entrepreneurship process.

Throughout this text, you'll read about entrepreneurs from many types of entrepreneurial businesses. Their stories will help you explore possible paths for building your own successful career. You'll also have the opportunity to assess your present career profile and strategy and contrast it with the approaches these entrepreneurs have developed. The career choices and paths you take are deeply embedded not only in relationships, but also in individual characteristics and valued outcomes. The course you follow will be based on a collected set of skills, knowledge, abilities, and experiences, as well as the recognition of unique opportunities.

AN ENTREPRENEURIAL PROFILE

Rebecca Smith is one of the most sought-after speakers in the United States. She was featured at the Working Woman's Summit of the most successful women entrepreneurs in 2001 and was a past winner of Ernst & Young's Entrepreneur of the Year and the Tampa Chamber of Commerce Small Business Award. She provides a model for a systematically programmed approach to building a successful entrepreneurial career. Smith began dreaming of starting a business of her own when she was a young child helping her father on home projects and watching him prepare engineering drawings in the evenings. Her fascination with the technical world of architecture and construction led to an early house design that won her a prize. However, it would be many years before she would step out of the corporate architecture world to launch her own business venture.

Smith earned her B.A. degree in architecture and her M.S. degree in building construction. After working for others, and with a small initial loan from her father and a lot of practical applied experience, she opened her own firm at age 29. Her business was not an overnight success, however. Smith's first priority was to be successful enough to pay back her father within the first year, which she did. Like many entrepreneurs, she learned what it was to struggle—a common denominator that links all business owners. Early on it was difficult for Smith not to compare her experience as a relatively new business owner to her previous work in a corporate environment. "When I was working for another company, I was building huge multimillion-dollar public-use facilities with costs exceeding $30 million," Smith recalls. "When I started my own business, for lack of capital, I was building anything short of a doghouse that rolled in." Today she is a Class-A Certified General Contractor and the founder and president of A. D. Morgan Corporation, a commercial general construction company with offices in Tampa and Melbourne, Florida.

Smith's path to becoming a successful entrepreneur followed a series of stages: obtaining a strong educational background, acquiring corporate experience and skill, and using a supportive network to launch her own business. Her approach was one of many that can lead to success, but each requires identifying an opportunity, extending a vision by careful strategic planning, being capable of doing even the most miniscule task, and having the will to persevere when times are rough.

AN ENTREPRENEURIAL PERSPECTIVE

The word *entrepreneur* comes from the seventeenth-century French word *entreprendre*, which refers to individuals who "undertook" the risk of new enterprise. Early entrepreneurs were also "contractors" who bore the risks of profit or loss, and many were soldiers of fortune, adventurers, builders, and merchants. Early references to the *entreprendeur* spoke of tax contractors—individuals who paid a fixed sum of money to a government for the license to collect taxes in their region. Tax entrepreneurs bore the risk of collecting individual taxes. If they collected more than the sum paid for their licenses, they made a profit; if not, they lost money.

Today, the definition of entrepreneurship includes more than the mere creation of a business; it also includes the generation and implementation of an idea. Understanding this team concept is critical if you wish to be a successful entrepreneur. The idea of a sole individual being able to take on enormous risks, attempt innovations, leap without the appropriate background research, and succeed by working long hours and persevering at all costs is no longer relevant in today's global economy. Entrepreneurs also communicate effectively, not only to their teams, but also to external "stakeholders" such as investors, bankers, and corporate partners, which are necessary components of their growth path.

HOW THIS BOOK IS DIFFERENT FROM OTHER TEXTBOOKS

Patterns of Entrepreneurship is different from other books on entrepreneurship in four key ways.

1. This book provides a practical, detailed roadmap that defines the entrepreneurial strategic process and the skills you need for real-world business practices.
2. As authors, we have both practical and academic backgrounds. We have distilled our experiences gained from launching many successful ventures into relevant tips, issues to consider, and solutions that are distributed throughout the book.
3. This book includes special chapters on topics that are only recently emerging as especially important for entrepreneurs in today's rapidly changing world. They include subjects such as the art of innovation, evaluation of intellectual property, creative business models, and ways to communicate to different stakeholders.

4. This book offers you an interactive learning experience that addresses the challenges, issues, and rewards faced by entrepreneurs as they start a venture. Extensive Web-based projects and cases focus on the strategic implications of the successes and failures of entrepreneurs, strategic goal setting, as well as business plan examples, tools, and future expectations. It is our firm belief that entrepreneurship skills can only be learned by interacting with real cases and experiencing first hand what it is like to be an entrepreneur.

Therefore, the Web-based portion of the book includes:

- **Personal Entrepreneurial Skills Assessment.** You will test your understanding of entrepreneurship by completing a Personal Entrepreneurial Skill Assessment on the Web site. This assessment will help you determine how capable you believe you are in performing entrepreneurial tasks and how interested you are in starting a business.[3]
- **Interviews and Insights.** You can click on links that will download entrepreneurs' insights into various aspects of entrepreneurship and examples of an "elevator pitch" and full investors' presentations.
- **Self-Assessment Exercises.** These include short essay questions that require you to think deeply about entrepreneurship, techniques, and processes.
- **Downloadable Documents.** You can download class PowerPoint presentations, sample legal agreements, and business plans.

The Structure of the Book: Mastering the Essentials of the Entrepreneurial Process

Entrepreneurs can increase their chances of success if they understand, follow, and implement the basic five-stage entrepreneurial process described in this section. These five stages, summarized in Figure 1-1, form the backbone of the entrepreneurial process. Each of the key stages includes a main focus activity, discusses tactics for completing tasks, and identifies the estimated amount of time required for each stage. Costs are also provided for each activity, which can be used to plan budgets. We'll also analyze the risks inherent in each stage and make suggestions for reducing potential problems.

Stage 1: Conducting Opportunity Analysis

The basic objective of this stage is to define the criteria that would make a business opportunity worthwhile. In this stage, the founder identifies the opportunity and creates a *vision for the company*. If there is no vision for the venture, the new idea is just a dream. Chapter 2 discusses the role of innovation in the economy and how entrepreneurs can learn to innovate new business concepts, as well as how you screen these business ideas and opportunities. We'll also discuss various techniques that are used to evaluate the different categories of opportunities. Specifically, we'll look at:

- Evaluating business ideas (determining the idea's value and relevant factors, as discussed in Chapter 2)
- Protecting the idea (screening questions for patent protection and using a mutual nondisclosure agreement)

Stage 1 **Conducting Opportunity Analysis** **(Chapters 2 and 3)**	• Innovate and create the vision • Conduct market analysis and research • Evaluate the competition • Research pricing and sales strategies
Stage 2 **Developing the Plan and Setting** **up the Company** **(Chapter 4)**	• Set goals and objectives • Start writing the plan • Investigate new processes and technologies • Determine pricing, market and distribution channels
Stage 3 **Acquiring Financial Partners/Sources** **of Funding** **(Chapters 5 and 6)**	• "Bootstrap" the company • Secure early-stage funding • Secure growth funding
Stage 4 **Determining the Resources Required** **and Implementing the Plan** **(Chapters 7, 8, and 9)**	• Determine value of licenses, patents, and copyrights • Prepare the organization for growth • Develop a business model to maximize value retention • Manage the finances

Stage 5
Scaling and Harvesting the Venture
(Chapters 10, 11, and 12)
	• Prepare a full business plan
	• Discuss options and alternatives
	  - Sell or merge
	  - Go public
	  - Form a strategic alliance
	• Communicate the opportunity

Figure 1-1   **The Five-Stage Entrepreneurial Process.**

- Building the vision and conducting market analysis to sustain a competitive advantage and learning how to "think big"
- Preparing a competitive analysis (as described in Chapter 3)

This stage usually takes at least a year because it details the pricing and sales strategies required. For example, Bill Gates and Paul Allen were in college when they saw a computer on the cover of *Popular Mechanics* magazine, which set their plan in motion. It took them over two years to complete the business planning process that led to the creation of Microsoft, an undeniably successful venture.

Stage 2: Developing the Plan and Setting Up the Company

In this stage, ideas are discarded and strategies are documented and converted to an outline business plan. The focus at this stage is not on producing a fully fledged business plan, but at least on documenting the main concepts for the company and the route planned for its growth. A full business plan is a vital, yet dynamic, document for the company; however, rarely, if ever, does a newly formed company precisely follow its original plan. In addition, any plan must be tailored for the audience for which it is intended. For example, when raising money from investors or banks, one version might be required; when selling the company either to another corporation or to the public, other versions are needed; and, of course, a plan is needed to guide your management team as the company grows. Because the business plan is such a vital tool for the entrepreneur we have devoted a full chapter just on this topic (Chapter 11).

Chapter 3 describes how to undertake competitive analyses, determine marketing strategies, and develop a pricing scheme for your products or services.

Chapter 4 describes how many entrepreneurs dedicate much thought and planning to starting their businesses and determining the structure of the company. Others establish their companies without much regard to how the business should be structured. Regardless of the amount of forethought, one of the most important decisions to make is how to legally structure a business. The legal form of the business proprietorship—C-Corporation, S-Corporation, partnership, and Limited Liability Company (LLC)—should be determined in light of the business's short- and long-term needs. We'll examine the pros and cons of each of these business structures as well as how to prepare a checklist to start a business.

Stage 3: Acquiring Financial Partners/Sources of Funding

Armed with a well-conceived plan, the next challenge is to focus on acquiring financial investors and partners. In most cases, entrepreneurs may not be aware of the many financing options available that would best meet the needs of the business. Therefore, it is important to know the expectations and requirements of various sources of funds.

The two chapters in this section each deal with two fundamentally different types of companies. Chapter 5 focuses entirely on funding a closely-held company in which the founder(s) wish to remain fully in control of their company. Control restricts the company from certain sources of money, and the entrepreneur must creatively "bootstrap" the company in order not to give up any ownership position to outsiders. Bootstrapping is a vital skill for all entrepreneurs; therefore, this chapter is also valuable even if the intention is to seek outside owners by selling "equity" or shares in the company. This form of financing is discussed in detail in Chapter 6.

Early-stage funding sources include self-funding, family and friends, "angels", banks, and government sources. We'll discuss these and other options used to raise capital in both chapters. Each potential source has certain criteria for providing financing, and these criteria are the focus of this stage. To increase chances of success, we'll specify what sources are available for early-stage funding and discuss the requirements of financial partners. Chapter 6 also discusses the sources for growth funding. We'll look at using private placements, attracting venture capital, and securing sources of debt financing, as well as examples of valuation of deals. The chapter describes the different valuation methods and how much of the company to sell, at what price, and for what percentage of the deal. We'll also explain the risks involved in financing in terms of timing and the emotional stress and patience required.

Stage 4: Determining the Resources Required and Implementing the Plan

Chapter 7 explores the value of intellectual property and how to file patents, trademarks, and copyrights to gain a competitive advantage in the marketplace. The chapter provides an explanation of these forms of intellectual property (IP) and guides you toward effectively developing, protecting, and promoting your own IP.

Chapter 8 deals with an emerging and important issue that all entrepreneurs must tackle, namely, the creation of a business model or framework that enables the new company to retain the value of its efforts and not have them quickly eroded by competition such that profits rapidly decline. Using a number of stimulating examples, we illustrate how it is possible to apply innovation to the overall business, not just to new products or services, and how to create a sustainable, highly profitable

"Don't give up. Don't ever give up. And when things look worst, just don't give up."

RICHARD FOREMAN
Former President & CEO—Register.com

business that will retain its value and be an attractive opportunity for investors and, eventually, purchasers. In this chapter, we show how the Internet can be used to build value and how information on customers' behaviors can be mined to build barriers to competitors.

Entrepreneurs are asked to plan operations and evaluate decisions using financial accounting information. An understanding of managing financial operations will contribute to the success of the entrepreneurial business. Chapter 9 thus discusses financial statements, how to analyze these statements, and how to prepare budgets, ratios, and cash flow forecasts.

Stage 5: Scaling and Harvesting the Venture

Chapter 10 highlights the methodology, procedures, and options available for entrepreneurs to scale the venture or consider an exit strategy. We'll discuss how to sell an equity stake to a partner, sell the business, merge with another company, and implement a leveraged buyout. We'll also discuss planning for a public offering that offers an option to sell a portion of the venture and scale the business for growth. The objective of this chapter is to help entrepreneurs identify the best exit plan and be in a strong position to manage the process.

Chapter 11 covers all aspects of the business plan. The plan pulls together all the topics covered in the earlier sections of the book. As we mentioned earlier, the plan is only valid on the day that it is completed, and it must be continually updated as you learn more about your business, its customers, and competitors. Also, when seeking funding, selecting partners, or selling your company, the plan must be tailored for the targeted audience.

Finally, Chapter 12 provides you with a vital skill that all entrepreneurs need, namely, how to communicate their opportunity concisely and compellingly to new employees, investors, partners, and customers. No idea has any value unless others understand its potential, become excited about being involved, and are willing to participate enthusiastically in the venture. Here you will learn about the different forms of communications, how to prepare for a presentation, and what is expected at each stage of relationship development.

WHY BECOME AN ENTREPRENEUR?

People become entrepreneurs for many reasons. Some people are attracted to the perceived independence and freedom from the politics and restrictions of corporate America. Being able "to do your own thing," make your own decisions, and exert greater control over your working environment are attractive alternatives to the conformity—real or imagined—associated with life in a big company. Some may hit a plateau, see that they are blocked from further promotions, or recognize that they are not progressing as rapidly as they would like, and so these conditions become motivating factors. Other people believe that building a company can provide them with opportunities for sustained growth and mobility. For others, starting their own company provides them with the flexibility they seek in their lives. And, of course, for many, entrepreneurship offers a vehicle for creating huge financial rewards.

ENTREPRENEURSHIP: A LIFETIME CHOICE?

Until recently, people tended to think of the world of work in distinct categories. Most people either worked in someone else's business or in their own. The distinction between being an employee and being an entrepreneur was clear. The exceptions were those who worked inside an organization and created an entrepreneurial environment.

The rapid changes in the economy over the past two decades have blurred the lines between traditional employment and entrepreneurship. What counts now are portable skills and knowledge, meaningful work, on-the-job learning, and the ability to build effective networks and contacts, whether through teams or the Internet. Many people now follow less predictable, and even zigzagging, career paths. The distinction between managing your own operations and working for others has become blurred. Owning your own business may be a lifetime pursuit or just one part of your career.[4] Some people, called *serial entrepreneurs*, start, grow, and sell several businesses over the course of their careers. In any case, to be successful, you must develop the appropriate skill sets, strategic plans, and management team to enhance your possibilities of survival.

There are several different approaches to identifying entrepreneurial types. "Approaches to the types of entrepreneurship vary across a wide spectrum," states Ray Smilor, president of the Foundation for Enterprise Development and formerly vice president of the Kauffman Center for Entrepreneurial Leadership. His book, *Daring Visionaries*, recognizes three kinds of entrepreneurs: aspiring, lifestyle, and growth entrepreneurs.[5]

1. *Aspiring entrepreneurs* dream of starting a business; they hope for the chance to be their own bosses, but they have not yet made the leap from their current employment into the uncertainty of a startup. Findings by the Entrepreneurial Research Consortium, a public and privately sponsored research effort directed by Dr. Paul Reynolds at Babson College in Boston, indicate that at any given time, 7 million adults are trying to start businesses in the United States.

2. *Lifestyle entrepreneurs* have developed an enterprise that fits their individual circumstances and style of life. Their basic intention is to earn an income for themselves and their families. Lifestyle entrepreneurs, sometimes referred to as "small businesses" or "mom-and-pop shops," develop ventures that are essential to a community's well-being. More than 13 million Americans—25 million if you count part-time entrepreneurs—are now running their own businesses from home. Roughly half of these home-based businesses are service firms, from consulting practices to graphic design firms. The rest are sales (17 percent), technical and administrative support (15 percent), repair service (11 percent), and the arts (5 percent).[6]

3. *Growth entrepreneurs* have both the desire and ability to grow as fast and as large as possible. These firms are the most dynamic job generators in the American economy. The "gazelles" of this entrepreneurial group, as David Birch at Cognetics, Inc., in Cambridge, Massachusetts, calls them, are increasing. By his reckoning, in the United States there are over 300,000 entrepreneurial companies with more than 50 employees that are growing at a rate of more than 20 percent per year. The 2,100 members of the Entrepreneur of the Year Institute had revenues of $155 billion and employment of over 1.3 million while growing collectively at an estimated rate of 150,000 jobs per year.[7]

One of the major mistakes aspiring entrepreneurs make when starting out is NOT to closely question what they want to be "when they grow up." Choosing the path of a lifestyle company creates certain advantages and disadvantages that must be carefully considered. If the goal is to employ maybe 20 or 30 people, to create a comfortable lifestyle for yourself and family members, and to retain control of the company, then the lifestyle path is for you. However, this imposes certain limitations on how you can fund the company. This path eliminates the possibility of selling part of the company for cash to pay for growth. A lifestyle company will not provide a way for investors to get a return on their investment through the sale of their ownership position in the company. Not being honest with yourself at an early stage about the control and lifestyle issues will lead to serious and unpleasant conflicts with investors if you take money from them and do not provide them a way to "exit" their investment.

Growth entrepreneurs, on the other hand, are much less driven by control or lifestyle. They recognize that to grow quickly they will have to sell part of their company to raise cash. These investors will apply various levels of control. The aspirations of the founder and the investors are aligned; they both want to build a valuable company and then sell it either to an established company or to the public via an IPO (initial public offering). The entrepreneur is willing to trade control for growth and wealth creation.

There is a third route however—a lifestyle company that manages to grow fairly rapidly without taking in outside investors. These companies are a hybrid between the lifestyle company and the high-growth equity-financed company. We call these "growth bootstrapped" companies. In most cases, entrepreneurs do not plan it this way. They may start off as a lifestyle company and find that they can generate enough interest for their products or services that they can grow using the cash that they generate from sales. Or they may be in a place where there is little or no access to equity funds, or their business does not match the industry knowledge and interests of investors.

It is important for you to think carefully as you decide whether control and lifestyle are what drive you, or whether it is growth, visibility, wealth, or perhaps fame that fuels your ambition. Moving between these two different paths is so difficult that we devote two chapters (5 and 6) which explore the financing methods for each path.

PROFILE: PAUL SILVIS, HEAD COACH AND FOUNDER OF RESTEK CORPORATION

Before founding Restek in 1985, Paul Silvis worked at Supelco, Inc. as supervisor of the capillary research group and for the federal government's Mining and Safety Enforcement Agency. He received a B.S. in Chemistry/Life Science from the University of Pittsburgh in 1977 and later took chemical engineering courses at Penn State. Not satisfied with just working for a company, Paul decided that he had some ideas for a new business. He took the plunge in 1985 and started Restek Corporation in the Ben Franklin Matternville incubator. At the outset, Paul had a modest target of reaching $3 million in sales in five years. However, the company continually innovated new products and was able to finance its growth from the retained funds from sales of products. During this time, Paul retained control of the company. Perhaps taking in outside investors may have helped the company grow faster, but Paul chose to run a "bootstrapped" closely held company. Restek (www.restek.com) is now a leading manufacturer of chromatography laboratory supplies, with annual sales of over $30 million and offices and distribution centers in over 60 countries.

Paul's title, head coach, rather than president or CEO, more closely defines his role in the company. "The head coach puts the right players in the right positions; provides training, tools, and opportunities for them to become star players; encourages an atmosphere of support and honesty; helps to define the team's strategy for

"As professors of entrepreneurship, we are often asked if it is possible to 'teach' someone to be an entrepreneur. My response is that you can't teach someone to acquire the drive, the hunger, the passion, and the tenacity to pursue an entrepreneurial path. However, give me someone who has such 'fire in their belly' and we can help them to develop critical entrepreneurial skills which will guide them along their journey."

ALEX DENOBLE
Professor of Management and Director of Academic Entrepreneurship Program, San Diego State University Entrepreneurial Management Center

winning—all for the sake of creating a championship team of which each member can be proud!" Beginning with an idea and a rather small target for sales, Restek has migrated to a successful highly innovative growth company. It has grown every year since its formation and has always been profitable. The company did not have to sell an ownership position to grow. Here is Paul's view on running an entrepreneurial company:

> *Embracing problems and overcoming insurmountable obstacles is the key to any successful individual or venture. Envision "problems" like a track and field event, in which the athlete who jumps hurdles faster than the competitor wins the race. It is not the number or magnitude of the problems you have, but how fast you can jump over them and embrace the next one that wins the race.*

THE GROWTH OF ENTREPRENEURIAL COMPANIES

Despite the growing prominence of entrepreneurship, understanding its key features and development stages lags. Mainstream media coverage frequently emphasizes the most unusual successes, creating misconceptions about the nature and evolution of most successful entrepreneurial firms. In theory, entrepreneurship includes several subdisciplines, including small business, businesses owned by women, high-technology startups, home-based businesses, and family-owned businesses. Businesses in these groupings have received the most intensive study.

Relatively little research has been done, however, on the distinctive features of growth companies. This is an important point because in many respects, entrepreneurial companies are indistinguishable from small businesses until they enter a "growth" phase, during which they are transformed into an almost entirely different entity. An entrepreneurial firm is one that grows large enough to influence the environment and thus become a pacesetter. Yet we cannot use growth alone to evaluate the real pacesetters, as 86.7 percent of all U.S. businesses employ 20 or fewer people.[8] The past 15 years have been years of tremendous growth for entrepreneurial companies and for the individuals who make them thrive. During this time, entrepreneurs such as Bill Gates, Andy Grove, Steve Jobs, Meg Whitman, and Jeff Bezos have captured the public imagination and dominated the business news.

The reasons for this trend in entrepreneurship are clear. Each year, at least 700,000 new businesses are started in the United States, and of these, a small portion turn out to be the fast-growth companies that propel the economy forward. Each year, this small set of businesses creates a disproportionate share of the new jobs and fuels the economy in numerous ways.

THE GROWTH PERIOD

Most businesses "start small and stay small." On the one hand, the business may not offer any productivity improvement and therefore may have no significant potential for entrepreneurial growth. On the other hand, even if they do have growth potential, the business owner may prefer to grow the business only to a certain point. As we mentioned above, not all entrepreneurs want to grow their businesses. Many entrepreneurs work toward the goal of growing the business to a certain level to provide a relatively steady stream of income and employment. The true challenges for these entrepreneurs and small business owners are to avoid burnout from the daily operations and keep the entrepreneurial spirit that drove them into business in the first place.[9]

What distinguishes an entrepreneurial company from a small business is the ability of the venture owner to maneuver successfully through the transition stages necessary to handle distinctive periods of growth. In many cases, the growth period comes right from the start and is part of the initial vision for the company. In other cases, the growth period comes later or appears to arrive out of the blue. Each year, a certain number of small businesses make the transition to become entrepreneurial growth companies. One thing these growth companies usually have in common is an entrepreneurial mindset.

THE ENTREPRENEURIAL MINDSET

Professor Rita McGrath, in her book *The Entrepreneurial Mindset*, states that a key aspect of establishing an entrepreneurial mindset is "creating the conditions under which everyone involved is energized to look for opportunities to change the business model."[10] Someone with an entrepreneurial mindset might seek to redesign existing product offerings, reshape markets, and change products in novel ways. McGrath calls such people who have made careers of starting a new business *habitual*, or *serial, entrepreneurs.* These entrepreneurs have in common the skills to forge opportunity from uncertainty.

Defining Commonly Shared Entrepreneurial Characteristics

Entrepreneurs share a number of characteristics:

1. They passionately seek new opportunities and are always looking for the chance to profit from change and disruption in the way business is done. They register their greatest impact when they create entirely new business models. They revolutionize business models and examine how revenues are determined, how costs are incurred, and how operations are conducted.

2. They pursue opportunities with enormous discipline. Habitual entrepreneurs not only spot opportunities, but they make sure they act on them. Most maintain some form of inventory of unexploited opportunities. They make sure that they revisit their inventory of ideas often, but they take action only when it is required. They make investments only if the competitive arena is attractive and the opportunity is ripe.

3. They pursue only the very best opportunities, and they avoid exhausting themselves and their organizations by chasing after every option. Even though many habitual entrepreneurs are wealthy, the most successful remain ruthlessly disciplined about limiting the number of projects they pursue. They go after a tightly controlled portfolio of opportunities in different stages of development.

4. They focus on execution—specifically, adaptive execution. People with an entrepreneurial mindset *execute*; that is, they move forward instead of analyzing new ideas to death.

5. They engage the energies of everyone in their domain. Habitual entrepreneurs involve many people—both inside and outside the organization—in their pursuit of an opportunity. They create and sustain networks of relationships rather than

going it alone, making the most of the intellectual and other resources people have to offer, all the while helping those people to achieve their goals as well.[11] They communicate well with their coworkers and outsiders, and they lead by example rather than by dictation.

PROFILE: ANDY STENZLER, CHAIRMAN AND CEO OF COSI, INC.

In 1994, 34-year-old Andy Stenzler had just received his M.B.A. from the Stern School of Business at New York University and felt that the time was right for a new idea in casual restaurants. He knew that he liked cafés and people and he felt Starbucks was fine, but it fell short as a place for customers to linger. He opened his first restaurant in Hartford, Connecticut, in 1994, and he has been expanding ever since. In October 1999, Xando, Inc. merged with Cosi Sandwich Bar, Inc., and it now operates 66 casual dining establishments in 11 states. Andy's strategy and mission are to facilitate the rapid growth of the company and build high-quality nationwide service. He has raised over $125 million in capital from investors and investment companies in the last three years and plans to consider a public offering next year. He has been featured on the cover of *Entrepreneur Magazine* and was named in "40 under 40" by *Crain's New York Business* and in "35 under 35" by *New York Magazine*.

SUMMARY

The definition of an entrepreneur has evolved over time as the surrounding economic structures have become more complex. Today, *entrepreneurship* is defined as the process of creating something different by devoting the necessary time and effort; assuming the accompanying financial, psychic, and social risks; and receiving the resulting monetary rewards and personal satisfaction.

The entrepreneurial process consists of five stages: conducting opportunity analysis, developing the plan and setting up the company, acquiring financial partners and sources of funding, determining the resources required and implementing the plan, and scaling and harvesting the venture.

The study of entrepreneurship has relevance today not just because it helps entrepreneurs better fulfill their personal needs, but because of the economic function of new ventures. More than increasing national income by creating new jobs, entrepreneurship acts as a positive force in economic growth by serving as the bridge between innovation and application.

STUDY QUESTIONS

1. What are the five stages of the entrepreneurial process?
2. Why do people become entrepreneurs?
3. What are the different approaches to identifying entrepreneurial types?
4. What are the growth issues entrepreneurial companies face?
5. What is the entrepreneurial mindset? What characteristics do entrepreneurs often share?

6. If you start a company, will you expect to always be in control, or will you be willing to share control with others if that will help the company grow and make all the participants wealthier? Describe your reasons for your choice.

EXERCISES

1. What is/was your best business idea opportunity?

2. Who are/were the participants?
- The person with the idea _____
- Family _____
- Friends _____
- Other _____
  Explain.

3. What are/were the main risks?

4. What is the current status of your idea?
- On hold _____
- Abandoned _____
- Continuing _____
  Explain.

INTERACTIVE LEARNING ON THE WEB

Test your knowledge of the chapter using the book's interactive Web site. A Personal Entrepreneurial Assessment is available to test the roles and functions during the startup phase.

ADDITIONAL RESOURCES

Kauffman Center for Entrepreneurial Leadership at the Ewing Marion Kauffman Foundation

Ewing Marion Kauffman established the Ewing Marion Kauffman Foundation to pursue a vision of self-sufficient people in healthy communities. The Foundation, with an endowment of more than $2 billion, is based in Kansas City, Missouri. It directs and supports innovative programs and initiatives that merge the social and economic dimensions of philanthropy locally and nationally.

The Foundation's mission is to research and identify the unfulfilled needs of society and to develop, implement, or fund breakthrough solutions that have a lasting impact and give people a choice and hope for the future. In pursuit of its vision and mission, the Foundation works to help youth become productive members of society and to accelerate entrepreneurship in America.

Inspired by his passion to provide opportunity for other entrepreneurs, Ewing Marion Kauffman launched the Kauffman Center for Entrepreneurial Leadership, the largest organization focused solely on entrepreneurial success at all levels, from elementary students to high-growth entrepreneurs. The Center takes an innovative approach to accelerating entrepreneurship through educational programming and research. The Center's entrepreneurial activities are organized around three primary areas. (1) It develops and disseminates innovative, effective, and comprehensive curricula and support systems for adult entrepreneurs, from aspiring to high growth. (2) Its youth entrepreneurship efforts focus on creative initiatives for enhancing entrepreneurship awareness, readiness, and application experiences for K–12 youth and community college students. (3) It also promotes entrepreneurship with public policymakers, not-for-profit leaders, and in urban and rural communities of need.[12]

For more information, visit the Center's Web site at www.entreworld.org.

National Dialogue on Entrepreneurship

In the summer of 2003, the Public Forum Institute began work under a grant from the Ewing Marion Kauffman Foundation to develop a National Dialogue on Entrepreneurship (NDE) to improve awareness of the value of entrepreneurship. The project is building on the Forum's extensive background in national dialogues on economic issues and, in particular, a series of events and activities since 2000 focusing on women and entrepreneurship.

Though only in its initial stages, NDE has reached out to national and regional policymakers and begun a dialogue on the role and value of entrepreneurship to the United States. At the Web site you can find some useful information and also sign up for their regular newsletter.

For more information and to sign up for the newsletter, visit the Web site at www.publicforuminstitute.org.

Resource Conference Centers and Research Facilitators

American Women's Economic Development Corporation (AWED), New York. AWED, a premier national not-for-profit organization, is committed to helping entrepreneurial women start and grow their own businesses. Based in New York City, AWED also has offices in Southern California, Connecticut, and Washington, D.C. It has served over 150,000 women entrepreneurs through courses, conferences, seminars, and one-on-one counseling provided by a faculty of expert executives and entrepreneurs.

Catalyst, New York. This national nonprofit research and advisory organization founded in 1962 has a dual mission: (1) to help women in business and the professions achieve their maximum potential and (2) to help employers capitalize on the talents of women. Under the leadership of Sheila W. Wellington, president, the Catalyst library at 120 Wall Street offers resources on women for background research.

The National Association of Women Business Owners (NAWBO), Washington, D.C. NAWBO propels women entrepreneurs into economic, social, and political spheres of power worldwide. NAWBO offers assistance in securing access to financial opportunities to meet, exchange ideas, and establish business ventures; educational programs, seminars, and leadership training; chapter programs, regional meetings, and national conferences; discounts on products and services; an international network of business contacts; visibility and clout in political arenas; and procurement opportunities.

www.wiley.com/college/kaplan

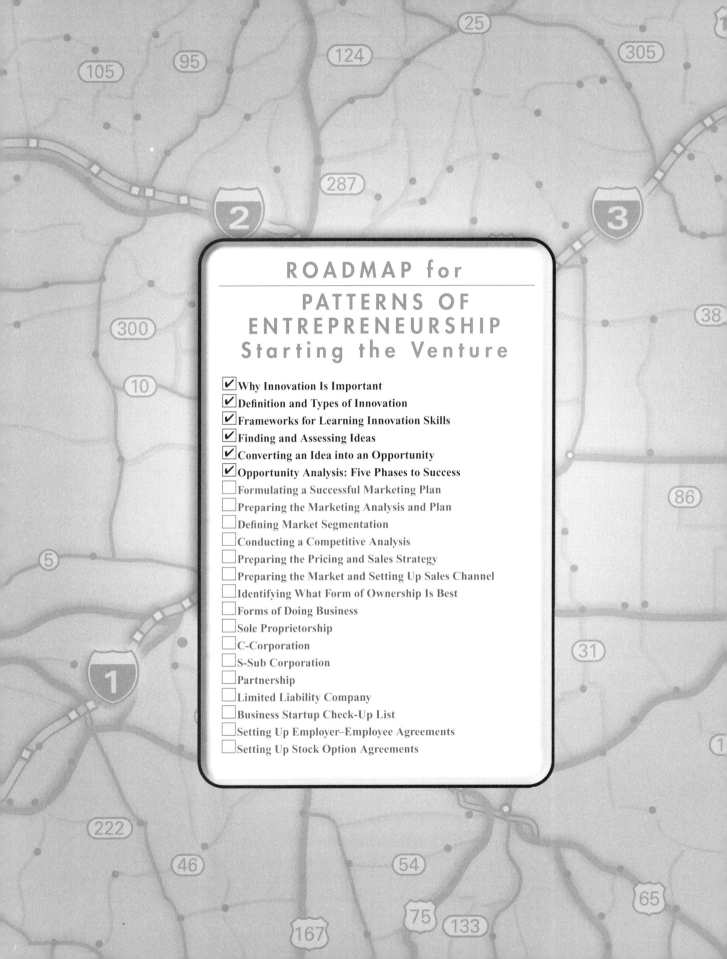

ROADMAP for

PATTERNS OF ENTREPRENEURSHIP
Starting the Venture

- ☑ **Why Innovation Is Important**
- ☑ **Definition and Types of Innovation**
- ☑ **Frameworks for Learning Innovation Skills**
- ☑ **Finding and Assessing Ideas**
- ☑ **Converting an Idea into an Opportunity**
- ☑ **Opportunity Analysis: Five Phases to Success**
- ☐ **Formulating a Successful Marketing Plan**
- ☐ **Preparing the Marketing Analysis and Plan**
- ☐ **Defining Market Segmentation**
- ☐ **Conducting a Competitive Analysis**
- ☐ **Preparing the Pricing and Sales Strategy**
- ☐ **Preparing the Market and Setting Up Sales Channel**
- ☐ **Identifying What Form of Ownership Is Best**
- ☐ **Forms of Doing Business**
- ☐ **Sole Proprietorship**
- ☐ **C-Corporation**
- ☐ **S-Sub Corporation**
- ☐ **Partnership**
- ☐ **Limited Liability Company**
- ☐ **Business Startup Check-Up List**
- ☐ **Setting Up Employer–Employee Agreements**
- ☐ **Setting Up Stock Option Agreements**

CHAPTER 2

THE ART OF INNOVATION—DEVELOPING IDEAS AND BUSINESS OPPORTUNITIES

"I think all great innovations are built on rejections."
(LOUIS-FERDINAND CÉLINE)

OBJECTIVES

- Understand the changing role of innovation.
- Create frameworks for innovating.
- Source and filter ideas and build them into opportunities.
- Analyze opportunities using a five-step analysis.
- Use a framework to evaluate a business opportunity.

CHAPTER OUTLINE

INTRODUCTION

Entrepreneurs are often considered highly innovative, always coming up with unique ideas for new businesses. In fact, entrepreneurs do not have to be innovative to be successful, but they do have to understand and manage the innovation process within their companies. They may use innovations found elsewhere or use those continually developed within their own company, even when they themselves are not the source of innovation. Therefore, it is important that an entrepreneur has a grasp of the nature of innovation and how it is generated and managed.

Innovation can have many facets. For example, Michael Dell is rightly considered an extremely successful entrepreneur. Yet for many years Dell has built similar products to its major competitors, Hewlett-Packard, Compaq, IBM, and so on. What is unique about Dell is the *way* that these products are sold, manufactured, and delivered to its customers. The business methods employed religiously by Dell are what make the company successful, not innovation of new products. (Chapter 8 has a more detailed discussion of Michael Dell.) In contrast, Steve Jobs of Apple fame is the driving innovator behind Apple's ability to continually come out with unique looking and functioning products. Therefore, we cannot understand entrepreneurship without exploring the entrepreneur's relationship with innovative processes. It could be claimed, of course, that Michael Dell was innovative when he conceived the direct sale, made-to-order business model that has driven the success of his company. His competitors, after all, failed to see this model; having been caught unawares and locked into their old ways of doing things, they have been unable to compete directly.

This chapter is about innovation in entrepreneurship. We begin with explaining the changing role of innovation in business, including definitions and types of innovation. We then show how you can learn to be innovative, how to seek out and screen ideas, and how to build them into creative new business opportunities.

The Changing World Around Us

We often hear such broad statements as "competition is becoming brutal," "markets are global," "the Internet has changed the rules of business," and so on. Let's look at some of the facts and see how they influence an entrepreneur.[1]

The Growth of the Internet and Access to Knowledge and Ideas

Relatively recently, computers (and other digital devices) have become connected in networks, and automated search techniques have been developed by companies such as Google. This is resulting in a cataclysmic shift from an emphasis on local products and productivity to global knowledge sharing. We are only just beginning to understand the implications and effects of this connectivity. Although it is notoriously difficult to accurately size the Internet, any estimate provides staggering statistics. According to research from Nielsen-Netratings in Feburary 2003, conservatively over 580 million people worldwide had Internet access. Extrapolating data from Nua Internet Surveys at www.nua.ie, we can expect this number to grow to 700 million quickly. At the same time, the information available to these Internet users is exploding, with over 7 million new Web pages being added daily to the several billion that already exist and many pages linking to other archived data sources.[2] Other estimates quote 50 million independent Web sites existing at the end of 2003,[3] growing at a compound rate of 200 percent per year.[4] Google claims that it regularly scans 12 billion Web pages; this may only be 1 percent of the total of so-called hidden pages that exist. Now it is just as easy to find an expert at a university in Melbourne, Australia, as in Melbourne, Florida; or a corporate partner in Cambridge, Massachusetts, as in Cambridge, England.

To remain competitive today, it is no longer sufficient to rely on local know-how; indeed, it is vital to access the best ideas, technologies, research resources, and experts, wherever they are. For example, the networked world can support a biotech company with headquarters in Seattle, basic research undertaken at universities in San Diego, Edinburgh, and Auckland, scale-up of production in Singapore, and clinical trials in the newest members of the European Union. Its advisory board will undoubtedly be international in makeup. A management challenge—yes—but by assembling appropriate resources to compete quickly and efficiently, more certain success is in the offing. These knowledge-centered structures are variously referred to as "virtual knowledge networks" or "virtual clusters." They are fluid and may form and dissolve in short shrift when they are no longer valuable, whereas geographical-based clusters may take years to evolve, with the danger then of being outmoded and redundant. We can envision a world not long in the future where nearly everyone will be able to search the world's knowledge, locate experts on demand, and do this more or less for free. For an entrepreneur, this means access to more ideas, more stimulation, and more expertise when conceiving and growing a business opportunity. The Internet should be one of the entrepreneur's major tools. Just remember, everyone else has access to this tool too!

The Internet and Customer Expectations

The Internet is also changing the way customers view suppliers. It enables us to find and compare products, even sometimes having the product "made-just-for-me," to order instantly, to choose when and how to have it delivered, and to decide how to pay or finance the purchase. This is true in both business-to-business (B2B) and business-to-consumer sales (B2C). We are being subtly educated to expect customized service and instant gratification to be part of our buying experience. Products are being surrounded by service. We want *our* problem to be solved, not a standard product to buy. This shift, of course, is at the center of entrepreneurial companies such as Dell, eBay, Amazon, and Google. Lesson: think service not product, personalized solution, not third-party handoff. As you will see in the many cases in this book, these ideas can be applied to the most mundane product areas.

Example: Greif Packaging (www.Greif.com)

A supplier of metal drums for shipping bulk chemicals, many of which are toxic, realized that it had no real competitive position and that profit margins were thin. An internal entrepreneur decided to listen carefully to customers. He saw there were unmet needs and new sources of value to be accessed. Customers did not want to buy and own steel drums; rather, they wanted to move toxic chemicals efficiently and safely. Nor did they want to deal with all of the details such as finding a licensed trucker, filling in the government forms, or washing, cleaning, and refurbishing the drums. To meet its customers' actual needs, Greif converted its business model into a "trip leasing" company for specialty chemicals—the FedEx® of problem chemicals. Now it solves the total trip problem for its customers—drum supply, cleaning, refurbishing, regulatory compliance, transportation, and tracking. Greif built a new Web application and became an "Internet company." Although it subcontracts out most support functions, it captures the value in the supply chain and builds long-lasting client relationships. Moreover, it buys support services in volume, and its database of trip costing enables the company to accurately quote on "trips" and to provide customized and traceable service. This shift has significantly improved its profits and cash flow, which it can direct to further innovations. The business model also builds barriers against competitors.

Barriers to Trade

Historical trade barriers for goods and services are rapidly being dismantled, opening up all markets to global suppliers. According to the World Trade Organization,[5] the number of international agreements signed annually to open up trade has ballooned from less than 10 in 1950 to close to 200 in 2000 and over 250 last year. Any new product can be copied within days, manufactured, and shipped into most markets in a few weeks. The entrepreneur's defenses against this happening are having a sound intellectual property strategy (see below and Chapter 7) and an innovative business model that supplies more than just a product (see Chapter 8).

Access to Capital

Simultaneously with the elimination of trade barriers for goods and services, restrictions on currency trading have also been almost entirely removed. Now daily cross-border trading in currency dwarfs the value of imports and exports. Although most currency trading is on a short-term basis, the lack of restrictions in the majority of economies to inward or outward foreign investment means that funds may now seek opportunities on a global basis and firms must *compete internationally* for finance. Fully 20 percent of mutual funds managed in the United States and a mainstay of U.S. personally managed pensions are now invested overseas. The year 2004 was a record one for U.S. investors to place their investment bets overseas, with $90 billion slated to flow into foreign corporations.[6] Geographical location no longer provides any significant advantage for access to major sources of capital. Venture capital (VC) remains one source of funding that prefers proximity; but overall, VC funds are a very small part of total growth capital. Even venture capital is trending international. As reported recently,[7] leading "Sandhill Road" VC firms are looking to target a significant part of new funds for investment in early-stage companies in Asia, hoping to bring their startup management skills into markets where U.S.-style venture capital is little known. Clearly, they are not finding sufficiently attractive opportunities nearby. For the entrepreneur, this means that the competition for growth capital is becoming tougher; therefore, the "bootstrapping" skills dealt with in Chapter 5 are most important.

Technological Obsolescence

We often hear that product life cycles are declining, but it is notoriously difficult to find hard data supporting this statement. (A product life cycle is the time that a product is able to command a high profit margin in the market before it becomes obsolete or becomes a commodity with intense competition.) Clearly, it is much more likely to be true for fast-moving consumer products such as food and detergents and for products in which the underpinning technology is driven by Moore's law,[8] or is impacted by major technological shifts. According to an internal study conducted in the mid-1990s by Hewlett-Packard (HP),[9] the average period that HP's products remained major contributors to sales had fallen from four years in 1980 to well below two years in 1995. More recent studies[10] measure product development times. These have declined from an average of 225 days three years ago to 207 days now. In the portable communication business sector populated by such companies as Motorola, Nokia, and Blackberry, market life cycles are now shorter than product development cycles; that is, it takes longer to develop a product than the time it will be successful in the market. This is a challenge to even the most efficient engineering departments.

To meet these pressures, companies are developing new methods to reduce their product development times by employing 24/7 activities spread around the world. For example, a Münich-based team hands over to Beijing at the end of the day, whose team, in turn at sunset, hands over to Denver, with all the information being sent over the Internet. In many cases, these teams may not be on the staff of the lead company, but may be joint development partners assembled quickly to meet an urgent deadline—so-called virtual organizations. Managing such complex projects across corporate, national, and cultural boundaries requires new skills that ensure the ability to "get it right the first time." There is no room for error.

Of course, in slower moving sectors such as machine tools and locomotives, the evidence for rapidly declining product life cycles is not so obvious. However, even here, the impact of low-cost electronic computing power and the ubiquity of the Internet are accelerating the upgrades that customers expect to provide them more than just a product; they anticipate nothing less than a total solution to their requirements throughout their ownership. These additional service components may cover not only financing and operator training, but remote condition monitoring for 24/7 online support and maintenance (for an example, refer to the Taprogge case in Chapter 8), performance guarantees with financial penalties, and even returns of the product for recycling at the end of its life cycle. For example, Dell has recently started a recycling service for used computers. Each of these service components demands implementation of new technologies within even the most traditional of engineering sectors.

The acceleration of product life cycles changes the way that intellectual property must be managed. In the past, the 17 to 20 years of protection afforded by a patent was often valuable over its full life. But when technology evolves rapidly, 20 years of protection loses its value. Research by one of the authors[11] shows that companies are reevaluating the ways that they protect their intellectual property and are carefully selecting areas for long-term patent coverage, usually on fundamental inventions, and are forgoing patents for trade secrets elsewhere. Patent law requires inventors to "teach" what they have done within the patent document; this inevitably exposes concepts and know-how that may be better kept secret rather than giving competitors a jump-start to catch up. An agile company[12] has moved on by the time patents are issued, and so the patents may be of more value to competitors than the owner. In the new innovation model, churning out patents is replaced by including the protection of intellectual property within the overall business strategy rather than a way of protecting an invention. And when patents are filed, they are written to protect both the "hard" invention and the unique business model surrounding it.

In some sectors, of course, patents will continue to be the principal method to retain protection from competition. For example, the long and expensive development cycles and regulatory hurdles governing pharmaceutical products encourage the use of patent protection. Even here, however, careful selection of what to patent and when, in order to retain maximum advantage after perhaps a 10-year development cycle, is a challenging task.

The budding entrepreneur can learn several lessons here:

- It is becoming more and more difficult to build a company around a single product idea without strong patent protection. This is particularly true for consumer products that have a very short product life cycle.
- Protective barriers must become part of any business model, whether via patents, trade secrets, uniqueness in the business model, or fast movement to market to stay ahead of competitors.
- Innovation is not a single event; one should never stop innovating!
- The entrepreneur should always imagine that there is someone, somewhere, having the same idea as he does. How can he protect it and build a strong position quickly?
- The entrepreneur needs to solve customers' problems. One should think service, not product.

WHY INNOVATION IS IMPORTANT

So we are in a world in which access to knowledge and expertise, labor, and capital is truly global and transparently accessible, and in which technology relentlessly advances. Technical breakthroughs are no longer confined to just a few centers of excellence such as Bell Labs or MIT; the next breakthrough can just as easily occur in Bangalore, Beijing, or Brisbane as in Boston, Bristol, or Basel. Shorter product life cycles and rapid technological obsolescence make patents lose their power in monopoly preservation. In addition, companies can no longer rely on the earlier protections of trade and monetary restrictions, local labor preeminence, and cozy knowledge clusters to provide competitive advantages. The only way that sustainable advantages can be earned is through continuous innovation—innovation not only in product development, but in all aspects of business activity and at an ever-increasing rate. Of course, there has always been innovation in corporations. Indeed, William Baumol[13] argues that the unprecedented wealth generated in the major economies in the twentieth century would not have been possible without innovation. However, until relatively recently, many firms could survive and prosper without innovating: they competed in a protected environment. Now, ***innovation is no longer a luxury; it is a necessity***.

DEFINITION AND TYPES OF INNOVATION

Definition of Innovation

In this book we will use the following definition.

Successful innovation is the use of new technological knowledge, and/or new market knowledge, employed within a business model that can deliver a new product and/or service to customers who will purchase at a price that will provide profits.

This definition is built on the generally accepted work of Alan Afuah.[14] In order to focus the discussion and to emphasize the new innovation, we have added the following:

"Successful . . . ." in order to emphasize that we are not interested in innovation that fails to deliver and maintain value for the innovating enterprise.

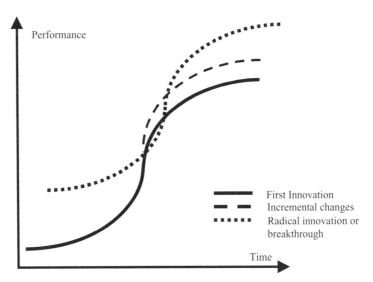

Figure 2-1   The S-Curve of Innovations.

"...**employed within a business model**..." in order to stress that innovation in the business model is as important, perhaps more so, than purely product or process technology. (This theme is developed further in Chapter 8.)

"...**that will purchase at a price that will provide profits**" in order to stress that success requires that the innovator be able to extract benefit from the value created and not allow it to migrate to partners, customers, or offshore manufacturers.

Types of Innovation

There are two major classes of innovation: incremental and radical. Incremental innovations are continual improvements on an existing product or service or in the ways that products are manufactured and delivered. Radical innovations are the result of major changes in the ground rules of competition, culminating in either a customer satisfying her needs in an entirely new way or in a totally new need being created through innovation.

The 'S' curve is often used to illustrate the difference in which the performance achieved by a new innovation is plotted against time (see Figure 2-1). When the innovation is first made, a period of experimentation ensues in which little performance improvement is made while the innovator tries different ways of reaching goals. As learning improves with experimentation, the advances in improvements accelerate quickly until a plateau is reached, at which time major efforts are required to make minor improvements—the region of limited returns. Usually, improvements can be made with *incremental* innovations pushing the original curve higher. Then along comes a new innovation—usually from another place—which goes through the same cycle until it ends up giving a higher performance than the first idea and takes a major part of the market away from the first innovation. This is the radical change.

Example: The Evolution of Lighting

When Thomas Edison invented the incandescent lamp, it took many years before lamps were in the mainstream of lighting. First, he encountered difficulties in encapsulating the filament to prevent burnout, and houses had to be wired to receive electric power. But after 20 years or so electric lighting became the preferred way. Electric lighting, a radical innovation, replaced candles. Since then, the electric lamp has undergone many incremental improvements, yet it remains fundamentally the same as Edison's original innovation. There are now only a few suppliers of lamps, and none of them makes a very high profit margin. Electric lamps are a commodity and are perhaps ripe to be replaced by the next radical innovation. We can only guess where that might come from. For example, the glow-worm's tail is a very efficient converter of electrical energy to light. With fuel costs rising rapidly, there is a big incentive to reduce energy consumption. Is the bio-lamp far away? What is assured is that it will not be developed by one of the existing lamp manufacturers, for they are focused on incrementally improving the old idea.

Edison's lamps nearly destroyed the candle industry—though not quite. There's money to be made in candles too!

Example: Candles for Everyone

In 1977 Robert Groegen, an entrepreneur, bought a small, just surviving, candle company in Brooklyn, New York. At that time the company had annual sales of about $3 million. He changed the name to Blyth Candles,[15] and since then he has built up the company to the point where it is the largest candle supplier in the United States, with annual sales of over $1.5 billion and profits before tax of $136 million. Groegen still owns 27 percent of the company, which is now publicly traded, making his personal wealth in the company's stock worth $365 million—not bad for a candlemaker! This has been achieved entirely via incremental innovations—perfumed candles for certain occasions and seasons, candles for outdoors, ornamental candle holders, and so on, and by buying smaller candle manufacturers that were not innovating at all.

Entrepreneurs therefore do not need a radical innovation to create a new, successful, and profitable company. Continuous incremental innovation can also be sufficient.

Disruptive Innovation

The term disruptive innovation is often used to describe innovations that *disrupt* the status quo. As companies grow, they develop cultures and procedures that create internal barriers to change. The greater the mismatch of the innovation to the current know-how and the more it threatens to destroy existing product sales, the tougher it is for a large company to respond. The change can arise from a new technology. Kodak is struggling with changing from being the leading supplier of photographic film and moving to an entirely new business based on digital imaging. All of the company's chemical know-how provides no advantage in the new world, and the more digital products that Kodak sells, the faster its film business will decline. Dell entered the PC market with a new "direct to customer" business model. Major competitors such as IBM and HP/Compaq have been unable to remain competitive, for a change to this business model would require completely removing their existing sales channels and compromising short-term revenues. The changeover is just too difficult. Again and again, it is entrepreneurial startups that can take advantage of the larger company's inability to respond to disruption. It was startup Intel that destroyed RCA's vacuum tube business, Amazon that is challenging established retail chains, and Netflix attacking the location-based Blockbuster chain.

To learn more about how large companies struggle with disruptive innovation, see Clayton Christensen.[16] And to learn how small entrepreneurial companies can partner with large companies see Baumol's article on the Internet. As evidence that

Table 2-1   Some Important Innovations by U.S. Small Firms in the Twentieth Century[17]

Air conditioning	Heart valve	Prestressed concrete
Air passenger service	Heat sensor	Prefabricated housing
Airplane	Helicopter	Pressure sensitive tape
Articulated tractor	High-resolution CAT scanner	Programmable computer
Cellophane artificial skin	High-resolution digital X-ray	Quick-frozen food
Assembly line	High-resolution X-ray microscope	Reading machine
Audio tape recorder	Human growth hormone	Rotary oil drilling bit
Bakelite	Hydraulic brake	Safety razor
Biomagnetic imagining	Integrated circuit	Six-axis robot arm
Biosynthetic insulin	Kidney stone laser	Soft contact lens
Catalytic petroleum cracking	Large computer	Solid fuel rocket engine
Computerized blood pressure controller	Link trainer	Stereoscopic map scanner
Continuous casting	Microprocessor	Strain gauge
Cotton picker	Nuclear magnetic resonance scanner	Strobe lights
Defibrillator	Optical scanner	Supercomputer
DNA fingerprinting	Oral contraceptives	Two-armed mobile robot
Double-knit fabric	Outboard engine	Vacuum tube
Electronic spreadsheet	Overnight national delivery	Variable output transformer
Freewing aircraft	Pacemaker	Vascular lesion laser
FM radio	Personal computer	Xerography
Front-end loader	Photo typesetting	X-ray telescope
Geodesic dome	Polaroid camera	Zipper
Gyrocompass	Portable computer	

entrepreneurs and small companies are the source of the most important innovations, see Table 2-1.

So don't be scared of those behemoths out there. Take advantage of their inability to respond to disruptive innovations, whether in products, services, or business models. Throughout this book you will find many examples of entrepreneurial ventures. Think about whether they are based on a disruptive innovation and how this will affect the existing larger firms. Can they respond?

FRAMEWORKS FOR LEARNING INNOVATION SKILLS

Debate continues as to whether innovators are born or whether such skills can be learned. The authors' research shows that, indeed, if someone has the desire to be an entrepreneur, then innovation skills can be effectively learned. The best way to achieve this expertise is by using examples and practicing the learned skills. In this section, we will outline some "innovation frameworks" that will help you in this regard. These frameworks are examples and not a complete list. In fact, you may be able to develop your own frameworks that you find more suited to your own personality and style.

Analogs

Why innovate from nothing when many ideas have already worked well? The idea of this framework is to help transfer innovations in one field to another. Chapter 12 quotes the example of LeafBusters. The company "outsources" the leaf collection and disposal services provided by municipalities to residents annually. LeafBusters claims that it can do this more efficiently because it can use the required expensive equipment for a longer season each year by "following the weather." Where did the founders of this company get this "obvious" idea? They read an article about crews that harvest crops under contract to farmers in the Corn Belt moving southward each year. The underlying drivers for the two businesses are the same: more effective utilization of expensive capital equipment through "following the seasons." The trick here is to analyze existing successful businesses and to get behind the immediate product or service to examine the underpinning drivers. Then ask "where else can these principles be applied"?

Let us work through another analog example. Dell is now supplying printers that connect to the Internet, and the printers have built in "ink management software." The software analyzes usage, recommending when to print in black and white only, when in color, and so on. When it is time to replace the ink cartridge, the printer has already forecasted the need, contacted Dell via the Internet, and had ink dropshipped just in time. This is a valuable service to the consumer. It also locks in the purchasing to Dell supplies, preempting competition from low-cost refill stores. The consumer is happy, and Dell grows its revenue and profits. What other products/services could be analogous to this example?

Consider that household appliances that connect to the Internet[18] are now also being offered. Initially aimed at monitoring performance so that service calls can be scheduled before the appliances break down, this feature could be used as follows. The washing machine monitors usage and injects into the wash the appropriate detergent, softener, bleach, and so on, depending on the needs for the load. Like the printer, detergent usage forecast enables a supplier to dropship just in time the consumer's needs, which are placed into holders built in to the machines. Currently, detergent manufacturers are not making any profits because they have to pay to have their products put on retailers' shelves and they compete in a commodity market with expensive advertising. There is little consumer loyalty, with products on "special" getting bought. Consumers do not like carrying the heavy containers of detergent. Perhaps there is an opportunity for a new detergent manufacturer to tie up with an appliance manufacturer such as GE, Whirlpool, or Maytag to provide the "total washing solution." This would benefit the consumer both in service and cost, for it would no longer be necessary to advertise detergents separately or to use the inconvenient and expensive retail distribution chain. Perhaps the companies that already deliver drinking water and therefore have the distribution network in place could be the logistics partner of this new venture.

Entrepreneurs learn to think like this: always analyzing intriguing innovations and thinking about where else the *principles of the concept*, not necessarily the details, can be applied. Get into the habit of questioning situations like this. And don't only look at successes; often, analyzing a failure can shine light on another situation where the reasons for failure may not apply.

Intersection of Technology Trends

We live in a world where technology is changing quickly. Watching cost and performance trends particularly where they begin to intersect can give rise to whole new innovative business opportunities. Let's consider digital photography, high-bandwidth communications, and ubiquitous wireless communications and think about some new business ideas. For example, imagine a digital camera with a wireless Internet connection. You could have your own personal Web site whereby your latest pictures are uploaded as soon as you take them. E-mails can be sent to friends and relatives immediately so that they can participate with you "in real time." Where is the business opportunity? What an interesting upgrade of services for a professional event photographer. Now at your wedding, bar mitzvah, and the like, a photographer can post pictures as they are taken, and those friends and relatives who are unable to be there in person can enjoy the event. The photographer can also sell more pictures and albums to a wider audience because they are more likely to buy when they are closely involved in the event.

Or again, take the B2B photography idea being developed by a company in Portland, Oregon. Advertising agencies, magazine publishers, and the like are always seeking images for their artwork and are often on a tight deadline. Until now, they have relied mostly on "canned" pictures already in picture libraries. Often they have to make compromises on their choices. Now, by signing up many of the world's best freelance photographers, a request can go out on the Internet, say for "a blond child holding a pink teddy-bear under a cherry tree in blossom," and one or more of the photographers can bid on the task and deliver the images within 24 hours—all made possible by the developments in high-quality digital photography and high-speed communications.

Solving "Points of Pain"

Entrepreneurs are quick to notice inefficiencies, inconveniences, and other forms of "points of pain" and to use these to build a new business opportunity.

Example: SmartPak, Inc.[19]

SmartPak was born of necessity. According to Becky Minard, a horse lover and founder of this company in Cape Cod, "Feeding supplements was a disaster at our boarding barn." I have a horse who needs daily vitamin E, joint supplement, and a dose of daily wormer. I assumed he was generally getting his supplements. Then I noticed that the vitamin E lasted months longer than it should have. It's a white powder, so I checked his feed tub (premade for the next morning) to see if it was in there. Nothing. No trace of white powder. The joint supplement was there, but it was hard to tell if it was one or two scoops. He did have a hefty dose of his daily wormer in there; may be that would explain why I was going through it twice as fast as I thought I should be. Now it's hard to blame the barn staff, since they have to feed 35 horses with an average of three supplements per horse. That works out to 105 supplements to be opened, measured, fed, and resealed. What a headache for them." Becky had just recognized the "point of pain" for both the horse owners and their minders.

Becky continues: "We wondered if others had the same problem so we went out and talked to boarders, owners, and managers at other barns. All sorts of other barns: big show barns, small private barns, lesson barns, and back yard barns. They had many of the same problems. In a few cases we found some moldy supplements or contaminated supplements (mouse droppings!). We found many outdated supplements (usually in those gigantic containers). The most consistent thing we found was that most of the feed rooms we visited had containers that had not been resealed after each use. Some were even left entirely open! Since then we have learned from manufacturers that oxygen, moisture, and sunlight are devastating to the potency of many supplements. Money down the drain!"

These "points of pain" were solved by creating "smartpaks." A horse owner can go to this Web site and order custom-packaged daily supplies for his individual horses. All the minder has to do is tear off the seal—just like those six-packs of yogurts—and empty the different food supplements into the horse's feed. Each patented pack comes clearly labeled with the horse's name and list of additives. The owner can now rest assured that his pet horse is well taken care of, the barn-helper's tasks are greatly simplified, and Becky has grown a substantial business built around noticing this one "point of pain."

Actually, Becky might have come up with the same idea by looking for an analog. Cardinal Healthcare (www.cardinal.com) does the same for hospital patients by taking over the internal pharmacy role. Patients' daily medicines are delivered, clearly labeled, to the bedside, reducing potentially dangerous errors and also costs by eliminating the large inventories at hospitals and consolidating suppliers at central locations rather than at individual dispensaries. Both Smartpak and Cardinal provide services around their products and solve their customers' problems.

Example: Netflix (www.Netflix.com)

Netflix provides rental DVDs through the mail rather than via bricks and mortar rental outlets favored by Blockbuster. The founders of Netflix realized that Blockbuster's customers had "points of pain"; they had to drive to the store, search through rows of movies, often not find the one they were seeking as it was already out, and pay late charges if they forgot to return it on time. Netflix solves these "points of pain" by mailing the movies (made possible by the DVD format taking over from tapes) directly to the customer, after a subscriber selects a queue wish list of movies she would like to watch. Movies can be kept as long as a consumer wishes with no late charges. When John Antioco, CEO of Blockbuster, first encountered Netflix, he did not see it as a threat, stating "no one will want to wait three days for a movie." In fact, having a wish list and allowing a subscriber to hold several DVDs simultaneously avoid this supposed disadvantage. And because inventory is stored centrally, a greater selection is possible. The Netflix business model innovation is "disruptive" to Blockbuster, which has invested much in stores and local inventories. It is interesting that Blockbuster did not see Amazon as an analog to Netflix, just as Barnes and Noble never saw Amazon as a threat until Amazon had taken a major share of the book market.

Entrepreneurs are continually noticing and analyzing "points of pain." Practice this in your daily life and challenge yourself to find the business opportunity.

Analyzing Existing Businesses

Understanding how existing businesses work, their cost structure, and customer "points of pain" can lead to ideas about how they can be effectively attacked. In our classes, students usually start with thinking of business ideas related to things near and dear to their everyday experience. This is often pizza! Their business idea is to open yet another pizza parlor, with the innovation centered around new product ideas—Thai-French or Indonesian curry pizzas, for example! But under questioning they expose a number of areas where the current pizza delivery services are unsatisfactory:

Customer Points of Pain:	*Owner's Challenges:*
Pizza arrives late	Location is bad
Pizza arrives cold	Rent is high
Phone takes forever to be answered	Labor is expensive and unreliable
Order taker is incomprehensible	It is difficult to schedule baking with deliveries
Pizza tastes of the packaging	

Digging further, an analysis of the cost of making and delivering a pizza shows that the storefront and labor overhead far outweigh the cost of food ingredients. And the customers are unhappy!

So let's think outside the pizza box, and let's think really BIG. Let's ask ourselves how we can totally restructure the pizza business on a national basis and grab the lion's share of the pizza market. Are there any technical advances that might impact the pizza business? Here you can get pretty creative. The following present some ideas culled from searching the patent database, surfing the Web, and talking to experts in a number of different fields. (Remember: use the vast sources of information now available at your fingertips.)

- Package delivery companies such as UPS and FedEx have invested heavily in software to optimize the most efficient routes for their vehicles depending on today's delivery addresses. How can this be applied to pizza delivery?
- Cars are commonly fitted with Global Positioning System (GPS) guidance systems that determine where the car is and then display a map and instructions on how to get to a desired location.
- Customers are increasingly becoming accustomed to using the Internet for ordering. Can this be applied to pizza ordering?
- Because labor reliability and costs are major issues for pizza outlets, Pizza Hut has developed working prototype robots for assembling pizzas automatically based on an order input. The robots make the pizza and then feed it into an oven. The time in the oven depends on the size and ingredients so that a perfect pizza comes out every time.

How can all these apparently unconnected developments be combined to create an entirely new pizza business?

Think about putting the robot and oven on a truck. Pizzas are made not in the sequence of the orders as they come in directly to the truck over the wireless Internet, but in the order that optimizes delivery time based on knowledge of the location of the vehicle, the optimum routing, and the oven scheduling. Labor is reduced to one person, the driver, and there is no storefront at all. Customers are informed by e-mail or phone exactly when their pizza will be delivered, and it will always be fresh having just come out of the oven as the driver pulls up. And there is no need for flavor-destroying packaging to keep the pizza hot for 20 minutes while the driver goes to other locations or gets lost.

Better service, better pizzas, lower cost of doing business! Think about starting out in one or two locations first and then either raising capital to expand into other markets or using a franchising model to cover the country (see Chapter 8 for a discussion on franchising). Look out Domino's and Pizza Hut! Think this is silly? Check out www.superfastpizza.com, a startup in Wisconsin following this model. Everyone thought Starbucks was a short-lived fad when it first started, yet it has grown to dominate the coffeehouse scene not only in the United States but worldwide. Even the most unlikely candidate areas can be ripe for entrepreneurial attack.

This example illustrates several ways in which entrepreneurs innovate. You may be surprised that it is a largely analytical process. The situation is deconstructed, ideas for stimulation are sought on the Internet, and then a synthetic process is initiated whereby the different inputs are rearranged until a possible solution emerges. Entrepreneurs are very good at synthesizing new opportunities from a collection of apparently disparate concepts. They recognize patterns that others may not find obvious. Get accustomed to looking for such patterns through analogs, technology confluences, "points of pain," and the like. You will find that you will quickly get better at this, and you may even develop your own personal frameworks for innovating. And do NOT be frightened to think big; often bigger is easier than smaller.

FINDING AND ASSESSING IDEAS

"During your life, you will probably generate many ideas for potential businesses. With proper training and skill development, your creativity can flourish. The value of entrepreneurship education is that you will learn how to critically evaluate your ideas to locate the best opportunities for commercial success. The pursuit of these opportunities will require significant work on your part, but the rewards are limitless."

SANFORD B. EHRLICH,
*QUALCOMM Executive Director
of Entrepreneurship and
Associate Professor of
Management,
San Diego State University
Entrepreneurial Management
Center.*

The previous sections show how to create new ideas for a business within innovation frameworks. For entrepreneurs just starting out, however, it may be necessary to seek some stimulation from idea sources. The world is full of ideas, but ideas are not opportunities, and opportunities are not ready-made to build a business around. Figure 2-2 shows how many ideas are required to start one business. The rest of the chapter therefore looks at idea sources and at how they can be built up and analyzed as real business opportunities.

Maybe you have some starting concepts but question how original they are. You may be surprised to hear that not all entrepreneurs come up with unique ideas. You can be innovative without that initial generative impulse. Here are five ways to build upon already existing material and still provide a profit-driven concept:

- Develop ideas as an extension or redesign an existing service (Marriott Senior Assistance Living; Sam's Club—an extension of Walmart).
- Re-segment and create an improved service (overnight delivery, such as Federal Express, or buying cheaper airline tickets from Priceline.com).
- Redifferentiate and market the product at a lower price (Internet shopping, Sam's Club).
- Add value to an existing product or service (linked brands, such as PCs just for the Internet).
- Develop or redesign a new version of an existing product (Snapple Ice Tea, fresh-baked chocolate chip cookies, and Krispy Kreme Doughnuts).

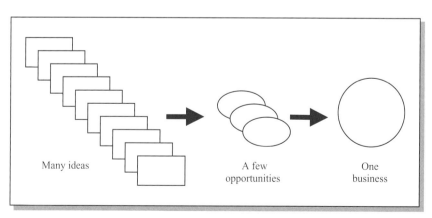

Figure 2-2   Many Ideas Are Filtered Down to One Business.

Idea Assessment

The first step for any entrepreneur is to generate an idea for a new business. The entrepreneur must then assess the opportunities available for putting the idea into practice. Is this something that has been overdone? Or has it been executed poorly in the past? Has anyone else thought of it? In short, is the idea a potential dead-end, a niche on an existing opportunity, or an entirely unexplored chance to create a business?

There are many sources for ideas. The Internet has made idea searching much faster and broader, and it also makes it easy to check whether an idea has already been discovered and put into a business. Entrepreneurs source ideas from many places.

To get you started, we have assembled a "starter-kit" of 27 general idea sourcing Web sites. The full list can be found on the book Web site at www.wiley.com/college/kaplan. The sites range from a pure list of ideas to franchising opportunities, patent auction sites, and sites committed to global scanning of new ideas. Take a look at some of the sites and then use a search engine such as Google to start searching on your own. You will be amazed at the wealth and breadth of idea triggers that will get you thinking.

One of the most underutilized sources for ideas are the U.S. and foreign patent databases. Chapter 7 deals with protecting your own ideas using patents. Here we discuss patents as *sources* of ideas. There are over 6 million patents issued in the United States. These can be searched by key words, owners, dates, and so on at the U.S. patent Web site, www.uspto.gov, or at a private patent database site, www.delphion.com. Many patents, of course, are filed to protect deep technology know-how. However, often forgotten are the simpler product ideas that their inventors may not have exploited for a number of reasons; perhaps they did not have the money or did not know how to develop a market, or perhaps the idea was "before its time" either because the market was not ready or the means of making them practical were not yet available. Also, every patent has to describe why the invention is important, including prior ideas, and why the idea is useful. What a great place to pick others' brains. In fact, only about 10 percent of existing patents have actually been commercialized; the remainder are still potential opportunities!

Example: Intuitive Controls Inc.

When Ted Graef and Scott Johnson left college, they were determined to start their own company. With engineering and business backgrounds, they felt comfortable looking for ideas where they could apply their skills. They started networking in their local community and were directed to an inventor named Ernest Merz who had been trying to create a business around two of his patents, 6543578 and 617606. These inventions are for one-hand "joysticks" for industrial equipment. Until Merz's ideas, controlling a crane for example, would require the user to manipulate several control handles for each direction of movement. This could easily lead to accidents, and Ted and Scott immediately saw the advantages of the idea for many applications. They reached an agreement with Mr. Merz to get rights to the invention and formed a company, Intuitive Controls Inc.[20], and created a range of products around the inventions. In order to sell the products, they entered into an agreement with a major supplier of controls systems to equipment manufacturers. As the sales started trickling in, the company presented its plans to a local group of "Angel" investors (see Chapter 6 for further discussions on Angels) and sold part of the company for a few hundred thousand dollars to sustain itself until sales were sufficient. Then the economy turned down, the marketing partner reduced its efforts to sell the products, and the company hit a brick wall. As Ted relates, "there are two sides to having a large company market your products—you do not have to pay for your own salesforce, which is a major cost saving for a small company short of cash, but if things do not go according to plan, you have no way to contact potential customers to generate sales, or to learn of their needs." However, their experience was not all wasted. They had learned a lot about safety products during their first attempt, and they had learned about "points of pain" for users of electronic speed monitors and traffic control equipment. Talking to potential customers such as police chiefs and township engineers, analyzing the shortcomings of existing products, and applying their hard-won philosophy of "intuitive controls," Ted and Scott developed a range of traffic management products and restarted their company in a new direction. Their new products are creating a stir in the market as they are embodying a service component into speed control systems. Now a police chief can monitor in real time, over the Internet, where it would be most effective to deploy patrols and place resources where they are needed immediately, making enforcement much more efficient and streets safer.

Lessons Learned from This Example

Learn and make corrections quickly. Time and time again, we have seen startup companies redirect their efforts when the first idea did not work out. Entrepreneurs learn to spot problems early and to make adjustments rather than pushing a "dead-horse" into bankruptcy.

Launch to learn. If you don't start at all, then you lose the opportunity to learn as you proceed until you uncover the really hot opportunity. Rarely, if ever, is the original plan correct and followed through.

Use "sleeping" patents. Launching can be aided by finding an underutilized patent and adding value to it.

Beware of having no access to the end user of your product or service. Even if you enter into a distribution agreement with an existing company to save money and accelerate sales, find a way to stay in contact with customers. They are a very good source of ideas, and you can observe their "points of pain" directly.

CONVERTING AN IDEA INTO AN OPPORTUNITY

Many new companies are built around a radical or breakthrough technology. As we explained earlier, major corporations are surprisingly bad at exploiting "disruptive" innovations. Indeed, as Table 2-1 shows, many of the major breakthroughs are discovered and taken to market by small firms. Of course, many of these breakthroughs are good enough that the small company grows into a large firm. Remember that all large firms started small! The important point to grasp is that breakthroughs are more likely to be conceived and developed in small companies. An entrepreneur need not be the developer of the technology. In fact, small companies can access a wealth of new technologies from a variety of sources such as universities and government-funded research laboratories and the companies that the government funds to carry out research and development (R&D). In fact, these sources are mandated by law to make the results of their research available to companies. (See the Bayh-Dole Act in the end-of-chapter appendix.)

Entrepreneurs require motivation, passion, and encouragement to develop a business idea. To convert the idea into a viable business opportunity, the entrepreneur will encounter many obstacles and roadblocks.

We have created two long lists of Web sites that you can visit to browse the technological inventions that are available, one for universities and the other from U.S. government sources. These lists can be found at the book Web site, www.wiley.com/college/kaplan.

The Evaluation Process

The entrepreneur will unquestionably need plenty of encouragement and support while developing a business idea. But in turning this idea into a concrete business, the entrepreneur will be faced with hard facts and cold reality. Armed with information gleaned from research, the entrepreneur is positioned to legitimately decide whether to proceed with the idea and work to sustain the venture.

Approximately 2 million businesses are started each year. Anywhere from 50,000 to 100,000 file for bankruptcy within a 10-year period. This total does not seem exceptionally high, but business failure extends beyond bankruptcy. Eighty-five percent of businesses actually fail within five years. They are not all bankrupt, yet their owners have decided to fold—for a host of reasons. Many lack the needed investment to carry them through the startup process (typically six months to a year between opportunity analysis and opening the doors for business). Others die because of poor business planning at the initial stages. Still others disappear owing to a lack of business resources, management expertise, and simple dearth of experience. For example, the short-sided ideas based on the fad for cabbage patch dolls is no longer a viable opportunity.

It's sobering to think that, of those initial 2 million ventures that start each year, only one in ten will reach its tenth birthday. But the entrepreneur should not allow an uncontextualized statistic to thwart a viable and potentially profitable business idea. Many startup owners conceive of their ventures as a sideline to their "real" profession. They never make the emotional and practical investments needed to ensure continued success. Note that 1.3 million of these businesses never legally register as corporations or partnerships because they don't intend to grow.

If the entrepreneur is committed, the odds of success rise considerably. A full-time owner has a one-in-four chance of keeping a new business going for eight years if it is incorporated. If ownership is then transferred, the business can be expected to survive another eight years, at that same rate of one in four. Putting the failure rates into context shows how those initial figures can be misleading. According to the Small Business Administration (www.SBA.gov) the actual eight-year survival rate for incorporated startups is about 25 percent.

What if the entrepreneur does not want the business to survive that long? The entrepreneur needs to identify his motives, goals, and the different outcomes that spell personal success by asking the following questions. Is it acceptable for assets to be tied up for a significant period of time, especially during periods of loss with the possibility of an eventual turnaround, or does the thrill lie in the rush of the startup period? Does success mean long-term survival or developing the company during a window of opportunity and then selling it at a high gain?

However long the entrepreneur ultimately decides to run the business, the fact is that in order to reap any kind of reward it will need to be developed in a logical and stable manner. Now that we've looked at the statistics and emphasized the need for research related to the specific needs of the venture, the next step is to formulate a plan and a schedule. This will assist the entrepreneur in conducting the most thorough inquiry yet into the potential of the idea/opportunity—otherwise known as the opportunity analysis.

OPPORTUNITY: FIVE PHASES TO SUCCESS

Identifying which business ideas have real commercial potential is one of the most difficult challenges that an entrepreneur will face. This section describes a systematic approach to reducing the uncertainties. The five-step model outlined in Figure 2-3 will help entrepreneurs to know a winning business area when they see one.[21]

Phase 1: Seize the Opportunity

The basic objective is to define the criteria that would make a business opportunity worthwhile to pursue. To start the process, think about how much value an opportunity can add to a business. The idea is to improve not only profits but profitability as well. Rita McGrath's *The Entrepreneurial Mindset* describes the techniques that can be used to create an opportunity register. The register is like an inventory of opportunities. It is a list of your ideas for improving, or even completely reinventing

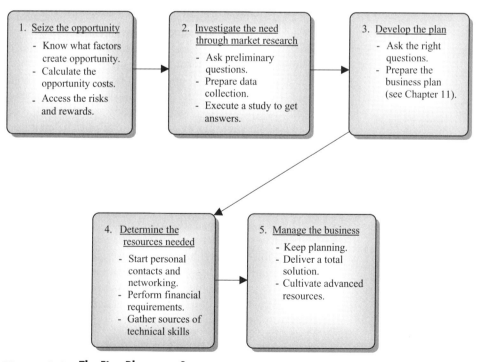

Figure 2-3   **The Five Phases to Success.**

the current business model or going into entirely new opportunity spaces. The entrepreneur wants to store good ideas so that they can be revisited to see how new ideas might fit in, determine whether the timing is right to implement older ones, or figure out what to eliminate as the direction becomes more defined. The register can take the form of a database because it is easier to review and update. The important aspect is to decide how to record and revisit ideas that are generated.[22]

To evaluate the business opportunity, review the sequence of events in Figure 2-3 and answer the following questions from the perspective of both a personal and professional experience.

- What are the indicators that lead to this idea and opportunity?
- What are the conditions that permit the opportunity to occur?
- How will the future of this new product or service change the idea?
- How great (in terms of time) is the window of opportunity?

Time Horizon

A window of opportunity is a time horizon during which opportunities exist before something else happens to eliminate them. A unique opportunity, once shown to produce wealth, will attract competitors, and if the business is easy to enter, the industry will quickly become saturated. In this situation, the entrepreneur must get in quickly and be able to get out before revenues become dispersed in an overdeveloped market.[23]

The entrepreneur gains the greatest ability to maneuver at the threshold of a startup idea by creating his or her own window of opportunity. Successful companies find and exploit markets that others have missed or that new technologies have suddenly created. For example, advertising has obviously been around for some time, but when DoubleClick started, Internet advertising was a brand new field. Its founder helped to create a wildly successful business by taking advantage of an unforeseen opportunity. The factors that help the entrepreneur create opportunity for the business are given in Figure 2-4.

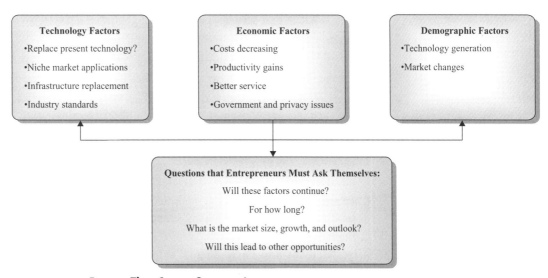

Figure 2-4 **Factors That Create Opportunity.**

Opportunity Costs

Opportunity costs are the value of benefits lost when one decision alternative is selected over another. For example, suppose a software company refuses to deliver a software program because writing the software code will require the company to miss a major deadline for another company. The order for the software program would generate revenue of $25,000 and additional costs of $14,000. Then the opportunity cost and the net benefit lost associated with the software deadline is $11,000 (i.e., $25,000 to $14,000).[24]

Phase 2: Investigate the Need Through Market Research

The first step is to identify, measure, and document the need for the product or service. This means making a specific financial forecast of the actual potential and anticipated return for this proposed product or service. This process is not the end; it's only the beginning. The topic of marketing will be explored more fully in Chapter 3—but for now, it will be considered as it fits into the opportunity analysis.

Marketing research need not be extensive, sophisticated, or expensive but must determine what customer satisfaction means for the target market. It should also provide other critical information about the target market used to develop marketing strategies. In some cases, the entrepreneur can survey the market to obtain information specifically tailored to the business's needs. However, judgment must be used in order to protect future marketing plans.

The questions below will assist in evaluating the actual climate surrounding the new company and preparing for the early stages of a new venture. Larger companies often outsource research to a marketing company, but this process will identify the steps and questions needed to custom-design the research and conduct it productively.

Preliminary Questions

At this point, the entrepreneur needs to solidify the purpose and object of the research. Those who are developing a particular product will want to focus on questions that can tell them about product features and distribution. A more service-oriented entrepreneur will consider other inquiries, directed at identifying the sources and beneficiaries of that service. Consider the goal now—it will save time and money later on. These areas and questions are meant to guide the direction of the research.[25]

Need. Will this product be serving customers' real needs? What is the overall market for the business? Are there special niches that can be exploited?

Niche/Competition. What is different about the product or service that will cause the customer to choose it over the competition's product or service?

Proprietary Questions. Can the product be patented or copyrighted? Is it unique enough to get a significant head start on the competition? Can the process be easily copied? Will the business concept be developed and licensed to others, or developed and sold?

Cost and Manufacture. How much will the customer be willing to spend for the product? How much will materials and labor time cost? How much will be needed in the future? Now?

Advertisement and Packaging. What type of advertising and promotional plans will be used to market the product? Will the promotional methods be traditional or innovative?

> "Find a need of the consumer that is currently not getting met, or inadequaely met, and fill that need in a way that is appealing to the consumer and profitable for you."
>
> PAMELA POMMERENKE
> *Assistant Professor,*
> *Department of Management*
> *Michigan State University*

Experts in the field	Contact well-known entrepreneurs to get advice.
Internet searches	Visit Web sites on companies and new products or technologies.
Library research	Use college libraries to access references and specialized biographies.
Questionnaires/surveys	Use the mail, phone, Internet, or professional interviews. Write and prepare questions to make sure you collect appropriate data.
Existing research	Use investment banking firms, advisory searches, or consulting firms to gather data on existing research.
Trade associations	Visit trade shows and read trade publications.
Market research firms	Hire a firm to prepare a report or market survey for the proposed idea.

Figure 2-5 **Sources for Finding Information.**

Sales. What distributions and sales methods will be used? Will the reliance be on independent sales representatives, company salesforce, direct mail, door-to-door sales, supermarkets, service stations, or company-owned stores?

Transport. How will the product be transported—via company-owned trucks, common carriers, postal service, or airfreight?

Employees. Can the company attract employees with the necessary skills to operate the business venture? Who are the workers? Are they dependable, competent, and readily available?

Start with Data Collection

The entrepreneur needs to find answers to the key questions about the potential business identified above. Data collection can come from a variety of sources. The sources to provide data collection are given in Figure 2-5. The more sources that are consulted, the more valid the results will be. However, it is not advisable to go overboard: the amount of available data can become overwhelming. Basically, the questions should be as specific as possible, the sources as relevant as possible, and the data collection only as extensive as needed for the initial investment and planning to run smoothly.[26]

Design and Execute a Study to Get the Answers

Once primary sources of data have been exhausted based on appropriate questions and expectations, the entrepreneur must identify secondary resources to support the preliminary research. This is the stage when the entrepreneur should consult directly with existing business owners and experts in the field and ask pertinent, key questions.

The entrepreneur should target a small number of representative businesses. First, the entrepreneur must identify companies with similar products or services and then inquire as to who may be willing to give advice or provide the names of other contacts without wasting a lot of time and money. Remember that the purpose of this exercise is to start a business, not to become a research expert.

Once the participants have been identified, solicit information from them to answer the key questions, which should be based on the most unbiased model available. To eliminate receiving questionable data, certain pitfalls must be avoided.

1. Ensure that all of the participants are asked the same questions in the same manner.
2. Get detailed—make certain that the answers are accurate by maintaining a precise, objective method of questioning.
3. Train and monitor survey recorders and telephone interviewers to ensure consistent results.

Analyze the Data

Once the primary data have been collected, they must be analyzed. What do the data reveal? How can they be interpreted? Examine the secondary sources that have been queried. How did the survey participants interpret their results? Write a final report modeled on the most thorough sources. This ensures that a record exists for the future and that others in the organization can refer to the study as necessary.

This may all sound too extensive—and expensive. Many entrepreneurs must do their market research with limited funds. Employ these cost-cutting recommendations:

- Use search engines, Web pages, and online databases.
- Use the telephone instead of mail surveys and door-to-door interviewing.
- Avoid research in high-cost cities.
- Test more than one product at a time.
- Avoid collecting unnecessary data.

One example of an inexpensive source is a local university. Professors and students are often involved in projects to help small companies develop marketing plans and undertake market research. Other examples include friends or relatives who own their own business, published interviews with successful entrepreneurs, and library resources.

Phase 3: Develop the Plan

Once an opportunity has been identified, decisions must be made regarding performance and staffing. Who is going to do what? How will decisions be made? The result of the business plan should fully capitalize on all of the company's assets while maintaining flexibility. It also should be sufficiently broad to incorporate unexpected changes in the aim for success and profitability.

A business plan charts the current and future components of the business in about 30 to 40 pages. Similar to a real map, it should answer some basic questions. How far will the business have to go? What is the exact destination or goal? How will the destination be reached? What is the anticipated arrival time at each of the various stops or milestones? A good plan will do the following:

- Determine the viability of the business and application in selected markets.
- Provide guidance in planning and organizing the activities and goals.
- Serve as a vehicle to obtain financing and personnel for the business.

The business plan is the backbone of the business. This single document guides the entrepreneur at three critical junctures:

1. It simplifies decision making during ***times of crisis.***
2. It is the roadmap at ***points of indecision.***
3. It is a motivational guide during ***setbacks or downturns.***

An extremely valuable outcome of preparing and writing the plan at this stage is identifying flaws and creating contingencies. The business plan compels the entrepreneur to carefully examine the prospective venture at its initial, planning stage before significant capital has been invested.

If the plan reveals insurmountable flaws, the entrepreneur may need to abandon that particular opportunity. Although it is discouraging to return to the idea stage, consider two facts:

1. The groundwork has been laid, and the initial learning curve has been completed.
2. Only a relatively small amount of time and capital have been invested.

The entrepreneur should not ignore serious misgivings. Walking away at this stage and beginning again with a new idea and a strong attitude will impress investors and others already involved with the project.

A more detailed version of the business plan is found in Chapter 4, but the entrepreneur can greatly benefit from considering these basic elements now.

Phase 4: Determine the Resources Needed

All businesses must address resource capabilities to foster venture development.[27] However, for a startup venture that uses new technology for its service or as its product it is crucial. The new business must have the skills to match—and triumph over—the competition. Much like Darwin's survival of the fittest, in the business world only the highly skilled will survive.

This section examines three aspects of assessing resource capabilities.

- **Personal contacts and networking**
  Resources are needed to identify, contact, and establish a network with appropriate clients and vendors. Who will devote time to meeting people by traveling? Phone work? E-mail correspondence? Time for networking may be a daily task, high on a priority list.

- **Financing requirements**
  Sufficient capital is required to sustain the company for a specific length of time, possibly a one- or two-year period. The entrepreneur must carefully consider the financial elements required for implementing the plan. Begin by answering the following questions:

  How much initial capital is needed? What resources are available for financial support?

  How long can the new business be self-financed, if necessary, and still withstand initial losses?

  How long will it take to make the business profitable?

What kind of profit margin will eventually result from the product or service?

How can the revenue and financial model be presented to investors for their involvement in the business?

After initial financing, new investors may be approached at a later date for further infusions of capital.

- **Sources of technical skills**
  The entrepreneur may have an idea but not possess the creative process and innovative technical skills to implement it.[28] In that case, external skilled labor is needed. This may be someone the entrepreneur already knows, such as a coworker, or he or she might need to hire someone through want ads or an employment agency. Training costs need to be calculated into startup costs. Furthermore, someone may be needed who can translate technical jargon to simplified terms for investors.

Phase 5: Manage the Distinguishing Features of the Business

So far in this chapter, we've evaluated the opportunity, begun developing the plan, and assessed resource needs. Phase 5 entails running the business, applying a specific management structure and style to any questions, as well as handling difficulties and roadblocks to successes that may arise. The emphasis here is on the act of investing. Substantial time, money, experience, and energy have been invested in setting up. Now the entrepreneur needs to break off from the path blazed by the most successful businesses and invest in people, operating procedures, and information technology. This involves the following sequence of events:

- **Deliver a Total Solution**
  Traditionally, small companies have assumed unchallenged territory and special distribution channels for their products. Today, however, all companies are playing in the same markets and providing the entire range of service for their customers. Investors and customers want to buy a total solution product or service.
- **Cultivate Advanced Resources**
  The layoffs of highly skilled workers from major corporations that abound create an important opportunity for a startup company. These trained and effective personnel are looking to apply their business skills and experiences to startups. The results to the business include access to small companies and major corporations, capital, and productive market knowledge.
  Consider an example of a new technology that effectively transformed day-to-day services and how a business plan was crucial in making that opportunity a business reality.

Use the Framework to Evaluate and Test the Five-Phase Opportunity Concept

Now that we have completed the five phases for the opportunity analysis, use this framework to evaluate the issues that are stronger or weaker for the market, competition, management team, and financial requirements for the new business concept.[29]

Criterion	Stronger Opportunity	Weaker Opportunity
Need	Identified	Unclear
Customers	Reachable; receptive	Unreachable or loyalties established
Payback to user/customer	Less than one year	Three years or more
Product life cycle	Long; recover investment	Short; recover investment
Industry structure	Competition or emerging	Aggressively competitive
Potential market size	$100 million sales	Less than $10 million sales
Market growth rate	Growing at 30 to 50 percent	Contracting less than 10 percent
Gross margins	30 to 50 percent	Less than 20 percent; volatile
Market share attainable (year 5)	20 percent or more	Less than 5 percent

Figure 2-6   Framework for Evaluating an Opportunity: Market Issues.

Tables 2-6 to 2-9 list in greater detail the factors to be considered in each of these four categories.

The most successful entrepreneurs know where they fit in the market and where they want to be. The framework plan should account for, and accommodate changes in, designing, testing, and marketing to prepare for the business opportunity. The issues that need to be described in more detail should include: determine the improvement needed and anticipate the necessary time frames and how to remain competitive at all times.

Know How to Protect the Idea or Product

One question that might be encountered while conducting research and formulating a business plan is whether or not the idea/opportunity/product/service needs to be protected.[30] The following evaluation screening identifies those conditions

Criterion	Stronger Opportunity	Weaker Opportunity
Profits after tax	10 to 15 percent or more; durable	Less than 5 percent; fragile
Time to: Break even Positive cash flow ROI potential	Under 2 years Under 2 years 25 percent or more per year	More than 3 years More than 3 years Less than 15 to 20 percent per year
Value Capital requirements	High strategic value Low to moderate; fundable	Low strategic value Very high; unfundable
Exit mechanism	Present or envisioned harvest options	Undefined; illiquid investment

Figure 2-7   Framework for Evaluating an Opportunity: Financial and Harvest Issues.

Criterion	Stronger Opportunity	Weaker Opportunity
Fixed and variable costs Production, marketing distribution	Lowest	Highest
Degree of control Prices, channels of resources/distribution	Moderate to strong	Weak
Barriers to entry Proprietary protection Response/lead time	Yes 6 months to 1 year	None None
Legal contractual advantage	Proprietary of exclusivity	None
Sources of differentiation	Numerous	Few or none
Competitors' mindset and strategies	Live and let live; not self-destructive	Defensive and strongly reactive

Figure 2-8   Framework for Evaluating an Opportunity: Competitive Advantage Issues.

whereby an idea may qualify for patent protection. See Chapters 8 for details on patent protection.

Evaluation Screening for Patent Protection

1. Is the service, product, or idea unique to get a head start on competition?

2. Does the service or product represent a breakthrough (either high-tech or different from others)?

3. Is the field changing so slowly that the innovation will be valuable for at least 10 years?

4. Have other, less expensive but adequate protective measures been explored?

5. Has an attorney discussed the options and recommended that a patent be pursued?

6. Is the fee for a patent search and application affordable?

If the answer to two or more of these questions was "yes," patent protection for the idea and opportunity should be seriously considered. However, if a disclosure document, which essentially protects the idea for the first two years (see Figure 2-10), will suffice, then that option should be considered first. What about marketing this idea to a large company as a customer? Most companies have their own internal research and development organization dedicated to monitoring and

Criterion	Stronger Opportunity	Weaker Opportunity
Management team	Existing, strong, proven performance	Weak, inexperienced, lacking key skills
Contacts and networks	Well developed, high quality, acceptable	Crude, limited, inaccessible
Risk	Low	High
Fatal blows	None	One or more

Figure 2-9   Framework for Evaluating an Opportunity: Management Team and Risk Issues.

meeting the needs of their product or service line. The best method for submitting an idea is to contact the company and ask for its disclosure conditions to review an idea.

Some companies, however, will sign a nondisclosure form, whereas others will not. Most will have their own protection form to sign, which essentially states that, while they may agree to review or discuss an idea, their research department may have already thought of the idea long before. Let an attorney have the last word. Get a second (or even a third) legal opinion before committing to any legal expenditure.

As these issues are contemplated, examine the mutual nondisclosure agreement in Figure 2-10 and consider using this agreement to protect the idea.[31]

SUMMARY

Every business starts from an embryonic idea that is analyzed to create an opportunity and then built up until a complete business concept has been reached. Ideas can come from many sources. They can be a result of an entrepreneur's own innovation, which is best accomplished using some simple analytical frameworks; or they can be found in searching the Internet or in observing "points of pain." Some good opportunities are the result of assembling what might at first seem to be unrelated ideas. Once an entrepreneur has identified an opportunity that is worthy of further consideration, the entrepreneur must assess its potential. Often, after a market approach has been selected and the necessary research conducted, the idea may require revision, adding refinement and sophistication to the original spark of an idea.

Generally, a great deal of useful information is readily available. Often our market research objectives must be modified to use available information. In some cases, the entrepreneur may choose to survey the market to acquire data designed specifically to fit the project's needs. In every case, the entrepreneur must apply some judgment to the data while trying to project future prospects.

Once this step is completed, the planning and developing process starts. All ideas must be screened and evaluated to determine the feasibility of the opportunity. The best ideas are evaluated through test marketing and managing the resources to successfully launch the business.

From the marketing research results, the plan must be fine-tuned. The following questions should be answered. What segment(s) of the market can it serve? What does the product or service have to offer the market? Who are the customers? How will the product or services be promoted and marketed?

The next chapter will address how to apply the marketing plan for a business.

STUDY QUESTIONS

1. Why is innovation important, and how is it changing?

2. What are the two types of innovation? Give two examples of each type.

3. What are the various ways to generate business ideas?

4. Briefly describe the various methods to research a business opportunity.

5. List the five phases to complete an opportunity analysis.

6. When does an idea need to be protected?

7. Describe the evaluation screening process.

THIS AGREEMENT is made on _____, [date and year], by and between _____, Inc., [name and address] _____, and [name and address] _____.

Purpose. The parties hereto wish to explore various business ideas and joint venture possibilities under which each may disclose its Confidential Information to the other.

Definition. "Confidential Information" means any information, technical data or know-how, including, but not limited to, that which relates to research, products, services, customers, markets, software development, source code, inventions, patents or patents pending, designs, drawings, engineering, marketing or finances, or licensing agreements. Confidential information does not include information, technical data or know-how which (i) is in possession of the receiving party at the time of disclosure as shown by the receiving party's files and records immediately prior to the time of disclosure; or (ii) prior to or after the time of disclosure becomes part of the public knowledge or literature, not as a result of any action of the receiving party; or (iii) is approved for release by the disclosing party.

Nondisclosure ofConfidential Information. The parties hereto agree not to use the Confidential Information disclosed to it by the other party for its own use or to compete with either party or for any purpose except to carry out discussions concerning and the undertaking of any business relationship between the two. Neither will disclose the Confidential Information of the other to third parties or to the first party's employees, except to third parties and employees who are required to have the information in connection with such discussions or in order to carry out the contemplated business ("Representative"). Both parties shall cause their respective representatives to comply with all restrictions set forth herein. Each agrees that it will take all reasonable steps to protect the secrecy of and avoid disclosure or use of Confidential Information of the other in order to prevent it from falling into public domain or the possession of unauthorized persons. Each agrees to notify the other in writing of any misuse or misappropriation of such Confidential Information of the other, which may come to its attention.

Return of Materials. Any materials or documents which have been furnished by one party to the other will be promptly returned, accompanied by all copies of such documentation after the business possibility has been rejected or concluded.

Patent of Copyright Infringement. Nothing in this Agreement is intended to grant any rights under any patent of copyright of either party, nor shall this Agreement grant either party any rights in or to the other party's Confidential Information, except the limited right to review such patent, copyright or Confidential Information solely for the purpose of determining whether to enter into the proposed business relationship between the parties.

Term. This Agreement shall remain in effect so long as the parties continue to exchange Confidential Information provided that either party may terminate this Agreement at any time upon thirty (30) days prior to written notice to the other party. Upon any expiration or other termination of this Agreement for any reason, each party's obligations with respect to Confidential Information received prior to such expiration or termination shall continue for a period of three (3) years after the date of such termination; provided, however, that with respect to Confidential Information which consists of software source code or related documentation, the obligation contained in this Agreement shall continue indefinitely.

Miscellaneous. This Agreement shall be binding upon and for the benefit of the undersigned parties, their successors and assigns, provided that Confidential Information may not be assigned without consent of the disclosing party. Failure to enforce any provision of this Agreement shall not constitute a waiver of any term or condition hereof.

Governing Law and Jurisdiction. This Agreement shall be governed by and construed under the laws of the state of _____ [state]. The federal and state courts within the State of _____ [state] shall have exclusive jurisdiction to adjudicate any dispute arising out of this Agreement.

Remedies. Each party agrees that its obligations hereunder are necessary and reasonable in order to protect the other party and the other party's business, and expressly agrees that monetary damages would be inadequate to compensate the other party for any breach of any covenant or agreement set forth herein. Accordingly, each party agrees and acknowledges that any such violation or threatened violation will cause irreparable injury to the other party, and that, in addition to any other remedies that may be available, in law, in equity or otherwise, the other party shall be entitled to obtain injunctive relief against the threatened breach of this Agreement or the continuation of any such breach, without the necessity of proving actual damages.

IN WITNESS WHEREOF, the parties hereto have executed this Agreement effective as of the date first above written in _____ [city and state].

FOR: (Company) _____   FOR: (Company) _____

BY: _____   BY: _____

TITLE: _____   TITLE: _____

Figure 2-10 **Mutual Nondisclosure Agreement.**

EXERCISES

1. Finding an Idea and Turning It into an Opportunity

Go to the book Web site, www.wiley.com/college/kaplan, and browse a number of idea source Web sites from the three lists. Use these as starters and browse until you find an idea that you think has merit for creating a business opportunity. Write a one-page synopsis of the idea, explaining why you think this is a good idea and how you would use it to build a business opportunity argument.

2. Preparing an Opportunity Cost Analysis

RJL Technologies provides custom services to its loyalty customers from Monday through Friday. David Lee, the co-owner, believes it is important for the employees to have Saturday and Sunday off to spend with their families. However, he also recognizes that this policy has implications for profitability, and he is considering staying open on Saturday.

David estimates that if the company stays open on Saturday, it can generate daily revenue of $2,500 each day for 52 days per year. The incremental daily costs will be $500 for labor, $50 for transportation, and $150 for an office manager. The costs do not include a portion of monthly rent.

David would like to know the opportunity cost of not working on Saturday. Provide an estimate of the opportunity cost and explain why you do not have to consider rent in your estimate.

INTERACTIVE LEARNING ON THE WEB

Test your skill-builder knowledge of the chapter using the interactive Web site.

1. Self Assessment:
2. Multiple Choice:
3. Matching of Key Terms:
4. Demonstration:
5. Case:
6. Video:

CASE STUDY: STARION INSTRUMENTS

This case was prepared by Bruce Melzer and Gile R. Downes Jr. under the supervision of Professor Murray B. Low as the basis for class discussion, rather than to illustrate effective or ineffective handling of an administrative situation.

The authors wish to thank Columbia Innovation Enterprise, Joseph R. Flicek, Michelle Monfort, and Dr. Michael Treat for their support in the development of this case. Copyright © 2001 by the Lang Center for Entrepreneurship, Graduate School of Business, Columbia University, 317 Uris Hall, 3022 Broadway, New York, NY 10027, 212.854.3244, www.gsb.columbia.edu/entprog.

Note: For competitive reasons, some financial figures—specifically, product production costs and marketing figures—have been altered or fabricated.

INTRODUCTION

In the spring of 1996, Dr. Michael Treat, a surgeon and professor at Columbia University Presbyterian Hospital, walked into U.S. Surgical Inc.'s New Jersey offices expecting to pitch his latest invention in a one-on-one meeting with the company's new technology scout. Instead, Dr. Treat found himself at the head of a sprawling boardroom table surrounded by 20 or so engineers, scientists and managers— "high-priced people," as he described them.

Dr. Treat had no formal presentation, no PowerPoint show, no overhead slides, not even a one-page handout. All he had was a Nike shoebox, from which he pulled an untested prototype of a surgical device he completed at four o'clock that morning.

The device had a pistol grip attached to a thin balsa wood arm with a pincers on the end. Its components included a model airplane switch, a surgical blade, a Ni-Cad battery and two pieces of heater wire Dr. Treat harvested from an old hair dryer. "It was like something out of Bomb Making 101," Dr. Treat recalled.

Although the execution was crude, the idea was elegant and simple. Dr. Treat created a grasping tool with a surgical blade and battery-heated tip that simultaneously cut tissue and cauterized it to stop any bleeding. In contrast to the existing devices that cost tens of thousands of dollars and relied on bulky complicated ultrasound technology, Dr. Treat's device fit the palm of his hand and could be built for a fraction of the price.

Having come to medicine with an engineering background, Dr. Treat had invented a tool that he believed would revolutionize electrosurgery. Moreover, he was convinced he had the right ingredients for a deal. He had sold concepts to U.S. Surgical before, and the company, one of the country's largest medical device makers, had the marketing clout and capital to make his device as common as forceps in the operating room.

BACKGROUND

The foundation of Dr. Treat's technology was built in the 1980s, when he and Dr. Larry Bass, a plastic surgery resident at Columbia, started experimenting with lasers in surgery. Begging and borrowing lasers and electrical gear from companies all over the country, the two surgeons filled Blakemore Laboratory, a small room on Columbia Presbyterian's 17th floor, with equipment for the new research. Together, Drs. Bass and Treat created the field of "laser tissue welding," using thermal energy to rejoin tissue severed in surgery. "We got to create this whole world—it was like Wayne's World. Mike and Larry were like Wayne and Garth; we made up this whole thing," Dr. Treat recalled.

But 10 years of tinkering and research produced few useful clinical results. By the late 1991, with Dr. Bass near the end of his residency, he and Dr. Treat shelved their laser work. But the ideas continued to percolate, and, eventually, Dr. Treat realized that he had it all wrong. It was the heat, not the laser's energy, that could seal tissue. It was then that he called U.S. Surgical to arrange the meeting in which he now stood.

After explaining how the device worked, the meeting moved downstairs to a laboratory, where Dr. Treat demonstrated the device on an anesthetized dog. The device worked as he predicted and the U.S. Surgical people were "blown away" by the results, Dr. Treat said.

Despite Dr. Treat's technical success and impressive demonstration, however, U.S. Surgical's team declined to invest in or purchase the idea. Surely someone else has done this before, the company argued. And how could something so simple ever be protected by a patent? Without a patent, U.S. Surgical would be vulnerable to competition, and they did not want to invest time and money developing and marketing a product they couldn't protect.

Dejected, Dr. Treat returned to his surgical and teaching practice at Columbia Presbyterian; his invention languished in its shoebox above his workbench.

Four years later, Dr. Treat's device is on the market. Medical entrepreneur Michelle "Shelly" Monfort joined forces with Dr. Treat, creating Starion Instruments to develop and market his electrosurgical devices.

The birth of Starion and Dr. Treat's progression from despair to deal exemplifies the entrepreneurial process. Ms. Monfort seized upon an inventor's idea, tested it against competing technologies, negotiated the rights to license the technology, and raised the funds to build a company. At each step along the way, Starion ran into roadblocks, and the future of the venture was never assured. "Obstacles are the rule. There's no such thing as smooth sailing. It's about overcoming the obstacles." Dr. Treat said.

IDENTIFYING THE OPPORTUNITY

Shelly Monfort, a Stanford-trained engineer, began her entrepreneurial career in 1986, working with Dr. Thomas Fogarty, a legend in the surgical world. His Fogarty catheter is a standard tool in operating rooms all over the world. The holder of at least 63 patents, Fogarty has a long record of turning ideas into money, and spinning off companies that get acquired by major medical companies.

First conducting research and development on devices and later helping to start and run companies to commercialize those devices, Ms. Monfort and two engineers, Ken Mollenaur and George Hermann, helped Fogarty create, fund, and take public six different surgical device companies between 1990 and 1996. The last company they worked on together was General Surgical Innovations; Ms. Monfort stayed with the company on and off until its IPO in 1996.

After working for others, Ms. Monfort was looking for a company she could call her own. She had experience, market and product savvy, and was searching out interesting technologies to bring to market. She also had the nucleus of a team. Ken Mollenaur was an engineer and wizard at designing and building prototypes. George Hermann, also an engineer, was an all around wise advisor, who could ask the probing questions, worry about details, and had extensive experience driving medical devices through the regulatory maze. All three were serial entrepreneurs, who knew what it took to bring an idea to market.

One of Ms. Monfort's first prospects was a laser-powered surgical tool that would cut and cauterize tissue. In the course of her research, she called her friend, Dr. Larry Bass, whom she knew had laser experience, to talk about a device. Dr. Bass said he knew of something even simpler and told her there was someone she needed to meet: Dr. Michael Treat.

Ms. Monfort met with Dr. Treat and was impressed by the simplicity of his solution and its advantages in the medical device marketplace, where complicated, expensive technologies are always at risk of being supplanted by products that are cheaper and better. She said of Dr. Treat's device, "[it's] the lowest common denominator; no one can make something simpler."

Ms. Monfort arranged for a head-to-head test of the laser and Dr. Treat's tool in the Boston laboratory of Dr. Steve Schwaitzberg, the surgeon who was championing the laser tool under consideration by Ms Monfort.

In a small veterinary operating room, Drs. Treat and Schwaitzberg operated on an anesthetized pig, while Ms. Monfort looked on. Each surgeon sliced the mesentery, the blood vessel-laced tissue that surrounds the intestines; then they compared the results. Dr. Treat says his device hung up on the tissue, while the laser cut a bit more cleanly and easily. Dr. Treat said, "Steve, yours works better than mine." But Schwaitzberg replied, "yeah Mike, but I didn't build mine in my basement and yours is going to cost about 100 times less."

Dr. Schwaitzberg's "honesty, his candidness, his unselfishness was crucial," Dr. Treat recalled. Dr. Schwaitzberg could have simply pushed the laser technology, but instead urged Ms. Monfort to put her money on Dr. Treat's tool. Ms. Monfort did not need much convincing. "We knew right there" that Dr. Treat's technology could be the basis for her new company, she said. "You put it on tissue and it worked." And she knew the market well enough to see that surgeons would embrace a device that could cut and seal in a single step.

THE STATE OF THE ART

Electrosurgical devices—those used for cutting and sealing or cauterizing tissue—are used in almost every major surgical procedure. The overall annual market for these devices is about $1 billion.

The most common electrosurgical tool is the monopolar device,[32] also known in the industry as a Bovie, after its inventor, William T. Bovie. With this technology, the patient is wired to a grounding pad that provides a path for the current to flow. The surgeon uses an electrode to pass a high-frequency electrical current through a patient to cut and cauterize tissue in a selected area. Bovie requires a generator that costs between $7,500 and $10,000 and lasts about seven years. Each operation requires disposable grounding pads and electrodes, whose combined cost is $5–$6 per procedure.[33] The disadvantages include (relatively rare) situations in which the device causes burns to the patient at the site of the grounding pad. Additionally, the Bovie's high-energy output can interfere with the ever-growing mass of electronic equipment in modern operating rooms. A more advanced technology than the Bovie is the UltraCision, also known as the harmonic scalpel. This device uses ultrasound to generate the heat needed to cut and seal tissues. Ethicon Endo-Surgery Inc., a Johnson & Johnson subsidiary, owns UltraCision, and Ms. Monfort estimates that the ultrasound-based products have annual sales of about $100 million. Like the Bovie, the UltraCision system requires a reusable power supply, which carries a list price of about $15,000. The system uses an electrical cable that lists for $630 and must be replaced after about 100 surgeries, and single-use tips that cost about $325.

UltraCision devices are used primarily in laparoscopy, abdominal operations in which surgeons use long tubular instruments and relatively small incisions to work inside the patient. Despite its growing popularity, laparoscopic surgery accounts for only 20 percent of the surgical procedures. More common is open surgery, where the surgeon fully exposes the area that he or she is working on.

The opportunity for Starion Instruments lay in Dr. Treat's and Ms. Monfort's vision of Treat's technology as not only a head-on competitor for Ethicon's UltraCision tool, but as a highly diversifiable device. In addition to the obvious laparoscopic application, they envisioned a specially modified forceps that could be used for the open surgery market. And that was just the start. Indeed, as Ken Mollenauer put it, "this technology can fit onto almost any style of surgical device that does clamping and cutting," and there are over 1,000 such devices on the market.

But all this was just talk. First, Ms. Monfort had to decide whether this was truly a technology around which she could build a company. "There's a big leap of faith you take at the very beginning," she said. "It was so simple; we just couldn't believe that it hadn't been done 30 years ago. We realized that everybody was saying that, and that there was something very simple that everybody had just walked right past and missed."

INDUSTRY CONTEXT

The medical devices industry is populated by a small number of major device manufacturers and diversified medical companies and a large number of small companies. Dominant players in the medical device industry include Johnson & Johnson, Baxter International, Becton Dickinson, Medtronic, Guidant, Boston Scientific, and U.S. Surgical, a unit of industrial conglomerate Tyco. The industry tallies total annual worldwide sales of $150 billion, with international sales accounting for approximately 40 percent of total revenues.[34] Standard and Poor's expects 2000 revenue growth to reach between 9 and 10 percent, down from the 14 percent growth in 1999.

Medical products and services companies invest about 8 percent of annual revenues in research and development, compared to 3 to 4 percent of all U.S. manufacturers, according to Standard and Poor's.[35] But these figures don't reflect the true path of innovation in the medical device industries. Small medical companies often serve as sources of innovations and new technology. Often, when a small company's device or technology establishes a firm foothold in the marketplace, the company either partners with a giant or is acquired by one.

MARKET CONTEXT

Medical equipment sales are a two-step process, requiring approval at both the user and hospital purchasing committee levels. The surgeon is the clinical buyer, the one who decides whether this new tool is one he or she wants or will use. Although the purchasing process varies widely from hospital to hospital, if the surgeon rejects a product, it won't get purchased. After the surgeon's approval, a committee, usually composed of the hospital or the clinic purchasing agent, the operating room supervisor, and the surgeon, makes the final buying decision. Expensive equipment purchases may be slowed because they may have to be charged to the hospital's capital budget. In some cases, medical equipment companies may loan or simply give a device to key researchers or industry leaders, hoping they will write about the device or discuss it in professional panels.

As a group, surgeons are open to innovation, but it is difficult to generalize how quickly they will adopt new technologies. On one hand, they are always looking to save time and save steps in a procedure. On the other hand, surgeons hone their skills by doing the same task, the same way, over and over again. And the risks to the patient can be high if a technology or procedure doesn't work properly, so surgeons tend to choose what's been tried and proven. Nevertheless, surgeons will go where the market pushes them, too. Part of the growth in laparoscopic surgery came because patients were demanding it, and surgeons who weren't performing common laparoscopic procedures saw their referrals and workload slow down.[36]

LICENSING

In the medical device industry, the combination of patents, extensive clinical trials, and research combined with federal government oversight can create significant barriers to entry that can protect device makers against competition.

The Food and Drug Administration is the primary regulator of medical devices, and its mandate is to ensure that devices that reach the market are safe and effective. Although the agency does not conduct clinical trials, it does require companies to submit documentation on the efficacy of any regulated device. Based on that documentation, the FDA approves products for sale. The agency has oversight of some 80,000 devices and medical instruments. In the 2000 fiscal year, the agency approved or cleared for use approximately 3,500 devices.

Two major questions hung over Ms. Monfort. First, is this technology unique enough to be patented? Second, could she make a device reliable enough to be used by thousands of different surgeons in thousands of different circumstances?

First, she had to undertake the patent search to find out if indeed the product was patentable. And if she concluded it was, the only way to find out if the technology was feasible was to build and test some prototypes. Since she didn't own the idea, she needed to get a license from the owner of the concept: Columbia University.

Under the 1980 Bayh-Dole Act (see Appendix 1), universities are entitled to claim royalties on inventions and discoveries made by their faculty members or employees using university facilities and federal research funds. As an assistant professor at Columbia University's Presbyterian Hospital, Dr. Treat's inventions are therefore not necessarily his to own exclusively. The university's policies on faculty inventions state: "Columbia University has the right to claim ownership of an invention developed in University laboratories and funded by federal, foundation, university, or corporate funds." Columbia shares the income it receives from licenses with the inventor or faculty member.

Dr. Treat duly reported his invention to the university. Prior to negotiating with Ms. Monfort, the university started taking the steps to apply for a patent on the invention. Like many research universities, Columbia created a technology transfer office—Columbia Innovation Enterprise (CIE)[37]—to patent, license, and commercialize intellectual property created by its researchers. Money raised from this office goes in part to the university and in part to the inventor. The printed policies of this office tell its inventors, "of the first $100,000 of net income from licensing your invention, you receive 50 percent and an additional 25 percent goes to your research activities. 'Net income' is determined by deducting a flat 20 percent of gross income to cover the University's expenses, including patent prosecution expenses."[38]

By the time Ms. Monfort started talking to Columbia in November 1997, the University had already filed a preliminary patent application, which triggered the process of determining whether Dr. Treat's technology was unique and could be protected. Using the patent research sites on the Internet, Ken Mollenauer conducted his own patent search on Dr. Treat's technology. Then he and Ms. Monfort brainstormed with Dr. Treat and other surgeons to devise the broadest possible patent protection. And even though Ms. Monfort didn't have a contract with the university, she fed that work to the university's patent lawyers, who were preparing a second, more comprehensive patent filing. "We helped out with the second filing knowing that we might lose the contract to develop the product," Mollenauer said.

THE CONTRACT

Joseph Flicek, Senior Technology Advisor at CIE, was handling Dr. Treat's invention. Ms. Monfort and Mr. Flicek spent a day coming up with a basic term sheet; then the lawyers took about four months to fill in the details. At times, the legal wheels turned so slowly that Ms. Monfort came close to walking away from the deal. But in retrospect, said Ken Mollenauer, the Columbia deal was quick relative to other university licensing deals.

In the end, the University gave Ms. Monfort's new company an exclusive license for the life of the patent. Ms. Monfort agreed to give the university 10 percent of the company, which would be diluted as new investors joined in later funding rounds. And she agreed to make cash payments when she reached specific milestones, such as closing her first round of funding and making the first product sale. She also agreed to make royalty payments based on the company's gross sales of products based on Columbia's patent. Any new patents developed by Starion were the company's property.

Summer arrived, along with a signed license, and by June 1998, the new company, Starion Instruments, could start building a staff and a product. With a deal in place, Dr. Treat flew out to Starion's California office and workshop, which was now well equipped with tools and supplies for building prototypes.

Starion decided that the first device should be a simple one that would work in open surgery. Rather than try to go head to head with Ethicon's UltraCision, Starion chose to develop a versatile device, a forceps with an electrically heated tip. Once they perfected the technology and understood how to turn Dr. Treat's idea into a real product, they would expand into the laparoscopic device market.

Dr. Treat and Mr. Mollenauer experimented with the technology and built prototypes. The task was tricky. They needed to create a device that would produce uniform results on any kind of tissue and would work in the hands of any surgeon, regardless of how much pressure they applied to the forceps. Testing their handiwork on pieces of beef liver and steak, Dr. Treat and Mr. Mollenauer developed a prototype that cut without a blade.

Next, Mr. Mollenauer figured out how to control the voltage, how to craft the hot tip, and how to design a product that could be built simply and cheaply. Every few months Dr. Treat, Ms. Monfort and Mr. Mollenauer would gather at Steve Schwaitzberg's Boston laboratory to test the latest version. The development process was neither quick nor easy. "A lot of unimaginable things will come up when you move from a working prototype to an actual product," Dr. Treat said.

In March 1999, Starion applied for critical approval from the Federal Food and Drug Administration and received approval within three months. But the company was still a year away from full-scale production.

With prototypes in hand, Ms. Monfort started making the rounds to potential investors in May 1999. "The people who are putting money in the company obviously want all the risk taken out of it. They want all the answers to all the questions, and when you're first starting you don't have them. So you rely more on making the box looks . . . smart and polished, and [you] make the prototype look really nice; [you] do your slide presentation in PowerPoint with the beautiful background because that's all you've got. And you just tell them, 'we don't have the answer to this, this, and this, but this is how we'll find out.'" Although her target was to raise $750,000 in capital, Ms. Monfort assembled $2 million from her own funds, family and friends, private investors, and a pair of venture capital funds. Shares were priced at $1, and Starion's pre-money valuation was $7 million. Her mentor, Dr. Fogarty, pitched in, and his credibility—as much as his cash—gave the fledgling company a boost.

In October 1999, Starion Instruments, represented by Dr. Treat, made its debut with a booth at the American College of Surgeons Conference, the single most important industry event for people who would buy and use the product. But sales were not the primary objective this time. Instead, Ms. Monfort wanted to raise enough buzz and attention that she could attract the next round of investors and amass the money to carry Starion's devices to market.

The company planned to hit the market with a package consisting of a single-use disposable forceps and a disposable battery pack. The forceps would carry a list price of $110, and the battery pack would list for $39. Concentrating initial marketing efforts on open surgery applications (which account for about 80 percent of procedures performed each year), Starion would eventually expand into laparoscopic devices.[39]

Starting with open surgery applications was intended to ease adoption of the product—if the new tool didn't work, surgeons could easily revert to their standard cut-and-suture techniques. Variable costs, excluding sales commissions, of both the battery and forceps were projected to equal about 40 percent of the list sales price. Fixed costs, excluding research and development, were projected to total $1.10 million in the first year of operation and $1.65 million the second year. R&D for the first year was projected at $1.25 million the first year and $1.45 million the second.

Meanwhile, Ethicon had been promoting its devices for use in ear, nose, and throat surgery. In an attempt to segment the surgical market and avoid going head to head with Ethicon, Starion marketed its cautery forceps as a timesaving tool for ligation—cutting and sealing blood vessels. Parsing the market even further, Starion decided to promote its forceps to ligate veins one-to-four millimeters in diameter typically encountered during hemorrhoid surgery. Under the standard method, a surgeon clamps off each side of the vein, snips it, then sews or seals each end. Using the Starion's instrument, the surgeon cuts and seals the vein in a single step. Moreover, Starion's device is an improvement over conventional Bovie, where the electrical current can cause muscle tightening and pain in patients. Starion estimated that some 200,000 hemorrhoidectomies are performed each year in the U.S. market alone. The company also saw a ready market for the forceps in axial dissection, a procedure that is part of some breast surgeries. Approximately 100,000 of these procedures are performed each year in the United States alone.

Starion started marketing through trade shows and was considering the best way to build a salesforce. One option was to build a 24-person salesforce of independent reps, earning 15 percent to 20 percent commission. It also considered setting up a direct salesforce, with salaries at the market rate of $30,000 to $50,000 and commissions of 10 percent of list price. A third option was to build a salesforce comprised of 50 percent in-house representatives and 50 percent independents."

Even as Starion looked at distribution options, Ms. Monfort was raising the second round of funding. She was seeking to raise $4 million at $3 per share, with Starion's pre-money valuation at $14 million.

U.S. Surgical, the company that once turned Dr. Treat away, was interested in the device and even talked of buying the company. U.S. Surgical had its own ultrasonic device on the market and was having trouble gaining market share against longtime competitor Johnson & Johnson. And U.S. Surgical's market position got even worse after it lost a patent infringement suit with Johnson & Johnson over the ultrasonic device. Suddenly, U.S. Surgical was desperate for another product to compete with UltraCision, and it focused on Starion.

But U.S. Surgical's parent company, Tyco, wouldn't buy a startup. Tyco, however, was in the process of creating its own small venture fund and through that fund plowed $4 million into Starion.

By the time she closed the second round of funding with $7.2 million, Ms. Monfort was practically turning away investors. "The excitement built on itself." When she started to close the round of funding, "we made it kind of scarce, . . . well then suddenly everybody is clamoring to get in. As a CEO you have to capitalize on that."

Separate from the Tyco investment, U.S. Surgical wanted to sell and distribute Starion's products. Ms. Monfort, who helped engineer product distribution deals with U.S. Surgical for her previous company, GSII, had a good relationship with U.S. Surgical's management. Although the details were not yet clear, U.S. Surgical would likely demand a 40 percent commission.

Ms. Monfort and her team were torn. Certainly U.S. Surgical had a massive, well-connected marketing organization. But would U.S. Surgical's salesforce really push the Starion product, or would they simply add it to the list of hundreds of items they already sold. Would it be wise for such a young company to relinquish control of its distribution so early in its life? Or could this be the way to pave a smooth path toward a swift and profitable buyout?

EPILOGUE

Ms. Monfort concluded that it was too risky for a young, small company to let such a giant company dictate her future, and she turned down the distribution deal with U.S. Surgical. Starion instead elected to develop a network of independent salespeople supervised by company staff. The issue of which distribution channels to use still generates debate within Starion, and the current CEO, Ed Cornell, said: "There are strong arguments for each, and I do not believe the final chapter has been written on the mix of opportunities we will use."

Starion spent much of the spring and summer of 2000 refining and manufacturing the first product, which looks like a fancy forceps with a battery pack. "There's just a lot of fussing to get it right," Ms. Monfort said.

Even production wasn't simple. Starion paid to have key components manufactured, but the manufacturers took months to deliver the product and often pushed the firm to the back of the line in order to do work for bigger customers. Product design delays and manufacturing setbacks delayed the full-scale rollout of the forceps until early 2001.

Starion developed and sought FDA approval for four other devices based on Dr. Treat's technology. Disposable, single-use versions of the instruments were created, and would cost between $80 and $300. Starion also changed the basic method for powering its devices, after concluding that the original power supply— a pack running on four D-cell batteries—was impractical due to the batteries' short

Starion Instruments Analysis

Starion Teaching Note Final Worksheet 2-20-01

Assumptions
Margin

List price	139
Variable manufacturing cost (% basis)	40%
Variable costs manufacturing amount (% x list price)	55.6
Variable sales (commission) average 20% x list price =	$27.80
Total variable unit cost	$83.40
Contribution margin	$55.60
Contribution margin % (contribution margin/sales price) =	40%

	Year 1		Year 2	
Revenues and Sales	Units	Revenue	Units	Revenue
Projected revenue	28,776	$ 4,000,000	57,552	$ 8,000,000

Fixed Costs (without sales force)	**Year 1**	**Year 2**
Fixed cost	1,100,000	1,680,000
Research and development	1,250,000	1,450,000
Total Fixed costs	2,350,000	3,100,000

Sales Force Calculations		
Number of people in sales force	24	24
Average salary	40,000	40,000
Fixed cost for staff sales force	960,000	960,000

Blended Staff and Independent Reps Fixed Costs	Sales force cost		
# of independents (commission only)	12	0	0
# of staff (at $40,000 salary)	12	480,000	480,000
Fixed cost blended sales force		480,000	480,000

Year 1 Distribution and Profit Analysis

	% Commission	Commission Amount($)	Total Variable Cost (Commiss + Mfg Cost)	Contrib. margin	Fixed Costs	Break Even Vol = (Fixed/ Contrib)	Net Income Based on $4 Million Revenue
Independent reps	20%	27.8	83.4	55.6	2,350,000	42,266.2	(749,916)
Staff	10%	13.9	69.5	69.5	3,310,000	47,625.9	(1,309,932)
Half staff, half ind. reps	15%	20.85	76.45	62.55	2,830,000	45,243.8	(1.029,925)
Distributor	40%	55.6	111.2	27.8	2,350,000	84,532.4	(1,549,691)

Year 2 Distribution and Profit Analysis

NI based on $8 m

	% Commission	Commission Amount($)	Total Variable Cost (Commiss + Mfg Cost)	Contrib. margin	Fixed Costs	Break Even Vol = (Fixed/ Contrib)	Net Income
Independent reps	20%	27.8	83.4	55.6	3,100,000	55,755,4	100,163
Staff	10%	13.9	69.5	69.5	4,060,000	58,417,3	(59,864)
Half staff, half ind. reps	15%	20.85	76.45	62.55	3,580,000	57,224.2	20,150
Distributor	40%	55.6	111.2	27.8	2,350,000	84,532.4	(749,782)

lifespan. The new, reusable power supply would draw 110 volts AC from the wall and utilize a step-down transformer to deliver 6 volts DC (battery voltage level) to the surgical instrument. Although the new power supply was more expensive than the battery pack (approximately $1,000), it was still cheaper than the power supply for lasers, UltraCision, and Bovie-type devices by a factor of ten.

The company expects to seek a third round of funding before it reaches profitability. In the autumn of 2000, Ms. Monfort's father, whom she called "my best friend," became seriously ill. She cut back on the amount of time she devoted to Starion to help care for him. In January 2001, Ms. Monfort stepped down as head of the company she founded, although she retained a seat on Starion's board. In January a new CEO, Ed Cornell, stepped in.

CASE STUDY QUESTIONS

1. Define the market potential and business opportunity.
2. What are the competitive advantages for the business model?
   a. Do you agree with the company's pricing and sales strategy?
   b. What licensing strategies should be considered?
3. Did the company select the right management and partners?
4. Is the technology unique enough to be patented?
5. What are your recommendations for the business?

APPENDIX: THE BAYH-DOLE ACT

For decades, some universities and research institutions have retained the rights to inventions developed by their employees or professors during the course of their university-based work. Many universities routinely require faculty to file disclosures of the inventions or technologies they develop.

The 1980 Bayh-Dole Act (P.L. 96-517, Patent and Trademark Act Amendments of 1980) helped strengthen some of the university and small-business claims on inventions created by their employees. Sponsored by Senators Birch Bayh of Indiana and Robert Dole of Kansas, the act allows small business and nonprofit institutions, including universities, to retain the rights to inventions created with federal research funds. Since the federal government dispenses research money through thousands of programs, the act created a uniform policy for dealing with the key intellectual property rights generated in the course of federally funded research.

Under the act, universities are encouraged to file patents for the inventions they hold and are encouraged to work with companies to promote the use of inventions developed with federal funds. Moreover, universities are expected to give small businesses preference in licensing new technologies and inventions.

The government retains a nonexclusive right to use or practice the patents that originated with federal funding. Critics of the act see it as a giveaway and say that the public should retain a greater share of intellectual property created with public money.

The legislation has helped create a technology transfer industry at universities around the country. The Association of University Technology Managers (AUTM), which tracks universities' commercialization efforts, reports that before the act fewer than 250 patents per year were issued to universities and research institutions. In 1998, the 198 U.S. and Canadian universities, teaching hospitals, and nonprofit research institutes that belong to AUTM generated 4,808 new U.S. patent applications and yielded 3,668 new licenses. Those new licenses in turn were the foundation for 364 new companies.

Feeding that patent machine were inventions and technologies developed by faculty and employees. In 1998, university faculty declared the development of 11,784 inventions or technologies, according to AUTM.

AUTM members received $725 million in gross income from licenses and options in 1998, which was up from $611 million in gross adjusted income and options the previous year. Much of that money has been recycled back into the universities for research.

Source: Daniel E. Massing, "AUTM Licensing Survey: FY 1998" (Norwalk, CT: Association of University Licensing Managers, 1999).

ADDITIONAL RESOURCES

- **Office.com (www.office.com):**   "This new way we work."
- **Digitalwork.com (www.digitalwork.com):**   "Your business workshop."
- **Onvia.com (www.onvia.com):**   "The premiere e-marketplace for small businesses."
- **Ideacafe.com (www.ideacafe.com):**   "A fun approach to serious business."
- **Smartonline.com (www.smartonline.com):**   "Small-business answers from small-business owners."
- **Workz.com (www.workz.com):**   "Helping small businesses grow and prosper online."
- **Edge.low.org (www.edge.low.org):**   "A peer-learning community for growing your company."
- **Entreworld (www.entreworld.org):**   "A world of resources for entrepreneurs."
- **Small Business Administration (www.sba.gov):**   "Helping small businesses to succeed."

www.wiley.com/college/kaplan

ROADMAP for:

ENTREPRENEURSHIP
Starting the Venture

☐ Why Innovation Is Important
☐ Definition and Types of Innovation
☐ Frameworks for Learning Innovation Skills
☐ Finding and Assessing Ideas
☐ Converting an Idea into an Opportunity
☐ Opportunity Analysis: Five Phases to Success
☑ **Formulating a Successful Marketing Plan**
☑ **Preparing the Marketing Analysis and Plan**
☑ **Defining Market Segmentation**
☑ **Conducting a Competitive Analysis**
☑ **Preparing the Pricing and Sales Strategy**
☑ **Preparing the Market and Setting Up Sales Channels**
☐ Identifying What Form of Ownership Is Best
☐ Forms of Doing Business
☐ Sole Proprietorship
☐ C-Corporation
☐ S-Sub Corporation
☐ Partnership
☐ Limited Liability Company
☐ Business Startup Check-Up List
☐ Setting up Employer–Employee Agreements
☐ Setting Up Stock Option Agreements

CHAPTER 3

ANALYZING THE MARKET, CUSTOMERS, AND COMPETITION

"The great secret of success in life is for a man to be ready when his opportunity comes."

BENJAMIN DISRAELI

OBJECTIVES

- Define a successful marketing plan and its relevance to new ventures.
- Learn how entrepreneurs prepare a marketing analysis plan.
- List the steps of a successful database marketing plan.
- Learn how to define market segmentation.
- Describe the methods of a competitive analysis.
- Learn the process to position a product or service.
- Describe the methods for a price and sales strategy.

CHAPTER OUTLINE

INTRODUCTION

By now, the entrepreneur has solidified the idea, has implemented the recommendations in Chapter 2 to investigate the worth of the idea, and has identified potential problems. The entrepreneur may already have approached others with the idea and gained their initial support. The next step is to start writing the business plan as will

61

be described in Chapter 11, in conjunction with analyzing the markets, customers, and competition explained in this chapter. In order to prepare the marketing section of the business plan, the entrepreneur must understand the customers' needs and desires, their profile, markets, and pricing, as well as be able to plan for the company's future strategies in each of these areas. This chapter provides the information and tools needed to do just that. Throughout, the two important elements to understanding the entrepreneur's role in marketing—and the key to understanding and dominating the competition—will be explained.

A number of techniques and strategies can assist the entrepreneur in effectively analyzing a potential market. By using them, the entrepreneur can gain in-depth knowledge about the specific market and can translate this knowledge into a well-formulated business plan.

This chapter addresses key issues in the marketplace and examines the major factors in marketing that entrepreneurs need to know. It also offers guidelines on attracting new marketing opportunities through e-commerce solutions. Electronic commerce is a form of marketing that is now a competitive necessity for many businesses. It can change the way an entrepreneur provides business and markets services and products. The business begins and ends with customers. Therefore, it is imperative to obtain and keep customers in order to sustain the business. By far, the best assets for business are its customers, from which market analysis begins.

FORMULATING A SUCCESSFUL MARKETING PLAN

How can marketing techniques be used to the entrepreneur's advantage? Consider the following areas and how each question can be answered to anticipate concerns from a marketing perspective. These topics will be expanded upon later in this chapter to guide the entrepreneur in preparing a marketing plan.

"Marketing is important, but there is nothing more important to the success of most entrepreneurs than personal selling. As the expression goes, 'Nothing happens until there's a sale!'"

GERALD E. HILLS
Coleman Foundation Chair of Entrepreneurship, University of Illinois at Chicago

1. **Set Marketing Objectives.** Marketing objectives are likely to be based on sales revenues and market share. They may also include related objectives such as sales presentations, seminars, ad placements, and proposals submitted to prospective customers.

   Remember to make all the objectives concrete and measurable. Develop the plan to be implemented, not just read. Objectives that cannot be measured, tracked, and followed up are likely to lead to implementation. The capability of plan-vs.-actual analysis is essential.

   Sales are easy to track and measure. Market share is harder because it depends on market research. There are other marketing goals that are less tangible and harder to measure such as positioning or image and awareness.

2. **Get the Product Out: Sales and Distribution.** Begin with how a business will deliver its products or services to customers. Will the business employ its own salesforce for direct marketing; or will dealers, distributors, or jobbers, or perhaps partners be used? Have any of these been identified or selected? On what basis will they be chosen? How will they be compensated? If the business will rely on its own salesforce, what skills and training will that require?

3. **Set a Pricing Strategy.** Pricing should be considered as part of the overall marketing strategy. Although nonprice factors have become more important in buying behavior in recent decades, price still remains one of the most important elements

in determining company market share and profitability. For example, the manufacturer of women's designer apparel might pursue a high-price strategy and then discount the apparel as a means of generating sales. However, this strategy may risk weakening the image of the upscale brand.

The entrepreneur needs to generate a rationale to explain the pricing strategy and anticipate its impact on gross profit. A detailed price list will be helpful whether the entrepreneur is handling the marketing of the product personally, getting advice from mentors, or outsourcing the marketing to a company that specializes in it.

4. **Raise Visibility: Advertising, Public Relations, and Promotion.** In many instances, public relations will play an important role in attempts to generate sales. Usually, the focus is on the concept and the creative content of the communications campaign, the media used, and the extent to which each will be employed.

Many startup or early-stage companies will not have a large advertising budget. For these companies, public relations may be the answer. Entrepreneurs may contact local media—newspapers, radio, and television—that often write or broadcast stories on new businesses in the community. A favorable response may translate into free advertising directed at a large audience. The Dyson case profile in Chapter 5 describes a novel approach using "personality marketing" for a cash-strapped company.

5. **Conduct a Site Analysis.** In some instances, particularly if the business has a retail focus, location must be taken into account in the marketing plan. The entrepreneur must think about the demographic and educational issues of the neighborhood, its environment, its accessibility and proximity to other businesses, and the cost of maintaining a facility there.

6. **Future Marketing Activities.** The marketing plan should consider sales strategies aimed at sustaining growth. For example, a company's immediate plans might involve penetrating only the domestic market, but in the future the same company might consider a license for its products in some international markets or perhaps even a joint venture or partnership with a company in similar or complementary markets. The Ultrafast case history on this book's Web site illustrates how this might be achieved.

"You can never do too much research. In-depth knowledge of your market, your customer, and your competition will create a strong foundation to carry you from early startup through the rocky stage of growth and expansion."

PAMELA POMMERENKE
*Assistant Professor
Department of Management
Michigan State University*

PREPARING THE MARKETING ANALYSIS AND PLAN

Marketing analysis is sometimes called a feasibility study or marketing plan. This process will help the entrepreneur develop a plan that leverages all of the strengths and accounts for any weaknesses in determining the demand for the product or service.[1]

Marketing analysis is also the process of determining a plan that provides the entrepreneur with a sense and an indication of demand. The analysis addresses the following questions. Is there a market to build a viable business? Who are the competitors? Will this venture be the first in the market or face competition? Is governmental regulation an issue? What new products are in the pipeline? How much financial support will be needed to start up? This analysis also describes the research for collecting and analyzing marketing information to make decisions about demographic and consumers' needs and buying habits.

Identifying Customers

The first step is to identify the most likely customer for the new business. Who will buy the product? Often the decision maker and the buyer are the same person, particularly with consumer product goods. A profile of the potential customer or the target audience being served should be developed.[2] This profile is usually based on the following four factors:

- **Market Identification.** The current market and service needs are determined. How profitable are the existing company services? Which of these services offer the most potential? Which (if any) are inappropriate, and which will customers cease to need in the future?

- **Current and Best Customers.** Identifying the company's current clients allows management to determine where to allocate resources. Defining the best customers enables management to segment this market niche more directly.

- **Potential Customers.** By identifying potential customers, either geographically or with an industrywide analysis of its marketing area, a company increases its ability to target this group, thus turning potential customers into current customers.

- **Outside Factors.** Identifying the changing trends in demographics, economics, technology, cultural attitudes, and the role of governmental policy may have a substantial impact on customer needs and, consequently, expected services.

Niche or Target Markets

A niche market is a small segment of a large market ignored by other companies. For many firms, niche markets are too small to be attractive to large competitors. Yet a startup firm can do well within them. The plan is to select a niche market in which the new business can grow and gain a competitive advantage. In the future, additional niches will open up as market efficiency improves.[3]

Target marketing is the strategy used by most successful businesses today. Usually, a company ignores segments that have limited growth because the product will not generate sufficient sales to sustain the company's profitability or allow the company to compete effectively.

The market segments are selected and targeted. Marketing tactics are developed for each target market, which is called *strategy market segmentation*. Once markets have been targeted, the entrepreneur should develop a marketing program for penetrating each segment. The business plan will help identify the markets and their selection. Each target market should be treated almost as a separate marketing program.

One-to-One Marketing

One-to-one marketing requires learning the profile or details about individual customers to identify which are most valuable to the company. By customizing the product or service, the value for the customer can be increased.

One-to-one marketing is rapidly becoming a competitive imperative.[4] As companies learn more about their customers, they can use this knowledge to create and sell products and services to breed loyalty. The key steps to becoming a one-to-one marketer are:

- **Identify customers, or get them to identify themselves.** Consider all options for collecting names: sales transactions, contests, sponsored events, frequent-buyer programs, 800 numbers, credit card records, simple survey cards, and quick one-question polls when customers call.

- **Link customers' identities to their transactions.** Credit card records are especially useful but not necessary. The best way to build individual customer transaction records is often to adopt a different business approach. Consider membership clubs to make it possible to link information about purchases with people.

- **Calculate individual customer lifetime value.** Knowing what a customer is likely to spend over time will help the entrepreneur decide which customers are most desirable (because their business is more profitable) and how much to invest in keeping them. In this light, unusual and seemingly expensive offers can make powerful economic sense.

- **Practice "just-in-time marketing."** Know the purchasing cycle for the product or service and measure it in months or years. Time the company's entry into the market to the customer's purchasing cycle. Time marketing material to meet the customer's needs rather than the company's quarterly sales goal. Send handwritten postcards or marketing materials or use a new catalog for selling.

- **Strengthen a customer-satisfaction program.** Survey questions can be tailored to a customer's wish list and buying preferences. Customize responses to meet the customer's demand.

- **Treat complaints as opportunities for additional business.** Don't ignore customer complaints; follow up with them to identify and correct the problem. By responding quickly, a disgruntled customer may turn into an advocate for the company.

- **Survey customers to find their "points of pain."** Listening to customers' problems can often lead to new products, services, or business models. The Greif and Smartpak cases in Chapter 2 illustrate this point.

- **Enhance product information.** Build in some form of information that will keep customers coming back. For example, the retailer, J. Crew, provides a $25 electronic gift card when customers make purchases in access of $200.[5]

The Value of Loyalty Programs

Marketing plans often place a great deal of emphasis on acquisition but not on customer loyalty. The reality is that for a startup to survive, regardless of industry, it must not only obtain but keep the right customers. A widely held view is that on average it costs a firm five to six times as much to attract a new customer as to keep one.

Not all existing customer relationships are worth keeping unless you can convert them to valuable client status. Careful analysis may show that many relationships are no longer profitable for the firm because they cost more to maintain than the revenues they generate. At times, firms may want to "let customers walk" if they prove unprofitable. Of course, legal and ethical considerations will influence such decisions.

In order to know how much the startup can spend on customer loyalty, one must have a general understanding of what the customers are worth. Generally, customers are worth more with a longer relationship (although this is not always true).

The following factors often underlie hidden profit potential:

1. *Profit derived from increased purchases*. Individuals may buy more or consolidate their purchases.

2. *Profit from reduced operating costs*. As customers become more experienced, they make fewer demands on the supplier. (For example, they may call the customer service center less frequently.)

3. *Profit from referrals to other customers*. This saves on acquisition costs.

4. *Profit from price premium*. Depending on the industry, new customers often benefit from introductory promotional discounts (phone service, magazine subscriptions, etc.).

Calculating the Value of a Loyal Customer

Calculating this value is an inexact science; the purpose of calculation is to ascertain which customer segments will be the most profitable and, therefore, the most viable investment.

Attempt to calculate the following revenues and costs. As the business grows and actual (rather than estimated) data become available, tweak the calculations accordingly. Table 3-1 is a work sheet to help you in this calculation.

DEFINING THE MARKET SEGMENTATION

Segmentation divides a market into workable groups or divisions. It divides a market by age, income, product needs, geography, buying patterns, eating patterns, family makeup, or other classifications. Good marketing plans rarely address the full range of possible target markets. They almost always select segments of the market. The selection allows a marketing plan to focus more effectively, to define specific messages, and to send those messages through specific channels.[6]

A market may be segmented in several different ways.

1. **Demographic Segmentations** are classic. This method divides the market into groups based on age, income level, and gender. Some marketing plans

Table 3-1   **Work Sheet for Calculating the Value of a Loyal Customer**

Acquisition Initial Revenue		Annual Revenues	Year 1	Year 3	Year 4	Year N*
Application Fee Initial Purchase		Annual Account Fee				
		Sales				
		Any Service Fees				
		Value of Referrals				
Total Revenues Discount Rate						
Initial Costs Marketing Costs Account Setup		Annual Costs Account Management				
		Cost of Sales Other				
Total Costs						
Net Profit (Loss)		Year N* represents customer's final year with business.				

Source: Christopher Lovelock, *Services Marketing* (Englewood Cliffs, NJ: Prentice Hall, 2001), p. 155.

focus mainly on demographics because they work for strategy development. For example, video games tend to sell to adolescent males; dolls sell mainly to preadolescent females. Cadillac automobiles generally sell to older adults, while mini-vans sell to adults (with families) between the ages of 30 and 50.

Business demographics may also be valuable. Government statistics tend to divide businesses by size (in sales or number of employees) and type of industry (using industry classification systems like SIC, the Standard Industrial Classification). If the business is selling to companies, then the focus is on segmenting by using types of business. For example, the business may want to sell to optical stores, CPA firms, auto repair shops, or companies with more than 500 employees.

2. **Geographic Segmentation,** another classic method, divides people or businesses into regional groups according to location. It is very important for retail businesses, restaurants, and services addressing their local surroundings only. In those cases, divide the market into geographic categories such as by city, ZIP code, county, state, or region. International companies frequently divide their market by country or region.

3. **Psychographic Segmentation** divides customers into cultural groups, value groups, social sets, or other interesting categories that might be useful for classifying customers. For example, First Colony Mall of Sugarland, Texas, describes its local area group as "25 percent Kids & Cul-de-Sacs (upscale suburban families, affluent), 5.4 percent winner's circle (suburban executives, wealthy), 19.2 percent

boomers and babies (young white-collar suburban, upper middle income), and 7 percent county squires (elite exurban, wealthy)."

4. **Ethnic Segmentations** are somewhat uncomfortable for those of us living in a country with a history of ethnic-based discrimination. Still, the segmentation by ethnic group is a powerful tool for better marketing. For example, Spanish-speaking television programming became very powerful in the United States in the 1990s. Chinese and Japanese television stations have also appeared in the major metropolitan areas.

5. **Combination Segmentations** are also quite common. You frequently see demographic and geographic segmentations combined—population groups or business types in a specific area are an obvious example, or ethnic groups in a certain city, or "boomers and babies" within reach of a shopping center. These are all combinations of factors. For example, Apple Computer has used a combination of business and general demographics by region, segmenting the market into households, schools, small business, large business, and government. It further divides each group into countries and regional groups of countries.[7]

ACTIONS

To determine the best segmentation, analyze what specific channel provides the best marketing potential. The goal is to select the right media messages and divide customers in a way that makes it easy to develop a marketing strategy and implementation plan.

Questions for Effective Segmentation

1. Do potential customer groups have different needs?
2. Does meeting customer needs require different capabilities than meeting the needs of other customers?
3. Can the customers that fit into a given segment be identified?
4. Are customers both willing and able to pay?
5. Is the segment large enough to be profitable?
6. Can the segment be reached in a cost-effective manner?
7. Can the segment be influenced to respond favorably?

Market Segmentation Factors

The nature of your industry will dictate what kind of segmentation is crucial. For some businesses, it will be driven mainly by demographics (e.g., beauty products). For others, it will be more psychographic-driven (e.g., bicycles where you would want to target individuals interested in fitness or in biking).

Whereas many segmentation schemes rely on compiled demographics and psychographics, technology firms oriented to consumers need to know the propensity of potential customers to purchase their products.

If your startup is a technology product, consider the following segmentation developed by Forrester Research, Inc.

Segmenting Technology Customers			
		Uses	
	Career	Family	Entertainment
Optimists	**Fast Forwards—** big spenders, early adopters for all uses	**New Age Nurturers—**big spenders but for home use	**Mouse Potatoes—**like online entertainment and will spend for it
Pessimists	**Techo-Strivers—** use tech to gain career edge (cell phones, pagers)	**Digital Hopefuls—** families with limited budget but still interested in technology	**Gadget Grabbers—**like online entertainment but lack cash to spend for it
	Handshakers— older consumers who avoid computers at work	**Traditionalists—** willing to use technology but slow to upgrade	**Media Junkies—** seek entertainment but can't formulate a plan

⬛ Less-affluent customers

Source: Forrester Research, Inc.; Paul Judge, "Are Tech Buyers Different?" *Business Week*, January 26, 1998, 65.

CONDUCTING A COMPETITIVE ANALYSIS

Creating a competitor profile provides the entrepreneur with a detailed assessment of the competitive environment. It is helpful to know the key players, their personalities, and marketed positions in each firm with which the company will be competing. How do they compete for business in terms of product, service, location, and promotion? In many situations, competitors use different methods to gain market dominance. Do the competitors vie for price? Some may pursue price-sensitive market segments, whereas others may seek the business of those who want improved service, quality, convenience, value, rapid delivery, or a wide selection of product options.

It is particularly important to identify which businesses will provide the most significant competition and predict what they will likely do.[8] Analyze the situation by asking the questions provided below regarding six key areas of competition.

PRODUCT OR SERVICE

- How is the competitive product or service defined?
- How is it similar or different?
- Does the competition cater to a mass or targeted market?
- What features of the product are superior?
- What strengths or weaknesses of the competition can be exploited?

PRODUCT OR SERVICE (cont.)

PRICE

- What is the competitor's pricing strategy?
- Is the competitor's price higher or lower?
- What is the competitor's gross margin for similar products?
- Does the competitor offer terms, discounts, or promotions?

INDUSTRY COMPETITORS

- Define the competition in terms of new, Internet, or potential threats of existing companies.
- What are the strengths and weaknesses of each?
- How will e-commerce companies affect the business?
- How can the suppliers or buyers affect the competition?

SELLING/PROMOTION

- How do the competitors advertise? Analyze their Web sites.
- How much do the competitors spend on advertising, Web development, and promotions?
- What marketing vision or plan are the competitors selling?

MANAGEMENT

- How strong is the competitor's management team?
- What is the team's background or experience?
- How does the company recruit new key employees?
- How does the company compensate their employees?

FINANCIAL

- Is the competitor profitable?
- What volume are sales and market shares?
- Do they spend money for R&D, Internet, and Web development?
- Are they properly capitalized? How strong is their cash flow?

Positioning the Product or Service

Figure 3-1 highlights attributes that should be measured in a competitive analysis. The marketing plan should also specify how you will position your product. Given the competition, how will the product appeal to a specific niche market, if any? What will customers think of the product versus that of someone else's?

| Factors | Attractiveness | |
	High	Low
Competition among existing firms	Competition is minimal but will become intense	The industry is declining and mature
Bargaining power of buyers	Purchase volume is high and they are willing to negotiate pricing	The buyer can replace the service
Bargaining power of suppliers	Many substitutes and sources are available	Limited supply; products are differentiated
Internet companies	No competition defined on the internet	Many companies are entering this market
Potential threats	Complex barriers and costs are high to enter the market	Few simple entry barriers to enter the market

Figure 3-1   Evaluating the Competition: Factors Affecting Attractiveness.

Positioning is the process of establishing and maintaining a distinctive place in the market for the startup and/or its product offerings. Effective positioning entails that the positioning be singular, providing one simple and consistent message.

The airlines industry, an overcrowded industry serving primarily a commodity service, provides fruitful examples. New entries into the industry have encountered great competition. Song (owned by Delta) and Jet Blue for instance, have positioned themselves as more "youthful," "playful," and "fun" airlines with whom to travel. When Song was first introduced on the market, its positioning was that it was not just "another carrier." It did not tout "tangible" or "hard" benefits such as low prices or convenience. Instead, Song played on the theme "Fly Away," suggesting the airline offered an escape from the ordinary. Marketing consultants to Song believed that to espouse the traditional benefits (low price, etc.) would not make the new carrier stand out among the clutter for consumers. However, Delta is now in bankruptcy and has canceled Song Airlines.

The outcome for this section of the marketing plan should be a positioning statement. This articulates the desired position of the organization in the marketplace. The plan should also identify any competitive threats to this positioning. For example, will an existing firm copy this positioning, realizing that this is an underserviced part of the market? Will an existing competitor feel threatened by the new strategy and take steps to reposition its own service so as to compete more effectively?

In order to show the firm's positioning versus that of its competition, one may want to add a positioning or perceptual map to the marketing plan. A map is usually confined to two- or possibly three-dimensional attributes. This map should indicate visually any future threats. Information can be garnered from customer surveys or inferred from published information such as past surveys, reports from staff, and benchmarking. If the firm is a startup, the entrepreneur will not yet know perceptions of the brand; however, for the marketing plan, complete this section for those of the competition.

PREPARING THE PRICING AND SALES STRATEGY

Once the marketing analysis and competition review are established, the entrepreneur should begin to develop the pricing and sales plan. Pricing is the key to the process of controlling costs and showing a profit. It is a very effective marketing tool that must be mastered. The price of a product or service conveys an image and affects demand. Preparing the pricing and sales strategy is also one of the most difficult tasks the entrepreneur must fulfill regarding the product or service.[9]

A number of other factors can influence the entrepreneur's ability to effectively price the product or service: notably, number of competitors, seasonal or cyclical changes in supply and demand, production and distribution costs, customer services, and markups.

Pricing procedures differ depending on the nature of the business, whether it be retail, manufacturing, or service-oriented. The general methods discussed below may be applied to any type of business. They also demonstrate the basic steps in adopting a pricing system and how that system should relate to the desired pricing goals. With this general method in mind, the entrepreneur can formulate the most appropriate pricing strategy.

Pricing Methods

Value

Demonstrating value is part of pricing a new strategy. Price should not be based simply on cost, plus a modest profit. Rather, it should be based on the value of the product or service to the customer. If the customer does not think the price is reasonable, then the entrepreneur should consider not only a price change, but also a new image for the product or service.

Rationale

The entrepreneur must explain why his prices differ from those of the competitors.[10] For instance, does the new business perform a function faster or more efficiently? Lower prices can be justified that way. Or is the new product created with greater care and better materials? A higher cost can communicate this idea.

To determine pricing, you need to know the breakeven point: that is, the sales volume at which a product or service will be profitable. This involves dividing the total fixed and semivariable costs by the contribution obtained on each unit of service.

Calculating Breakeven Points: Hotel Room Pricing Example

Assume a 100-room hotel.

Needs to cover fixed and semivariable costs of $2 million/year.

Average room is $120/night.

Variable costs per room are $20/night.

Average contribution per room is $100.

$2,000,000/100 = 20,000$ room nights per year out of 36,500 capacity must be sold
If prices are cut 20% (or variable costs rise 20%), new calculation is:
$2,000,000/80 = 25,000$ room nights per year out of 36,500 capacity must be sold

The marketing plan should estimate the following:

- **Fixed Costs:** the overhead for the startup; the economic costs of running the business even if no products or services are sold (Examples: rent, insurance, taxes, salaries and payroll taxes for long-term employees).

- **Variable Costs:** the economic costs associated with service for an additional customer (serving an extra hotel guest, making an additional teller transaction in a bank).

- **Semivariable Costs:** in between fixed and variable costs; represent expenses that rise or fall in stepwise fashion as the business volume increases or decreases (example: hiring a part-time employee to work in a restaurant on busy weekends).

- **Contribution:** difference between variable cost of selling an extra unit of service and the money received from that buyer of that service.

Depending on the startup, the ratio of fixed costs to variable will vary greatly. For example, an airline has very high fixed costs but relatively low variable costs (and airlines have reduced variable costs recently to compensate for higher fixed costs, like oil prices). Conversely, the beverage industry would incur high variable costs (cost of can, beverage, labeling, etc.).

This ratio of fixed to variable costs has important implications for pricing. High fixed cost industries like car rentals or airlines are willing to "give away" services, typically as rewards from customer loyalty programs, for many of these firms do not encounter additional costs as a result. Moreover, these industries are most likely to discount their products or services.

High variable cost industries cannot discount as readily, especially if their discounted price falls significantly below marginal cost or the cost of producing an extra unit.

Establishing Pricing Objectives

The marketing plan should be based on a clear understanding of the startup's objectives. There are three basic categories of pricing objectives:

- **Revenue-oriented:** the aim is to maximize the surplus of income over expenditures.

- **Operations-oriented:** typically, capacity-constrained organizations seek to match supply and demand to ensure optimal use of their productive capacity at any given time. (Example: hotels seek to fill rooms because an empty room is an unproductive asset; theaters want to fill seats.) When demand is low, organizations may offer special discounts. When demand exceeds capacity, these firms try to increase profits and ration demand by raising prices ("peak season" prices).

- **Patronage-oriented:** the aim is to attract customers, even at a loss, typical of grand opening sales. For example, a theater may give away seats for an opening night of a performance to create the image of excitement and popularity. Furthermore, if advertising is a major revenue draw, giving substantial discounts may pay off in higher advertising rates for the increased exposure.

Another concept that the marketing plan may address is price elasticity. The concept of elasticity describes how sensitive demand is to changes in price. When a small change in prices has a big impact on sales, demand for that product is said to be price elastic. The converse—a small change in price having little effect on demand—is price inelastic.

Price elasticity affects different industries to varying extents. For instance, the leisure airline passenger market tends to be price elastic. For this reason airlines are always discounting prices during the off-season to attract more customers. (They also must meet minimum flight capacities in order to stay profitable owing to their high fixed costs.) Conversely, business airline customers are far less elastic. Usually, a businessperson needs to travel (to conduct important transactions or affairs) regardless of airline prices. Knowing this, some airlines discount fares far more frequently for flights with more consumer than business travelers, typically during the off-season.

Here are some pricing issues to consider:

How much should be charged?

- Costs to the startup
- Margin you are trying to achieve
- Breakeven point
- Discounts offered
- Psychological pricing points ($9.95 vs. $10.00)

What is the basis of pricing?

- Execution of specific task
- Admission to service facility
- Units of time
- Physical resources consumed

How should prices be communicated to the target market?

The entrepreneur should also consider price bundling as an option. Often, companies will "bundle" a core service with a supplementary one—for example, concessions at a theater and an admission ticket sold under one price. This approach works well for motivating customers to try different types of products or services in addition to those they are already buying from the company.

PENETRATING THE MARKET AND SETTING UP SALES CHANNELS

The desired market penetration determines specific methods that can be used to sell products and services to customers. Some of the selling options include the following: direct sales, sales agents, and trade shows.

Direct Salesforce

The direct salesforce is a group of salespeople who work directly for the company and are paid either straight salary, salary plus bonus, or straight commission. The advantage of a direct salesforce is that, as full-time employees, they work for the company. The entrepreneur has complete control over training them to sell, price, and service the product. The disadvantage is the added expense in maintaining a full-time salesforce. Salaries, travel expenses, office support, and benefits must be paid for each salesperson.

Sales Agents

A sales agent works as a subcontractor to sell products or services. Agents are paid by commission, which is calculated as a specified percentage of the price. They receive their commission after the company collects from the customers. Sales agents pay for expenses such as product samples, travel, office, telephone, and supplies that are incurred in selling the product or service.

Sales agents usually work a specified territory where they can sell the product or service. In addition, they sign a performance contract, which specifies the minimum number of sales to be executed annually.

The advantage of using sales agents is that sales costs are not incurred until the product is sold. The entrepreneur can quickly build a large salesforce and sell the product or services nationwide in a relatively short period of time.

The disadvantage of using sales agents is that they usually sell other products or services as part of a complete line handled by the sales agent. They tend to push the easier-to-sell products or services and those for which they have already established a large customer following. The entrepreneur has little control over the sales agents since they are subcontractors and do not work directly for the company. Therefore, they can be extremely difficult to manage with regard to pricing, follow-up, and service.[11] An extension of the agent model is to use one or more corporate partners, where there is closer contractual relationship. Such partners gain additional value from selling your product or service if it helps them sell more of their own products or helps them sell against their own competitors. These issues are highlighted in the Ultrafast case on the Web site associated with this book. Similar advantages and disadvantages are met in such partnerships. If you use agents or partners in this way, it is recommended that you also employ some direct selling; this retains close interaction with customers, which may identify new needs or "points of pain" while making you less dependent on independent sales resources.

Trade Shows

Trade shows are good places to exhibit and sell products. Many trade shows are held year-round, but finding the right one can be difficult. The entrepreneur must carefully consider which trade shows to attend to meet target customers.

Selling products at trade shows has five major advantages:

1. Many prospective customers can be identified because they come directly to the trade show booth, rather than incurring additional costs to visit each one individually.
2. It is an excellent opportunity to interact with many people in the industry that the entrepreneur may not have otherwise met.
3. The company can demonstrate the products and answer any questions from prospective customers about the product or service.
4. The company can initiate a business relationship by inviting the customer to a follow-up breakfast, lunch, or dinner meeting.
5. The competition can quickly be assessed.

Prior to the trade show, the company should develop screening questions to identify solid sales leads. This is an excellent method to meet the key players in the industry and learn what is happening. The contracts that are made here can significantly increase business sales and better establish and increase market share.

Entrepreneurs should consider the variables of targeted audience, type of product, and cost to help make their choice in determining the type of advertising best suited to let potential customers know about their product or service.

SUMMARY

Writing the marketing plan is the first step in the marketing process and a vital component of a full business plan. The marketing plan is one of the most important parts of a business because it communicates most directly the nature of the intended business and the manner in which that business will be able to succeed. Specifically, the purpose of the marketing process is to explain how a prospective business intends to manipulate and react to market conditions in order to generate sales.

The entrepreneur must prepare a marketing plan that is both interesting and thought provoking. The plan cannot simply explain a concept; it must sell a prospective business as an attractive investment opportunity, a good credit risk, or a valued vendor of a product or service.

The degree of detail and support that should be provided may depend on the market share one requires in order to ensure success. If the market potential is commonly understood to be large and only a very small market share is projected, less detail and support information are needed. Conversely, this detailed information becomes more critical as relevant market share increases.

The marketing plan must establish realistic goals and objectives. The goals must address the market share, penetration, sales, and pricing strategies. Pricing strategies must consider such factors as market competition, customer demand, life cycle of products, and economic conditions.

The marketing strategy describes how the business will implement its marketing plan in order to achieve desired sales performance. This involves focusing attention on each salient marketing tool a company has at its disposal. Elements such as distribution, pricing strategy, advertising, promotion, site analysis, and related budgets all may merit discussion, depending on their importance in relation to the company's overall market strategy. Although meticulous detail is probably unnecessary, it is important that you gain a general understanding of how the business intends to actively market its product or service. Most importantly, the marketing plan should show that you have spent some time talking to actual or potential customers. This is called "primary research" and is one of the main factors that will influence your ability to raise funds to build your business. (For more details, see Appendix 1.) After all, there *is* no business without customers.

The plan should also detail major competitors, noting their strengths and weaknesses. For the plan to be more "strategic" rather than mere "reporting," it should suggest how the new company will vie within the competition—how it will serve an untapped niche. Perceptual mapping can visually illustrate this in two dimensions. Furthermore, a segmentation scheme of customers can be developed with an emphasis on which customer segments the new product or service seeks to capture.

Once the marketing analysis and competition review are established, the entrepreneur can begin to develop the pricing and sales plan. Pricing a product or service is one of the most difficult, but crucial, decisions a business owner must make. A number of factors can serve as guides for pricing a product or service, including the number of competitors, seasonal or cyclical changes in demand, distribution costs, customer services, and markups. The elasticity of demand, or the change in demand given an increase in price, will also influence discounting decisions. Finally, clear knowledge of the breakeven point of the business is crucial in calculating the largest discount the business can afford to give away.

With a marketing plan in place, later chapters will focus on setting up the company (Chapter 4), accessing money (Chapters 5 and 6), managing the company's finances and growth (Chapters 9 and 10), and preparing a complete business plan (Chapter 11).

STUDY QUESTIONS

1. What are the five steps to formulate a successful marketing plan?
2. List three kinds of segmentation. For what kinds of products or services would one kind be more important than another?
3. What is "positioning"? What is "perceptual mapping"?
4. What factors determine whether the business would offer discounts?
5. What are the three pricing objectives? Give an example of an industry that would use each.
6. You own a café in a large urban area that carries a total of $500,000 per year in fixed costs. Your café only sells coffee for $2.50 per cup. The average variable cost per cup (coffee mix, cup costs, etc.) is $1. How many cups do you need to sell per day to break even? If the price of the coffee decreased by 10 percent for a special promotion (with all other costs staying the same), how many cups would you need to sell to break even?

EXERCISES

Marketing Analysis Interview: Customer Analysis

1. Interview an entrepreneurial company and prepare the top five reasons people buy (or would buy) the product or service. Then complete the table.

Description	Importance (1–10)	Company/Product/Service Strength		
		Low	Average	High
1.				
2.				
3.				
4.				
5.				

2. When does a customer buy the product or service?
3. Describe a scenario in which a customer buys the product or service.
4. Where/how does a customer buy the product or service?
5. Describe the target customer (age, sex, income, interests, education, career, etc.).
6. How many target customers are within the geographic market (or are within reach of the distribution and marketing mechanisms)?
7. What percentage of these people would buy a product or service similar to the entrepreneurial company?
8. Do you expect this number to change? Why or why not?

9. Draw three perceptual maps (using two attributes for each map)

Marketing Analysis Interview: Competitor Analysis

1. List all of the major competitors and complete the table with descriptions and figures:

Name	Approx. Sales	Target Market	Product/ Service	Price
1.				
2.				
3.				
4.				
5.				

Marketing Analysis Interview: Risk Questions

1. Complete the following table by describing the company's exposure to the risks listed on the left and the company's planned response or strategy should these risks be realized.

Area of Potential Risk	Company Exposure	Company Response/ Strategy
Industry Growth		
Product Liability		
Economic Changes		
Weather		
Legal and Government		

INTERACTIVE LEARNING ON THE WEB

Test your skill-builder knowledge of the chapter using the interactive Web site.

1. Self Assessment:

2. Multiple Choice:

3. Matching of Key Terms:

4. Demonstration:

5. Case:

6. Video:

CASE STUDY: SMART CARD LLC MARKETING PLAN

Smart Card LLC uses its expertise in smart cards and magnetic stripe technology to develop applications and solutions to meet the rapidly growing demand for marketing frequency programs. Existing and previous loyalty programs have normally been too expensive, complicated, and paper-intensive, thus leading to lack of customer participation. As competition increases in retailing and other industries, companies are searching for new ways to understand customers and retain them. Smart Card LLC offers a smart card solution for these companies.[12]

Smart Card LLC's strategy is focused on using smart cards for frequency programs that can benefit the customer. The company enables its clients to identify:

- Their most profitable customers
- What these customers purchase (how often, how much)
- Their buying preferences

Clients use these smart card solutions to better understand their customers and their purchase habits in order to introduce new services that create added value for their customers. The Smart Card LLC also uses a marketing database to drive all aspects of the marketing mix: advertising, promotion, pricing, and site selection; and it can be customized to meet the individual client's needs.

The objective is to establish an ongoing relationship with the client that will enhance the company's return on investment. Industry surveys have found that 80 percent of revenues are generated by 20 percent of customers. The Smart Card LLC can help companies identify that 20 percent segment of their customers.

REVIEW OF THE PRODUCT ANALYSIS

SMART CARD MARKETING OPPORTUNITIES
• **Product**
➤ Compelling use: Application must attract critical mass of users.
➤ Versatility: Multiple uses→ more value.
➤ Cost effectiveness: Is services' perceived value worth the delivery cost?
• **Price**
➤ Startup: New high-tech products command price premium.
➤ Transition to maturity: Will price cover costs? Eliminate unprofitable services.
➤ Maturity: Will competitive price begin cutting?
• **Selling**
➤ Direct salesforce versus distributors for selling smart cards. The sale is complex, and direct sales provides better service and control.
• **Promotion**
➤ Smart card's promotional issues: The industry must create a need for new technology and replace existing magnetic stripe cards.

Figure 3-2   **Marketing Opportunities for Smart Cards.**

Participant	Advantage	Description
Cardholder	Convenience	• No need for correct change • Easier than carrying cash
Merchant	Reduced costs	• Reduced cash handling • Reduced vandalism/theft
Issuer	Additional revenue	• Float/interest • Unused balances • Additional fee income • Expanded cardholder base
Acquirer	Additional revenue	• Additional merchant services charges • Expanded merchant base

Figure 3-3   **Advantages of Smart Cards.**

The product's quality and features should be directly compared to those offered by competitors. Unique attributes that are important to customers should be identified and highlighted in the memory of the card. As an example, smart cards can hold one to ten pages of customer-related information.

Other important marketing characteristics for smart cards are:

- *User-Friendliness*: Will customers feel comfortable using the product?
- *Reliability*: Will the card work? Will the user feel 100 percent confident about the card's reliability? What backup system is in place?
- *Cost-Effectiveness*: How does delivery cost compare to the customer's perceived value of the service?
- *Compelling Use*: The initial application must be universal and valuable to compel a critical mass of people to accept it. Does the product fit the bill?

Figure 3-2 summarizes the marketing opportunities for smart cards, and Figure 3-3 shows the advantages of smart cards as they relate to the cardholder, merchant, and issuers.

Other issues the company considered were to use specialists and generalists as salespersons and to strategically assign sales territories. The number of accounts to be assigned to an individual salesperson was determined, and compensation included salary and commission.

To promote smart cards, a complex product, the company used a more sophisticated promotion approach—a combination of trade shows, press kits, Web sites, demonstrations, and other promotions.

SUMMARY OF THE COMPANY'S STRENGTHS AND WEAKNESSES

The model in Figure 3-4 measures the company's strengths and weaknesses as they relate to the factors of management financing, product sales, and marketing. The

Factor	Attractiveness	
	High	**Low**
Management team	Proven	People with right skills not available
Financing	You have comfortable cushion or can raise capital if needed	You have a narrow time horizon to make money
Product development	Complete product line	One product of limited life
Salesforce	Strong contacts: specialist skills	Limited contacts: generalist skills
Marketing	Deep and tightly focused	Untargeted
Operations	Strategic alliances help improve execution	Learning in a vacuum

Figure 3-4   **Summary of Company's Strengths and Weaknesses.**

company preparedthe factors that affect the business and how attractive each is in terms of high or low priorities.

CASE QUESTIONS

1. Assess the market feasibility:
    (a) Had the management team done enough research to quantify the size of the market?
    (b) How valid was their assessment of probable market acceptance of the product?
2. Assess the advantages for smart cards as listed in Figure 3-3.
3. Assess the various outside threats to the Smart Card LLC model:
4. Assume that you are a team member:
    (a) Would you want to pursue the opportunity? Would you put your own money into it? Why or why not?

APPENDIX: MARKETING RESEARCH TECHNIQUES

Market Research to Aid Writing the Marketing Plan

Chapter 3 outlines the key parts of a marketing plan. In order to write a more substantial plan, the entrepreneur may consider marketing research for many purposes, including the following:

Market Dynamics
- To size up a market or industry in terms of annual sales revenue and potential for growth
- To forecast revenue and profit projections for the startup
- To quantify the strengths and weaknesses of competitors in terms of market share and other competitive metrics

- To quantify untapped niche markets, like underserved demographic groups, for the product or service

Consumer Behavior

- To gauge potential customers' reactions to a proposed product or service
- To test a name or concept
- To test price points
- To measure customer satisfaction with competing products or services
- To ascertain consumers' perceptions of competing products or services
- To understand customer behavior at different points in the "buying experience"
- To learn the most effective means of reaching customers
- To gain insight into which advertising appeals are most and least effective

Two Types of Market Research

Market research can be described as information gathered in order to obtain a more comprehensive understanding of an industry, product, or potential clientele. The two basic types of market research are primary and secondary.

Primary market research consists of specific information collected to answer specific questions. A few examples include user surveys, focus groups, phone interviews, and customer questionnaires. Many times specific studies are commissioned by private or public entities and are conducted for a fee by market research firms that specialize in various methods of data collection. Results are then published and may or may not be considered proprietary and thus may or may not be made publicly available.

Primary market research may be accessed directly from the vendor who conducted the research or via various services that collect several providers' reports, called *aggregators.* Many market research vendors, as well as aggregators, make reports and tables of contents accessible via the Internet as well as through database services such as Dialog or Profound. Entire reports can range in price from a few hundred dollars to several thousand. Many times, vendors will sell sections of various primary market research reports for much less than the entire report would cost. This is referred to as "cherry picking" and can be a cost-effective alternative to purchasing the entire report. Another cost-effective strategy can be to access the vendor's white papers, which are generally available for free at their Internet site. These are summary papers that are published when a new study is released, and many times they contain valuable bits and bytes of information. A few of the many potential sources of primary market research are:

- www.mindbranch.com (MindBranch)
- www.imrmall.com (International Market Research Mall)
- www.ecnext.com (ECNext Knowledge Center)
- www.marketresearch.com (MarketResearch.com)

The dilemma for the small-business owner is that, properly done, market research is quite expensive, takes time, and requires professional expertise. Acquiring all the necessary data to reduce the risk to your venture may cost so much and take so long that you may go out of business. The answer is to find a quick and inexpensive way of getting enough data to help you make the right decision most of the time.

An entrepreneur can conduct surveys and focus groups himself or farm them out to a research firm. The cost of conducting primary research, however, may be prohibitive. Therefore, the entrepreneur may consider a "quick and dirty" study that will not be as statistically reliable but will at least provide some initial insights into the business. Two ways of conducting low-cost research are:

- *Informal focus groups.* Gather a group of likely customers for two or three hours and ask pointed questions about the product or service. Ask open-ended questions and probe responses. Use visuals like competitors' products to gain reactions.
- *Online surveys.* Write questions about potential customers' thoughts and reactions to the proposed product or service. Consider a brief consultation with a statistician to ensure that the survey has reliability. (If it were repeated it would yield the same result.) Purchase e-mail lists of potential customers and e-mail the survey with incentives to participate. Analyze the tabulated results for key findings. (See the reference section for more information.)

Secondary market research is information that has been gathered and repackaged from already existing sources. At one time or another in its life cycle, most marketing research has been considered primary research; someone somewhere identified the information to be gathered and contracted some entity to collect, repackage, and perhaps distribute or publish the data. Most of the information sources familiar to librarians and their patrons are considered secondary sources of market research.

Secondary market research is by far the most cost-effective information solution and generally the best place to start the information-gathering process. This information is extracted from industry studies, books, journals, and other published resources and are readily available at most public libraries. Many times they are accessible for free via the Internet as well. You should look to both sources for a complete picture.

Information to Garnish from Secondary Research
- *Basic demographic information.* The age, sex, geographical region, marital status, and so on of your existing and potential customers and clients. More in-depth demographic information provides details on their personal preferences and buying habits.
- *Customer ideas and opinions.* Information such as product quality preferences, motivators of buying decisions, and color preferences.
- *Buying cycles or patterns.* Do they buy weekly, monthly, yearly? Are the purchases spontaneous or planned? Is the purchase for self or a gift for others?
- *Trends for new or improved products and services.* What needs do they want to have filled? What's missing in the marketplace?
- *Strategic alliance opportunities.* Who else is doing what you do? What companies could complement your product or service offerings if you worked together?
- *Opportunities for beating your competition.* What's important to your customers? Price? Quality? Features?

ADDITIONAL RESOURCES

- **Lexis/Nexis,** Reed Elsevier, P.O. Box 933, Dayton, OH 45401; (800) 227-4908; www.lexis-nexis.com

- **Direct Marketing Association,** 1120 Avenue of the Americas, New York, NY 10036; (212) 768-7271; www.the-dma.org

- **Business Marketing Association,** 400 North Michigan Avenue, 15th Floor, Chicago, IL 60611; (800) 664-4BMA; www.marketing.org

- **Marketing Research Association,** 1344 Silas Deane Highway, Suite 306, Rocky Hill, CT 06067; www.mra-net.org

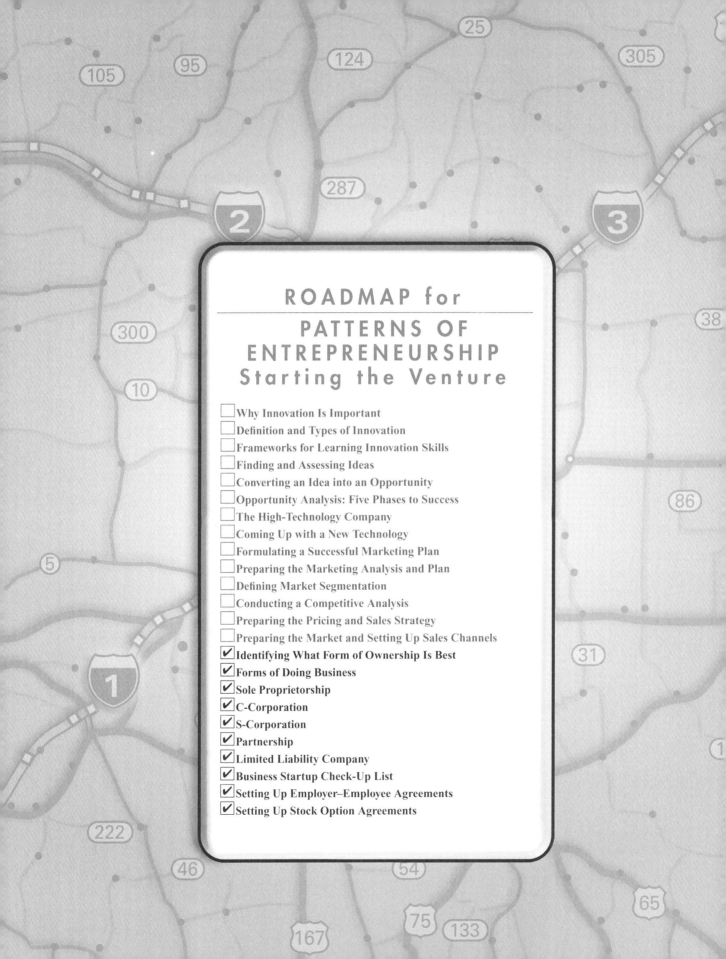

ROADMAP for

PATTERNS OF ENTREPRENEURSHIP
Starting the Venture

- ☐ Why Innovation Is Important
- ☐ Definition and Types of Innovation
- ☐ Frameworks for Learning Innovation Skills
- ☐ Finding and Assessing Ideas
- ☐ Converting an Idea into an Opportunity
- ☐ Opportunity Analysis: Five Phases to Success
- ☐ The High-Technology Company
- ☐ Coming Up with a New Technology
- ☐ Formulating a Successful Marketing Plan
- ☐ Preparing the Marketing Analysis and Plan
- ☐ Defining Market Segmentation
- ☐ Conducting a Competitive Analysis
- ☐ Preparing the Pricing and Sales Strategy
- ☐ Preparing the Market and Setting Up Sales Channels
- ☑ Identifying What Form of Ownership Is Best
- ☑ Forms of Doing Business
- ☑ Sole Proprietorship
- ☑ C-Corporation
- ☑ S-Corporation
- ☑ Partnership
- ☑ Limited Liability Company
- ☑ Business Startup Check-Up List
- ☑ Setting Up Employer–Employee Agreements
- ☑ Setting Up Stock Option Agreements

CHAPTER 4

SETTING UP THE
COMPANY OBJECTIVES

"The ladder of success doesn't care who climbs it."

FRANK TYGER

OBJECTIVES

- Assess the factors in deciding which form of ownership is best suited for a potential business.
- Outline the advantages and disadvantages of a sole proprietorship and partnership.
- Explain the corporate form of ownership and describe how a business is incorporated.
- Understand the S-Corporation and the Limited Liability Company (LLC).
- Understand how to register a business with government entities.
- Know how to set up stock options and employment agreements.
- Learn how to choose an attorney.

CHAPTER OUTLINE

INTRODUCTION

Some entrepreneurs start businesses and determine the structure of the company with lots of thought and planning. Others find themselves establishing a company without much regard to how the business should be structured. However, one of the most important decisions to make is how to legally structure a business.[1]

Before deciding how to organize a company, the entrepreneur needs to identify the legal structure that will best meet the requirements of the business. This is due to the tax laws, liability situation, and ways to attract capital.

Many companies provide added incentives for keeping key employees by offering an ownership or equity interest in the company. This is usually in the form of common stock or options to acquire common stock. In this chapter we will discuss how companies should establish a qualified stock option plan and how selected employees receive options to purchase stock in the company.

The legal form of the business, whether sole proprietorship, C-Corporation, S-Corporation, partnership, or LLC, should be determined in light of the business's short- and long-term needs. In this chapter, we will examine the pros and cons of each of these forms and how to prepare a checklist to start the business. The entrepreneur's specific situation, circumstances, and issues will determine the choice.

PROFILE: ROY WETTERSTROM, PRESIDENT OF MICRO MODELING ASSOCIATES

Remaking the Company from Top to Bottom

Micro Modeling Associates (MMA) grew out of the need for automated tools in the Merchant Banking Division of First Bank System (now U.S. Bancorp) in Minneapolis, where Roy Wetterstrom worked as an analyst. Soon, his Lotus 1-2-3™ models became the department's standard. Eventually, Wetterstrom was placed in charge of building a state-of-the-art Windows™-based corporate finance model in Microsoft Excel™. With the bank's permission, Wetterstrom and a partner marketed the model to Wall Street. Merrill Lynch was impressed and promised to keep Wetterstrom and his partner busy for three months. With this promise and $40,000 that Wetterstrom and his partner scraped together from various sources, Micro Modeling was born. MMA also secured a $20 million equity investment from TA Associates, a Boston-based investment firm and a $15 million line of credit from Fleet Bank, Boston.

Initially, the company was organized as an S-Corporation. The purpose was to limit ownership in the company, pass through losses to the owners, and maintain control for future growth. However, as the business grew, Wetterstrom's $54 million client/server consulting business required changes in structure and strategy. The plan was to transform Micro Modeling Associates into a top-tier Internet service, strategy, and developmental company. To meet this mission, the company changed its name to "Plural" and became a Delaware C-Corporation. This name and structure change positioned the company to become a top-tier Internet player and give "Plural" the power of a potential public offering. The new strategy also includes discounted rates to dot-com companies for services and making up the difference by taking an equity stake in the client companies. Roy's goal was to build a mutual fund of pre-IPO dot-com companies and use the equity to retain employees and attract new talent. In addition, a search firm was hired to recruit a president and chief marketing officer to meet and complete the transformed new company image.

When Wetterstrom and his partner first started the firm, it was virtually the only company doing Excel-based applications for the financial industry. Since that time, by organizing the company structure and strategy, the firm has expanded its client base to other industries while consistently keeping ahead of the technology curve. The firm is now on the cutting edge of Internet and E-solutions consulting development.[2]

IDENTIFYING WHAT FORM OF OWNERSHIP IS BEST

In choosing a form of ownership, entrepreneurs must remember that there is no single "best" form; what is best depends on the individual's circumstances. To determine the form of ownership, be prepared to address the following issues.[3]

FORMS OF OWNERSHIP QUESTIONS

1. How big can this business potentially become?
2. How much control do you need in the decision-making process of the company? Are you willing to share ideas and the business's potential profits with others who can help build a more successful business?
3. How much capital is needed to start the business?
4. What tax considerations are important? What sources of income are there, and how are they to be sheltered?
5. In case of failure, to what extent are you willing to be personally responsible for debts created by the business?
6. Is it important that the business continue in case of owner capacity or death?
7. Who will be the sole or major beneficiary of the business success? Is the owner the type of person who doesn't mind taking all the risks but expects to reap all the benefits if successful?
8. Can you put up with the time-consuming bureaucratic red tape associated with more complicated forms of ownership? What is the emotional reaction to government regulations and their accompanying paperwork requirements?

FORMS OF DOING BUSINESS

The legal form of the business (sole proprietorship, C-Corporation, S-Corporation, partnership, or LLC) should be determined in light of the business's short- and long-term needs. Because there are significant tax and nontax differences among the forms, the results and requirements of each form should be carefully considered to ensure that the business form chosen best meets the requirements. A brief analysis of each form of doing business is presented to meet business requirements.

SOLE PROPRIETORSHIP

A sole proprietorship is a form of business in which a single owner does business himself or herself and only requires business licenses to open. If the plan is to operate a business under a name other than that of the owner, the business name must be filed as a "doing business as" registration with a state and/or local filing authority (for example, Jack Smith doing business as Jack's SmartCard Consulting). The business can be terminated at any time and always ends with the death of the owner. The sole owner has the right to make all the decisions for the business. However, the owner is personally liable for all debts and contracts of the business. Since there is no distinction between personal and business debts, if the business cannot pay its bills, the creditors can sue to collect from the owner's personal assets. In matters dealing with taxes, profits and losses from the business flow directly to the owner and are taxed at individual income tax rates on the owner's personal tax return. If the owner does not plan to take a salary, income is the profits of the business. There is no carryback or carryforward of losses for tax-reporting purposes.

Advantages of a Sole Proprietorship

Sole proprietorships are popular because they have a number of attractive features:[4]

- *Simple to Initiate Business.* One of the most attractive features of proprietorships is how fast and simple it is to begin operations. If a proprietor wishes to operate the business under his or her own name, one simply obtains the necessary licenses, if any, and begins operations. In a sole proprietorship, the proprietor is the business. It is not difficult to start up a proprietorship in a single day if the business is simple.

- *Low Start-Up Fees.* In addition to being easy to begin, the proprietorship is generally the least expensive form of ownership to establish. Legal papers do not need to be credited to start the business. Rather, if required, the proprietor goes to the appropriate state and/or county government office and states the nature of the new business in his or her license application. The government assesses the appropriate fees and license costs. Once these fees are paid, the owner is allowed to conduct business.

  If the proprietorship is to do business under a trade name, a Certificate of Doing Business under an Assumed Name must be filed with the state and/or county in which the business will operate. The fee for filing the certificate is usually nominal. Acquiring this certificate involves conducting a name search of previously filed names to determine that the name to be used is not already registered

ACTIONS

Entrepreneurs have a number of legal forms of business to choose from including sole proprietorship, C-Corporation, S-Corporation, partnership, or LLC. Entrepreneurs should determine which business form is best for their short- and long-term needs. In choosing a form of ownership, entrepreneurs must remember that there is no single "best" form; what is best depends on the individual's circumstances.

as the name of another business or as a trademark or service mark for another business.

- *Profit Incentive*. One major advantage of the proprietorship is that after all the debts are paid, the owner receives all the profits (less taxes, of course). Profits represent an excellent scorecard of success.
- *Total Decision-Making Authority*. Because the sole proprietor is in total control of operations and can respond quickly to changes, this becomes an asset in rapidly shifting markets. The freedom to set the company's course of action is another major motivation for selecting this ownership form. For the individual who thrives on the enjoyment of seeking new opportunities and then modifies the business as needed, the free, unimpeded decision making of the sole proprietorship is a must.
- *No Special Legal Restrictions*. The proprietorship is the least regulated form of business ownership. In a time when government requests for information seem never-ending, this feature has much merit.
- *Easy to Discontinue*. When an owner cannot continue operations, he or she can terminate the business quickly, even though such persons will still be liable for all outstanding debts and obligations of the business.

Disadvantages of a Proprietorship

As advantageous as the proprietorship form of ownership is, it does have its disadvantages:

- *Unlimited Personal Liability*. The greatest disadvantage of a sole proprietorship is unlimited personal liability; that is, the sole proprietor is personally liable for all business debts. The proprietor owns all the assets of the business. If the business fails, these assets can be sold to cover debts. If there are still unpaid debts, creditors can sell the owner's personal assets to cover the remaining debt. Failure of the business can ruin the owner financially. Because the law views the proprietor and the business as one and the same, the debts of the business are considered the owner's personal debts. Laws protecting an individual's personal assets to some degree may vary from one state to another. Most states require creditors to leave the failed business owner a minimum amount of equity in a home, a car, and some personal items. The new Federal Bankruptcy Law protects retirement assets from creditors. Bankruptcy or other insolvency protection may be needed to protect a failed business owner. Because laws vary, picking the proper jurisdiction in which to do business is critical.
- *Limited Skills and Capabilities of the Sole Owner*. The owner may not have the needed skills to run a successful business. Each individual has skills and talents reflective of education, training, and work experience. However, the lack of skills and knowledge in other areas is what often causes failure. If an owner is not familiar with an area such as finance, accounting, or law, he or she will tend to

gloss over these areas thinking that they do not seriously impact his or her business or that this is a way to save money by ignoring these services even when needed. The sole owner who fails may have been successful if he or she had had previous knowledge of possible problems in one or more of these areas and had obtained good, timely advice. Sole owners need to recognize their shortcomings and then find help in those areas in which he or she is not proficient.

- *Limited Access to Capital.* For a business to grow and expand, a sole proprietor generally needs financial resources. Many proprietors put all they have into their businesses and often use their personal resources as collateral on existing loans. In short, proprietors, unless they have great personal wealth, find it difficult to raise additional money while maintaining sole ownership. The business may be sound in the long run, but short-term cash flow difficulties can cause financial headaches. Most banks and lending institutions have well-defined formulas for borrower's eligibility. As a result, a proprietor may not be able to obtain the funds needed to operate the business, especially in difficult times.

- *Lack of Continuity for the Business.* Lack of continuity is inherent in a sole proprietorship. If the proprietor dies or becomes incapacitated, the business automatically terminates. Unless a family member or employee can effectively take over, the business could be in jeopardy. If no one is trained to run the business, creditors can petition the courts to liquidate the assets of the dissolved business and the estate of the proprietor to pay outstanding debts.

C-CORPORATION

The C-Corporation is the most common form of business ownership. A corporation is a separate legal entity apart from its owners and may engage in business, issue contracts, sue and be sued, and pay taxes. The owners of a corporation hold stock in the corporation. Each share of stock represents a percentage of ownership. The actual business of the corporation is conducted by the directors and officers of the corporation.

When a corporation is founded, it accepts the regulations and restrictions of the state in which it is incorporated and of each state in which it does business. Corporations doing business in the state in which they are incorporated are domestic corporations. When they conduct business in another state, that state considers the corporation to be a foreign corporation. Corporations that are formed in other countries but do business in the United States are alien corporations. Where and how a corporation does business has an impact on its ability to operate and its tax liability. Also, a corporation may be taxed in every jurisdiction where it is incorporated or doing business.

Generally, the corporation must annually file in its state of incorporation and in every state in which it is doing business. These reports become public record. If the corporation's stock is sold in more than one state, the corporation must comply with federal and state regulations governing the sale of corporate securities.[5] For most small businesses the selling of stock will not involve registering the stock as a security. However, there may be reports that are required to be filed showing an exemption from registration.

A corporation has three primary sections: the stockholders, the Board of Directors, and the officers. It is important to understand the specific functions of each section.

The stockholders are the owners of the business.

When a corporation is established, its equity is divided among a number of shares of stock that are issued to the investors in proportion to their investment in the corporation. A general protocol for the company's operations, called the "by-laws," is adopted by the stockholders. Sometimes these by-laws can be amended or changed by the board of directors, sometimes only by the stockholders. The ultimate power and control of every corporation lie in the hands of the stockholders.

The Board of Directors has responsibility for the overall operation of the company.

The stockholders elect the board and have the power to remove board members. The board establishes the general policies of the company and, to a greater or lesser extent depending on the particular corporation, can become involved in various details of the operating procedures. The Board of Directors elects the officers of the corporation to handle the day-to-day affairs.

The usual officers in a corporation are president, secretary (or "clerk" in some states), and treasurer.

The functions of each officer are defined by the Board of Directors. The president is in charge of day-to-day operations under the directives of the Board of Directors. The secretary is charged with handling the paper work of the corporation, such as preparing minutes of stockholder and directors' meetings, sending out notices, and preparing stock certificates. The treasurer is charged with guardianship of the corporate finances. However, there are differences in the functions of the officers among different corporations.

Additional officers may include vice presidents, who are sometimes charged with a specific aspect of operations such as engineering, finance, production, and sales. There may also be assistants for each of the offices, such as assistant secretary and assistant treasurer.

You do not need the services of an attorney to set up and maintain a corporation. The days when a corporation was a rigid structure with reams of rules for the precise keeping of records and holdings of meetings are gone. The various states have revised the corporate laws to allow great flexibility in creating and maintaining a corporation. Nevertheless, if you wish to have the benefits offered by a corporation, you must treat the business as a corporation, not as a proprietorship. We'll say more about this presently.

The specific requirements for forming a corporation vary from state to state. The easiest way to start is to request information and forms from the office of your local secretary of state. This will tell you the fees and generally how to prepare the papers for filing.

What State to Register

Delaware is a popular state for incorporation, so we will use that as a practical example.[6] If you are not a resident of Delaware, you must have an agent in the state who is empowered to accept service in the event the corporation is sued. In other words, if you incorporate in a particular state, the corporation can be sued in that state even if you conduct no other activities there. Such agents represent the corporation for a relatively modest annual fee. A list of acceptable agents in Delaware can be obtained by writing to the Department of State, Division of Corporations, P.O. Box 898, Dover, Delaware, 19901. Similar lists for other states are available from the secretary of state in that state. After obtaining the list of agents, you can then write to them to inquire about their annual fees and the "extra" fees for performing additional special functions.

After selecting a local agent, the next step is to select the corporate name. The name must include an indication that the entity is a corporation. In many states, you could not, for example, call your corporation "The SMITH Company." You could call it "The SMITH Company, Inc." or "the SMITH Company Corp." You should find out just what corporate indicators are required in your state of incorporation. In Delaware, the permitted corporate indicators are "Association," "Club," "Company," "Corporation," "Foundation," "Fund," "Incorporated," "Institute," "Limited," "Society," "Syndicate," "Union," or any of these abbreviations: "Co.," "Corp.," "Inc.," or "Ltd."

You can ask your agent to check on the availability of the name; this can usually be done by telephone. If the name is available, it can be reserved for 30 days without charge. "Availability" means that no other corporation has a prior registration of the same name or one sufficiently similar that it might cause confusion. If "SMITH Incorporated" is already incorporated in your state, you cannot use the name "SMITH" even if you change the other parts of the name. You can still incorporate in another state where the name has not been usurped, but this is not likely to be a practical solution because before a foreign corporation (a corporation formed in another state) can do business in your state, it must register there as a foreign corporation. This will not be permitted if another local or foreign corporation has the same or a confusingly similar name.

The next step is to prepare the Certificate of Incorporation (sometimes the Articles of Incorporation). The following is a typical form ready for forwarding to the agent, along with the filing fee and the first annual charge for the agent:

> "To raise capital for early stage companies, a C-Corporation is preferred and provides the most flexible structures for various rounds of private equity investments."
>
> MICHAEL BUCHEIST
> *Managing Partner,*
> *Advanced Infrastructure Ventures*

CERTIFICATE OF INCORPORATION OF SMITH INCORPORATED

A Corporation

1.: The name of this corporation is SMITH Incorporated

: Its registered office in the State of Delaware is to be located at (here insert the address of the Delaware agent you have selected). The name of the registered agent is (name of registered agent).

Third: The nature of the business, and the objects and purposes proposed to be transacted and carried on, are to engage in any lawful act or activity for which corporations may be organized under the General Corporation Law of Delaware.

Fourth: The amount of total authorized capital stock of the corporation is divided into 3,000 shares of no par common (the maximum number of shares with minimum tax).

Fifth: The name and address of the incorporator is:
Jane Vista

CERTIFICATE OF INCORPORATION OF SMITH INCORPORATED (cont.)

345 Boulder

Austin Texas Boulder 29555

Sixth: The powers of the incorporator are to terminate upon the filing of the Certificate of Incorporation. The name and mailing addresses of the persons who are to serve as directors until their successors are elected are as follows:

Jane Vista

345 Boulder

Austin Texas Boulder 29555

Seventh: All of the issued stock of the corporation, exclusive of treasury shares, shall be held of record of not more than thirty (30) persons.

Eighth: All of the issued stock of all classes shall be subject to the following restriction on transfer permitted by Section 202 of the General Corporation Law.

Ninth: The corporation shall make no offering of any of its stock of any class which would constitute a "public offering" within the meaning of the United States Securities Act of 1933, as amended.

Tenth: Directors of the corporation shall not be liable to either the corporation or to its stockholders for monetary damages for a breach of fiduciary duties unless the breach involves: (1) a director's duty of loyalty to the corporation or its stockholders; (2) acts or omissions not in good faith or which involve intentional misconduct or a knowing violation of law; (3) liability for unlawful payments of dividends or unlawful stock purchases or redemption by the corporation; or (4) a transaction from which the director derived an improper personal benefit.

I, the undersigned, for the purpose of forming a corporation under the laws of the state of Delaware do make, file and record this Certificate, and do certify that the facts stated herein are true; and I have accordingly set my hand.

Dated:

_____Incorporator

Corporate Stock

The ownership of a corporation lies in the stockholders and is evidenced by stock certificates issued to the shareholders. There may be several classes of stock. The most usual is no-par value common stock. Common stock most often has voting power equal to one vote per share. However, there may be more than one class of common stock. For example, a Class A stock may have voting rights, while Class B stockholders own, say, 95 percent of the corporation, but the entire corporation is controlled by the 5 percent of the outstanding stock held by the Class A stockholders.

A specific number of shares of each class is authorized in the Articles of Incorporation, and more than that amount may not be issued without first amending the Articles of Incorporation. Provision may be made for converting one class of stock into another. For example, Class B stock might be convertible, at the option of the holder, into Class A stock on a share-for-share basis or any other specified ratio.

Another class of stock is called "preferred" because it usually has a preferred position with respect to dividends or receiving distributions should the company go into bankruptcy. For example, a corporation might issue preferred stock for $100 per share that carries a normal dividend of, say, $8.00 per share. Those dividends would ordinarily have a preference to dividends paid on the common stock. So someone investing in preferred stock could expect a return of 8 percent on the investment, if the company is sufficiently profitable to pay the dividend out of profits.

Dividends on preferred stock may be either cumulative or noncumulative. If the dividends are noncumulative, a lost dividend is gone forever. The company may subsequently become profitable, pay the current dividend on the preferred stock, and then pay dividends on the common stock without making up for the missed dividend. If the dividend is cumulative, all missed dividends on the preferred stock must be paid before any dividend on the common stock can be paid. Preferred stock may be convertible into common stock at the option of the holder, or the Board of Directors may have power to compel conversion under some preestablished formula or some defined event (such as being sold or "going public"). Preferred stock usually has no voting power. It is permissible for preferred stock to have voting power, but usually voting rights are limited to common stock. Different classes of stock may have different voting powers. For example, Class A common could have three votes per share, Class B common could have two votes per share, and the preferred stock could have one vote per share.

There is great flexibility in establishing classes of stock, voting rights, and rights to dividends, so you can tailor your corporation to best meet the needs of your particular situation.

"Par value" is an archaic concept that is still applied to stocks; it is the monetary value assigned to each share of stock in the Articles of Incorporation. Such stock must be issued for an amount of money, or other property, equal to at least the par value of the stock. If par value stock is issued by the corporation without such remuneration, the stockholder could be liable to creditors for the difference between the par value and the amount actually paid. Once the stock is issued, the par value of the stock bears no relationship to its actual value. "No par value" common stock has no stated valuation in the corporate charter. In practical terms, the difference in par value stock from no par value stock lies in the tax area. In some states, as in Delaware, the corporate tax may be less par value stock than for no par value stock.

Taxes

Annual taxes are usually based on the number of shares of authorized stock and on whether the stock has a par value. Currently in Delaware, the minimum annual tax on a company with 500,000 shares of authorized no par value common stock is almost $1,770.55. If the stock has a par value, the minimum tax on the same amount of par value stock may be as little as $40.00. Before sending in your annual corporate tax to the state of incorporation, read the tax law carefully because the rules can be somewhat misleading. Delaware, for example, sends the company with 500,000 shares of authorized stock having a par value of $0.01 per share an official notice in which the tax is calculated as $1,770.55. The busy businessperson might just send a check for the full amount. However, the fine print on subsequent pages of the tax notice describes a rather complex method of computing an alternate tax based on the assets of the corporation. If the corporation has few assets, the actual tax due may be only the minimum of $40.00. If you inadvertently pay the larger sum to the state of Delaware, you can, with some red tape, likely recover the overpayment. If you intend to create a Delaware corporation and plan to issue more than 3,000 shares, consider making it par value stock, because the alternate tax computation method cannot be used for no par value stock. There is no logical reason for the legal distinctions drawn by the Delaware tax law—but logic is never a strong point among lawyers who write tax legislation.

Shares Authorized

The number of shares you will want to authorize depends on the particular circumstances. Suppose only one or a few people are to be stockholders, then 10 or 100 shares might be sufficient. Usually, some number of shares can be authorized at the minimum tax rate. In Delaware it is 3,000. The maximum might as well be authorized, so that if needed in the future additional shares can be issued without amending the Certificate of Incorporation.

There may be a psychological reason for authorizing more shares. If a corporation, for example, intends to make stock options available to its employees and has only 100 shares issued, an employee getting an option for an amount of stock representing 1 percent ownership of the company receives an option for one share, which doesn't sound like much. If the ownership of the corporation is represented by 2 million shares, then 1 percent ownership is represented by 20,000 shares. Sounds like a lot more! There is, of course, no difference, but many individuals may not be aware of that. Even if I do know the difference, I'd still rather show 100,000 shares in my portfolio than only one!

SETTING UP A CORPORATION (C)—OWNERSHIP

SUMMARY OF PROS AND CONS

- Separate legal and tax entity
- Shareholder liability limited to invested capital
- Existence continues after shareholder's death
- Easier to raise equity capital

PROS

- Limited liability
- Most appropriate structure for an IPO
- Tax benefits such as loss carryforwards and easy to set up stock option plans
- Ease of transferability of interests
- Structure that a venture capitalist requires

SETTING UP A CORPORATION (C)—OWNERSHIP (cont.)

CONS

- Double taxation
- High administration compliance costs
- Directors held accountable
- Well-defined corporate governance rules and laws to follow

Advantages of a C-Corporation

- *Limited Liability of the Stockholders.* The corporation allows investors to limit their liability to the total amount of their investment in the corporation if they adhere to the terms of the Certificate and the by-laws. A corporation cannot just be set up and run as if it were a sole proprietorship. Business must be conducted in the name of the Board of Directors through the officers using separate books and records from the personal books and records of the shareholders. This legal protection of personal assets beyond the business is of critical concern to many potential investors. Because startup companies are so risky, lenders and other creditors often require the owners to personally guarantee loans made to the corporation. By making these guarantees, owners are putting their personal assets at risk (just as in a sole proprietorship), despite choosing the corporate form of ownership. However, it is possible to limit the scope of a guaranty so that not all assets of a person may be at risk.

- *Ability to Attract Capital.* Based on the protection of limited liability, the corporation has proved to be the most effective form of ownership to accumulate large amounts of capital. Limited only by the number of shares authorized in its charter (which can be amended) and subject to the laws on registration of securities, the corporation can raise money to begin business and expand as opportunity dictates. Professional or "institutional" investors such as venture capitalists (Chapter 6) demand this form of incorporation.

- *Ability of the Corporation to Continue Indefinitely.* Unless limited by its charter, the corporation as a separate legal entity theoretically can continue indefinitely. The existence of the corporation does not depend on any single individual.

- *Transferable Ownership.* If stockholders in a corporation are displeased with the progress of the business, they can sell their shares to another individual, subject only to restrictions on transfer of shares. Stocks can be transferred through inheritance to a new generation of owners. If any person wishes to own some shares in a firm and there is someone who would like to sell his or her interest in that firm, an exchange is possible. During all this change of ownership, the business continues.

- *Skills, Expertise, and Knowledge.* Unlike the proprietor who is often the only active member of management, the corporation can draw on the skills, expertise, and knowledge of its officers and Board of Directors, and people whose knowledge and experience can be used to shape the direction of the firm. In many cases, the board members act as advisors, giving the stockholders the advantage of their years of experience.

Disadvantages of a C-Corporation

- *Cost and Time Involved in the Incorporation Process.* Corporations can be costly and time-consuming to establish. The owners are creating an artificial legal entity, and the startup period can be prolonged for the novice. In some states an attorney must handle the incorporation, but in most cases entrepreneurs can complete the requirements. However, the complexity of the requirements leads many entrepreneurs to employ an attorney even in states where one is not required so that one does not go afoul of the legal and registration requirements. Failure to properly register and follow the corporate form may cause loss of the ability to limit shareholder liability.

- *Double Taxation.* Corporations are taxed on their profits. Rates range up to 35 percent. In addition, when shareholders are distributed profit in the form of a dividend, taxes on the dividend up to 35 percent may be incurred.

ACTIONS

Corporations offer limited liability to the owners, which means owners cannot be sued for the debts of the business unless they have personally guaranteed those debts. Therefore, the potential loss for owners is limited to the capital they have invested.

S-CORPORATION

The S-Corporation, often referred to as a Sub-S Corporation, is a corporation that elects under federal and state tax laws to be taxed like a partnership. Its profits and losses are recognized for tax purposes at the individual shareholder level. It is the shareholder's responsibility to report the profits or losses on his or her individual income tax returns. To become an S-Corporation, the following must occur:[7]

- The company must be a domestic company.
- Only one class of stock is allowed.
- Only individuals and certain trusts may own stock.
- Shareholders cannot be nonresident aliens.
- There can only be a maximum of 100 shareholders.
- The shareholders must elect to become an S-Corporation at the federal and state levels.

Advantages of an S-Corporation

The S-Corporation retains all the advantages of a regular corporation such as continuity of existence, transferability of ownership, and limited personal liability. The most notable provision of the S-Corporation is that it avoids the corporate income tax (and the resulting double taxation) and enables the business to pass through operating profits or losses to shareholders. In effect, the tax status of an S-Corporation is similar to that of a sole proprietorship or partnership.

Entrepreneur Fanny Chin, who launched Creative Calendar in 1998 as an S-Corporation, maintains that form of ownership today. "Since there were no shareholders except me, I didn't see any advantage to C-Corporation status since my earnings would have been taxed twice."

Disadvantages of an S-Corporation

An S-Corporation has restrictions on use of its losses and tax recognition on sales of its assets different from those of a C-Corporation. These may be disadvantages to the owners. Thus, although one may face double taxation as a C-Corporation, the loss of flexibility on the sale of assets or stock of the corporation may require one to remain a C-Corporation and ultimately gain the most profit upon the sale of a business. In addition, if the entrepreneur's intention is to raise capital from third parties, such as venture capitalists, the company will have to be restructured into a C-corporation before this can occur.

SETTING UP AN S-CORPORATION

SUMMARY OF PROS AND CONS

- Corporation but with "flow through" tax benefits.
- As a corporation, an S-Corporation is a separate entity and therefore has limited liability for owners and stockholders.
- Limited to 100 owners, only one class of stock allowed, and no foreign shareholders.

PROS

- Offers liability protection.
- Enjoys corporation status, but owners pay the taxes.

CONS

- Stringent rules necessary to maintain S-Corporation status.
- Qualification requirements necessitate administrative and cost burdens.
- If failure to comply with S-Corporation rules, tax consequences can be disastrous.
- Not eligible for qualified employee stock options.
- Investors cannot receive preferred shares as in a C-Corporation.

When Is the S-Corporation a Wise Choice?

Choosing the S-Corporation status is usually beneficial to startup companies anticipating net losses and to highly profitable firms with substantial dividends to pay out to shareholders. In these cases, the owner can use the loss to offset other income, or the owner is personally in a lower tax bracket than the corporation, thus saving money in the long run.[8]

Small companies with these following characteristics, however, are not likely to benefit from S-Corporation status:

- Highly profitable personal service companies with large numbers of shareholders, in which most of the profits are passed on to shareholders as compensation or retirement benefits
- Corporations in which the loss of fringe benefits to shareholders exceeds tax savings
- Corporations with sizable net operating losses that cannot be used against S-Corporation earnings

PARTNERSHIP

A partnership is usually defined as an association of two or more people carrying on as co-owners of a business for profit. There are typically two types of partnerships. The first type, a general partnership, contemplates that each partner participates in all profits and losses equally or to some previously agreed upon ratio. Normally, a general partner has unlimited liability, which includes personally owned assets outside the business association. A partnership can be created either by a formal agreement or an oral understanding. In addition, it must be banded together for profit-producing motives and is generally not considered a legal entity separate from the partners. A general partnership may not sue or be sued in the firm's name. Each partner shares potential "joint and several" liabilities.

The second type of partnership, a limited partnership, limits the liability of the partners to the extent of their capital contributions. A limited partnership must have at least one general partner so at least one person or entity's personal assets must be at stake. In many instances, the general partner is a corporation so that only the corporate assets are at stake.[9]

Advantages of a Partnership

- *(General Partnership) Easy to Establish*. Like the proprietorship, the general partnership is easy and inexpensive to establish. The partners must obtain the necessary business license and submit a minimal number of forms. In most states, partners must file a Certificate for Conducting Business as Partners if the business is run under a trade name. Limited partnerships require registration to be official.
- *Complementary Skills of Partners*. In a sole proprietorship, the owner must wear many different hats, and not all of them will fit well. In successful partnerships, the parties' skills usually complement one another. For example, one partner in a software firm says, "My co-owner provides the vision, energy, and enthusiasm needed in a deal situation. I am more negative and careful. Together we're a solid team."
- *Division of Profits*. There are no restrictions on how profits must be distributed as long as they are consistent with the partnership agreement and do not violate the rights of any partner.
- *Larger Pool of Capital*. The partnership form of ownership can significantly broaden the pool of capital available to the business. Each partner's asset base improves the ability of the business to borrow needed funds. Therefore, each

individual has more to contribute in equity capital, and together their personal assets will support a larger borrowing capacity.

- *Ability to Attract Limited Partners*. There can be any number of limited partners as long as there is at least one general partner. A partnership can attract investors who, with limited liability, still can realize a substantial return on their investment if the business is successful. A great many individuals find it very profitable to invest as limited partners in high-potential small businesses.

- *Flexibility*. Although not as flexible as a sole proprietorship, the partnership can generally react quickly to changing market conditions because its organizational structure does not stifle its quick and creative responses to new opportunities.

- *Taxation*. The partnership itself is not subject to federal taxation. Its net income is distributed directly to the partners as personal income, and the partners pay income tax on their distributive shares. General partners are allowed to use partnership losses on their personal returns. The partnership, like the sole proprietorship, avoids the double taxation applicable to the corporate form of ownership.

Disadvantages of a Partnership

- *Unlimited Liability of at Least One Partner*. At least one member of every partnership must be a general partner. The general partner has unlimited personal liability.

- *Capital Accumulation*. Although the partnership is superior to the proprietorship in its ability to attract capital, it is generally not as effective as the corporate form of ownership. This is because the partnership usually has limitations and restriction to raising capital.

- *Restrictions of Elimination for the General Partnership*. Most partnership agreements restrict how partners can dispose of their share of the business. It is common to find that partners are required to sell their interest to the remaining partners. But even if the original agreement contains such a requirement and clearly delineates how the value of each partner's ownership will be determined, there is no guarantee that the other partner(s) will have the financial resources to buy the seller's interest. When the money is not available to purchase a partner's interest, the other partner(s) may be forced either to accept a new partner who purchases the partner's interest or to dissolve the partnership, distribute the remaining assets, and begin again. When a general partner dies, becomes incompetent, or withdraws from the business, the partnership automatically dissolves, although it may not terminate. Even when there are numerous partners, if one wishes to disassociate his or her name from the business, the remaining partners will probably form a new partnership.

- *Lack of Continuity for the General Partnership*. If one partner dies, complications arise. Partnership interest is often nontransferable through inheritance because the remaining partner(s) may not wish to be in partnership with the person who inherits the deceased partner's interest. Partners can make provisions in the partnership agreement to avoid dissolution due to death if all parties agree to accept as partners those who inherit the deceased's interest.

- *Potential for Personality and Authority Conflicts*. Friction among partners is inevitable and difficult to control. Disagreements over what should be done or what was done have dissolved many a partnership. For example, when the cofounders of a successful communications company got into a dispute over its future direction, the firm lost its edge and momentum in the market. While the partners fought over buyout terms, the business floundered. Ultimately, the business was sold at a very low price.

LIMITED LIABILITY COMPANY (LLC)

An LLC is a blend of some of the best characteristics of corporations, partnerships, and sole proprietorships. It is a separate legal entity like a corporation, but it is entitled to be treated as either a sole proprietorship or a partnership for tax purposes, depending on whether there is one or more members. Therefore, it carries with it the "flow through" or "transparent" tax benefits that corporations do not have. It is very flexible and simple to run. As long as the terms of the governing document called the Operating Agreement are adhered to, the LLC may be operated more like a sole proprietorship or a partnership than as a corporation.

The owners are called members, who can be individuals (residents or foreigners), corporations, other LLCs, trusts, pension plans, and so on.[10]

An LLC is formed by filing an Article of Organization form with a secretary of state and signing an LLC Operating Agreement. The corporation division of most secretary of state offices handles the filing of LLC papers. Most states require that an annual report be filed to keep them apprised of the current status of an LLC. The LLC is not a tax-paying entity. Profits, losses, and the like flow directly through and are reported on the individual member's tax returns unless the members make an election to be taxed as a corporation.

Advantages of an LLC

- Owners do not assume liabilities for debt.
- They **may** offer different classes of **memberships.**
- There are no restrictions on the number and types of owners.

Disadvantages of an LLC

- There may be difficulty in business expansion out of state.
- Transferring ownership is restricted. Requirements are different for each state.

SETTING UP A LIMITED LIABILITY CORPORATION (LLC) — OWNERSHIP

SUMMARY OF PROS AND CONS

- Owned by "members," not shareholders.
- A combination of characteristics of corporations, partnerships, and sole proprietorships.

SETTING UP A LIMITED LIABILITY CORPORATION (LLC) — OWNERSHIP (cont.)

PROS

- Liability protection (a separate legal entity as in a C-Corporation).
- LLC is not a tax-paying entity (tax benefits to members).
- Statutory meetings are not required.

CONS

- Unlikely that a venture capitalist would invest in a LLC.
- Cannot take the company public.
- Different shareholder interests result in complex operating agreements.
- Restrictions on transfer of ownership.
- Management and member rules different in each state.

Business Organizational Structure Comparison Chart

Characteristic	C-Corp	S-Corp	LLC
Limited liability for all owners	Yes	Yes	Yes
Owners can participate in management without losing liability protection	Yes	Yes	Yes
Easy to form and without maintaining extensive records	No	No	Yes
Number of owners	1 or more	1–100	1 or more
Restrictions on ownership	No	Yes	No
Double tax	Yes	No	Maybe
Able to deduct business loss on individual return	No	Yes	Maybe
Basis for loss includes owner's share of company debt in owner's tax return	No	Yes	Maybe
Can increase basis by "step-up" election	Yes	Yes	Yes
Can specially allocate terms of income and expense	Yes	Yes	Yes
Contributes and distributes property tax free	Yes	No	Yes

Moving to the Next Step

Now that you have a good beginning to understand the legal forms of the organization, a business startup checklist is presented. This checklist will be your guide for the first 30 days, 60 days, and your first year-end activities.

BUSINESS STARTUP CHECK-UP LIST

Now that you know the forms of doing business, the next steps are to begin the process of starting a new business:[11]

First 30 Days

- Obtain an Employer Identification Number from the IRS by completing federal form SS4.
- Select a lawyer.
- Select an accountant.
- Prepare a business plan.
- Select a banker or banking institution.
- Select an insurance agent.
- Obtain business insurance.
- Order business cards and letterhead.
- Obtain a business license or permit from the city hall or county office.
- Establish bank accounts.
- Establish Merchant Credit Card Service allowing your business to accept major credit cards (if applicable).
- Pick a year-end date.
- Corporations hold an organizational meeting where:
- By-laws are adopted.
  1. A Board of Directors is elected.
  2. Share certificates should be distributed to shareholders once purchased, and these transactions should be recorded on the corporation's stock ledger.
  3. Company members and/or managers and officers are elected.
  4. Any corporate business that needs immediate attention is addressed.
- An LLC should have an organizational meeting where:
  5. An operating agreement is adopted.
  6. Membership certificates are distributed.
  7. Company members and/or managers are elected.
  8. In some states, publishing is required of your operation or an LLC.

First 60 Days

- Establish presence on Internet with domain name registration.
- Contact suppliers.
- If selecting S-Corporation status, file Form 2553 within 75 days.
- Obtain business insurance (liability, health and dental, workers' compensation, etc.).
- Join a professional organization.
- Some states such as Nevada require a list of officers and directors to be filed with the state.

By First Year End

- Obtain federal tax forms.
- Obtain state tax forms.
- Pay corporate franchise tax or annual state fees.

- Order mail-forwarding service.
- Obtain financing.
- Establish a line of credit.

Selecting Your Attorney

The legal requirements for setting up a company can vary greatly from state to state. An attorney should be consulted to ensure you meet the legal requirements facing the business. An attorney can provide assistance in formating the business, filing necessary documents with appropriate governmental authorities, and preparing employment contracts, stock ownership agreements, and other documents for equity holders. An attorney can also assist in preparing documents for the hiring of employees and independent contractors (confidentiality agreements, work for hire agreements, noncompetition agreements, nonsolicitation agreements, etc.) and those required for raising capital.[12]

In selecting an attorney, the most important element is finding one that can competently meet your needs. Selecting an attorney based on price is not a good idea. The intricacies of forming and operating a business require that an attorney be knowledgeable in corporate law, securities law, taxation, contract law, employment law, and license and trademark law. Therefore, one should find out how experienced an attorney is in rendering services for a business. One should also get recommendations from other business owners and consult guides that list attorney credentials and rate their ability. An attorney should always be interviewed before being engaged for his or her services. A competent attorney should be able to answer all of your questions in your initial interview. The attorney should also be able to give an estimate of cost for establishing a business. If you are not satisfied with the answers received, then you should consult another attorney. As you grow your business, you are likely to need additional legal advice in specialist areas such as exporting, franchising, and patenting. Ask your first corporate attorney what affiliations he or she has with specialist legal offices.

Selecting Your Accountant

The accountant should be a practical business advisor who can set up a total financial control system for the business and render sound financial advice. At the outset, the accountant should work to establish accounting and reporting systems, cash projections, financing strategies, and tax planning. In addition, as the company matures, the following services can be provided:[13]

- Vendor services and payment options
- Cash management or fiscal accounting
- Cost-reduction planning using invoices
- Compensation plan for employees
- Merger, acquisition, and appraisal assistance
- Management information systems to determine the accounting software requirements

Name Registration

A business that adopts an assumed business name must register the name with the state of incorporation and with each state in which the business is doing business.

This should be done before taking any other steps to do business in the state. The registration will protect the name from infringement. The amount of registration fee varies by state.

In most states, a corporation's name must include the word "corporation," "company," "incorporated," "limited," or an abbreviation of one of these words. Limited Liability Companies must include LLC as part of their name. A competent attorney can assist with this phase of establishing a new business.

Federal Identification Number

A business must obtain an identification number from the Internal Revenue Service, except for a sole proprietorship that has no employees other than the owner. An identification number can be obtained by using Form SS-4, "Application for Employer Identification Number."[14] One may get an Employer Identification number (EIN) by calling the IRS or going online.

Insurance Issues

Most businesses require insurance of one form or another. In addition, state law may require some forms, such as workers' compensation. The entrepreneur should shop around to find the insurer who offers the best combination of coverage, service, and price. Trade associations often offer special rates and policies to their members.[15]

Even though not required by law, the entrepreneur should consider the following forms of insurance to protect the business.

- Fire, employee, health, and life
- Crime coverage, which reimburses the employer for robbery, burglary, and vandalism losses
- Business interruption, which compensates the business for revenue lost during a temporary halt in business caused by fire, theft, or illness
- Key man insurance, which compensates the business for the death or disability of a key partner or manager
- Liability, which protects the business from claims of bodily injury, property damage, and malpractice
- Product liability

Other issues the entrepreneur should address in the business are:

- Directors and officers Insurance may be required as the company grows to protect against personal lawsuits associated with the company's business activities.
- State registration.
- Most state taxing authorities require a business, whatever its form, to register. The purpose of this registration is to receive sales tax registration numbers or exemptions and to receive the proper forms for filing wage withholding. Each state in which an entity does business must be contacted to determine how to do this registration.
- Web site registration.
- Domain name registration is a separate form of registration from registering a business name with a government entity. One should register a domain name as

soon as possible. If a name is already registered, a business cannot use it on the Internet. Domain names can be bought and sold. This is an expensive alternative to direct registration. One should "reserve" one's domain name prior to filing with any government authority. This will prevent the costly process of changing the name on government registrations to the domain name after one has registered with government authorities.

ACTIONS

The best employment agreement serves as an incentive for the employee and provides protection against the employee damaging the company subsequent to employment. The incentives may include stock options, payments for inventions, or bonuses.

SETTING UP EMPLOYER–EMPLOYEE AGREEMENTS

It is important to establish employment agreements for your management team and key employers in the company. The agreement describes the obligations of the employer and employee and varies widely among companies and even among employees within the same company. Usual provisions included in the agreement should emphasize the following employee issues:[16]

- They cannot disclose any confidential information about the company either during or subsequent to employment.
- They must return all materials that belong to the company at the time of termination of employment.
- They cannot engage in a new business during the period of employment without the consent of the employer.
- They will not compete with the company for a period of time subsequent to employment.
- They will disclose and assign to the company all inventions during their employment.

Employment agreements can present an element of coercion. The employee may assume that because he or she is given the agreement for signature, the employee has little choice but to sign it or seek employment elsewhere. If the employer tries to enforce an agreement, the sympathies of the court usually lie with the employee. Seldom will a court enforce an employment agreement if it deprives the ex-employee of the means of making a living. For these reasons, employment agreements should be drafted, read, and agreed to prior to actual employment.

SETTING UP STOCK OPTION AGREEMENTS

Many companies provide added incentives for keeping key employees by providing an ownership or equity interest in the company. This is usually in the form of common stock or options to acquire common stock. Companies should establish a qualified stock option plan under which selected employees receive options to purchase stock in the company. Qualified stock options are restricted to employees and are not available to others. The word "qualified" indicates that the plan is qualified for certain tax benefits under Section 422A of the Internal Revenue Code of 1986. Under such an arrangement, the employee pays no tax at the time the option is granted. Another feature of the option plan is that the ownership of the options can vest over a period of years, so that if the employee is terminated prior to the terms of the option, only a portion of the options is received.[17]

A qualified employee stock option plan must meet certain requirements. Some of the most important features to consider are as follows.

- A "plan" must be adopted by the Board of Directors and approved by the stock-holders of the company. The Board can adopt the plan and put it into effect, subject to approval by the stockholders, at the next annual or other meeting within 12 months.

- The plan must state the aggregate number of shares being set aside for the options and the employees or class of employees (for example, "key employees") for which options will be made available.

- No options may be granted more than 10 years after the plan is put into effect without board approval.

The option must not be transferable and is exercisable during the lifetime of the employee.

Shares Issued for Compensation and Tax Implications

Attracting and maintaining talented employees are necessary for the success of a new organization. The "carrot" used to attract these employees might take many different forms. For example, competitive cash compensation, retirement plans, transferring property (automobiles, real estate, equipment, etc.), and equity, along with many other forms, could be used to attract employees.

The Internal Revenue Code (IRC) Section 83 governs the tax treatment accorded to transfers of almost any kind of property to employees in the course of their employment. The key point of Section 83 is that when an employer transfers property to an employee, in connection with the performance of services, the difference between the price paid (if anything) for the property and its fair market value at the time the employee's interest is substantially vested is treated as compensation—that is, included in the employee's gross income in the year ownership is vested. In addition, under this section, the employee stockholder would be required to pay taxes on the amount seen as income (the spread) upon it fully vesting at the tax rate of 35 percent, or whatever the employee's individual income tax rate is at the time.

As an alternative to the tax structure, the employee stockholder can elect the use of IRC Section 83(B) to pay in the year the stock was received and the income tax on the spread. When the stock is later sold, the employee will pay a capital gains tax on future appreciation of the gain.[18]

Example of Tax Implications

In year 1, a startup company sells stock to a key employee, Allison, at $8 per share. The fair market value of the stock is $10 per share. In year 5, when the restriction lapses, the fair market share of the stock is $110 per share. The restriction is that

	83(a) Default	83(b) Election
Tax implications for Allison in year 1	None	The difference between fair market share and the price sold to Allison is taxed at ordinary income. Tax rate = 35 percent Tax due = $0.70 per share
Tax implications for Allison in year 5 (when restriction was removed)	$110 − $10 = $100 = taxable compensation Tax rate for ordinary income = 35 percent Tax due = $35 per share	Taxed only if stock is sold Taxed at long-term capital gains rate of 15 percent on the amount stock has appreciated above original value. If sold, tax due = $15 per share
Tax implications for Allison upon selling the stock	Taxed on further appreciation of stock above is $110 at 15 percent.	Taxed on appreciation of stock at 15 percent. Benefit of additional tax deferral. If the stock were not sold prior to Allison's death, the gain would never be taxed.

Allison must still be working for the company in five years. If she quits, she must sell the stock back to the company at the cost of $10 per share. (See accompanying table.)

Nonqualified Stock Options (NQSOs)

This type of option allows the employee to purchase shares of employer stock at a stated price over a given period of time. This option plan is not subject to strict regulations and allows for flexibility in setting the exercise price and term of conditions. The terms of the plan usually include the following provisions:[19]

- *Exercise Price*. This is usually equal to the fair market value of employer shares at the time of the grant. Any difference between the option exercise price and the fair market value of the option at the date of grant is a compensation expense and would reduce earnings for accounting purposes.
- *Vesting Restrictions*. Vesting in equal installments over a three- to five-year period is most common.
- *Term*. Ten years is a typical term. Option values increase with the length of the exercise period; a shorter term may be appropriate if the recipient is close to retirement or the employer anticipates quick and extreme appreciation of the shares and is concerned about the potential dilutive effects of outstanding options.
- *Post-Termination Exercise Restrictions*. Most limit the post-termination exercise period to 90 days or one year following death or disability.
- *Form of Payment*. Payment may be in cash or by surrender of currently owned shares. Shares used for payment should be owned for at least six months to avoid potential Section 16(b) issues under the securities laws.

Advantages of Nonqualified Stock Options
- To the individual or employee:
  (a) The possibility of a large gain is not limited by any accounting considerations.

(b) The employee can choose the time to exercise the option for maximize gains.

(c) There are no statutory limitations on exercise after retirement.

- To the employer:

   (a) The company can take a tax deduction.

   (b) There is no charge on the income statement, although there may be a negative impact on earnings per share.

   (c) It provides an increase in capital to the company.

   (d) The plan is simple to design and administer.

   (e) Setting up is by board resolution, or shareholder approval may be required in some states.

   (f) There is no need to establish specific performance standards; value is determined by the price of stock.

Disadvantages of Nonqualified Stock Options

- The employee may need to borrow the cash to exercise the option. A program can be arranged through a broker to pay the purchase price.
- The profit or gain may not meet the benefits for employment.
- The compensation may not provide the cash rewards based on the particular performance of the employee.

Setting Up Incentive Stock Options (ISOs)

These options provide the right to purchase shares of stock at a stated price over a given period of time. ISOs, however, must satisfy certain statutory requirements:[20]

- The option price is not less than the fair market value of the stock at the time of the grant.
- The option by its terms is not exercisable after the expiration of 10 years from the grant date.
- The option is nontransferable other than by will and exercisable during the life of the agreement.
- Individuals owning more than 10 percent of the outstanding shares are subject to a minimum exercise price of 110 percent of fair market value at the date of grant and a maximum exercise period of five years.
- The plan must be approved by shareholders, state the number of shares to be granted, specify who is eligible, and be granted within 10 years of the shareholder approval.
- The value of all options vesting in a given year per individual may not exceed $100,000. This provides limitations to senior executives.

Disadvantages of the Incentive Stock Options Plan

- Mandatory waiting period of two years from date of grant and one year from date of exercise to qualify for long-term capital gain treatment.
- Three-month exercise limitation after termination of employment, including retirement. One-year limitation on exercise after death or disability.
- Limitations on the maximum amount of $100,000 that may vest in any year.

- No grant to an executive owning more than 10 percent of the voting power of all classes of stock before the option is granted unless the option expires within five years of grant and exercise price is 110 percent of FMV on date of grant.
- Need for the individual to borrow cash to finance the option.
- Action required by the Board of Directors and shareholder approval.
- No tax benefit to the company.

SUMMARY

This chapter provides a good beginning for understanding the legal forms of the organization. It presents guidelines on the best legal form most appropriate for a particular situation.

In choosing a form of ownership, entrepreneurs must remember that there is no single "best" form; what is best depends on the individual's circumstances. Ask the questions that will help determine which form of ownership is best:

1. How big can this business potentially become?
2. How much control do you need in the decision-making process of the company? Are you willing to share ideas and the business's potential profits with others who can help build a more successful business?
3. How much capital is needed to start the business?

A sole proprietorship is a form of business that has a single owner and only requires business licenses to open. If the plan is to start a business under a name other than that of the owner, one must file a name in order to operate as "doing business as" (for example, Jack's SmartCard Consulting). The business can be dissolved or closed at any time, and it always ends upon the death of the owner.

The C-Corporation is the most common form of business ownership. It is a separate entity apart from its owners, and it may engage in business, issue contracts, sue and be sued, and pay taxes. When a corporation is founded, it accepts the regulations and restrictions of the state in which it is incorporated. A corporation doing business in the state in which it is incorporated is a domestic corporation. When it conducts business in another state, that state considers the corporation to be a foreign corporation. Corporations that are formed in other countries but do business in the United States are alien corporations.

The S-Corporation is a corporation that is treated like a partnership for tax purposes in that profits and losses are typically taxed directly to the individual shareholders. It is the owner's responsibility to report the gains or losses on individual income tax returns.

A partnership is usually defined as an association of two or more people carrying on as co-owners of a business for profit. There are typically two types of partnerships. The first type, a general partnership, contemplates that each partner participates in all profits and losses equally or to some previously agreed upon ratio. Normally, a general partner has unlimited liability, which includes personally owned assets outside the business association. A formal agreement or an oral understanding can create a general partnership.

An LLC is a blend of some characteristics of corporations, partnerships, and sole proprietorships. It is a separate legal entity like a corporation, but it is entitled to be treated as a sole proprietorship or a partnership for tax purposes and therefore carries with it the "flow through" or "transparent" tax benefits that corporations do not have. It is very flexible and simple to run, and, like a sole proprietorship, there is no statutory necessity to keep minutes, hold meetings, or make resolutions, which can trip up many corporations' owners.

The chapter summarizes the major forms of the legal organization, sole proprietorship, partnership, and corporation. The advantages and disadvantages of each are discussed, and a list of questions are highlighted to help you decide which form of ownership is best for you. In addition, a checklist has been prepared to assist you in the first 30, 60, and year-end periods to maximize the best performance for the business.

You should also seek legal advice to assist in preparing charters, name registration, and other documents to ensure the proper registration of the form of business.

STUDY QUESTIONS

1. What are the factors in deciding what form of ownership is best suited for the potential business?
2. Briefly describe the advantages and disadvantages of a sole proprietorship and partnership.
3. Explain the corporate form of ownership and how a business is incorporated.
4. List the differences between the S-Corporation and the Limited Liability Company.
5. Explain the difference between qualified and nonqualified stock option plans.
6. Describe the advantages and disadvantages of stock option plans for the employer and the employee.

EXERCISES

Starting a New Health Care Service Company

In the fall of September 2001, Peter, the chief technology officer for a health-care technology company resigned from his position. He then contacted Jennifer, who was the director of marketing for a hospital in charge of advertising and promotions. Both discussed an idea to start a company that offers health-care providers claim processing services. Peter and Jennifer committed to start a new company called New Health Claim Processing. This name was important, for it would carry great weight in the industry. Peter and Jennifer had developed a unique business model to process claims at a very low cost while providing a high degree of customer service. The company would lease all the backend hardware and write the software necessary to operate the business. The company would also provide all implementation, maintenance, and other ongoing support that would be required to utilize the service.

Peter and Jennifer invited Andy and Grace to join their effort. The four had met in Professor Jack Kaplan's Entrepreneurship Course at Columbia Business School. They were all technology savvy and had outstanding grades and extensive relevant work experiences. Their credentials would look good for raising capital. This core group of four refined Peter and Jennifer's initial ideas and started drafting a business plan.

As part of the business plan, the group decided that they needed a CEO in order to attract the venture capital they believed they needed. Before the business plan was complete, they called their friend, Michael, with a proposition. They promised that they would make it worth his while if he would lead the company as the CEO.

Two months later, the business plan was complete. The group of five was very excited as Michael took the lead in seeking funding for the venture. Michael's early contacts were successful. Within weeks of completing the business plan, he had scheduled an appointment to present the business plan to the first venture capital firm.

During the presentation, the venture partners became interested in the company's vision and strategy, and in the business processes for delivering customer service. However, as the due diligence questions got around to technology, Michael became quiet as the partners questioned the type of company formed and the ownership of the business. A moment of silence occurred when one partner asked who owned the company. Michael, as CEO, had not yet settled how the ownership would be divided.

At the end of the all-day session, one of the venture partners told Michael in frank terms that he had handled the ownership questions poorly. He referred Michael to a partner at a local law firm who was a close friend of his. Michael immediately made an appointment with the partner, Cathy, for the next day.

Cathy was an expert in organization and stock option incentives programs. She began by asking Michael for a retainer, which he paid out of his personal funds. Michael gave her a brief overview of the situation and arranged to bring all members for questioning.

Cathy soon uncovered the following:

- Jennifer had left her previous company three months ago but, did not tell him that she was still on a retainer by the company. She also had signed a nondisclosure agreement on the day she left.
- Cathy also learned that Peter had taken his client list and index of all his personal contacts. He

also took a notebook and articles on health-care products.

Peter also received a letter from his previous company stating, "It has come to our attention that you may have in your possession confidential documents belonging to the company."

Based on the foregoing information, please answer the following questions:

1. Identify the legal structure and issues involved in starting the business.

_____
_____
_____
_____

2. Identify the issues raised by the conduct of the startup team.

_____
_____
_____
_____

3. Identify three ethical business issues presented in the case.

_____
_____
_____
_____

4. What is your decision: to proceed, or not to proceed?

_____
_____
_____
_____

INTERACTIVE LEARNING ON THE WEB

Test your skill-builder knowledge of the chapter using the interactive Web site.

1. Self Assessment:

2. Multiple Choice:

3. Matching of Key Terms:

4. Demonstration:

5. Case:

6. Video:

CASE STUDY: D-MARC TECHNOLOGIES, INC.

INTRODUCTION

As the chill of 1999's winter descended upon New York City, Jack M. Kaplan, the president and founder of D-Marc Software, Inc. (D-Marc), a provider of customer loyalty programs using smart card technology, faced two classic strategic entrepreneurial problems. The first, how would he determine and secure the most effective and beneficial means of financing the company's growth (or possibly lose the near-term competitive advantages that the company had struggled so hard to achieve)? The second, how must the company's organizational structure change to successfully make the leap from a loosely organized, entrepreneurial focused group of individuals to a clearly defined, professionally managed company?

The environment in this infant industry was changing since the company was founded in 1994. Many players were entering the field and competing for more new business. Kaplan recognized that D-Marc had about a 12- to 18-month window of opportunity whereby D-Marc must leverage its strengths and maintain its competitive advantages in an all-out effort to grow the company.

The choices available for its growth and for maintaining the company's advantages while building upon new opportunities were (1) internal financing through increased sales revenues, (2) strategic partnership(s) with another company(s) with complementary fit, and/or (3) venture capital investment. The choices suitable for redefining the company's management structure were far less tangible. How would he determine whether certain employees, who were invaluable in the early stages of D-Marc's development, could adapt to a new internal structure? How would each employee fit into his newly defined role? If an employee could not adequately make the transition, what would be the consequences? Would he need to hire outside professionals who possess necessary business skills and contacts to lead D-Marc forward?

Kaplan struggled with these issues as he tried to best lead his company away from a small-business mentality into a growth-driven orientation. He had come to realize that he would need approximately $2.5 million to effectively finance the expansion of D-Marc's business. He was considering setting up a C-Corporation in New Jersey or Delaware and could not decide which would be best. He also recognized that D-Marc could not efficiently utilize its potential new funding without a more professionally organized management team. On top of all this, D-Marc would require additional personnel, equipment, hardware and software, and larger facilities to attract and service a growing client base in the burgeoning marketing data-capture industry. Kaplan understood that he was destined to make many strategic decisions in a relatively short period of time that would affect D-Marc's competitive positioning as it entered its growth phase in the following spring. His decisions would determine how quickly D-Marc could leverage its strengths to penetrate this new market, capture share, and harvest investment potential.

COMPANY DESCRIPTION AND HISTORY

D-Marc Technologies, Inc., in operation since 1994, is a marketing-driven technology firm and a leading provider of electronic customer loyalty programs in the United States and North America. It has developed a program design that can easily offer the benefits of a comprehensive loyalty and relationship marketing program for the retail, restaurant, telecommunications, oil and gas, travel, and entertainment industries. Transaction processing services and software licensing fees constitute its primary means of generating income. Considering the changing nature of consumer tastes and buying habits, its product set offers distinctive advantages to consumer product and service organizations seeking to maximize their opportunity to generate sales growth. Its unique solutions offer proven tools that allow precise marketing data to be captured and utilized to the fullest. Functioning similar to the airline frequent flyer programs, D-Marc's programs utilize smart card, magnetic stripe, and bar code technology to reward loyal customers and to capture nonfinancial customer data and transaction histories. Through detailed data manipulation and processing techniques, D-Marc's proprietary technology allows its clients the distinct competitive advantages of providing a loyalty program.

The History

D-Marc Technologies, Inc. was conceived by Jack Kaplan, who continues to serve as president of the company. Jack had received a request to consult with a major corporation to develop a customer loyalty program. Although the project was never launched, Jack's vision took shape, and D-Marc was born.

The company embarked upon its first loyalty project in early 1994. D-Marc was challenged to assume control of an existing card-based loyalty system that had been handled by a previous company. The company was handling transaction processing for a restaurant chain loyalty pilot program running in 21 locations in Canada and was in the process of going out of business. Operations had to be transferred within 30 days for the deal to go through. D-Marc rose to the challenge, meeting the first of many seemingly impossible timelines and creating a defining moment in the company's evolution. The restaurant chain project was a regional program and was successful, but it failed to gain corporate funding for a national rollout due to budgeting constraints. The program was phased out at the end of June 1995.

Following a technical outsourcing relationship with a large computer company in 1994 that proved to be too costly, D-Marc saw the need to build up its own technological capabilities and subsequently developed proprietary software for a loyalty system for a major sporting goods company that began in June 1995.

Shortly after launching the sporting goods pilot, D-Marc signed a contract with a petroleum company. The mission was to convert the petroleum company's paper-based loyalty system to an electronic, magnetic card program. Negotiations were finalized in June of 1995, and the revamped electronic loyalty system was in field test by September of the same year. To meet the needs of this client, D-Marc developed in-house customer service, technical support, and a call center software product.

In retrospect, it is clear that the choice to develop a strong technological team was important. With each new project, valuable team project managers and technical staff were needed. The plan was to set up a stock option plan for employees and provide additional incentives as needed.

PRODUCTS AND SERVICES

Patron Plus™ Customer Loyalty Programs

Personalized relationship marketing can create sales growth, increase customer retention, and provide measurable results. Whether companies are looking to improve an existing program or seeking to create a customer loyalty system, a solution to fit client needs is only a telephone call away. D-Marc has proven successful with large-scale frequency shopper programs. It supports all facets of a comprehensive, result-oriented customer loyalty, frequency, and relationship-marketing platform. When considering both the lifetime values of a customer and the significant expense involved with attracting new customers, loyalty-enhancing platforms can be a sound investment in the future. We have created a variety of targeted consumer loyalty platforms that will maximize sales growth, provide immediate, measurable feedback, and help clients build a personalized relationship with customers.

D-Marc's marketing professionals can engineer and design all components of a program. This can include award structure, application form, management reports, targeted marketing campaigns, data utilization, and overall consulting services. Its significant experience and knowledge of customer loyalty/frequency programs work to complement our technical and system programming know-how.

Its loyalty experts can show clients how to generate sales growth in targeted markets and measure responses. Clients will own the customer database, which is updated each time a program participant makes a purchase. Custom reports are formatted to capture the information the client requests.

D-Marc offers:

1. **Turnkey Solutions**
   - Hardware and software
   - Programming
   - Program design
   - Point of Sale (POS) integration
   - Smart, bar code, magnetic stripe, and thermal-print card expertise
   - Account access via the Internet
   - Flexible promotional coupons

2. **Transaction Processing and Database Maintenance**
   - In its efforts to provide a total solution, D-Marc offers in-house data processing and record maintenance services. Customer account and transaction data are downloaded in electronic format from participating locations at regular intervals. The data is collected at a central data center where the information is processed and reconciled. D-Marc utilizes its Patron Plus™ transaction-processing platform for this purpose. New point/rebate totals and customers' award statuses are determined at this time. D-Marc provides options to support both batched and online processing systems depending on the program requirements.

3. **Enrollment/Data Entry**
   - D-Marc offers enrollment processing and data cleansing services. It can provide data entry services, accept customer information via electronic feed, or handle enrollment processing over the telephone or on the Internet. Its facility

provides all of the necessary tools to custom fit the enrollment process to a client's existing processes. These data can be further augmented with demographic and psychographic information from third-party databases.

4. Customer Service and Technical Support

- Our dedicated customer service professionals are available to answer cardholder inquiries, process service requests, as well as report comments and complaints. D-Marc's call center software offers the ability to maintain detailed call-tracking records that can help identify operational and program concerns.

- D-Marc also offers help-desk support to assist our clients in maintaining smooth program operation. It can support routine terminal maintenance, installation, and initialization, as well as provide diagnostic and replacement service.

- Its call response center features:
  - ➤ interactive voice response service
  - ➤ 24 × 7 phone support for Patron Plus™ platforms
  - ➤ fast response and strong customer focus
  - ➤ automated call distribution
  - ➤ 17,000 calls per day capacity
  - ➤ detailed call tracking with regular feedback

How Patron Plus™ Works

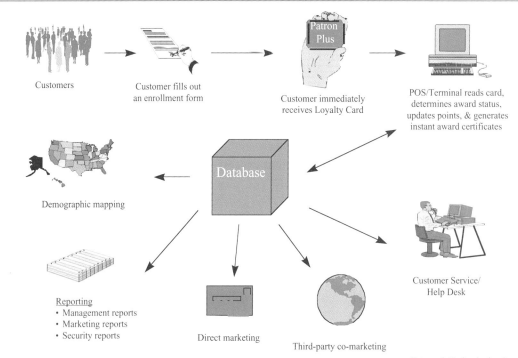

Customers

Customer fills out an enrollment form

Customer immediately receives Loyalty Card

POS/Terminal reads card, determines award status, updates points, & generates instant award certificates

Database

Demographic mapping

Reporting
• Management reports
• Marketing reports
• Security reports

Direct marketing

Third-party co-marketing

Customer Service/ Help Desk

Datamark Technologies, Inc.

Figure 4-1   D-Marc's Patron Plus System.

> ➢ personalized messaging
> ➢ point and click access to multiple client databases
> ➢ proactive daily service review
> ➢ call tracking cross reference for technical and nontechnical problem reso-
> lution
> ➢ installation and replacement service for selected terminals

Figure 4-1 shows how Datamark's Patron Plus system works.

E-Gift™ (Electronic Gift Certificate Program)

The E-Gift™ design resembles that of a prepaid telephone card in that the value for the gift certificate is automatically debited with each use. Receipts are provided to gift certificate customers with up-to-date balance information, which can be printed instantly at the point-of-sale. The technology allows the capture of customer trans-action and demographic data and offers an activation/registration feature that can be used to protect the gift certificate from loss or theft. Reduced paper, automated recordkeeping, and time saved during issuance and redemption are just a few of the benefits of this system.

E-Gift™ can be configured to work in two ways. The system can be loaded on a stand-alone terminal or integrated into the point-of-sale system. Often the stand-alone terminal option can be designed to share space on an existing credit card terminal. In many cases, no additional hardware is required.

As a result of this program, one client has experienced 14.2 percent savings by using cards instead of paper and 100 percent savings on bookkeeping and administration costs, resulting in 33 percent savings overall compared to a paper gift certificate program. Figure 4-2 illustrates how the E-Gift™ system works.

Project Life Cycle

A typical D-Marc implementation lasts three to five months and involves:

- *Specifications* (two weeks): D-Marc prepares specifications for the loyalty sys-tem in conjunction with the client. The specifications describe how the system will be implemented, what database analyses are required, and the costs/benefits of competing technologies (i.e., smart cards vs. mag-stripe or bar coded cards).

- *Installation and Pilot Program* (two to three months): After the approval of the specification, D-Marc will proceed to promptly install the system at a Beta site. This will be done in accordance with a mutually agreed upon schedule and with the specifications. A successful Beta site test typically leads to a re-gional pilot and eventually to full rollout among the client's locations world-wide.

- *Rollout Services* (one to two months): During the initial implementation phase and the full rollout, D-Marc will conduct training sessions for the client's staff.

- *Ongoing Maintenance and Support*: For the full life of these systems, D-Marc provides maintenance and customer support, including a client support help desk, hardware maintenance, free software upgrades, and consulting services.

Electronic Gift Certificate System

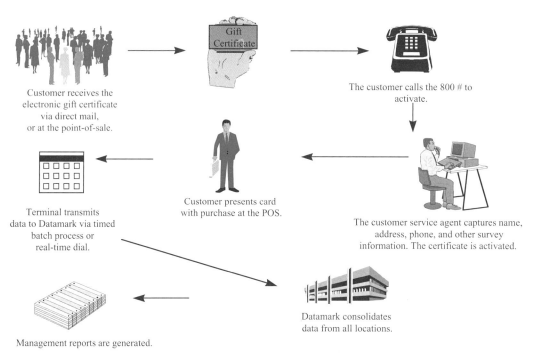

Customer receives the
electronic gift certificate
via direct mail,
or at the point-of-sale.

The customer calls the 800 # to
activate.

Terminal transmits
data to Datamark via timed
batch process or
real-time dial.

Customer presents card
with purchase at the POS.

The customer service agent captures name,
address, phone, and other survey
information. The certificate is activated.

Datamark consolidates
data from all locations.

Management reports are generated.

Datamark Technologies, Inc.

Figure 4-2   The Electronic Gift Certificate System (E-Gift™).

D-Marc's Success Factors

1. *Highly Lucrative Rollout Process*
   The company provides a turnkey loyalty service that details all of the services required for a loyalty program. Its POS software provides clients with instant awards and innovative technology and services for instant redemption and point totals. Once a company signs with D-Marc for a frequency pilot program, it is likely that the company will be a customer of D-Marc's over the next two to three years at a minimum. This is true because D-Marc retains control over the fundamental aspects of the program, making it very costly and time consuming for the client to switch to another vendor. Because of a pricing structure that creates large profits for D-Marc after the costs associated with the initial implementation, the company benefits tremendously from such a long-term relationship with its clients.

2. *D-Marc's Patent Positions*
   D-Marc has two patents with multiple claims covering multi-application data cards. The company believes that these patents will create a barrier to competition and will provide significant ongoing licensing revenues.

3. *Strong Smart Card and Marketing Expertise*
   D-Marc differentiates itself from much of its competition by being a marketing-driven firm with technical expertise. Its management team combines outstanding marketing talent with highly experienced smart card experts who have been associated with the technology practically from its advent in the United States.

4. *Low-Cost/High-Quality Programs*

D-Marc's frequency programs and its Customer Allegiance™ software are all positioned to be among the lowest cost solutions in the industry. The company prices its applications on a per store basis and has developed breakeven analyses for its clients. Usually, the installation needs only to generate less than 5 percent in additional sales to reach breakeven, while D-Marc's programs have consistently demonstrated more than 20 percent increase in customer visit frequency and average check size.

Stored Value Solutions

Benefits	Competitive Advantage
• Gift certificate sales lift (30%)	• Primary business is offering complete turnkey solutions for large-scale loyalty and stored value programs.
• Increased float and breakage	
• Sleek image/industry trend	• Extremely price competitive
• High perceived value by customers	• Provides a customized, detailed reporting, tracking, and analysis system that is far superior to our competitors' capabilities in this area
• Improved process for sales associates	
• Reduced administrative/reconciliation costs	
• Mitigation of fraud/theft	• Quick implementation and flexible solutions
• Time saving in issuance and redemption	
• Streamlined procedures at POS	• Offers loyalty programs in addition to only stored value
• Enhanced brand reinforcement	
• Automatic tracking/reporting	• Ability to offer issuance and redemption through a catalog department or via the World Wide Web
• Ability to capture customer data	
	• Equity partner, GE Capital, provides strong financial resources.
	• Co-located server for disaster recovery

Attributes

- Multi-use card
- Reloadable
- Nondenominated or fixed denominated cards
- POS activation
- Potential for additional revenue steams (via manufacture tie-ins, etc.)
- Leverage existing networks for competitive real-time connectivity

COMPETITION

To the best of its knowledge, D-Marc faces minimal direct competition in its electronic customer loyalty market. A number of companies presently offer electronic frequency systems to secure customer loyalty, and several companies offer customer database analysis programs. However, most companies are smaller, in terms of revenue, than D-Marc. D-Marc is considered the largest customer loyalty provider for card-based loyalty projects, offering turnkey services for hardware, software, programming, program design, customer support and service, POS integration, loyalty licensing software as well as smart, bar code, and magnetic stripe cards.

In addition, D-Marc presently has 4,500 client sites online and is projecting over 6,000 sites next year. Its programs have an excess of 4 million registered loyalty cardholders with 20,000 to 30,000 new enrollments per month.

D-Marc's primary competitive advantages rest with its turnkey solutions, including both data capture and PC-based real-time analysis, its low-cost, open systems approach, and its ability to manage large-scale or large-volume transaction loyalty programs.

There can be no assurance, however, that the companies listed in the charts for loyalty programs will not change their policies or that other companies will not appear in the market. In addition, as the smart card market grows in the United States, direct competitors to D-Marc will almost certainly appear.

Below and on the next page are several charts listing D-Marc's potential competitors:

Companies Offering Electronic Loyalty Programs and Related Services

Electronic Loyalty Programs

The following loyalty competitors are smaller in size than D-Marc and offer limited technology for their programs.

Company/Location	Product/Service	Customer/Market
PCS, Inc.	Frequency programs Transaction processing POS software Database analysis	Retailers Fast-food restaurants
SCS, LLC	Smart card software Loyalty software	Retailers (high end) Entertainment related
CK	Software and hardware for loyalty programs	Restaurants
TS, Inc.	Frequency programs	Retail Restaurants Malls
DC USA, Inc.	Restaurant loyalty programs Database analysis	Restaurants Retail

Electronic Gift Certificates/Stored Value Cards

The following competitors are much larger in size than D-Marc and offer similar-based technology and services.

Company/Location	Product/Service	Customer/Market
SVS	Card-based prepaid & gift certificates	Oil and gas Mass merchants
VL	Card-based prepaid & gift certificates	Retail
AEGC	Stored value gift card services	Retail

Potential Competitors

The following companies offer loyalty programs that include database marketing, incentive marketing, and fulfillment services. They do not offer a front-end POS loyalty component that D-Marc has expertise in.

Company/Location	Product/Service	Customer/Market
M	Frequency loyalty and database programs	Travel Leisure Financial Retail
CM	Frequency programs Retail marketing services	Oil and gas Travel related Automotive Cosmetics Community based
FMI	Backend loyalty programs	Retail Travel Oil and gas

D-Marc Technologies, Inc.

Balance Sheets

ASSETS	December 31, 2004	2005
Current assets		
Cash	45,746	125,440
Investments	52,145	130,689
Accounts receivable, net	718,882	263,263
Deferred taxes	125,000	75,000
Prepaid expenses and other	12,967	7,398
Total Current Assets	954,740	601,790
Property and equipment, net	156,962	264,978
Security deposits	18,000	23,000
Total assets	1,129,702	889,768
LIABILITY AND SHAREHOLDERS' EQUITY		
Current liabilities		
Accounts payable and accrued expenses	368,814	227,151
Current portion of capitalized lease	79,565	71,422
Notes payable to affiliate	140,000	75,000
Notes payable to bank	250,000	250,000
Bank line of credit	50,000	40,000
Total Current Liabilities	888,379	663,573
Long-term liabilities		
Capitalized lease, net of current portion	42,150	84,651
Total liabilities	930,529	748,224
Shareholders' equity		
Preferred stock	6,742	6,742
Paid in capital—preferred	2,493,258	2,493,258
Common stock	19,904	19,904
Paid in capital—common	483,631	483,631
Accumulated deficit	(2,804,362)	(2,861,991)
Total shareholders' equity	199,173	141,544
Total liabilities and shareholders' equity	1,129,702	889,768

D-Marc Technologies, Inc.
Projected for Years 2003–2005

	Jan-Mar	Apr	May	Jun	Jul	Aug	Sep	Oct	Nov	Dec	2000	2001	2002
Sales	325,911	89,884	102,701	274,396	138,599	184,793	250,876	322,526	412,172	519,400	2,621,258	5,205,432	6,437,353
Cost of sales	220,344	88,860	100,633	135,527	111,775	130,203	152,400	175,565	202,656	228,235	1,546,197	2,543,868	2,897,566
Gross profit	105,567	1,024	2,068	138,869	26,824	54,590	98,476	146,961	209,516	291,165	1,075,061	2,661,564	3,539,787
Gross margin	32.4%	1.1%	2.0%	50.6%	19.4%	29.5%	39.3%	45.6%	50.8%	56.1%	41.0%	51.1%	55.0%
Operating expenses:													
Research & development	207,720	79,806	88,903	86,158	83,636	89,527	83,681	86,868	96,629	93,832	996,760	1,238,579	1,362,437
Sales & marketing	104,356	46,216	50,985	49,501	48,135	51,212	48,091	49,742	49,522	48,112	545,873	635,084	698,592
General & administrative	150,962	47,673	51,590	50,363	49,221	51,758	29,189	50,540	50,379	49,204	600,879	649,495	714,445
Total operating expenses	463,038	173,695	191,478	186,022	180,992	192,498	180,961	187,149	196,530	191,148	2,143,512	2,523,158	2,775,474
Operating income	(357,471)	(172,672)	(189,410)	(47,153)	(154,168)	(137,908)	(82,485)	(40,188)	12,987	100,017	(1,068,451)	138,405	764,313
Other income (expense)													
Interest income	3,969	1,500	1,500	1,500	1,500	1,500	1,500	1,500	1,500	1,500	17,469	10,000	10,000
Interest expense	(7,212)	(4,583)	(4,583)	(4,583)	(1,250)	(1,250)	(1,250)	(1,250)	(1,250)	(1,250)	(28,461)	(30,000)	(30,000)
Other, net	0	0	0	0	0	0	0	0	0	0	0	0	0
Total other income (expense)	(3,243)				250	250	250	250	250	250	(10,992)	(20,000)	(20,000)
Net income	(360,714)	(175,755)	(192,493)	(50,236)	(153,918)	(137,658)	(82,235)	(39,938)	13,237	100,267	(1,079,443)	118,405	744,313

CASE STUDY QUESTIONS

1. Assess the organizational structure

   (a) Describe why a C-Corporation is best suited for this type of business.

   (b) What types of people would you look for to fill the various positions?

   (c) What employee agreements should be in place for growth?

   (d) What type of structure and qualities would you look for to attract new employees?

   (e) How would you set up a stock options plan? Consider nonqualified or incentive stock options.

2. Assess the market feasibility in the context of early 2001:

   (a) Had the management team done enough research to quantify the size of the market?

   (b) How valid was their assessment of probable market acceptance of the product?

3. Assume that you were one of the team members:

   (a) What are the strengths and weaknesses that the management faces for both the short and long term?

   (b) How will competition affect this business opportunity?

   (c) What are the recommendations for the company?

ADDITIONAL RESOURCES

- Thomas Register of American Manufacturers   www.thomasregister.com
- Hoover's Corporate Information   www.hoovers.com
- IMB Patent Server   www.delphion.com
- U.S. Patent and Trademark Office   www.uspto.gov
- Copyright Resources On-Line   www.library.yale.edu/%7Eokerson/copyproj.html
- IPWorldwide   www.ipworldwide.com
- Inventors Resource Homepage   www.Gibbsgroup.com
- Licensing Executives Society   www.lesorg.com
- Everything you want to know about SEC filing   www.10kwizard.com
- American Intellectual Property Law Association   www.aipla.org
- Franklin Pierce Law Center   www.fplc.edu
- Investors' Alliance   www.investorsalliance.org
- Patent Café   www.Patentcafe.com
- Investors' Digest   www.investorsdigest.com
- ABOUT.COM Investors' Page   www.investors.tqn.com
- U.S. Copyright Office   www.loc.gov/copyright
- World Intellectual Property Organization (WIPO)   www.wipo.org/eng.main.htm

- European Patent Office   www.european-patent-office.org
- Japanese Patent Office   www.jpo-miti.go.jp
- Internet Corporation for Assigned Names and Numbers (ICASNN) www.ican.org
- TMEP   www.uspto.gov/web/offices/tac/tmep
- Copyright Law   www.loc.gov/copyright/title17
- Rules/Registrations   www.loc.gov/copyright/title37
- Federal Registration   www.access.gpo.gov/nara/index.html3fr
- CAFC   www.findlaw.com/casecode/courts/fed.html
- USPTO Patent and Trademark Data   www.uspto.gov/web/menu/search.html

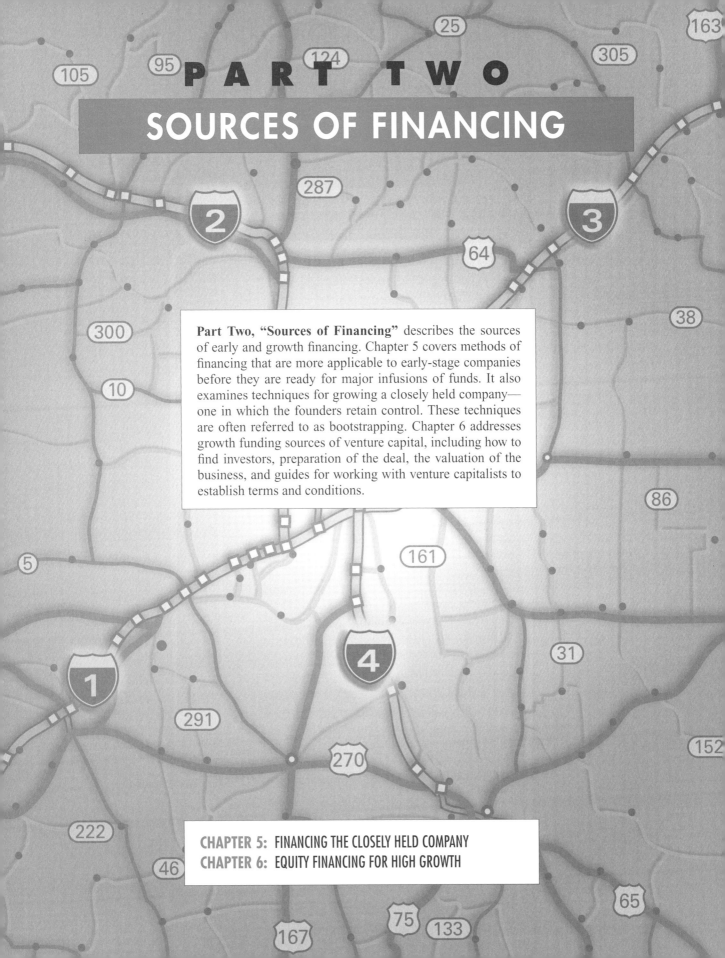

PART TWO
SOURCES OF FINANCING

Part Two, "Sources of Financing" describes the sources of early and growth financing. Chapter 5 covers methods of financing that are more applicable to early-stage companies before they are ready for major infusions of funds. It also examines techniques for growing a closely held company—one in which the founders retain control. These techniques are often referred to as bootstrapping. Chapter 6 addresses growth funding sources of venture capital, including how to find investors, preparation of the deal, the valuation of the business, and guides for working with venture capitalists to establish terms and conditions.

CHAPTER 5: FINANCING THE CLOSELY HELD COMPANY
CHAPTER 6: EQUITY FINANCING FOR HIGH GROWTH

ROADMAP for

PATTERNS OF ENTREPRENEURSHIP
Sources of Financing

- ☑ Securing Early Stage Funding
- ☑ Bootstrapping
- ☑ Using Bank Loans as a Source
- ☑ How to Use Commercial Banks
- ☑ Preparing a Loan Proposal
- ☑ Applying for a Loan
- ☑ Establishing the Terms of Debt
- ☑ Building a Relationship with a Banker
- ☑ Using Government Sources
- ☑ Small Business Innovative Research
- ☐ Angel Investors
- ☐ Understanding the Venture Capital Process
- ☐ Guide to Selecting a Venture Capitalist (VC)
- ☐ Private Placements
- ☐ Learning How to Value a Business
- ☐ Earnings Valuation
- ☐ Asset Valuation
- ☐ Discounted Cash Flow Valuation
- ☐ Net Present Value (NPV) Method
- ☐ Internal Rate of Return (IRR)

CHAPTER 5

FINANCING THE CLOSELY HELD COMPANY

"Very early on, the founders of startups make an important choice. Do they want success or control? Neither is bad so long as the choice is explicit."

JOE KRAUSE, FOUNDER OF EXCITE AND JOTSPOT

OBJECTIVES

- Understand bootstrapping and its importance.
- Identify the different methods of early-stage funding and access other resources.
- Learn the problems and issues in raising capital from friends and family.
- Learn how to use commercial banks to acquire a loan.
- Learn how to prepare and apply for a loan.
- Build a relationship with a banker.
- Identify government financing programs.

CHAPTER OUTLINE

INTRODUCTION

In Chapter 1, we described the different types of startup companies and the aspirations of entrepreneurs. It is important that every entrepreneur look deeply inside himself at the outset and choose one of two routes for his company. If control and remaining the chief executive of the company is of paramount personal importance, then the company should in no way seek funding by selling part ownership to outside investors. This way of raising money is called equity investment. Equity investors provide money to companies in exchange for part ownership in the form of shares in order to get a financial return on their money. Because early-stage companies are risky investments, such investors typically seek an annual return on equity investments of 30 percent at a minimum. This is clearly well above the 5 percent or so they can earn by putting their money into Treasury Notes or Bank CDs.

In order to provide investors with a return on their money, the company must create a "liquidity event." Otherwise its money stays locked up in your company and is "illiquid." To unlock the value, the stock of the company must be purchased by another company through an acquisition (the most usual way), by a sale of stock to the public through an initial public offering (IPO), or in very rare cases by the company generating so much cash that there is enough left after internal funding requirements that it can afford to buy back the stock from outside investors. If the founders wish to retain control of the company, they have no incentive to create such a liquidity event and therefore are unable to provide a real return to their investors. This misalignment of objectives between founders and investors is the principal reason that startup companies end up with major conflict problems. If control is your prime objective, then you should not seek equity financing. In this case, other means of attracting resources, both financial and otherwise, are required. The techniques for doing this are broadly referred as *bootstrapping*—a term deriving from "pulling oneself up by the bootstraps."

If, on the hand, an entrepreneur is comfortable with trading control with an interest in acquiring significant personal wealth, then seeking outside investors should be considered. This may even lead to stepping aside as CEO, should the entrepreneur not have the appropriate skills to manage hectic growth. Raising outside equity investment is the subject of the next chapter.

Even if the eventual aim is to seek equity investment, however, the contents of this chapter are highly relevant. The further a startup company has progressed successfully with its plans before selling stock, the higher the value of the company is likely to be, and therefore the lower the percentage of the company that must be sold to raise an equivalent amount of money. Typical milestones that can trigger a jump in the value of the company include developing a working prototype, gaining a few paying customers, having a patent awarded, receiving a government grant, and signing up a larger company to test the results of the development. Therefore, it nearly always makes sense for entrepreneurs that plan on seeking outside investors to delay this event until as late as possible. Also, investors like to see that entrepreneurs are not totally dependent on their funding but know how to complement their money with other sources of funds and resources. Every entrepreneur therefore needs to learn how to bootstrap her company whether for reasons of control retention, increasing valuation before taking in equity investments, or perhaps out of necessity.

We will examine a number of options in this chapter, including self-funding, various forms of bootstrapping, family and friends, early-stage loans, and government sources such as the Small Business Administration and Small Business Innovation Research Programs. Finding the source that is best for you will depend on many different factors, including the amount of funding required, when it is needed, and how long and when it can be repaid. It is important to remember to plan ahead and not let your financial requirements be a surprise. Arranging financing takes time, and rushing decisions can be costly to the entrepreneur and his or her new venture. Running out of money is the most common reason for small companies to fail. Generally speaking, it takes twice as long to raise money than anticipated. Forecasting cash requirements is therefore very important and is dealt with in detail in Chapter 9. Starting early to make sure that the funds are available when they are needed and having contingencies in place are extremely important considerations and cannot be overemphasized.

PROFILE: JAMES DYSON

James Dyson[1] studied at the Royal College of Arts in England where he focused on furniture design. While still at college he invented several new products such as the "ball-barrow" and the "sea-track" boat (see www.dyson.com). His first and only job was as a sales manager for a small company in the west of England called Rotork (www.rotork.com). He rose rapidly to become a director of this small engineering firm where he furthered his skills in product engineering. Yet he felt confined in this position and left the company in 1978 to branch out on his own, using some cash that he had earned from his first ideas. While vacuum-cleaning his old cottage in the bucolic Cotswold Hills, he noticed that the sucking power was quickly lost as the paper bag filled. He had observed a "point of pain" and decided to tackle the problem of making a "bagless cleaner." His idea was to spin the air flowing through the cleaner, throwing the dirt to the outside where it could be collected. He built exactly 5,127 prototypes in his basement workshop before he felt he had reached a satisfactory outcome. Now was the time to cash in on these efforts, so he filed a number of patents on the invention. His initial business model (refer to Chapter 8 for more discussion on this topic) was to license his ideas, and he took to the road providing demonstrations to all of the existing vacuum cleaner companies around the world. He thought they would readily grab the opportunity to make and sell his "much better" performing products. After two years and no interest, he decided to start manufacturing and selling his products. He was unable to raise any venture funding, however. The idea of breaking into a well-established but dull market dominated by large companies with deep pockets was hardly alluring to venture capitalists when there was a lot more fun to be had with high-tech "dot.com" startups, which were in fashion at that time. Moreover, Dyson did not match the profile of a super-techie high-flyer living in one of the startup hotbed regions of the United Kingdom (UK). He was simply seen as a "country-boy" inventor playing around with vacuum cleaners.

The constant process of learning and refining led to several cash shortages before the product was launched in the UK in 1993, forcing Dyson to sell the patent rights in Japan for just $70,000 in 1986 and the U.S. rights for $100,000 in 1988. He later bought back the rights for both countries but at vastly inflated prices. Dyson paid $2 million to buy back the U.S. rights in 2002 after having success in the UK market. With little money left, he had to be creative in how he introduced the first "cyclone" product to the market in 1993. A combination of cameo appearances on popular television programs such as *Friends*, combined with what Dyson describes as word-of-mouth recommendations, helped to raise sales. He also decided to price the product well above the entrenched competition that on average sell for $150; Dyson's cleaners sell in the range of $399 to $1,500. The distinctive bagless vacuum cleaner has managed to grab a 20.7 percent share of the $2.3 billion U.S. market in just over two years, leaving Hoover trailing with only a 15.6 percent share at the end of 2004. In 2003, Dyson had only a 4.5 percent share of the U.S. market, but sales of 891,000 units—a threefold increase—over the next year catapulted it to the top. These strong U.S. sales, which now make up 40 percent of worldwide revenue, helped Dyson to more than double profit from $70 million to $185 million, while sales grew by 54 percent. To date, over $10 billion in sales of Dyson's cleaners have been sold worldwide.

So why didn't one of the existing companies take up the offer? Perhaps their reticence had something to do with the large profits they were making on the disposable bags which, without any marketing or selling expenditure, provided revenues of $500 million every year. Hoover was locked into a business model that prevented it from responding. According to Mike Dutter, a Hoover executive, "I do regret that Hoover did not take the product technology off Dyson—[in our hands] it would have lain on the shelf and not been used." As Dyson states, "Hoover wouldn't give me the time of the day. They laughed at it. They said 'Bags are best. Bags will always be best.' Then they copied it." This copying, which came after Hoover realized that this little startup was beginning to take away its market and profits, forced Dyson to sue for infringement of his patents. Again straining his cash for payment of legal fees, he won the case after 18 months of litigation.

Dyson is not satisfied yet with his success. With the cash now coming in, he has repurchased the Japanese business, which, as in the United States, has also accelerated sales in Asia. In 2004, sales—which are now running at 14,000 units a month there—rose fourfold. Expansion in Japan demonstrates Dyson's continued focus on research and its ability to shape its technologies to new markets. Since Japanese apartments tend to be smaller than those in the United Kingdom or United States, his team has devised a compact vacuum cleaner that uses a digital motor rather than a traditional mechanical one. The resulting machine is not only half the weight and size and more powerful than its larger contemporaries, but the digital technology allows customers with problems to hold the machine up to the phone and have faults diagnosed online. In this way, Dyson is embedding services into his products. If sales increase, the company is hoping to make a mark in China. As Dyson says: "It may be taking coals to Newcastle but it is the biggest market in the world for domestic appliances." The company is also planning to launch a new washing machine. Dyson is now working on another "point of pain." It takes a few minutes to wash by hand, so why must it take over an hour for a washing machine to do the same thing. Watch out, Maytag, Whirlpool, and GE!

Dyson's company, which he and his family still own 100 percent, employs 1,200 people in Malmesbury, Wiltshire, UK. Last year Dyson paid himself and his wife approximately $30 million, a prize worth waiting for after facing bankruptcy on more than one occasion.

There are many ways of accessing resources including cash, without taking major risks, or selling part of your company. Be creative to find ways to "bootstrap." Take the company as far as you can before bringing in investors or putting your personal assets at high risk.[2]

---

1. Self-funding
- Moonlighting
- Bootstrapping

2. Family and friends

3. Bank loans

4. Government programs

Figure 5-1 **Sources of Nonequity Funding.**

SECURING EARLY-STAGE FUNDING

Most entrepreneurs and business owners know when the company requires financing. However, it is much more difficult for entrepreneurs to judge what type of financing is appropriate and realistic for the business. In addition, after a string of recordbreaking years in which public and private companies have created high wealth, investor interest in entrepreneurial companies was at its height. Bank lending was readily available and affordable. Now, with the capital market returns low and interest rates going up, what are the best financing prospects for entrepreneurial companies? Raising funds can be confusing, so careful review and analysis are necessary to learn the process.

The various nonequity sources of funding available to the entrepreneur are listed in Figure 5-1.

In contrast, Figure 5-2 lists sources of funding using other and later stage sources for growth. (These sources are covered in detail in the next chapter.)

Self-Funding

The vast majority of businesses—about 90 percent—according to Venture Economics Report in 2001[3]—start with less than $100,000; close to a third start with less than $10,000. This form of financing is usually available to entrepreneurs who are highly motivated and committed to using personal resources to launch a venture. The majority of new businesses are usually started with self-funds that come from personal savings or various forms of personal equity of the founder(s). This form

---

1. Angels

2. Institutional venture capital

3. Private placements

4. Other debt funding sources: factoring, asset-based lending

5. Strategic partnerships/joint ventures as an equity partner

---

Figure 5-2 **Equity and Later Stage Funding Sources.**

of capital reflects the business founder's degree of motivation, commitment, and belief. Personal investment can also include what is called *sweat equity*, where owners either donate their time or provide it at below market value to help the business get established. Sometimes it is possible to pay the first hires with some ownership in the company rather than with a salary. However, it is important that the aspirations of these hires be in line with those of the founder(s); otherwise a conflict may arise later similar to that which arises when investors seek an exit. Also, in some cases, entrepreneurs use profits from previous endeavors to invest in their new enterprise.

When considering self-funding, carefully decide how much financial risk you are willing to take. This is a very personal decision and should involve other family members. Some entrepreneurs will stretch themselves to the limit and use every cent they have, including pledging all of their assets—their house as well—to the bank. Others are much more cautious. However, investors and lenders alike expect entrepreneurs to put some of their own assets at risk and so entrepreneurs must learn to be comfortable with this scenario.

PROFILE: LIZ ELTING, PHIL SHAWE, AND TRANSPERFECT TRANSLATIONS—A SELF-FUNDING BUSINESS

A major in Romance languages and a chance meeting in business school led to the founding of one of the largest, if not *the* largest, privately owned translation service in the United States. Liz Elting majored in Romance languages in college and wanted to be able to use her love of language in her professional life. While pursuing her MBA, she met Phil Shawe, and together they started Transperfect Translations, while working out of a dorm room.

They started the business with no outside funding and a strong desire to create an extremely high-quality translation company that would serve the most demanding of clients. From day one, they only utilized translators whose native language was the one being translated in the document. This policy ensured greater accuracy and use of appropriate idioms. Also, an understanding of each culture helped ensure that no offensive translations would be made. Other than the translations themselves, Phil and Liz performed all related functions that first year, including marketing, bookkeeping, and administration. As a result, the company has been profitable from that first year.

Utilizing their marketing skills, they carefully marketed their company to large law firms and corporations, which typically required rapid turnaround of large documents, with a critical requirement for accuracy. Using what is now an army of 3,000 translation subcontractors, Transperfect Translations can now translate documents into over 100 languages.

Transperfect has had a history of controlled growth. It has been consistently profitable, and its expansion has been entirely self-financed from its start in a dorm room. Today, it has 15 offices in the United States and 5 overseas.[4]

Moonlighting

Many businesses are begun while the founder is still working a full-time job. The income from the job can both help support the owner during negative or low cash flow and provide working capital to augment the business's cash flow. Usually, when the business begins paying as well or better than the regular job, the entrepreneur can leave the job and devote all her time to building the new business.

Part-time Consulting

Most people have skills that are valuable to existing companies on a part-time basis, perhaps as an advisory expert. You may have some deep technical knowledge, design skills, the ability to write computer code, or the like, which are currently in demand on a part-time basis. Perhaps your existing employer is willing to have you work for six months or so in a part-time capacity continuing your current work while a replacement is found. This may be a better solution for both parties than having you just walk out one day. Having a source of "survival" income while you are getting your company started removes a lot of stress and improves the chance of success. If you take a technical consulting assignment, you must make it clear who owns the result of your work—usually your client. Therefore, document what areas you consider to be your property so that you do not compromise your future opportunity by questionable ownership of the intellectual property.

"Entrepreneurship is creating something of value from practically nothing."

JEFFRY TIMMONS,
Franklin W. Olin Distinguished Professor of Entrepreneurship, Babson College, MA.

BOOTSTRAPPING

Bootstrapping,[2] a type of self-funding often applied in a current business, can reduce costs from the current operation and overhead. It is usually overlooked as a source to business owners. The process of analyzing the operation to save and improve efficiencies will also allow the entrepreneur to learn more about the company. By becoming more efficient and cost conscious, the entrepreneur will be in a stronger position to qualify for additional financing. A multitude of bootstrapping techniques are available, and it is not possible to catalog all of them. Indeed, an entrepreneur can be just as innovative in developing her or his own methods as in developing the original business opportunity. The following discussion describes some bootstrapping techniques that may suit your own and your company's needs.

No or low rent. Start by using a residence for office and workspace. Paying extra rent to a landlord takes away cash that can go directly into the company. The term *garage startup* is not a myth. Hewlett-Packard was started by two fresh graduates in a now-famous garage in Silicon Valley. When it comes time to move out and have a separate location for the business, avoid signing long-term leases in expensive locations. Often incubator space is available, which may be subsidized by an economic development grant for just this intermediate phase. Incubators usually have shared services, too, so money need not be spent on copiers, conference room furniture, and full-time office support staff since they are shared with other startups (see Appendix for more details on incubators). Investors and lenders like to see that "unproductive overhead" spending is being kept to a minimum. Unless the business is a beauty parlor or a wealth management consulting firm, opulence is usually a waste of hard-to-find funds. If you do sign a lease for more space than you need at the moment, make sure you can sublet to offset some of the costs.

Bartering of goods and services. Perhaps you can trade some Web site development work for a local small engineering firm in exchange for their machining the first prototypes of your product—or the other way around.

Trading of intellectual property rights. Dyson traded international rights when he desperately needed cash. At that stage in his company, he could not enter overseas markets anyway, so using these "sleeping assets" was one way to continue. Alternatively, you may be developing technology that has multiple applications, perhaps a new glue for rapidly assembling metal parts. Your interest may lie in the high-value but smaller aircraft market. You could sell the rights for the automotive sector to an existing company in order to fund your field of interest. The Ultrasfast case in Chapter 8 provides another example of this method.

Renting or leasing of equipment. Often an expensive piece of equipment may be needed only in the startup phase. Rather than buy, rent or lease the equipment only while it is needed.

Used equipment. Usually, the latest high-speed machines are not needed in the early stages of manufacturing and test marketing. It is often possible to find a piece of used equipment, often at a scrap price, that with a little work will fill short-term needs. The same applies to office furniture. Look for large companies that are moving, or companies in bankruptcy; they will often give away or sell for a song perfectly good furniture they no longer need.

Access to expensive equipment. Check out universities and government labs. They often have programs to help small companies and may allow access to equipment that an entrepreneur could only dream of owning.

Suppliers' help. Suppliers may be willing to help in many ways with the hope that, in the future, a new company will become a major customer. Help may include access to experts, supplies of test materials, introduction into their supplier and customer networks, technical support, sharing of market data and reports, and perhaps even an option to license some of their proprietary know-how. They may also be willing to help with funding inventory until you have been able to receive payment from your customers. Establishing a close and honest relationship with suppliers will help.

Customers' help. Similarly, engaging with customers early on can provide a range of benefits, even perhaps financial, by prepaying on a future delivery or paying for product development work to meet their specific needs. Also, a purchase order from a large company in good standing, even if it is contingent on delivery of product or service to a defined specification, may help in securing a working capital loan (see below).

Cooperative purchases. As companies begin to scale up, often they can find ways to work with other small companies to create a buyers' club. The first area to look at is health insurance costs, which are exploding. Often, professional society membership can provide access to reduced costs in a range of areas.

Outsourcing. A new growing company will need a number of professional services that are not required full-time and, indeed, may make sense to outsource entirely. These include payroll services, bookkeeping, and tax return preparation, which can usually be found as a service or by using part-time flexible workers. Legal, accounting, and other consulting services will always be purchased as needed. These professions are usually accommodating with regard to payment schedules. Find more about outsourcing in Chapter 8.

Contingent litigation. A small company does not usually have the financial resources to fight a major lawsuit against a large infringer of its patent rights such as James Dyson faced. If the case looks as if there is a good chance of prevailing, then there are some patent law firms that will take the case "on contingency" whereby the settlement, if the case is won, is shared by the legal team and the company filing the case. Some major law firms specialize in such cases, and just signing up with them can send a strong message to the alleged infringer, perhaps prompting an early settlement.

Example

Ron Chasteen[5] was awarded a patent for a fuel-injection system for snowmobiles in the late 1980s. He and his partner, John Balch, approached Polaris Industries in Minnesota about a possible supply agreement. "When we first met with their chief engineer, he told us we had made a massive leap in technology," states Chasteen. Initially, Polaris wanted to buy rights to the system outright. But Chasteen didn't want to sell. Eventually, a deal was struck, and Polaris agreed to purchase systems. After about a year of collaboration, Polaris claimed it was not after all going to proceed in selling fuel-injected snowmobiles, and so the relationship ended.

Chasteen was shocked when, soon after, Polaris launched a fuel-injected snowmobile. Examination of the product immediately showed that the snowmobile was very similar to the product Chasteen had developed. "We were furious, they'd simply cloned ours." Chasteen and Balch decided to sue—not only Polaris but their component supplier, Fuji Heavy Industries. It took several years, a lot of money, and five different patent law firms before they found one that agreed to take the case on a contingent-fee basis. "They were all happy to just take our money with no end in sight," Chasteen says. "We got nowhere, just a lot of bills." The case was eventually taken by the Chicago law firm of Niro, Scavone, Haller & Niro. According to Joe Hosteny, a partner at the firm, "Contingent-fee litigation is for individual inventors and small- to medium-size businesses which would have trouble affording normal patent or trade-secret litigation. Without contingent-fee litigation, big corporations could steal solo inventors' ideas with no one to stop them."

After almost 11 years, Chasteen and Balch finally got their justice—a check for $70 million. Other well-known cases include $120 million paid out by Microsoft for using the "Stacker" data[6] compression software developed by small Stac Electronics, and Robert Kearns, an individual inventor, received a payment of over $10 million from Ford Motor Company for infringing his patent on intermittent windshield washers.[7]

Credit cards. Credit cards have always been a source of funding for a new venture. If the options of equity or bank loans are not available, the entrepreneur may contact all the major credit card suppliers to compare prices and options. As with a bank, the entrepreneur should ensure that there are opportunities to increase the borrowing limit (and add on other financing sources, such as equipment leasing) as necessary, once the company is proven to be a good customer. Credit card funding is quick funding of the business and is more viable now than ever before. MasterCard or Visa cardholders with good credit now often receive credit limits of $10,000 and above. By carrying more than one credit card, the entrepreneur can considerably boost the total amount tapped into at any given time. Entrepreneurs may also take advantage of the regular offers of "no interest for six months" and keep rolling over their credit.

Unfortunately, use of credit cards in this way can adversely affect personal credit ratings if done too often. Credit card interest rates on cash advances vary considerably, from as high as 21 percent to 10 percent or lower. Annual fees can also range from over $50 down to zero. Therefore, when obtaining credit cards, it is wise to investigate getting the best deal. It may be advantageous to cancel one or more of the high-interest cards and transfer the balances to lower cost credit cards. The disadvantage is that obtaining funds through credit cards costs much more than bank loans. If the enterprise is not successful, the credit card payments will continue and may place the entrepreneur in a personal financial squeeze.[8]

The above is a short list of the many bootstrapping techniques entrepreneurs use to get through their early stages either to defer the search for equity funding or to retain control of the company.

> "Finding money from friends and family is much better then professional investors for several reasons: (1) it has higher probability of success for a startup company, (2) you do not give away 30 to 45% of the company at a very low valuation while you are just getting started, (3) you have freedom to make major changes as you validate the market opportunity and product development approach."
>
> JAMES B. SANDERS
> *President, Columbia Group,*
> *Investor and Consultant to*
> *High-Tech Startups, Adjunct*
> *Professor of Entrepreneurship*
> *University of Maryland*

Family and Friends

Friends and family members are a very popular source for startup capital because they are not as worried about quick profits as professional investors. However, there are problems associated with this method. Usually, friends and family do not investigate the business very well and are not familiar with all the risks of the business. In many cases, friends and family accept the word of the entrepreneur without any analysis or detailed review of the business venture. To guard against the risks of failure and to avoid being blamed for not disclosing all the important information about the proposed venture, the best method is to provide the same disclosure to a friend or relative that would be provided to the most sophisticated investors. Entrepreneurs should always resist the temptation to keep the venture on an informal basis and not document the details of the company's risks and financial requirements.[9]

PROFILE: WOO SONG, FOUNDER OF INTRASPHERE

Raising Money from Friends and Family

When he was a 12-year-old boy, Woo Song immigrated to America with his family from South Korea. His father left a comfortable job in Korea to give his children an opportunity to receive a better education and unlimited career opportunities in the United States.

Woo Song was a very good student in South Korea but did not fare as well in New York owing to his difficulties with the English language. Woo overcame this obstacle and eventually was granted admission to Stuyvesant High School. Then Woo transferred to undergraduate studies at SUNY Albany. Unable to maintain his grades, he transferred to Stevens Institute of Technology where he spent two years but never earned a degree.

Woo's first entrepreneurial effort was a consulting firm that specialized in applying technology to manage market risks. The business was moderately successful, servicing clients such as Bankers Trust and Pfizer. While consulting on a project at Pfizer, Woo met his current partner, Bill Karl. Woo attributes a large portion of his success to the relationship they developed. In 1996, Woo formed Intrasphere for the purpose of building a company to develop custom enterprise solutions by using the latest technologies while leveraging clients' existing investments in legacy systems. In other words, the company could provide clients with the ability to connect their existing mainframe technology with the latest technology. Intrasphere's largest customers are in the financial services and pharmaceutical industries.

Currently, Intrasphere has approximately 120 employees and produced $10.9 million in revenues for the year ended December 31, 2000. Woo raised $500,000 from friends and family and another $500,000 of subordinated debt through the New York City Investment Corporation, a consortium of banks organized to fund small businesses. Although the business was growing at the height of the technology/ Internet craze of the late 1990s, Woo did not seek out venture capital or additional debt financing. His future plans for Intrasphere are to replicate its industry-focused business model in other markets. In addition, the company has plans to expand into Europe.

USING BANK LOANS AS A SOURCE OF CASH

It is important to understand debt financing and its appropriateness for the business. The primary advantage of debt financing is that the entrepreneur does not have to give up any part of ownership to receive the funds. However, the loan has to be paid back with interest and may require the entrepreneur to personally guarantee part or all of the money. In addition, many loans have certain conditions ("covenants") that come with them. Often these conditions are tied to certain milestones or events that the company must make in order for the loan to remain in place and not be recalled. These covenants are not so different from conditions that might be applied by equity investors, and therefore they often remove some control of the company from the founders until the loan is repaid. Bank loans are more suitable for companies that have a track record of sales and growth. For the formative stages of a company, before any substantial sales, an entrepreneur will most likely have to secure the loan with personal assets or seek out loan programs underwritten by federal, state, or local economic development agencies.

Bank loans, commercial banks, loan proposals, and government sources are some of the major terms used in the search for debt capital. This section outlines a range of credit options regarding debt financing from a commercial lending institution. Not all of these sources are equally favorable. From a bank's perspective, the most important consideration is the degree of certainty that a loan will be paid back on the agreed schedule of intent and timing. In addition, we describe what lenders look for in preparing a loan proposal and the guidelines to improve the entrepreneur's chances for a loan approval.[10]

PROFILE: LISA ABRAMS, FOUNDER OF MUSIC SOUNDS INC. — SHOPPING FOR A LOAN

Lisa Abrams[11] started her first company out of her college dorm room 13 years ago and landed her first line of credit for $50,000 four years later. It took Lisa a long time to realize that the bank was primarily interested in supporting her not because they really understood or believed in her business concept but because as a minority, female business owner, she had public relations value to the bank.

At first, the more aggressively she pursued growth, the more the bank rejected her demands for a loan. The company, a mail-order house for instruments, grew dramatically to $4 million in sales revenues, but the margins were slim. Six years ago she established a new market in the instrument-rental business that serves local schools. This time the margins were much higher, so she decided to apply for another loan and received approval for a $1 million-plus loan package. The approval was based on the track record of her first company, her personal commitment to secure assets, and her personal signature on the note. Her advice: "If you're unhappy with your banker, move on quickly. If he or she only wants to support you because you're a woman, minority or whatever, don't waste your time. And above all else, don't expect a bank to know what's best for your business. You've got to know that and how to communicate it to them."[12]

Bank Loans

Many companies depend on bank loans. When the U.S. Small Business Administration last studied borrowing by small companies, it found that a majority of companies at every size level obtained financing from commercial banks. In the past few years, both the number and the amount of bank loans to companies have increased. Below are the numbers for all loans of less than $1 million made in 1999 and 2000. (Totals for 2001 are not yet available.)[13] Some statistics on small business loans are shown in Table 5-1.

Table 5-1   Small Business Loan Data

Total number of bank loans of less than $1 million (in millions)

1999	8.21	10%
2000	9.0	growth

Total amount of loans of less than $1 million

1999..$370.5 billion

2000..$398.5 billion

Average amount of each loan (rounded)

1999..$45,000

2000..$44,000

Source: SBA Small Business Administration 2001.

HOW TO USE COMMERCIAL BANKS

Most commercial loans are made to small businesses and can be either unsecured or secured. An unsecured loan is a personal or signature loan that requires no collateral; it is granted on the background and strength of the borrower's reputation. Such loans are made at fair market interest rates if the borrower can demonstrate that the business is sound. To most banks, that will mean having an operating history of at least two or three years. Banks often require that the borrower maintain appropriate deposits with them. In addition, most banks will require personal guarantees for newer companies. Secured loans are those with security pledged to the bank that the loans will be paid. Several types of security and collateral are used in loans:

Types of Security and Collateral Loans

Co-maker: person who signs as secondary principal

Endorser: person who pledges to back loan

Guarantor: person who personally guarantees loan

Real property: real estate, leaseholds, and land

Securities: stocks and bonds that can be pledged

Equipment: capital assets that include machinery, computers, and instrumentation

Inventory: usually finished goods

Accounts receivable: items receipted as sold with verifiable credit outstanding

Insurance policies: cash surrender value of policies

Not all commercial banks are willing to grant loans to early-stage businesses.[14] In most instances, the entrepreneur must seek loans through community banks that make it their business to serve the small-business sector. Talk to the owners of other small companies locally to learn about the most receptive banks for small companies and to get an introduction if possible.

Community banks are independently chartered and serve local clients; consequently, they thrive on small businesses. The entrepreneur should first find out which banks are most active in making loans in state. If no local institutions are available, reference the Small Business Administration Publication for friendly out-of-state banks. Many of the 567 banks that make business loans of less than $100,000 cross the state lines in the process. Also, the entrepreneur should reference the SBA's report on small-business lending in the United States, which ranks about 9,000 commercial banks by state based on their lending practices. Other reports are available at www.sba.gov/adov/lending/nusz.html or at (800) 827-5722. The entrepreneur may also want to visit www.entrepreneur/money/bestbank.html for a recent listing of the banks friendlier to small businesses.

PREPARING A LOAN PROPOSAL

All bankers want to hear how the loan they will provide will improve the worth of the company. To improve the chance of coming away with the loan, the entrepreneur should tailor the presentation to address this question. A loan proposal consists of eight parts. Using the information from the business plan, the entrepreneur should shift the emphasis toward the new audience to convert it into a loan proposal. Here are some guidelines to assist the entrepreneur in preparing a loan proposal:[15]

1. *Summary.* On the first page, the entrepreneur should give his or her name and title, company name and address, nature of business, amount sought, purpose, and source of repayment.

2. *Management Team Profiles.* A biography should be prepared on the entrepreneur and the management team, with emphasis on business background, education, experience skills, areas of expertise, and accomplishments. Bankers seek their ultimate security in experienced management.

3. *Business Description.* Details on the legal structure, number of employees, union status, and current business assets should be provided. The products and markets as well as customers and competitors should also be defined, along with the

inventory in terms of size, rate of turnover, and market ability. The status of your accounts receivable and accounts payable should also be reported.

4. *Projections*. The entrepreneur should show projections on the current share of the market and describe how he or she plans to exploit these opportunities for the next three years. The alternative and fallback plans, as well as a realistic timetable for achieving the goals, also need to be listed. Bankers judge plans and goals in terms of the industry's practices and trends.

5. *Financial Statements*. The entrepreneur should prepare a balance sheet and income statement for the past three years (if available). Bankers are more comfortable with audited statements. If the entrepreneur cannot afford a full audit, he or she should ask the accountant for a financial "review." Though less convincing than an audit, this new intermediate procedure gives the banker more assurance than an unaudited statement. Two sets of projected balance sheets as well as income and cash flow statements should also be prepared, one predicated on receiving the loan and the other on proceeding without it. Though critical to proving the entrepreneur's claim that the loan will increase company worth, the projections must be realistic. Bankers match projections against published industry standards, searching for padded earnings and meager cost estimates. Personal financial statements, including tax returns for the past three years, must also be submitted, since the entrepreneur's own net worth is a factor. Bankers check the entrepreneur's personal credit rating in addition to the company.

6. *Purpose*. The purpose of the loan should be stated. A request for "working capital" will elicit questions, not money. Instead, explain specifically what the intended use of the working capital is—for example, to build up Christmas inventory by increasing production, starting in late summer.

7. *Amount*. The entrepreneur should ask for the precise amount needed to achieve his or her purpose and support the figures with estimates or previous cost figures. Bankers know costs, so the entrepreneur should not ask for a high amount, expecting his or her request to be negotiated. The banker will verify all requested amounts.

8. *Repayment Plans*. The asset must match the loan. Any asset the entrepreneur wants to finance must last at least as long as the loan period. Also, the asset should generate the repayment funds by increasing sales, slashing costs, or heightening efficiency. Weaving these into a repayment schedule is a complex task, but the entrepreneur will not be required to do it all alone. Lending officers anticipate calls for advice on this and all other elements of loan proposals. They look to the entrepreneur to be an expert only on the business; however, he or she will be expected to come in with all the requisite financial data.

HOW TO APPLY FOR A LOAN

Lenders are looking for a company's ability to repay its debt. No matter how successful a company is, usually a lender has only the promise of being rewarded with steady payments of principal and interest. Although a borrower may become a better customer of the bank as the business grows, the bank will not necessarily prosper in direct proportion to the company's success. When lenders consider a loan request, they concentrate on what are sometimes referred to as the "four Cs" of credit: character, cash flow, collateral, and (equity) contribution.[16]

Character

Character is a crucial element in an individual's attempt to secure a loan. "Character" is of course a subjective, "soft" criterion that enters into the lender's decision process. Nonetheless, the lender must have confidence in the individual he or she is dealing with or the lender will not proceed with the venture. Such traits as talent, reliability, and honesty are used to describe character.

One aspect of character that is always used is credit history. Credit history in terms of a commercial loan is a one-way street. A bad credit rating will often eliminate the potential for a new business to obtain credit. A good credit history, on the other hand, has little upside. In the final analysis, even with a positive credit history, a banker's decision comes down to intuition: How capable is this individual? Will he or she run the business ethically and keep the bank honestly apprised of the real status of the business? How much faith can the bank have that this individual can successfully run a business and pay the monthly debt service?

Cash Flow

Banks need to be satisfied that cash flow will be adequate to cover debt service throughout the term of the obligation. Most loans are structured with interest payments due every month beginning in month 1, and principal payments also due, usually beginning in month 1. In some instances, principal payments can be deferred but usually no more than a year.

The business must be solid to meet debt service and operating obligations, and still have enough available cash to address uncertainties. The entrepreneur must remember that projections are imperfect and must therefore provide for deviations. Lenders will want to be assured that the margin for error has been considered and provided for amply.

Effectively projecting cash flow requires sound judgment and intuition. However, the entrepreneur should project cash flow with sensitivity to industry norms and standards, and should give a logical explanation if the plan shows a projected departure from these norms.

Collateral

No good lender will make a decision to loan money based solely on strong collateral. But every good lender will try to get the best collateral possible on the loan. This normally involves securing the lender's interest by liens or mortgages against tangible assets such as real estate or equipment. In addition, most lenders will require the entrepreneur's personal signature as evidence of the borrower's real commitment to the business.

As an example, one may keep personal assets in the name of other family members, most often a spouse or child. Also, a lender cannot take assets held jointly by spouses unless the lender has both spouses' signatures on the note. Incidentally, most lenders will ask for both signatures if the collateral is insufficient. The issues related to personal liability and loan repayment are complex, and it is often important to have advice from a lawyer when making borrowing arrangements.

Contribution

Almost all lenders require a significant commitment by the entrepreneur to ensure the success of the financing. The commitment also serves to reduce the lender's

The entrepreneur will generally be required to have some type of collateral to support a loan. The types of securities used for collateral include endorsers or co-signers, accounts receivables, real estate, stocks and bonds, and personal savings.

exposure relative to the deal's total size, providing a cushion to allow the lender to come out "whole" in the event of default.

In addition, different industries customarily have different ratios of debt to equity, commonly known as leverage. Some industries have traditionally been highly leveraged with debt three to four times greater than equity, often because of high success rates and good collateral. Real estate and the apparel industries are good examples of highly leveraged businesses. An unusually high failure rate or poor-quality collateral may result in relatively low leverage in an industry, as exemplified by the restaurant business. Because of these varieties, it is difficult to generalize as to how much the entrepreneur must contribute to a venture.

ESTABLISHING THE TERMS OF DEBT

The term of the debt (the length of time over which the obligation is amortized or paid off) usually depends on the life of the asset financed. If a lender really wants to make a deal, he or she can give some latitude in order to structure the debt in a way that makes sense economically and so that cash flow is sufficient to amortize the debt. Working capital loans are usually paid off over the shortest periods of time, and real estate loans are usually paid off over the longest. Remember: the longer the term is, the lower the monthly payment (principal and interest) will be, but there will be more monthly payments, more interest accruing, and more money paid in total to meet the debt requirements. Failure to meet interest payment typically constitutes loan default. Normally, on default, the entire principal amount outstanding becomes immediately due.

Rates

Most business debt today is provided at a variable interest rate, usually fluctuating with the prime rate (the rate banks charge their "best" customers). This rate is usually quoted as "prime plus" multiplied by percentage points, often 0.5 to 2 percent, but it can be as much as 3 or even 4 percent above prime, depending on risk and other variables that motivate the lender. This rate can change as often as the prime rate changes; therefore, each monthly payment can be different.[17]

There will also be other covenants, rules, and restrictions to the loan, which may constrain the entrepreneur's management freedom. This can include not giving raises to senior management without the lender's approval or obtaining further financing or reaching certain sales milestones.

The loan officer will make a determination of the entrepreneur's financial position based largely on the company's earnings statement and balance sheet, which measure growth potential and financial stability. The lender will be particularly interested in the company's net worth or equity as well as general information on:

Debtors can only sue the business and can claim only the assets of the business. For this reason, banks will usually require business owners to sign or guarantee any loans.

1. Receivables and Payables
   - Accounts receivable turnover
   - Percentage of total accounts owed by the largest account
   - Reserve for doubtful accounts
   - Condition of each client's payables
   - Ratio of debt to net worth
2. Inventories
   - Need for markdowns
   - Amount of raw material versus work in process versus finished goods
   - Obsolescence of inventory
3. Fixed Assets
   - Condition of equipment
   - Depreciation policy
   - Future plans for additional purchases

BUILDING A RELATIONSHIP WITH A BANKER

Setting up a checking account at a bank is one of the first steps in building a relationship with a lending institution. It will provide the opportunity to meet a loan officer who can be crucial in developing the business. The best borrowing relationships often depend on a loan officer who knows the business and will take a personal interest in the entrepreneur and his or her company. The entrepreneur should consider the following questions before making a choice:[18]

How much lending authority does the banker have, and what is the approval process?

Can the banker understand the business? Is there any interest?

What experience does the banker have with similar companies?

Issues to Avoid

The entrepreneur needs to identify the following issues prior to building a relationship with a banker:

Picking the wrong bank and banker. Some banks are much more aggressive in their lending practices, focusing on small companies. Others will do everything possible to avoid small-business loans. The entrepreneur should find a bank—and a banker—who understands the financial needs of small companies, especially those in his or her industry.

Being inadequately prepared to make loan requests. Bankers expect more than just a handshake and a "Hi, I'd like to borrow $50,000 for my business" from entrepreneurs. They want to see a complete business plan and forecasts showing how the loan will benefit the company and exactly how the entrepreneur intends to repay it.

Paying too little attention to financial details, especially cash flow. Even though financial projections are sometimes just "best guesses" of what is likely to happen, they are an integral part of any loan request. Bankers want to be sure that the entrepreneur understands the tools of financial management and cash flow analysis, because they are essential to business success.

Omitting a marketing plan. An idea for a great product or service is meaningless without a solid marketing plan. The entrepreneur must include a customer-focused marketing plan as part of the loan request. It must explain how the entrepreneur plans to sell his or her product, how the product will be priced, to whom the product will be sold, and why customers will want to buy it.

Being overly optimistic. Entrepreneurs are famous for being optimistic; bankers are equally famous for being pessimistic, especially when reading business plans and loan requests. The business plan should be based in reality, not fantasy, and the entrepreneur's financial projections should convey this reality. "When you're looking at a business plan and someone projects astronomical growth in five years, you tend to think that this person is not someone that you really want to put a lot of faith in," counsels one bank executive.

Failing to sell the strengths of the management team. Every banker would rather see a strong experienced team of managers working together to make a company successful than a strong entrepreneur trying to do everything all alone. A solid business plan is essential, but the entrepreneur must have the management team to fulfill it.

Failing to recognize problems and weaknesses. Too often, entrepreneurs are tempted to gloss over or to omit totally their businesses' problems and weaknesses. Bankers, however, are very good at finding them. Omitting problems and weaknesses is a sure-fire way to lose all credibility with a banker. The entrepreneur should emphasize strengths, but be straightforward about weaknesses, too.

USING GOVERNMENT SOURCES OF FUNDING

Many sources of financing are available to small businesses from federal, state, and local governments. The main source of funding from the federal government is the

Small Business Administration (SBA). Many state governments provide funding for businesses through their state departments of Commerce, Economic Development, Trade, or Industry Development. Local resources include city governments and regional authorities anxious to further economic growth in their area.

Federal Sources of Funding

The major source of government financing available to small businesses is the Small Business Administration (SBA). The SBA was established in 1953 to "aid, counsel, and protect the interests of the Nation's small business community." The agency works with intermediaries, banks, and other lending institutions to provide loans and venture capital financing to small businesses unable to secure financing through normal lending channels.

Many other federal programs are operated through government departments and agencies. The Small Business Innovation Research (SBIR) program and the Advanced Technology Program (ATP) are among other federal programs that provide funds to small businesses to develop new technologies.

Small Business Administration Programs

The Small Business Administration (SBA) was established by an act of Congress in 1953; in 1957, four years after its setup, the SBA was granted permanent status.

The SBA is involved in several aspects of small-business financing. There are financial programs whereby the SBA guarantees loans for small businesses to help them get financing when they cannot meet normal bank conditions. The SBA runs an investment program—the Small Business Investment Company (SBIC). The SBA also assists small businesses in obtaining government procurement contracts. Counseling and development services are offered to small businesses, including SCORE (Service Corps of Retired Executives), and many programs are designed to assist minority-owned businesses. The 57 Small Business Development Centers (SBDCs) across the country, with a network of over 1,000 service locations, provide advice and training to new and existing business owners.

For a business that is looking for startup funds, applying for a SBA loan is considered an alternative approach. The first step in obtaining SBA financing is to locate a commercial or savings bank that is a certified SBA lender. The SBA does not directly fund the loan. What it does is guarantee up to 85 percent of the loan for the lending institution. The key advantage is to repay the note over an extended period of time. The SBA is not in the business of guaranteeing bad loans. Once the institution accepts the credit, it recommends the company to the SBA.

General Description of SBA Loans[19]

For most SBA loans, there is no legislated limit to the total loan amount for which a business could apply. Typically, the maximum amount the SBA guarantees, however, is approximately $750,000. The SBA can guarantee up to 85 percent of loans of $100,000 and less, and up to 75 percent of loans above $100,000. Businesses could, therefore, receive over $1 million from a lender once approved by the SBA. The main considerations in the loan application for the SBA are a business's ability to repay the loans from cash flow, the owner(s') exhibit of good character and management ability, and the amount of collateral available and the owner's equity contribution. All owners of 20 percent or more are required to personally guarantee SBA loans.

Several types of financial assistance may be obtained through private lenders and then guaranteed by the SBA. These programs, which vary somewhat from state to state, include regular and special loans.

Regular Loans   Most regular SBA loans are made by private lenders (such as commercial banks, savings and loans, and insurance companies) and are then guaranteed by the SBA. The average size of a guaranteed loan is approximately $100,000 with a maturity of less than 10 years.

Special Loans   There are several types of these loans.

- *Local development company loans:* to groups that want to improve the economy in their area. The loan can be used to assist small businesses in the construction, expansion, and acquisition of plant or equipment.
- *Small general contractor loans:* to small construction firms with short-term financing. Funds can be used to finance residential or commercial construction or rehabilitation.
- *Seasonal line of credit:* to small firms with seasonal loan requirements to provide short-term financing.
- *Energy loans:* to companies engaged in manufacturing, selling, installing, servicing, or developing energy measures.
- *Handicapped assistance loans:* to owners of small businesses who are physically handicapped and private nonprofit organizations, which employ handicapped persons.
- *Microloans:* short-term loans of up to $35,000 for working capital and nonprofit childcare centers.

The SBA determines eligibility on the basis of four factors: type of business; size of business; use of loan funds; and special circumstances. Businesses are obliged to operate for profit and to do business in the United States. They also must have reasonable owner equity to invest and are obliged to use alternative financial resources first, including personal assets. The definition of a small business according to the Small Business Act is one "that is independently owned and operated and not dominant in its field of operation." This definition varies from industry to industry. The SBA size standards define the maximum size of an eligible small business (see Table 5-2).

Table 5-2   SBA Small Business Size Standards (1996)

Industry	Size (revenues/employees)
Retail and service	$3.5 to $13.5 million
Construction	$7.0 to $17.0 million
Agriculture	$0.5 to $3.5 million
Wholesale	No more than 100 employees
Manufacturing	500 to 1,500 employees

Table 5-3   The SBA Loan Application

1. Applicant Information	Names of owners, background, addresses, business name, date started, and other statement of business
2. Use of Loan Proceeds	Description of how the loan will be used in business operations
3. Collateral Pledged	List of all business and personal assets to secure the loan
4. Disclosures	List existing or previous government financing, personal and business debts, bankruptcies, and lawsuits
5. Personal Balance Sheet	Balance sheet on borrower(s)
6. Financial Statements	Cash flow, income, and use-of-funds statements

Borrowers must have appropriate collateral as security; the SBA does not accept unsecured applications. Collateral includes assets normally considered as security by lenders, including real estate, machinery, inventory, equipment, personal property, and receivables. The SBA will also consider as security co-signed endorsements by the guarantors; these are evaluated in the same manner as they are evaluated by commercial lenders. The application must be accompanied by cash flow projections and several other documents, together with a description of how the business will use the loan proceeds. A summary of SBA application requirements is shown in Table 5-3.

When the loan is approved, the SBA will restrict use of the money. For example, SBA loans cannot be used to repay past-due executive salaries or consolidate personal liabilities. They must underwrite operations or business expansion. As a result, the ability of the business to generate cash flow to repay the loan is the single most important consideration in the loan application.

SMALL BUSINESS INNOVATION RESEARCH (SBIR) PROGRAM

One of the best opportunities for obtaining funds is participation in the federally funded SBIR Program. This program allocates in excess of $1 billion annually to businesses with proposals for developing scientific innovation, and it has three phases:[20]

Phase I: There is a grant award up to $100,000 for the purpose of investigating the feasibility of an innovation. The award recipient has six months to prepare a feasibility plan that includes prototypes, market research, and report development.

Phase II: The report is reviewed, and, if feasible, an award of up to $1 million can be awarded for operating expenses. There is a two-year deadline to complete this phase, which can include further testing and market research. A report must be prepared to review the results that were achieved and how the funds were spent.

Phase III: This is not a funded stage of the program but includes selling the developed products or services to a federal government agency. Funding for development and commercialization must be obtained through private financing, which may be helped by having a purchase order from a creditworthy customer on hand.

How to Qualify

To begin the process, the entrepreneur should remember that the SBIR receives more than 8,000 proposals each year with fewer than 1,000 grants being approved. Under the Small Business Innovation Development Act, applicants must be independently owned companies with 500 or fewer employees and be able to demonstrate the capability for scientific or technological research. Through the first eight years of SBIR grants, award recipients have had, on average, under 35 employees, with nearly half of all initial Phase I grants awarded to companies with fewer than 10 employees. The SBIR grant program provides operating money to companies and is not a loan. There is no assumption to repay the amount of the loan. One problem the SBIR program presents for entrepreneurs is the time it may take for the relevant agency to make a decision on grants, leaving a gap in cash flow. To reduce this problem, some granting agencies have a fast track.[21] For more information on the SBIR Program, contact:

Small Business Administration

Office of Innovation Research and Technology

1441 L Street, NW

Washington, DC 20416

(202) 653-6458

Small Business Technology Transfer Program

The Small Business Technology Transfer (STTR) program is similar to the SBIR program in that it fosters R&D by small businesses. The major difference between the programs was that funding was provided to joint ventures or partnerships between nonprofit research institutions and small businesses. Like the SBIR, the STTR programs have three phases. An award of $100,000 is made during the year-long phase I. Phase II awards are up to $500,000 in a two-year expansion of Phase I results. Funds for Phase III of STTR must be found outside the STTR program. By this time, however, the research project should be ready for commercialization. The STTR Pilot program began making awards in fiscal year 1994.

SBA Express

SBA Express was intended to reduce the paperwork and time frame needed to apply for a Small Business Administration-backed loan. Bank-qualified business owners can borrow up to $150,000 without going through the standard SBA application process and are guaranteed a loan decision within 36 hours. Since the loans are guaranteed by the government and only at 50 percent of their face value, many of the eligible "preferred" lenders with good track records are not active. To track down active lenders, contact the SBA district office.[22]

Financing for Minorities and Women

The definition of a minority-owned business is one that is 51 percent or more owned by one or more owners, either a minority or a woman. Federal assistance is available, for example, to Native American-owned businesses and programs that promote the business and economic development of reservations.

The SBA division of the Office of Minority Enterprise Development (MED) assists economically and socially disadvantaged business owners. The act provides assistance, through the Division of Management and Technical Assistance, to "socially and economically disadvantaged individuals and firms owned by such individuals, businesses located in areas of low income or high unemployment, and firms owned by low-income individuals."

Other federal offices and agencies that give assistance to minority firms and individuals for business expansion and development are the Bureau of Indian Affairs, the Office of Small and Disadvantaged Business Utilization, and the Minority Business Development Agency.

Other Government-backed Financing Sources

The Farmers Home Administration (FmHA) provides guaranteed long-term loans for rural development. These loans are limited to applicants who reside in cities or rural areas with a population of less than 50,000. Although FmHA is viewed as a "farmer's program," it exists to help any rural enterprise with startup working capital, equipment purchases, and expansion.

The Department of Housing and Urban Development (HUD) provides loans and grants for rehabilitation of city areas. HUD operates predominantly in metropolitan areas, and funds are administered through local authorities. Funds are used for remodeling downtown stores, refurbishing historic sites, as well as converting older buildings for residential and commercial use.

Small Business Investment Companies (SBICs) and Minority Enterprise Small Business Investments Companies (MESBICs) are licensed by the SBA and may provide management assistance as well as equity funding to emerging businesses. These loans are arranged through lenders, and regulations vary from state to state. They are targeted to businesses capable of enhancing economic growth within the state.

State and Local Small-Business Financing Initiatives

Most states have programs that provide financial assistance or incentives to small businesses. Such programs are administered by departments and agencies within state and local government. Many different programs are available in each state, but most states have a department of trade or commerce that runs loan assistance, investment, procurement, and other programs. Small-business assistance at the state level can be in the form of direct financial assistance, tax benefits, technical assistance, or small-business incubators.

Contact city and county or township governments for assistance. In many areas, local development authorities can also be useful resources in locating financing for new or existing businesses.

SUMMARY

Depending on funding needs, the entrepreneur faces a number of options. To increase the chances of success, the entrepreneur must know what sources are available and understand the requirements of the financial partners. Preparing a business and financial plan before beginning the search helps the entrepreneur determine which sources would be most likely to assist in capitalizing the business.

This chapter examined the many sources of nonequity early-stage capital. Determining which source is best will depend on many different factors, including amount required, when it is needed and for how long, and when it can be repaid. The development stage for the company and the goals and objectives must be considered. Entrepreneurs become expert at using a range of bootstrapping methods to bridge the gap from starting the company to the stage where either they can acquire equity or bank loan funding for growth, or the company becomes self-financing through retained profits from sales.

Most commercial loans are made to small businesses and are either unsecured or secured. An unsecured loan is a personal or signature loan that requires no collateral. The loan is granted on the background and strength of the entrepreneur's reputation. Such loans are made at fair market interest rates if the entrepreneur can demonstrate that the business is sound. To most banks, that will mean having an operating history of at least two or three years. Banks often require that the borrower maintain appropriate deposits with them. In addition, most banks will require personal guarantees for newer companies. In either case, banks tend to be cautious about lending and carefully weigh the four Cs of lending: character, cash flow, collateral, and contribution.

Lenders are looking for the ability of a company to repay its debt. No matter how successful a company is, usually a lender has only the promise of being rewarded with steady payments of principal and interest. An idea for a great product or service is meaningless without a solid marketing plan. The entrepreneur must include a customer-focused marketing plan as part of the loan request. The plan must explain how the entrepreneur plans to sell the product, how the product will be priced, to whom it will be sold, and why they will want to buy it.

Every banker would rather see a strong experienced team of managers working together to make a company successful than a strong entrepreneur trying to do everything all alone. A solid business plan is essential, but the entrepreneur must have the management team to implement it.

The SBA guarantees 80 percent of the loan, allowing banks to lend money to businesses that might otherwise be refused. The Small Business Administration (SBA) is the most active federal agency in assisting small businesses. Loans guaranteed by the SBA are the prevalent means of obtaining government support, but direct loan assistance is available under certain programs.

The Small Business Innovation Research Program (SBIR) provides direct grants to businesses engaged in scientific development. With a SBIR Phase I grant, entrepreneurs are provided up to $100,000 for development feasibility plans; Phase II grants can be as much as $1 million for commercialization of their innovations.

STUDY QUESTIONS

1. What sources of funding are available to entrepreneurss at the early stage of the company?
2. What are the major techniques for bootstrapping?
3. Why is bootstrapping important for (a) closely held companies and (b) early-stage, high-growth companies that plan to seek equity investors?

4. What steps should entrepreneurs take to prepare a loan proposal?

5. Describe how you would build a relationship with a loan officer?

6. Describe three government funding programs.

EXERCISES

1. Refer to the Dyson Profile in this chapter and consider the following questions:
   (a) What personal attributes led to Dyson's success?
   (b) Give three reasons why you think Hoover rejected Dyson's offer of a license?
   (c) Describe three ways that Dyson creatively "bootstrapped" his company when he did not have enough cash to proceed?
   (d) Name two other large consumer companies with household brand names that are still privately owned and were therefore bootstrapped from their very beginning.

2. With regard to establishing early-stage funding:

   Select and briefly describe a business idea that will require early-stage funds to get started.

   Establish the amount of startup capital needed to fund the venture for one year.

   Describe where the venture will get sources of funding and other resources it may need. Use a mix of personal funds, family, friends, bank loans, and creative bootstrapping.

   Prepare an oral presentation to bankers for any loans you seek.

INTERACTIVE LEARNING ON THE WEB

Test your knowledge of the chapter using the book's interactive Web site.

CASE STUDY: hIDe

Read this case to

(a) Analyze the problem

(b) Review alternative funding solution

(c) Make recommendations

CASE: EARLY-STAGE FINANCING FOR A NEW VENTURE

The four Columbia University graduate students were putting the finishing touches on the first draft of a business plan in the spring of 2001. Jerry Adriano, Beth Hinshaw, Chris Callahan, and Vas Rajan had all spent considerable time doing research, testing, and writing the final plan for hIDe. The idea was originally conceived by Rajan, who sought to find a way to ensure privacy for online e-commerce purchases by consumers.

The idea was simple: find a way for a consumer to conduct online or other remote purchases, pay for them, and receive the products, all while maintaining total anonymity in the midst of the information revolution. The hitch was to provide this service without the consumer having to trust any intermediary. Rajan had been frustrated with certain companies' claims that they protected consumers' identities. He knew that this protection relied on trust of the company and that the only way to be truly protected was to be truly anonymous. The only privacy schemes out there at the time relied on the consumer trusting a bank or other company. There were only limited pilot tests of anonymous debit card systems in progress. Virtually no one had addressed the shipping issue. Lastly, there was no integrated solution.

The plan was to raise early-stage financing by going to friends, angels, and family members of the team. The venture capital firms would not be interested in investing until the company could demonstrate revenues and profit potential. They also considered a bank loan but questioned what assets or guarantees they could provide. Other issues weighed heavily as well, such as using credit cards to get started, differentiation, sustainability, the regulatory environment, and competitive threats. Although the plan addressed these and other issues, only time would tell if the concept was viable for early-stage funding.

OVERVIEW

Consumer privacy was the latest product of the information revolution to gain consumer attention. The backlash against the use of consumer data for targeted marketing had expressed itself in privacy legislation, consumer activism, and ultimately in the buying habits of some consumer segments. Major media polls indicated that 73 percent of the respondents were somewhat concerned or very concerned about threats to their personal privacy on the Internet. hIDe was designed to provide individual consumers with identity privacy during all stages of product acquisition, from searching to purchasing to delivery. It was not a pretense of privacy, where the consumer must trust a financial intermediary; rather, it was purchasing anonymity, where not even the transaction enabler could know the users' identity.

This case was written by Jerry Adriano, Beth Hinshaw, Chris Callahan, and Vas Rajan, EMBA 2001, under the supervision of Professor Jack Kaplan as a basis for class discussion. The authors may have disguised certain names and other identifying information to protect confidentiality.

Using a prepaid debit card platform, hIDe would offer consumers the ability to navigate the Internet anonymously and use cash to purchase a card that could be used like a credit card and was linked to one or more major credit card systems. The hIDe concept would thrive in the cashless society of the growing online transaction market. Global e-commerce revenue was predicted to top $100 billion in 2001, with estimates of $250 billion for 2003. hIDe was designed to appeal strongly to individuals who acted based on pro-privacy principles, as well as individuals who used other forms of payment for purchases to which they would rather not be linked.

Other companies had tested or launched businesses that addressed one or more of the features of hIDe. In most cases, hIDe was unique in that it did not require that the consumer's name be given and it facilitated not only anonymous purchases, but also the anonymous receipt of parcels hIDe's full-service platform, which include balance transfers/reuse, assistance for vendors in their obligations for age verification, and alignment with well-known and respected service providers. hIDe would generate revenue through premium-sharing agreements with credit card systems, issuing banks, and shippers.

The main strategy of hIDe was to bridge the gap between the trust mechanism that modern credit and debit card systems provided and the anonymity that only cash could provide, thus meeting a need driven by the growing mistrust of merchant use of consumer data.

The milestone objectives were to develop a system with a major credit card company to create the debit cards, such that they would work on a major credit card system and partner with retail distribution channels (such as convenience stores) and develop an online site to sell the cards.

hIDe PRODUCTS AND SERVICES

hIDe was designed to enable consumers to purchase goods and services anonymously where one accepted method of payment was a major credit card. hIDe offered consumers the ability to use cash to purchase a debit card linked to one or more credit card systems and navigate the Internet anonymously, without fear of tracking. hIDe was positioning to be the premier strongest brand provider of such services.

The business model is derived from that of the popular phone debit cards. The customer would purchase hIDe from a retailer or online (where the purchase would *not* be linked to the purchaser's credit card). The card would make use of the existing credit card infrastructure. The user would then purchase goods or services at a retail or online outlet while maintaining total anonymity. In the case of goods purchases, the end user could elect to have the shipper (a major shipper partnered with our company) distribute the product to a local holding facility or warehouse of the consumer's choosing (presumably at a location close to the consumer's home, office, school, etc.). He or she would then go to the facility and present a coded (or encrypted) receipt (proof of ownership) in exchange for the package.

In addition to this basic functionality, hIDe would offer services that followed the entire life cycle of the product, in order to make it easy to use. For example, small remainder balances on a card could be transferable to a new card via a convenient online system, or at retail channels. New credit could be purchased online, with hIDe agreeing to destroy all transaction data immediately after the transaction. In order to facilitate age verification, three different types of cards would be available, based on the age of the purchaser, with the sales agent being responsible for age verification at the time of sale.

hIDe would generate revenue through agreements with the credit card systems, issuing banks, and shippers, whereby premiums were shared. For example, part of the credit card premium charged to vendors would be assigned to hIDe, and/or shipping fees could be enhanced and then split.

THE MARKET

This product was targeted primarily at individual consumers in the United States. The team, having "grown up" in corporate America, felt that the product did not offer the audit trails and transaction visibility that business customers would demand. As a form of payment, the product was to compete primarily with cash and debit cards. hIDe could be used anywhere a major credit card was accepted. However, the primary market was intended to be the Internet transaction market. The team's preliminary research regarding market size was promising. Total spending on online sales was $6.1 billion in December 2000. Nearly 20 million households shopped online, spending an average $308 per person. Global e-commerce revenue was predicted to top $100 billion in 2001. Business to customer was estimated to climb to $250 billion by 2003 (March 2001 eMarketer Inc. study).

The hIDe goal was to be the market leader among a subset of that market, those who favored cards offering anonymous purchasing, anonymous parcel delivery, and anonymous Web navigation services. The market had many new entrants but no clear-cut leader and no integrated solution provider.

In order to achieve market leadership, the team figured on rapid market entry, for they felt that the industry would grow rapidly with relatively low barriers to entry rising along the way. They also felt the need for the name recognition of a well-established card company, and a reliable and well-known shipping company.

THE VALUE PROPOSITION

hIDe would offer security to its users by way of total anonymity. That could be valuable for a number of reasons:

To avoid recognition of personal or private preferences (services and/or goods)

To limit fraud exposure since funds are limited

To enable transactions for those who cannot participate in other credit mechanisms

To provide an alternative to cash in many ways, such as gift giving

To protect a consumer who wishes to avoid triggering unwanted market solicitation when shopping and purchasing online

Because so many payment methods existed, hIDe would be most successful if it could create a category need that was not recognized by many mainstream consumers of the day. Consumers typically rated their credit and debit cards on features such as acceptance, rates, annual fee, rewards programs, and protection. hIDe would have to create the awareness of anonymity and raise its importance level in the eyes of the consumer.

THE CONSUMER

One of the biggest questions on the mind of the team was who would buy the service. The team realized that intuition alone would not identify the consumer segments, particularly because the team was comprised of a fairly homogeneous demographic. However, intuition was a good starting point. Combined with an online survey and secondary research, the team identified four distinct consumer segments based on four attributes: access to credit cards, the things they buy, whether they would use or give the card for personal use, and attitude toward consumer privacy:

1. *Cardless Surfers*: Individuals who need a credit card payment option for online purchases but for some reason are restricted in their access to or use of traditional credit cards.

2. *Lascivious Lifestyles*: Purchasers of restricted or brown-wrapper items, including adult magazines and videos.

3. *Shy Shoppers*: Individuals who purchase over-the-counter medications and other socially sensitive products (Preparation H, Just for Men hair color, intimate apparel, etc.) with cash because they do not want these items to show up on credit card purchase summaries.

4. *None of Your Business*: Consumers who reject consumer information gathering on principle. These consumers will incur cost and inconvenience to prevent the government, credit card companies, and others from obtaining information on their purchases and habits.

A fifth segment, *Shady Suspects*, represented those who use this product for illegal activity (e.g., underage purchase; purchase of parts used in terrorism). While

Value Assigned to Feature by Segment (and substitutes)

Product Feature	Cardless Surfers	Lascivious Lifestyles	Shy Shoppers	None of Your Business	Gift Givers	Practical Parents
Enables online purchase		(Credit)	(Credit)		(Credit)	
Retail purchase anonymity		(Cash)	(Cash)	(Cash)		
Online purchase Anonymity:		✓	✓	✓		
Ship and hold option		✓	✓	✓	✓	
Limit is controllable						(Credit)
Easy to carry					✓	(Credit)
Can obtain online		✓	✓		✓	✓
Can obtain locally		(ODC)	(ODC)	(ODC)	(ODC)	✓

ODC = Competitors' Online Debit Cards

the business model would not target those consumers from a marketing standpoint, it would still need to be mindful of their needs and potential use of the product, and ensure that the processes had effective controls and that liability was minimized.

Each of these segments would respond to different features of the product and to different marketing messages. The following chart shows the attributes of the product that the team expected to be valued by each group, and substitute payment forms, if available.

An informal survey of potential card users validated the segmentation of the frontrunner segments: Shy Shoppers, Lascivious Lifestyles, and None of Your Business. The team found that these segments expressed interest in the concept of an anonymous credit/debit card substitute, but differed in their attitudes toward purchasing in privacy. In contrast, Cardless Surfers, Gift Givers, and Practical Parents represented unique value sets that the team felt would be relatively more difficult to attract initially.

COMPETITION

At that time, there were various direct and indirect competitors; it was an attractive new market with relatively low barriers to entry. Typically, these players focused on smart card or debit card functionality that enabled online purchase. They did not advertise heavily; however, a party looking for their services could find them easily enough.

Direct competitors included:

- Large credit card companies that had tried pilots of similar programs. Only one company had a true cash equivalent card that was sold through retail distribution channels, but even that did not have other services, such as shipping. Other large credit card companies had implemented debit card schemes but for other purposes, such as preset spending accounts for children. In addition, the large credit card companies also had tried one-time-use numbers for anonymous purchasing; but again, these schemes relied on trust in the credit card company.
- Several companies allowed anonymous Web surfing. These companies could only be loosely defined competitors, for they also were potential distribution channels or partners. For about $50 per year, a person can surf the Web anonymously.

- The relatively low profile of competing firms most likely related to industry structure, to the disruptive nature of the technology (initial low acceptance), to low parent company expenditures on marketing, or to other factors, including the lack of a clear technological standard for key parts of the process.
- Indirect competitors included firms using technologies and applications that could potentially be expanded to have a broader range of uses.
- Cash and money orders.
- Prepaid card applications ranging from telephone cards to mass transit cards.
- EZ-Pass™ and related toll payment systems.

Cash and money orders were indirect competitors because they both allowed someone to remain anonymous when completing a transaction. Cash was not accepted on the Internet, but it was of course accepted everywhere else. Money orders were accepted in lieu of cash for most purchases, but they were an inconvenient way to purchase something on the Internet since they had to be mailed to the seller of Internet merchandise or services before the transaction could be completed.

PATENTS AND REGULATORY ENVIRONMENT

Several patents had already been issued in this space. Even though the team had yet to research their specific affects, they believed there was room for entry into the market. Numerous online privacy bills had been drafted at the state and federal government level. Although there had been much debate and discussion about passing some legislation regarding online privacy, none of the bills had yet made significant headway in Congress. The public pressure to pass some legislation was growing, but several industry groups, namely, the Online Privacy Alliance, argued that the best way to guard privacy was through new technology, not new legislation. Therefore, the team felt that hIDe was well positioned as either a stand-alone privacy guard or as a complement to new legislation to guard privacy.

The end-to-end anonymous purchase process was unique to hIDe. Accordingly, management intended to file for a business process patent to prevent imitation. Furthermore, hIDe would seek intellectual property protection separately for the vendor integration method for anonymous payment. Lastly, hIDe would seek to reach agreements with various government and regulatory agencies that would not only enable hIDe to operate in this business but also create a process that substantially hindered or prevented others from entering the business without providing for the public good.

DIFFERENTIATION

Since hIDe would not be unique in its ability to provide totally anonymous purchasing power, and may have only temporarily been unique in totally anonymous shipping, its emergence as a market leader would be a function of attracting consumers for whom the privacy functionality would be paramount. Branding and strategic partnerships would be required to create an arena for effective competition.

hIDe therefore had two types of differentiation challenges: differentiating from currently popular forms of payment (easier) and differentiating from other firms' entry into this market (more difficult). The team believed that differentiation in the near term would likely be a greater function of positioning and branding than would the inherent capabilities of the product.

FINANCIAL OUTLOOK

Abridged revenue and cash flow projections are shown on the following pages. The models show the sales, pricing, and other factors that were realistically expected by the team when drafting the plan. They also list all of the pertinent assumptions for each revenue stream. Overall, the outlook is positive as the business model makes financial sense.

With only a few months of school left until graduation, the team needed to evaluate the viability of the plan and make a decision as to whether or not to pursue the idea. Was it viable? Would it sell? Would people like the idea but not the implementation? Most importantly, would friends, family, and/or angels be interested in funding it?

CASE STUDY QUESTIONS

1. Assume that you were one of the hIDe team members:
   a. Would you want to pursue the opportunity? Would you invest your own money in the company? Why or why not?
   b. Would you ask your friends and family members to invest in this early-stage venture?
   c. Assuming that you intended to move forward, what method(s) to fund growth should hIDe seek? (Bootstrapping, moonlighting, or going for a bank loan?) Explain your choice.

2. Based on your answer above, what resources do you think hIDe would need to get started in terms of cash or facilities? Be sure to explain how the resources would suffice until operations were self-sustaining and additional funding was available.

3. Had the management team done enough research to quantify the size of the market?
   a. How valid was their assessment of probable market acceptance of the product?
   b. Did they target the right segments, or was their approach for segment identification and description valid?
   c. How realistic is it to attract capital from various constituents/partners/suppliers (credit card company, shipper, distribution channel, corollary services, government)?

4. What is the likelihood and potential magnitude of competitive threat from large and small players?

5. Assess the organizational structure of hIDe:
   a. What type of corporate structure would you recommend for starting out the business and why? (S-Corporation vs. LLC, etc.)
   b. Assume for a moment that you accept the revenue and cash flow models as presented. Based on those models, what staffing structure would you propose, and why? Which positions would be important to fill, and what would be the schedule for filling them?

Revenue Forecast
(000's)

	Nov-01	Dec-01	Jan-02	Feb-02	Mar-02	Apr-02	May-02	Jun-02	Jul-02	Aug-02	Sep-02	Oct-02	Nov-02	Dec-02	Jan-03
Cards Sold	100	125	128	131	135	138	141	145	149	152	156	160	176	180	185
Face Value of Cards	7,500	9,375	9,609	9,850	10,096	10,348	10,607	10,872	11,144	11,423	11,708	12,001	13,201	13,531	13,869
Card Fees	175	219	224	230	236	241	247	254	260	267	273	280	308	316	324
Transactions	150	188	192	197	202	207	212	217	223	228	234	240	264	271	277
Transaction Revenue	6,000	7,500	7,688	7,880	8,077	8,279	8,486	8,698	8,915	9,138	9,366	9,601	10,561	10,825	11,095
Transaction Fees	60	75	77	79	81	83	85	87	89	91	94	96	106	108	111
Shipping	15	19	19	20	20	21	21	22	22	23	23	24	26	27	28
Shipping Revenue	225	281	288	295	303	310	318	326	334	343	351	360	396	406	416
Shipping Fees	23	28	29	30	30	31	32	33	33	34	35	36	40	41	42
Fee Revenue	258	322	330	338	347	355	364	373	383	392	402	412	453	465	476
Card Balances Outstanding	1,275	2,869	4,502	6,177	7,893	9,652	11,455	13,304	15,198	17,140	19,130	21,171	23,415	25,715	28,073
Card Balances Redeemed	6,225	7,781	7,976	8,175	8,380	8,589	8,804	9,024	9,249	9,481	9,718	9,961	10,957	11,231	11,511
Float Revenue 0.417%	5	12	19	26	33	40	48	55	63	71	80	88	98	107	117
Lost Card Revenue	75	94	96	98	101	103	106	109	111	114	117	120	132	135	139
TOTAL REVENUE	**338**	**428**	**445**	**462**	**480**	**499**	**518**	**537**	**557**	**578**	**599**	**620**	**683**	**707**	**732**
Cumulative Cards Sold	100	225	353	484	619	757	898	1,043	1,192	1,344	1,500	1,660	1,836	2,017	2,202
		Growth Rate													
Transactions		2.5%	2.5%	2.5%	2.5%	2.5%	2.5%	2.5%	2.5%	2.5%	2.5%	2.5%	10.0%	2.5%	2.5%
Cards		2.5%	2.5%	2.5%	2.5%	2.5%	2.5%	2.5%	2.5%	2.5%	2.5%	2.5%	10.0%	2.5%	2.5%

Assumptions

	Percentage	Transaction		Total	
Transaction Fees	1.00%	$	40.00	$	0.40	Percentage Fee
Shipping Fees	10%	$	15.00	$	1.50	Percentage Fee
Per Card Fee				$	1.75	Flat Fee
Avg. Card Denomination	$	75			
Lost %	1% of balances				
% of Customers That Ship	10%				
Cost per Card	$	0.25			
Transaction: Cards Sold Ratio	1.50				
% Collection in Current Month	50%				
% Collection in Next Month	50%				

Cash Flow Statement

	May-01	Jun-01	Jul-01	Aug-01	Sep-01	Oct-01	Nov-01	Dec-01	Jan-02
Cash Inflows									
Accounts Receivable	$ -	$ -	$ -	$ -	$ -	$ -	$ -	$ 169	$ 214
Monthly Sales	$ -	$ -	$ -	$ -	$ -	$ -	$ 169	$ 214	$ 222
Total Cash Receipts	$ -	$ -	$ -	$ -	$ -	$ -	$ 169	$ 383	$ 436
Cash Outflow									
Card Costs 2,000 per order	$ -	$ -	$ -	$ -	$ -	$ 500	$ -	$ -	$ -
Distributor Fees	$ -	$ -	$ -	$ -	$ -	$ -	$ 34	$ 76	$ 85
Salaries	$ 143	$ 143	$ 143	$ 143	$ 143	$ 143	$ 143	$ 143	$ 143
Benefits	$ 18	$ 18	$ 18	$ 18	$ 18	$ 18	$ 18	$ 18	$ 18
Taxes	$ 22	$ 22	$ 22	$ 22	$ 22	$ 22	$ 22	$ 22	$ 22
Rent/Utilities	$ 20	$ 20	$ 20	$ 20	$ 20	$ 20	$ 20	$ 20	$ 20
Research and Development	$ 50	$ 50	$ 50	$ 50	$ 50	$ 50	$ 50	$ 50	$ 50
Advertising and Promotion	$ -	$ -	$ -	$ 50	$ 75	$ 100	$ 100	$ 100	$ 25
Supplies and Other	$ 1	$ 1	$ 1	$ 1	$ 1	$ 1	$ 1	$ 1	$ 1
Professional Fees	$ 13	$ 13	$ 13	$ 13	$ 13	$ 13	$ 13	$ 8	$ 20
Total Cash Disbursement	$ 267	$ 267	$ 267	$ 267	$ 342	$ 867	$ 400	$ 438	$ 384
Operating Cash	$ (267)	$ (267)	$ (267)	$ (267)	$ (342)	$ (867)	$ (232)	$ (55)	$ 52
	$ (267)	$ (533)	$ (800)	$ (1,067)	$ (1,408)	$ (2,275)	$ (2,506)	$ (2,561)	$ (2,509)
Less: Interest Payments									
Interest on Debt 12%	$ 50	$ 50	$ 50	$ 50	$ 50	$ 50	$ 50	$ 50	$ 50
Interest on Line of Credit									
Less: Notes Payable Principal Payment									
Add: Beginning of Month Cash Balance		$ 4,544	$ 4,089	$ 3,633	$ 3,178	$ 2,647	$ 1,592	$ 1,171	$ 928
Cash Balance before Funding	$ (317)	$ 4,228	$ 3,772	$ 3,317	$ 2,786	$ 1,731	$ 1,310	$ 1,066	$ 930
Line of Credit Principal Payments	$ 139	$ 139	$ 139	$ 139	$ 139	$ 139	$ 139	$ 139	$ 139
Dividends									
Additional Funding									
New Equity	$ 5,000								
New Debt									
Line of Credit Borrowings									
Ending Cash Balance	$ 4,544	$ 4,089	$ 3,633	$ 3,178	$ 2,647	$ 1,592	$ 1,171	$ 928	$ 791

APPENDIX: STARTUP ENTREPRENEURS AND BUSINESS INCUBATORS

Business incubators are organizations designed to assist and accelerate the growth of small business. They typically provide business assistance in the form of coaching and training, access to investors, and access to office services and space on flexible terms. Incubators are short-term assistance programs. They are designed to provide concentrated critical resources during the key development period. Most incubators have time limits ranging from six months to three years. Business incubators have become one of the most concentrated and useful methods for obtaining business assistance.

Types of Incubators

Incubators have been around for 40 years and have helped produce more than 20,000 successful businesses. Today there are more than 800 in the United States and another 2,000 worldwide. The 800 U.S.-based incubators are divided into three types based on their sponsorship and objectives:

1. **Publicly sponsored (45 percent of U.S. incubators)**
   These incubators are organized through city economic development departments, urban renewal authorities, or regional planning and development commissions. Job creation is the major objective of publicly sponsored incubators.
2. **University related (27 percent of U.S. incubators)**
   Most of these incubators are focused on science and technology companies. Many of them develop business based on research started at the university. The major goals of this type of incubators are technology commercialization, along with a return on investment.
3. **For-profit incubators (33 percent of U.S. incubators)**
   These incubators are organized and managed by investors with the goal of receiving a return on their investment. A recent study by Harvard Business School found that most of the for-profit incubators were investor led, focused on the Internet, and designed to accelerate the speed and size of the startup.

   The study identified 345 for-profit incubators worldwide; 58 percent were new organizations founded by investors to maximize investment return, 31 percent were operated as part of a venture capital firm, 5 percent were holding companies designed to develop and then manage growth, and 6 percent were founded by established companies as a way of fostering innovation in the larger firm. As an example, see the accompanying diagram of the Austin Incubator's services.

   Incubators give entrepreneurs the opportunity to focus on business creation activities while providing essential at-cost and time savings.

Incubator Services and Advantages

Flexible Space and Flexible Leases
Most incubators provide facilities for startup companies. The biggest advantage they offer is flexibility in committing to space based on the growth of the business. Traditionally, incubators provide space at below-market rates. Many incubators are now pricing at the market and are focusing on business assistance services as a major value offering.

Administrative Services
Look closely at the services an incubator offers. Most incubators (88 percent) provide shared copiers, fax machines, telephone systems, computers, and high-speed Internet access. Access to equipment is a big time saver. Many incubators also provide administrative staff assistance such as answering telephones and clerical support.

Management Help
Management help can be the most important service you receive. It often begins with a consultation to help you evaluate the concept or growth prospects for a going concern, and it continues with regular reviews of the business. Incubators typically provide support on business basics such as developing business plans, refining the business concept, and marketing assistance. Roughly 75 percent of all U.S. incubators also provide help with accounting and financial management services.

Expert Advice
Expert advice from university business professors, other business owners, lenders, and accountants can help keep your business on track.

Specialization
Some incubators are industry specific; examples are food service, software, and biotech, Internet, art, or ceramics. Others focus on service businesses or specific social goals. For example, Entergy Arts Business Center in New Orleans started as an incubator specifically for individual artists and arts-related businesses. Other incubators serve specific groups, such as women or minority business owners. For example, the San Francisco-based Women's Technology Cluster is a high-tech incubator for women entrepreneurs. The Cluster helps startups get off the ground, hosts weekly seminars on business basics, and offers services such as help with hiring, finances, public relations, sales, and Web design.

Increased Credibility
Acceptance represents a kind of *Good Housekeeping*® seal of approval. Most incubators are highly selective about who they admit. High-quality meeting rooms, professional telephone coverage, and reception areas all improve a startup's image.

Easy Networking
This includes opportunities to chat with other tenants or make formal presentations to potential investors. It's often easier to get your phone calls returned when you are physically located at a known incubator in a normal business building.

Funding
Funding is not usually available directly from incubators, but many will help arrange meetings with potential investors. A few public incubators will provide funds to get you started. For example, the Austin incubator will provide $500,000 in seed money. For-profit incubators usually provide investments but take on average 45 percent equity versus the 2 to 5 percent common in nonprofit incubators. For-profit incubators differ from VCs in that they are willing to fund small seed rounds (those below the VC radar screen), they take a more active role, and they usually are willing to stay in longer.

GUIDELINES FOR SELECTING AN INCUBATION PROGRAM

TRACK RECORD

- How well is the program performing?
- How long has the program been operating?
- Does it have any successful graduate companies, and if so, how long have they been in business independent from the incubator?
- What do other clients and graduates think of the program?

GRADUATION POLICY

- What is the program's graduation policy; that is, what are the incubator's exit criteria?
- How flexible is the policy?
- How long, on average, have clients remained in the program? (Incubators typically graduate companies within three years.)

QUALIFICATIONS OF MANAGER AND STAFF

- How long has the current staff been with the program?
- How much time does the staff spend onsite?
- Have they had any entrepreneurial successes of their own? Do they actively engage in professional development activities, or are they a member of a professional/trade association to keep them up to date on the latest in incubation best practices?

FOR MORE INFORMATION

Information about Joining an Incubator

Directory of Incubators
www.nbia.org/links/index.php

Recent Articles

Henricks, Mark, "Incubate Your Biz," *Emerging Business*, November 1, 2000
    http:// www.ebmagz.com/articles.asp?magID=1062001&deptID=10&articleID= 86

Rosenwein, Rifka, "The Idea Factories," *Inc.* magazine, November 1, 2000
    http://www.inc.com/incmagazine/article/1,3654,ART20906_CNT53,00.html

Pfeil, Sherri, "Incubators Help Hatch Successful Companies," *Employment Review*, June 2001
    http://www.employmentreview.com/2001-06/features/CNfeat04.asp

Singer, Thea, "Inside an Internet Incubator," *Inc.* magazine, July 1, 2000
    http://www.inc.com/incmagazine

WEB SITES OF LEADING FOR-PROFIT INCUBATORS

CMGI: www.cmgi.com

IdeaLab: www.idealab.com

Research Articles

Adkins, Dina, Wolfe, Chuck, and Sherman, Hugh. 2000. *Best Practices in Business Incubation*. Study performed for the Maryland Technology Development Corporation (TEDCO). www.marylandtedco.org.

Chappell, David S., and Sherman, Hugh. 1998. "Methodological Challenges in Evaluating Business Incubator Outcomes." *Economic Development Quarterly* 14 (November).

Hansen, Morten, Chesbrough, Henry, Nohria, Nitin, and Sull, Donald. 2000. "Networked Incubators: Hothouses of the New Economy." *Harvard Business Review* (September 1).

McKinnon, Susie, and Hayhow, Sally. 1998. *State of the Business Incubation Industry*. Ohio: NBIA Publications.

Molnar, Lawrence A., Grimes, Donald R., and Edelstein, Jack. 1997. *Business Incubation Works*. Ohio: NBIA Publications.

ADDITIONAL RESOURCES

There are many articles and case reports of entrepreneurs' bootstrapping ideas published by popular magazines. You can search for articles for ideas and tips at:

www.entrepreneur.com

www.inc.com

www.fastcompany.com

The following sites provide further information about certain aspects of government grants:

www.nttc.edu/resources/funding/current.asp has details of all 10 units of SBIR and 5 units of STTR sources.

www.winbmdo.com/ lists all contact information, has links to relevant Web sites, and so on. This agency, now known as MDA, has traditionally funded riskier projects.

www.fedgrants.gov/Applicants/index.html lists all active federal grants programs.

www.acq.osd.mil/sadbu/sbir/overview/index.htm covers most SBIR and STTR documents.

www.acq.osd.mil/sadbu/sbir/solicitations/sttr04/index.htm lists solicitations from the DOD, which includes Army, Navy, Air Force, DARPA, and MDA with contact information. The DOD constitutes about 50 percent of the total SBIR/STTR funding, over $500 million.

grants1.nih.gov/grants/oer.htm is a link to grant opportunity, policy and guidelines, and contact information for the National Institutes of Health, the second largest funding source. At this site, click on "Small Business Funding Opportunities."

www.nsf.gov/home/grants.htm is a link to grant opportunity at the National Science Foundation.

www.nsa.gov/programs/msp/grants.html refers to the National Security Agency (NSA) Mathematical Sciences Program (MSP), which funds high-quality mathematical research in the areas of algebra, number theory, discrete mathematics, probability, statistics, and cryptology.

A particularly useful source is an up-to-date reference book on *all* federal R&D funding programs entitled *Federal Technology Funding Guide, 2004*. It can be downloaded free at: www.larta.org/Research/PublicationDetail.asp?Pub=FTFG2004.

For finding technologies available at government labs, see www.nttc.edu/techmart/default.asp.

Using University Outreach Programs

Certain business schools have venture funds that review opportunities for investment presented by students and outside entrepreneurs. We give two examples here from the authors' universities. These resources may also provide more than access to funding; they may provide student teams to work with startups in order to help them evaluate various options for their business. They are typical of resources that can be found at leading business schools. A list of contacts can be found at the National Consortium of Entrepreneurship Centers Web site, www.nationalconsortium.org/. Two examples of university out reach programs are the Columbia Business School and Smeal College of Business.

Columbia Business School—Eugene Lang Entrepreneurial Initiative Fund

Purpose and History

The Eugene Lang Entrepreneurial Initiative Fund was established in 1996 by an initial gift of $1 million from Eugene Lang, MS '40, founder and chairman emeritus of REFAC Technology Development Corporation. Its objective is to foster an entrepreneurial environment at Columbia Business School by providing students who conceive qualified business initiatives with seed capital for carrying them out after graduation. It also seeks to provide the Business School with the opportunity to share in the success of funded ventures through negotiated equity or other participation.

Eligibility

All students enrolled in Columbia Business School's MBA program are eligible to submit business plans for funding consideration in accordance with specified procedures. Students may work individually or with a partner.

Criteria

Proposals for all types of enterprises—small- or large-scale; high- or low-tech; startups or acquisitions; service, manufacturing, or retail operations—will be given consideration in relation to the following criteria:

● Feasibility of the proposed venture and its prospects for success

- Strength of the student's commitment to the venture and his or her qualifications to make it succeed
- Prospects for raising additional funding as may be required
- Technical or conceptual originality or social value

Mentoring and Assistance

Students will have a variety of resources available to them to assist with the development of their proposals. These include the school's entrepreneurship courses, faculty advisors, the Lang Fund Advisory Panel, volunteer mentors and relevant external sources, and the Lang Fund Board of Directors.

For further information, visit the Web site: www.gsb.columbia.edu/entprog.

Eugene M. Lang Center for Entrepreneurship

3022 Broadway

317 Uris Hall

New York, NY 10027

Phone: 212-854-3244

Fax: 212-280-4329

E-mail: entprog@columbia.edu

Smeal College of Business, Pennsylvania State University—Bette and John Garber Venture Capital Center, www.smeal.psu.edu/fcfe/garber.html

Purpose and History

The fund, established in 1999 through a $5 million commitment from Penn State Alumnus Dr. John Garber and his wife Bette, brings reality to the teaching of entrepreneurship and venture capital by enabling MBA students to become actively involved in the process of equity investment and new ventures. Students examine current investment opportunities and decide whether to invest from the fund in a particular transaction. Interaction with external private equity groups provides an opportunity for students to experience the complexities and pressures of the volatile private equity sector and to link applicant companies to other sources of help and funding.

Eligibility

Any early-stage company seeking help and investment can apply for analysis by teams of students within the Smeal College MBA program. To request consideration, nonconfidential outlines should initially be sent to fcfe@smeal.psu.edu.

Criteria

Proposals for all types of enterprises from entrepreneurs within the United States will be given consideration, provided that:

- The entrepreneur is in an early stage of building an investment and is seeking no more than $500,000 in this round.

- The entrepreneur is willing to make an investor's presentation and interact with a student team for several weeks.
- The business is sufficiently challenging that it can provide a learning experience.

Mentoring and Assistance

Students, themselves mentored by experienced faculty within the Smeal College, work closely with the entrepreneur providing valuable input.

www.wiley.com/college/kaplan

ROADMAP for

PATTERNS OF ENTREPRENEURSHIP
Sources of Financing

- ☐ Securing Early-Stage Funding
- ☐ Bootstrapping
- ☐ Using Bank Loans as a Source
- ☐ How to Use Commercial Banks
- ☐ Preparing a Loan Proposal
- ☐ Applying for a Loan
- ☐ Establishing the Terms of Debt
- ☐ Building a Relationship with a Banker
- ☐ Using Government Sources
- ☐ Small Business Innovation Research
- ☑ Angel Investors
- ☑ Understand the Venture Capital Process
- ☑ Guide to Selecting a Venture Capitalist (VC)
- ☑ Private Placements
- ☑ Learning How to Value a Business
- ☑ Earnings Valuation
- ☑ Asset Valuation
- ☑ Discounted Cash Flow Valuation
- ☑ Net Present Value (NPV) Method
- ☑ Internal Rate of Return (IRR)

CHAPTER 6

EQUITY FINANCING FOR HIGH GROWTH

> "The most important thing for a young man is to establish credit—a reputation, character."
>
> JOHN D. ROCKEFELLER

OBJECTIVES

- Learn when and how to attract angel investors.
- Describe how to attract venture capture financing and use a private placement.
- Learn the process of finding investors and targeting the right firm.
- Prepare a term sheet.
- Understand how a venture is valued.
- Understand corporate sources of funding.

CHAPTER OUTLINE

INTRODUCTION

This chapter describes the financing options for private entrepreneurial companies that are anticipating fast growth. The first sections describe the three main sources of attracting equity funding, namely, angels, "institutionalized" venture capital (VC), and formal private placements of stock. Equity funding means selling part of the ownership of the company to investors through the purchase of shares. Once entrepreneurs sell part of their company, their lives fundamentally change as the outside shareholders' primary objective is to earn a substantial return on their investment. The anticipated return will depend on the stage of the company when the investment is taken—usually the earlier the investment, the riskier the venture and therefore the higher returns that are expected. Investors can only derive the benefit of their investment when a "liquidity event" occurs and an "exit strategy" is fulfilled. This means that a new entity agrees to buy the stock in the company held by the current shareholders. The most common way for this to happen is for the company to be sold to a larger firm.

Alternatively, the company may be sold to the public via an "initial public offering," or IPO, although this is relatively rare. Clearly, if the founders' intention is to retain control of the company, and manage it for their own benefit and lifestyle, there will be a fundamental conflict of interest between the inside entrepreneurs and the external shareholders. So the golden rule is DO NOT TAKE CASH FROM EXTERNAL SHAREHOLDERS UNLESS YOU INTEND TO BUILD THE COMPANY FOR SALE. Note that this is regardless of HOW MUCH of the company you sell; sale of only 1 percent of the company fundamentally changes the way the company must be run. Many entrepreneurs starting out make the mistake of thinking that if they sell less than 50 percent of the company, they are still in control. As we shall see, investors with a minority interest can still determine how the company is run.

In the second part of the chapter, we look at how a company is valued using the different methods such as earnings and asset valuation, adjusted book value, discounted cash flow comparatives, and market valuation. A discussion of evaluating investment opportunities using the time value of money that addresses net present value and internal rate of return is also presented. The chapter closes with structuring a strategic partnership or joint venture as an alternative to seeking a private equity investment.

PROFILE: KEVIN O'CONNOR OF DOUBLECLICK—TWO SUCCESSFUL IPOs

In 1995, Kevin O'Connor, then 34, decided he wanted to start an Internet company, but he didn't really know how. He spent eight months holed up in his basement in Atlanta with his friend Dwight Merriman, looking everywhere for the "right idea"—a business that could take advantage of the Web's ability to link up with users, track their behavior online, and tailor data to them. Advertising, he thought, might fit the bill. They ended up developing a new company called Internet Advertising Network (IAN). IAN's first service was the e-mail White Page directory, Internet Address Finder.

At the same time, Poppe Tyson formed DoubleClick as its new media division in an experiment to sell ads on the then emerging Internet. In early 1996, these two ideas came together when Poppe Tyson bought IAN and merged its know-how with DoubleClick's client network. O'Connor became CEO of the new DoubleClick (www.doubleclick.com). The company raised $2 million from Poppe Tyson's parent, privately held Bozell Jacobs (since acquired by True North), and within three months, DoubleClick was delivering ads to some 30 Web sites. Later that year, DoubleClick announced it would make its tracking technology DART available to sites not in its network.

In late 1998, DoubleClick announced a public offering of 2.5 million shares of common stock for $34.43 and raised $86 million. It bought software maker NetGravity for $650 million (Net Gravity was merged with DoubleClick's Technology Solutions division), and in 1999, it bought marketing firm Abacus Direct for $1.7 billion to offer a complete suite of data targeting and marketing solutions. Again in 2000, a public offering of 7.5 million shares of common stock was sold for $90.25 per share, and $67 million was raised. Acquisitions continued into 2000 as DoubleClick took a 30 percent stake in performance-based ad network ValueClick and merged with FloNetwork to provide e-mail tools.

Kevin O'Connor, now chairman, continues to make DoubleClick Inc. a leading provider of comprehensive Internet advertising solutions for advertisers and Web publishers. He relies on his vision, perseverance, and his being at the right place at the right time to create his path to success. He is inspirational in the sense that without having an initial breakthrough idea or a background in the industry (he started in advertising), he still managed to become the CEO of a major Internet company.

EQUITY INVESTMENT FUNDAMENTALS

Public Stock

There are two basic classes of ownership in companies. The first, with which most people are familiar, is by holding shares in publicly traded companies. Usually associated with larger well-known corporations such as Ford Motor, J&J, and Citibank, public companies trade freely on stock exchanges, such as the New York Stock Exchange (NYSE) and NASDAQ, both of which are designed for trading the stock easily and transparently. In fact, many smaller companies also trade on these exchanges, which provide a "liquid market" in their stocks. Any member of the public can buy and sell these shares in this type of company. This liquidity enables inside shareholders to turn their shares into cash. When a privately held company "goes public," several benefits accrue. The private stock can now be traded openly, and insiders can convert their "illiquid asset" into cash. The company can also sell some of its own stock and hence raise further money for growth and acquisitions, and also have an easy way later, should more cash be required to sell more stock in a "secondary" offering. No wonder therefore that most entrepreneurs have a dream to "go public."

Not many of these dreams come true. Going public requires a significant amount of expensive legal work to prepare the company for such an event. Timing is critical. The stock market is very volatile, and synchronizing an IPO for a particular company with the right market timing is extremely difficult and uncertain. Often, an IPO is withdrawn on the day prior to the event, because there is not enough public demand at the price the company finds attractive. The public is fickle and follows fads, as was clear during the dot.com boom. After the bust, it was impossible to take an Internet company public for several years even if it was potentially a great company.

Private Stock

The second class of equity is ownership in private companies. When an entrepreneur starts a company, he or she, and perhaps a few other cofounders, agree how the company should be owned and issue stock in the company (see Chapter 4). They own "private equity" in their company usually in the form of common stock or participate as members in a partnership or LLC. For brevity, this is now referred to as private equity.

When a company is founded, legal contracts called membership or shareholders' agreements must be in existence as soon as there is more than one owner. An attorney should be used for preparing these contracts. They should clearly state how ownership can be transferred under different situations and how the company will be valued in these cases. For example, if one of the owners should die, there must be a way that the ownership position can be valued both for probate reasons and also to set a price for which this ownership can be bought back by the company or other designated shareholders.

Private equity has limited liquidity. Trading is usually confined to the existing shareholders of the company, and this internal trading may also have restrictions. So ownership in a private company has real value only when a liquidity event occurs.

Using Private Equity for Raising Funds

One way that a privately held company can acquire funds for its operations and growth is to sell an ownership position in the company to willing investors. Usually, a company will not need all the money to reach its goals immediately, and therefore, investments are divided into "rounds." The entrepreneur and investors have to balance several factors in choosing the size and timing of each round.

- The earlier in the company's life that the investment is sought, usually the less a company is worth. Therefore, to raise say $250,000 when there is little more than an idea and a business plan could cost the founder 50 percent of the company, for the idea at this stage is only worth $500,000. Clearly using the bootstrapping techniques described in the previous chapter to move the company further along its development path will reduce this early loss of ownership. This loss is called "dilution." In this case, the entrepreneur will have "suffered a 50 percent dilution on the first round."

- This dilution will discourage the entrepreneur from asking for more funding, even if the plan really needs $1 million to reach a key milestone.

- On the other hand, raising very small amounts of money in dribs and drabs can be a tremendous drain on the founder's time, leaving little time to actually build the company.

- Not raising enough money in the first round, and therefore being unable to meet a key milestone, could actually damage the company's reputation and make it even more difficult to raise the next round. In fact, it is not unusual in these cases that the investors demand a "down" round—that is, one in which the company's value is lower than in the previous round. This, of course, creates an even greater dilution of the ownership for the company's founder, who can end up with little ownership if things go wrong.

- The investor may not insist on too low a valuation, however, because once the ownership position of the founder is diluted down to a few percentage points, then there is no motivation left for the insiders to work hard to create value, little of which they will ever see. Smart investors are careful to leave "enough on the table" for the entrepreneur(s) so that there is enough alignment of objectives left for both parties.

These complex forces are at play every time an entrepreneur raises equity finance, and it is advisable if possible, until sufficient experience is gained, to find a trusted advisor who has gone through the process several times, to guide the negotiations.

Before seeking private investments, it is vital that a sound business plan has been prepared stating clearly when funds are required, the key milestones, and how the funds will be used. This enables the entrepreneur to determine the right time, amount, and potential sources for the funds.

Table 6-1 shows the likely targets for investments at different stages of a company's growth.

Table 6-1   Rounds of Financing.

Round	Status	Likely Sources of Funds	Expected IRR
Pre-seed	Barely an idea, rough business plan	Friends/family, bootstrapping, grants	0–10%
Seed	Prototype or proof of principal, no sales	Angels, grants, possibly a local VC firm	20–40%
A Round	Development nearly complete, first trials with customers	Angels, early-stage VC	30%+
B Round	Customers, first growth phase	VC, or other institutional sources of funds	30%+
C/D Rounds	Sufficient to get to cash flow neutrality or exit	Late-stage VCs in syndicate	20%+
Mezzanine	Prepare for sale or IPO, acquisitions	Large private equity funds	15–20%

The fewer rounds of investment that a company must go through prior to "exit," the less dilution both the founders and the early-stage investors will experience. If the company needs large amounts of capital to fulfill its plans, different investors will likely be required for later stages. It is usual for investors to work together to share the risk if the cash demands get too high for their risk profile. This is called syndicating. Investors like to choose their own syndicating partners and usually have relationships in place for this role. Entrepreneurs should question potential investors about their own "appetite" for funding and their access to syndicating partners if this is required in later rounds.

The table indicates that friends and family are usually undemanding on the annual return (internal rate of return, IRR) that they expect. They are usually helping out for personal, not financial, reasons. It is rare, however, that they have "deep enough pockets" to see the whole venture through. Other professional investors expect high rates of returns for the risk they are taking.

Classes of Stock

Once an entrepreneur seeks equity funding beyond his or her close friends and family, the structure of the investment becomes more formal. Any professional investor will require that an LLC or partnership is converted into a full corporation, usually a C-Corporation. The founders and any employees who own stock will have common shares that carry few rights except their ownership position. Investors will demand a different class of stock entitled "preferred." These shares carry with them certain preferences, the most important of which is "preference on liquidation." This means that if the company is sold at a low price or files for bankruptcy, the preferred shareholders receive their investment back first before any distribution to the founders holding common stock once any debt is paid off.

Another form of investment often used is "convertible preferred." In this case, the initial investment is made in the form of a loan sometimes referred to as a debenture. This loan will carry interest, typically a few percentage points above the current prime rate. The interest is normally accrued and not paid to the investors but of course increases the debt owed by the company. The loan can be converted at the investor's option to a defined class of preferred stock within a given time and at a valuation of the company that has normally been agreed to beforehand; the interest becomes part of the debt that is converted to equity at the time the option is taken. If the conversion is not requested, then the investor usually has the right to recall the loan plus interest. This gives the investor greater flexibility. If the company does not appear to be meeting its growth objectives and moving toward a liquidity event, then the investor can get the original sum plus interest out of the company. This is also a protection for the investor in the case that the founding entrepreneur(s) run the company as a "lifestyle" business. Calling the loan can effectively give the investor control should this happen, for it is unlikely that the company is financially strong enough to pay back the full sum owed.

As the company moves forward, additional rounds of investment will likely be required. The first investors will have insisted that they have the first right to make investments in subsequent rounds. Thus, the entrepreneur will enter into a negotiation before the funds are needed to try to reach mutually agreeable terms. This can result in the following scenarios:

- The investors are pleased with how the company is developing and wish to take all of the next round of investment. In this case, it is usually easy to reach satisfactory terms. However, the entrepreneur also has the right to find other investors who might be willing to invest at a higher valuation of the company, thereby reducing the dilution experienced by the existing shareholders. The existing investors are entitled to be informed of this intention and meet the terms that the entrepreneur finds. It is important to be open and retain a good relationship with the current investors.

- The investors do not want to make the full investment in the next round but are willing to co-invest with new sources of funds. Co-investment is common in later rounds and is called *syndication*. It allows investors to "diversify" their risk portfolio much in the same way that individual investors are advised to do for their retirement funds. In this case, the entrepreneur should negotiate the terms of the next round and then approach other investors to see if they wish to participate on these terms, or perhaps better terms. Asking the existing investors to find other sources of funds through their own networks is by far the best approach here.

- The investors decline to invest in the next round. It is important to understand the reasons for this decision. If they do not have sufficient funds to "go to the next level" or their investment objectives are not to invest at later stages, then having them talk to new investors can help raise the next round—there are legitimate reasons for no further participation. On the other hand, if they are dissatisfied with the company's performance, the entrepreneur may have difficulty attracting further investments. Any new investor will insist on talking to the existing external shareholders, and this will make them very cautious in making an investment. In this case, any new investor will likely view this as high risk, and the round will be at a lower valuation than the previous round. This will significantly dilute all the old shareholders, and the "new money" will dictate the terms of the deal. Often, in this case, the earlier investors will lose their preferences and downgrade to a common stock ownership position. Clearly, this is a bad situation for the entrepreneur and is to be avoided if at all possible

Warrants

Investors may also negotiate to receive warrants when making an investment. Warrants convey a right to purchase a certain number of shares, common or preferred as defined, within a given time period and at a stated price. The "exercise" of the warrants is at the option of the investor, not the company. As an example, assume that an investor purchases 10 percent of a company for $1 million by buying 100,000 preferred shares at $10 each. Each share purchased may have an "attached" warrant to allow the investor to buy one-half of an additional share of common stock for $6.00 within two years from the original investment. Within a two-year period the investor may exercise all or part of this right and buy more of the company at a slightly higher valuation than the original investment—$12.00 a share rather than $10.00. In this case, this new stock is common rather than preferred, and therefore the investor will have to feel pretty confident about the company's progress to buy it. On the other hand, he or she has two years to watch the company before this decision is made. If the company is not doing well, the investor is unlikely to come up with the extra funds and the warrants will run out.

Note: The question is often asked, "how much more is a preferred share worth than a common share"? The answer depends on the actual preference terms and the health and stage of the company's development. As a rule of thumb, in the very early and uncertain stages, the ratio can be as high as ten times. As the company approaches a suitable exit point for investors, this ratio approaches unity. Thus, in the warrant case above, the investor would take into account how far the company had moved forward toward an exit plan before exercising the warrants. If there was little progress, then the warrants would be worth as little as $1.20 a common share, and the purchase of the warrants would not be attractive. The company may have to raise money in a down round, which would be a better opportunity for the investor's participation.

Pre- and Post-Money Valuation

These two terms are commonly used at the time an equity investment is made. The pre-money valuation is the value that the entrepreneur and the investor agree upon as to how much the company is worth prior to any investment. The post-money is the valuation of the company immediately after the investment is made. The simplest way to reconcile these two numbers is just to add the pre-money valuation to the amount of the investment. For example, a company that is valued at $10 million upon receiving $5 million in equity investment will now be worth $15 million—the original company plus the $5 million cash now in the company's bank account. Of course, now that the money is in the bank, other possibilities for the company have opened up, and the post-money valuation may be considered higher than this number

ACTIONS   Investors will undertake a detailed analysis of your company before providing any cash. You can reduce the chance of future antipathy by being completely open with them AND carefully checking out whether they are the best partners for you, too.

for various reasons. However, the simple calculation is a good guideline to use in most cases.

Due Diligence

The term *due diligence* refers to the investigative process that prospective investors undertake prior to making an investment. This is usually broken down into at least two phases. The first is a quick evaluation on key claims made by the entrepreneur. Investors are loath to spend significant efforts until they have made some checks to see whether there are any obvious "show-stoppers." They may want to do some background checks on the principals, make sure that they own title to any intellectual property, do a short analysis of existing and potential competitors, and talk to some existing or future customers. If these check out, then they will start a complete and detailed investigation on all aspects of your business and plans. Appendix 1 shows a due diligence checklist that is typical for a professional investor. (A similar list may be used by a bank before approving a loan.) It is broad and thorough. It is mandatory that the entrepreneur provides full and complete access to this information and offers any other information that may be relevant. This is called *full disclosure,* and it is a legal responsibility imposed on anyone seeking funds from an investor or bank.

In addition, the entrepreneur should undertake due diligence on the potential investor(s) to make sure that the deal is a good fit to their investment criteria, that they have deep knowledge in the business area, that they will take an active role to help and be there for a follow-up round or can provide access to a network of future investors, and, most importantly, that they will be easy to work with during times of stress. There will be such times for sure, and investor(s) should be good partners, not enemies, when this happens. The best way to check this is to call the CEOs of companies who have already received investment from the investors and question them on the quality of the relationship. Poor due diligence and an entrepreneur's unrealistic expectations when seeking equity investment are common causes of future conflict. Building a company is difficult enough in any case; doing it with misunderstanding and with a misalignment of objectives between an entrepreneur and investors makes it impossible.

Bridge Financing

Timing investments to match a company's plans is extremely difficult. In today's climate, the time between identifying the need for additional funds and actually getting money in the bank can range from a minimum of six months to over a year. There is always the danger therefore that a company fails to raise the funds needed before running out of cash. In this case, it may be appropriate to seek "bridge" funding. Remember: a bridge spans between two places and does not hang in midair. Bridge deals require an event to happen that terminates the interim financing. An example well known to many is a bridge loan that allows someone to own two homes

Table 6-2   **Bridge Loan Example.**
Terms for $4 Million Bridge Loan for Acme Inc.

Amount	A total of up to $4 million to be done in an initial closing of $1 million and a secondary closing of $1 million and if necessary a third closing of $2 million
Institutional support	Beta Venture Partners LLC
Interest rate	6% simple interest to be paid in stock
Repayment	At the earlier of Series C close or December 31, 2004
Security interest	UCC filings on all assets (and if applicable in the Patent and Trademark Office)
Warrant coverage	Note holders will receive a warrant to purchase one share of common stock for every $2.50 invested in the bridge note.
Warrant term	5 years
Warrant exercise price	$0.01
Commitment to Class C Round	BVP will commit $7 million to the Series C Financing and will work with management to secure the $9 million follow on financing to fill out a $16 million Class C round.
Conditions of closing	Satisfactory completion of customer reference checks
Date of closing	The date of the first closing will be August 15, 2003, the date of the second closing will be October 1, 2003, and the date of the third closing, if necessary, will be November 1, 2003, unless otherwise agreed upon by the company and BVP.

at the same time during a move. If there is a contract to purchase your original home from a qualified buyer, then the bank will provide bridge financing for the period between buying the new home and selling the first home. The bridge loan is secured by the first house, and the loan is repaid precisely when the first home is sold. Bridge loans are expensive but convenient. For a company strapped for cash, current investors may agree to provide enough funding until the company has closed a new round of funding. The bridge financier must be relatively confident that the new money will be secured, so that the bridge money can be extracted or at least the investor made safe.

As expressed in the loan offer in Table 6-2, the current investors, BVP, are not willing to continue to fully fund this company, which requires $16 million of additional financing. It is willing to invest a maximum of $7 million. In order to bridge the company to its next "C" round, it will lend the company an interest-bearing sum of $4 million in stages. In addition to the interest, which will be paid in stock and not cash, the company will have a right to further invest at a very low rate for five years by exercising warrants. Both of these terms significantly dilute the ownership of the founders. The loan is secured by all of the company's assets. BVP will, however, commit to providing nearly half of the next round, which will greatly help the company raise the rest of the money. Clearly, the company has not achieved its expectations, and the deal is punitive for the company and the founders. However, they have little alternative at this stage.

Preferences and Covenants

The terms negotiated by investors when making an investment will contain several conditions that provide certain advantages over the common stockholders and certain rights to protect their interests. Private equity investment terms can become rather complicated, and the company will require the services of an attorney specializing in venture investments to guide it through the negotiations and contracts. The following list describes some of the more important terms that are met.

- *Board membership.* Board seat(s). Investors usually request a board seat in the company. If several investor groups or VCs participate (i.e., the deal is syndicated), then one investor will be the "lead." This means that they will negotiate the terms of the investment, agree on it with the co-investors, and usually take on the board representation. Investors look for a balanced board, not control of the board. Other investors might request "board visitation rights," which enables them to observe but not participate in board meetings or have voting rights.

- *Management decisions.* Investors owning preferred stock may request a right to change the management team if certain conditions are not met. This is often an emotional topic; however, it offers a wonderful chance for each party to understand its objectives. A smart entrepreneur will know whether she is the right leader to "take it all the way," or her management skills will be sorely tested once the company reaches 50 employees, for example. Often, it is better to step aside for more seasoned management to be brought in with mutual consent and take on a chairperson or technology officer role. Remember: control is not equivalent to ownership or wealth creation. Have this discussion up-front before the investment is made. It will avoid major problems later.

- *Registration rights.* Investors will insist on having "registration rights" should the company go public. This means that, in this event, their shares will convert automatically to common shares and have the same rights to be included in the public offer.

- *Later rounds.* A right of first refusal to participate in future investment rounds is granted. Investors fear that they will be diluted out of the company ownership or the company will bring in investors that the original investors do not like or trust.

- *Antidilution rights.* Antidilution provisions protect an investor from the company not meeting its objectives and from a subsequent round of investment being made at a lower valuation (i.e., a "down" round). In this case, the investors are freely issued an amount of common stock to bring their ownership position back up to their original stake so that they do not suffer dilution. The dilution in this case then falls onto the shoulders of the founders. This arrangement is also referred to as a *ratchet* clause.

- *Forcing exit.* The investors may request a *forced buyout* term, which means that if the company has not created a liquidity event within a stated time frame, the investors can take independent action and find a buyer and impose it on the board of the company. This is intended to protect investors from the founding entrepreneurs wishing to preserve the company as a lifestyle firm and not to lose their perceived control. If this clause is invoked, then clearly there is significant animosity between the insiders and the investors. A similar clause, called *demand registration rights*, allows the investors to force an IPO on the company by an agreed-upon date. These clauses are rarely exercised in full as the ability to create a viable exit may depend more on externalities. However, the existence of these clauses does enable investors to force the board to take action.

- *Piggybacking.* This gives all shareholders holding such rights to sell their stock at an IPO. An IPO may be used to sell the company's stock ("treasury stock") only in order to raise further funding for the company. It is not automatic that shareholders can offer their stock at the same time. Normally, the investment banker managing the IPO makes these decisions.

These terms and conditions may sound very complicated; indeed, they can be. However, there is one guiding principle in private equity financing that must be remembered: at each new round, EVERYTHING can and usually is renegotiated. For example, if an investor in an "A" round does not have enough capital to invest when the company looks for a "B" round investment, the new investor will often require the first investor to forego all of their preferences and rights, converting their shares to common. In the parlance of private equity, "last money in calls the shots." If the company is exceeding everyone's expectations, then the entrepreneur may be in a good position to negotiate great terms on later rounds. Unfortunately, this is not usually the case, and the entrepreneur takes the brunt of the dilution and loss of rights before any investor.

This happens for the following reason. In order to get investors to finance the company, an entrepreneur, always the optimist, will write a business plan that looks fantastic—*if* everything goes according to plan. The financial forecasts will have a "hockey-stick" sudden rise in sales and positive cash flow in year 2. If the plan is not so aggressive, then it is unlikely to attract investment. The entrepreneur knows this, but so do the investors. They are already discounting the plan when they evaluate the investment. The overenthusiastic plan therefore can be used to the detriment of the entrepreneur when they do not reach their goals by the time the next round of investment is required—usually earlier then planned. A better approach is to have a conservative plan as well as a more aggressive plan, which the company can follow if things go better than expected. Funding should only be sought for the first phase of the more conservative plan. This leaves space for slippage, and yet the situation has been set up for raising more capital at a much higher valuation should things really take off. Investors are always ready to continue funding if an entrepreneur is exceeding the plan. Startup companies rarely, if ever, follow their business plan; they will change direction many times as they learn about their environment and understand more about the opportunity they are creating. Investors welcome this flexibility, as can be reflected in the structure of the capital raising.

ANGEL INVESTORS

Angels[1] are an excellent source of raising capital and sometimes represent the best method for the entrepreneur to pursue when self-funding and friends are not a viable option. Angels are "high net-worth" individuals who have some funds they are willing to risk in startup companies. They usually invest locally because they like to have personal interaction with the entrepreneur. Often they look for investments in areas that they know well, which could range from retail stores to health products, or from real estate management to high-tech manufacturing. They may have a social agenda attached to their investments. For example, one group in Pennsylvania has invested in a chain of drug rehabilitation centers and a company that provides software for school districts to help the "no child left behind" program. They are often willing to become actively involved, and they are usually well networked into the local professional service firms. They may operate individually; more often, they work as an investment partnership. Angels are usually less rigorous in their due diligence and their push to reach an exit strategy. However, as the VCs are moving to later stage investments, and angels take over more of the earlier stage funding, they are themselves becoming more professional and demanding in their style and governance.

Angels are different from venture capitalists in that they invest their own money, in the range of $50,000 to $500,000 that companies need to get started. However, as a group the investments are significantly higher. One group funded by "angel" Michael Egan, former chairman of Alamo Rent-A-Car, invested $20 million in The Globe.com's startup. VCs, by contrast, invest institutional funds, and typically they are likely to invest later in a company's life, supplying $1 million or more to both early-stage and mid-stage companies. Angels always review potential deals carefully. They review business plans, require a strong management team, and perform financial review and analysis. Angels also expect the companies they invest in to go public or to be acquired in five to seven years, not one to two years. Angels require an equity stake and a return of 20 to 35 percent on their investment, and some require a seat on the Board of Directors.[2]

The best method to locate angel investors is through word of mouth. It is best to come recommended or to seek a referral from a friend or business associate. Another option is to receive an invitation to present to a local angel group. Angel groups offer an opportunity to present the company to a group of angels in one session and determine the financial viability quickly. Entrepreneurs should explore friends, acquaintances, the Chamber of Commerce, and any entrepreneurial groups in the state. Angel networks and matchmaking services set up by universities and state development agencies are other sources to utilize.[3] Sometimes for a small fee ranging from $100 to $300 your company can be listed in the organization database. (Investor contacts and angel networks are listed in the resource section at the end of this chapter.)

Sourcing Angel Opportunities

Angels are always looking for new deal opportunities; this is called *sourcing*. The best angels are those who can bring contacts, experience, and long-term financing. Contacts means helping the company find customers, employees, and partners to assist the company. For experience, the angel should understand the business and be able to assist the company in deals and important issues. The financing of the business may require additional funds in the future; the ideal angel has the financial support to continue to support the company.

The number of angel investors grew at 60 percent during the stock market boom years, but since then they have become more reticent in investing, as their own net worths have significantly declined with the fall of the public stock markets. Nevertheless, they are still an important source of funds. Organized groups of angels are increasing and are investing substantial sums. Table 6-3 provides data on angel investing.

Table 6-3   **Typical Profile of Angels Investors.**

Average number of members in an angel group	10–25
Average group investment per year	$2 million to $5 million
Average group investment in a startup	$350,000
Percentage of companies funded, out of all that presented	33 percent
Estimated total invested per year by angels	$54 billion

UNDERSTANDING THE VENTURE CAPITAL PROCESS

How VC Firms Work

Nearly all venture capital firms (VCs) are organized as a partnership. A group of professional managers gets together to manage high-risk private equity investments for investors who wish to participate in this sector of the investment market. The managers form a legal partnership and assume the role of general partners. (More about partnerships can be found in Chapter 4.) This means that they have the authority to make decisions on investments that the partnership makes. The partners prepare a "prospectus" describing in detail how much money they are trying to raise for their VC fund and how the money will be used. It also details how the profits from the fund will be distributed back to the limited partner investors. A typical VC fund has a defined life, typically 10 years; this is called a *closed-end fund*. At the end of this period, all the assets held by the partnership must be converted into liquid assets and the proceeds distributed according to the terms of the partnership agreement. There may be a provision by which certain assets can be held for up to, say, three years further in order to create a higher value for the fund, but after 10 years no further investments can be made.

The general partners use the prospectus to solicit commitments to their fund. Typical sources of money are corporate, state, and university pension funds and endowments, high net-worth individuals, and large funds under management by other money managers. All of these sources of money are looking to diversify their own investments by putting a small percentage of their cash into a high-risk, high-gain fund managed by professionals who understand the small company environment. The size of funds raised has grown significantly, and now a fund of $500 million would be considered a small to mid-sized fund. As the size of funds has grown, it has resulted in VC investments moving toward later stage opportunities. This is a direct result of the difficulty of putting so much money to work; it takes just as long to undertake due diligence for a $250,000 investment as a $10 million investment. If the partnership has raised $500 million, then there is just not enough partner time to make many small investments and sit on a myriad boards. Thus, these funds look to put a total investment of over $10 million into one opportunity, even if it is in two or three rounds.

Once the partnership has commitments for the amount it was seeking by having sufficient "subscription agreements" signed, the partners then actively look for opportunities to invest in. Usually, any VC firm is very focused on what sort of companies it seeks (see below). When an opportunity is found, one or two of the partners undertake a full due diligence exercise, perhaps taking several months, before an investment decision is made (see Appendix 1). Prior to making this large investment in time and resources, the VCs agree on the terms of a possible investment, which is memorialized in a "term sheet." Although this is a "good faith" rather than a binding document, it does restrict the entrepreneur seeking other investors during the period of the agreement. Most VC firms use a standard form of term sheet; a typical pro forma is shown in Appendix 2. If the due diligence meets the partners' requirements, a vote is taken; usually a majority or sometimes a unanimous agreement is sought before the investment is made. Attorneys then draft the final shareholders' agreement, and the investment is made. The VC general partner makes a "call" on the limited partners who have a short time to transfer the funds to the company. Should they default, they lose all rights, including the value of the investments in which they may already have participated. At the same time, each general partner is usually required to invest personally alongside the limited partners, thus aligning their interests and making sure they "have some skin in the game."

In order to pay for the running of the VC office, including partners' salaries and expenses, the investors pay a fee of typically 2.5 percent of funds invested annually. When a liquidity event occurs so that one of the investments is turned into cash, the distribution agreement determines how the proceeds will be used. Typically, the limited partners receive all of their investment back first, and then the rest is split 80:20 between the limited partners and the general partners. As an example, let us assume that an investment of $10 million has been made in Acme Inc. and the company is sold returning $100 million to the VC's. Then the limited partner investors would receive $10 million "off the top" and $72 million of the remainder. The general partners would share $18 million between them.

The most important thing for an entrepreneur to understand about a VC firm is that all interests are focused to maximize the return on investment; there is no other agenda. If the company is successful and achieves a high value upon exit, then everyone wins. If the VC firm fails to help the company and does not make sure that the management is well motivated, they and their investors lose too. So negotiating with a VC firm becomes easier if the entrepreneur understands these motivations and realizes that the aim is to make the pie bigger for everyone rather than to make the entrepreneur's slice smaller.

Venture capital firms look for generally larger deals and more impressive returns than angel investors. Also, angels will invest in the early stages of a company, whereas venture capitalists usually do not invest until a product or service can be demonstrated or a prototype is ready for commercialization. Some venture capital firms specialize in very early-stage funding, but this is the exception rather than the rule. Many venture capital firms want to invest where the time horizon is relatively short, since they must liquidate their investments and provide cash returns to their investors over a comparatively short period of time. Some venture capital firms focus on specific industries or stages of investment, such as bridge financing. In addition to raising capital, venture capitalists can be a valuable asset to the company in terms of their contacts, market expertise, and business strategy. As with angels, it is imperative to locate potential investors whose skills, experience, and reputation complement the entrepreneur and the company. The most critical element in a successful venture capital relationship is the close alignment of the entrepreneurs' objectives with those of the venture capitalists. The entrepreneur should reach agreement on several key aspects when negotiating a deal with venture capitalists, including, What are the investment objectives? How much control will be given up? And are the entrepreneur's needs compatible with the venture capitalists for a successful result?

The factors that might influence a venture capital firm's funding decisions are:

- **Specialized Industries for the Venture**
  Many venture capitalists specialize in a narrow set of industries. Some specialize in semiconductors, others in health-care devices, biotech, or Internet services. Still

others invest in "low-tech" businesses such as retail stores and service businesses. Knowing what industries a venture capital firm invests in will help in locating appropriate funding and demonstrate past performance in similar cases.

- **The Location of the Venture**
  Some venture capitalists are located in Silicon Valley, California, because traditionally, a large number of technology startups began in this geographic area. Others are located in large cities. This does not mean the firm will invest only in their area. Although venture capital firms prefer to invest in companies that are located near them, others have a national or global scope. However, entrepreneurs will fare better if they are located within two hours' driving time of the VC head office, for they are likely to receive more help and attention from the senior partners than from more junior staff.

- **Stage of Fund**
  In a 10-year life fund, investments made early on have a longer time to mature to an exit, and the VC firm will have more patience. As the fund nears the termination date, it is unable to make longer term investments. This would not be a good fit with, say, an early-stage biotech opportunity that may take 10 years of patient investment to reach an exit. However, late-stage funds may be suitable for a short bridge finance.

- **Stage of Development**
  Although some firms like to invest in a startup company, others like to invest in later stages of development. The key stages of development that venture firms consider are divided into three sectors—early stage, expansion, and acquisitions/buyout—and are based on the type of financing each requires. The following details each of these stages.

  Early-Stage Financing
  - Seed financing is the initial investment required to prove a concept (e.g., to build a prototype or conduct market research) and qualify for startup financing.
  - Startup financing is typically required to build a management team and bring a product service to market.
  - First-stage financing is often needed when startup financing is depleted and a company needs to expand its marketing and/or sales capabilities to grow the business.

  Expansion Financing
  - Second-stage financing is used by companies that are shipping products (or delivering services) but need additional funds for working capital requirements and to grow faster than internal cash flow will allow.
  - Mezzanine financing is typically used to fund substantial growth and/or expansion of companies that are up and running and are beyond breakeven volumes. Capital to fund a plant expansion or to move into a new geographic market is often categorized within this class of funding.

  Bridge financing is sometimes needed when a company is about to go public and requires capital until the IPO event. Usually, bridge financing is short term and is repaid with proceeds from the public offering. This form of bridge financing is less burdensome than that taken when the company is under duress.

  Acquisitions/Buyouts Financing
  - This type of financing is used to fund the acquisitions or buyouts of existing businesses. In many cases, these are mature businesses that are funded

Venture capitalists can also be a valuable asset to the company in terms of their network of personal contacts to attract customers, assist in building partners, and as board members participate in business strategy. Make sure to find potential investors whose experience and reputation complement the venture.

with a large component of debt or equity capital (leveraged buyouts). The KKR [Kohlberg Kravis Roberts & Co. (www.KKR.com)] acquisition of RJR/Nabisco was one of the more famous (and largest) examples of this type of transaction.

Table 6-4 shows the level of recent VC investing. These numbers should be compared with those in Table 6-3. Note that angels actually invest *more* than professional VC firms. Together, however, they represent only a minority of the funding accessed by early-stage companies, indicating the importance of the financing methods discussed in Chapter 5.

Table 6-4   **Recent Venture Capital Statistics.**

Venture Capitalists' Cash Flow[4]

VC Investments in 2003 (in billions)	**19.2**
VC Investments in 2004 (in billions)	**21.4**
Venture capitalists as a group invest huge amounts of money.	
VC Investments in 3rd Quarter in 2004 (in billions)	**4.6**
VC Investments in 4th Quarter in 2004 (in billions)	**5.3**
A small fraction of new companies ever receive venture capital	
Number of deals in 2004	**2,878**

This is well down from 2000 when the number of deals was 5,380, however; we are still recovering from the "dot.com" bubble.

COMPANIES USE VENTURE CAPITAL FROM THEIR RESEARCH DEVELOPMENT BUDGET

Fortune 500 companies use funds from their Research and Development Budget to invest in startups and growing businesses. Small investments by large corporations can have an impact on the future of new products and services. Investment funds from corporations can range from $2 million to $25 million depending on the opportunity. The initial equity they receive can be 20 percent plus, for a $250,000 to $500,000 investment.

Future investment in the companies is based on performance milestones. The companies usually take a board seat on the Board of Directors to observe the company goals and plans and to provide guidance as needed. An example is

COMPANIES USE VENTURE CAPITAL FROM THEIR RESEARCH DEVELOPMENT BUDGET (cont.)

United Parcel Service, which established a 2+ million fund. The group reviews over 100 business plans and invests in only 5 to 10 percent. A sponsor group in the company who may have a need for the business ideas justifies the investments. As an example, UPS invested in Vidco Networks—a digital document security. Recently, there has been a trend for corporations to co-invest with professional VC firms.

"The single best thing any startup can do is to find a beta customer or a customer sponsor as early as possible. This immediately gives you legitimacy in that you have moved from a business concept in a plan to solving a real problem. It also makes you smarter about what real customers want and will pay for. Ideally these beta sites become references and sources of funding."

JAMES B. SANDERS,
President, Columbia Group, Investor and Consultant to High Tech Startups. Adjunct Professor of Entrepreneurship University of Maryland

GUIDE TO SELECTING A VENTURE CAPITALIST (VC)

1. *Scrutinize the business with a critical eye*. Can the business give the returns that a venture capitalist demands? Work out solid financial projections to prove the results to the venture capitalist.

2. *Beef up management*. Venture capitalists invest in startups, but they usually don't want unseasoned executives. Everyone has strengths and weaknesses. Hire staffers who can make up the deficits.

3. *Keep a high profile so the VCs will visit*. For example, Edison Venture Fund, a venture capital firm in Lawrenceville, New Jersey, initiates contact with about 35 percent of the companies it funds. "We've already heard good things about the company and have researched their potential," says managing partner John Martinson, who also serves as chairman of the National Association of Venture Capitalists.

4. *Target the search*. Look for firms that specialize in the industry and the size of investment.

5. *Keep a lookout*. Look for smaller VC firms that may be more flexible and more receptive to investing in a company.

6. *Investigate possible venture partners*. One should treat the method of locating venture capitalists as though they were a customer. Find out what the needs are for the venture capitalist so that when a visit is made, the meeting can be more successful.

Venture capitalists like to invest in companies that include some "bootstrapping" techniques in their plans as a way of reducing their investment and risks.

ROADMAP

ACTIONS

A private placement memorandum is another alternative for raising capital. A business plan and a prospectus explaining the risks, issues, and procedures of the investment are offered. Private placements should be done with the advice of an attorney who knows the federal laws as well as those of the state in which the business will operate.

PRIVATE PLACEMENTS

A private placement involves selling stock in a private company to investors. Federal and state laws regulate these activities and determine how the offerings are made. The investors are solicited with a private placement memorandum that involves a business plan and a prospectus explaining the risks, issues, and procedures of the investment. Private placements should be done with the advice of an attorney who knows the federal laws as well as the laws of the state in which the new business will be run. Private placements are less expensive and take less time to achieve than a public offering. Each state has standardized disclosure and offering documents that must be followed. Some states require a registration process and others do not. Also, private placements are not exempt from the issue of antifraud provisions. This means that the company must give potential investors the information they need to make a well-informed decision.[5]

The Securities Act of 1933 states that securities may not be issued unless they are registered or an exemption from registration is available. The typical exemption would be Regulation D, adopted by the SEC in 1982. This details the SEC rules governing the exemptions from registration for private placements and limited offerings. The intent was to make capital markets more accessible to businesses and to simplify the private offering process for investors who met the requirements. The exemptions under regulation D used for a private placement are commonly referred to by their rule number as follows:

The Rule 504: Sell up to a $1 million limit in 12 months' time to the number of investors, whether or not they are sophisticated. No requirement of disclosure and no advertising restrictions on resale of stock are required. Sophisticated refers to investors who have a net worth of $1 million or salaries over $250,000 annually for the previous two years.

The Rule 505: Sell up to $5 million in 12 months of unregistered securities. There can be no more than 35 unaccredited investors, no requirement of disclosure to accredited investors but disclosure to nonaccredited investors, no advertising, or restrictions on resale.

The Rule 506: There is no limitation to selling stock. There is a maximum of 35 nonaccredited investors (nonaccredited investors must be able to evaluate merit and risks), and there is no requirement of disclosure to accredited investors.

LEARNING HOW TO VALUE A BUSINESS

Any private equity investment requires that the entrepreneur and the investors reach an agreement on the pre-money value of the company, for this determines how much of the company the investors will own on closing the transaction. A number of valuation methods can be applied. The later the stage of the investment round, when there is likely to be a history of sales and operations and it is easier to predict future performance, the more precise the valuation. In this case, financial analytical techniques can be used. However, in early rounds when there is little history on which to base future performance, and there are still many unknowns to be explored, it is much harder to establish a valuation. This section describes the various valuation methods and when they are applied.

Early-Stage Investments

The first step taken by investors looking at a seed or early-stage company is to estimate the company's future value by looking at forecasted earnings (profits) at the planned exit date of usually three to five years, and multiplying those earnings by a factor that is relevant to the industry. In growth industries, such as computing or telecommunications, investors might use an earnings multiple between 15 and 25. In a consumer-oriented business, a multiple of 2 to 10 times earnings might be used. For example, a health-care company forecast annual sales of $3 million at the end of three years, with a profit of just over $1 million. Multiplying the forecasted profit by 10 yields an estimated value of $10 million. This is the value one could assume for a company if it went public or were offered for sale. Investors use this figure to indicate whether a company will be large enough someday to make their investment worthwhile and to determine whether their percentage of ownership in the company would be commensurate with the amount of their investment.[6] In this case, assume an annual internal rate of return of 30 percent is sought after three years. This is equivalent to an increase in value of 2.2 times over this period. Thus, the present value of the company to provide this level of return is $4.55 million, postinvestment. If the investors provide $1 million for the company now, they need to own 22 percent of the company to meet their goal. This calculation provides the investor with a starting point for negotiating the value. However, they will discount the exit value, knowing that the company will probably fall short of its plans, which are overoptimistic. Therefore, the exit may be later than anticipated. More details on how to calculate an internal rate of return are covered later in this chapter.

The investors will consider other factors regarding exit valuation. As illustrated in the CoreTek case at the end of the chapter, the valuation at exit of $1.35 billion was high, not because of any earnings forecast, but because the oligarchical structure of the market sector drove the value up. An everyday analogy is the price that an owner of a key piece of real estate might capture if it is the last house blocking a major subdivision development by a major real estate investor. The value is related to the overall project and not the simple value of the house as a dwelling. Thus, an investor is likely to look at the structure and dynamics of the industry sector targeted for an exit to determine whether this might provide a premium over a purely financially driven sale. Concentrated markets where there are well-defined and intense competitive forces produce higher valuations than unstructured sectors where there are no clear competitive factors at play. Investors will also look for similar transactions ("comps") where a comparable company in the same field has recently been acquired or been taken public and can be used to benchmark a potential exit price. Entrepreneurs must also realize that certain fields become "hot" when valuations greatly exceed any that can reasonably be quantified on purely financial calculations. This was certainly the case during the dot.com bubble where companies with no believable plans to ever be profitable still attracted enormous valuations in what is termed a "feeding frenzy" by investors and acquirers. We are now well past this phase, and valuations have returned to levels that can be more soundly justified based on purely financial grounds.

In the end, all of the valuation methods, though helpful in establishing a basis for discussions, are overridden by the negotiations between the company's board and the investors where other factors come into play.

At later stages in the company's growth, the major factor that determines the value of a business is the cash flow and generation of profits in the marketplace. Other valuation factors include the history, characteristics, and industry in which the business operates as well as the strength and weakness of the management team and risks in investing in the business.

Motivational Issues

Investors must take into account the need to maintain the enthusiasm and drive of the key persons in the company. Entrepreneurial founders seeking equity finance expect to create a significant amount of personal wealth by building their dream company. In this regard they are aligned with the investors. However, if the investors, in order to get a high return, insist on taking too much of the company, this may demotivate the insiders, reducing the company's passion to succeed. This hurts everyone, and investors, especially at the earlier rounds of investment, are wise to accept a somewhat higher valuation. They are, after all, receiving preferred stock, which protects their investment to some extent, and they are in a position to readjust their ownership position during subsequent rounds, where there are more data available to establish an firmer valuation. Entrepreneurs usually have an inflated view of what the company is worth in the first round of investment and may have to accept a valuation well below their expectations. They should not base the decision solely on the valuation offered, but on whether they believe the investors are acting as partners and will help to grow the company. A good rule for any negotiation in business is: "if both parties feel that they did not get what they hoped for but feel that they can live with the deal and are keen to proceed, then the chance of a solid, lasting partnership is high." If one party believes that it "got one over" on the other, there is a high chance that the partnership will hit rough water later when the going gets tough.

Later-Stage Valuation: Key Factors

Valuation skills to guide entrepreneurs for business decisions are prerequisites for success in today's competitive environment. As an example, the key issue companies confront when raising equity funds or going public with an IPO is determining a valuation for the company and how much the new investors will receive for funding the company. Business valuations should always be considered as a starting point for the buyer and seller.[7] The goal is to determine a working valuation from which one can negotiate a fair price. The key factor in the value of any later-stage business is the focus on the company's cash flow and its ability to generate consistent profits in the marketplace. Other valuation factors include the history, characteristics, and industry in which the business operates, the strength and weakness of the management team, the growth trajectory of the company, and risks in investing in the business. Another financial factor to consider in the analysis is comparing the company to other companies in the industry and the stock price of similar companies in the industry. This can include the price to earnings ratio of similar companies and understanding the company's financial condition.

The valuation process involves trial and error; there is no single best method. The best is a combination of valuation methods that may apply to a given situation.

PROFILE: RON HEFFERNAN OF LEAD DOG DIGITAL

Then: Started a design and application company and was acquired
Now: Bought back the company

You don't have to talk to Ron Heffernan very long to realize that he is a true entrepreneur. He is dedicated to his employees, and he is proud of his office, the business, and the creative ideas that are generated from within its walls. However, true to the entrepreneur, his growth and success have not come without making mistakes, learning from them, and overcoming many challenges along the way. And few, like Ron, experience the unique reward of selling their original company only to buy it back because of a belief in the product and a dedication to those who helped build it in the first place.

The idea to start Lead Dog Design (LDD) in 1994 was inspired by Ron's wife (then girlfriend), Lucia Chang. Ron was witness to Lucia's late nights and frustration stemming from the unacceptable work she was receiving from the creative consultants working for her firm at the time. One night when Lucia came home complaining, Ron said, "quit and we will start a design ship." And so Lead Dog Design was born. Having never been involved in the Internet, Ron and his partners had to learn the business from the ground up, creating and implementing every procedure and process on their own.

As LDD continued to grow and established itself, others began to take an interest. In 1999, Lead Dog Design was courted and eventually acquired by Iconixx. However, because of a changing economy and the crash of the dot.com world, Iconixx started to downsize dramatically. At this stage Ron could have taken an admirable severance package and headed for the beach, but he felt that by doing so he would have failed his employees who would lose their jobs and get nothing from the deal. These are the same people who Ron believed were truly responsible for building the company to its worth before the acquisition. Instead, Ron negotiated the repurchase of the company under the new name of Lead Dog Digital.

EARNINGS VALUATION

Earnings Valuation
This approach is more suitable for a company with an established track record[8] and involves valuing the business based on:

- Historical earnings: valuation based on how profitable the business has been in the past.
- Future earnings: the most widely used method of valuing a business that provides the investor with the best estimate of the probable return on investment.

Once the buyer or seller has decided on the time frame (i.e., historical versus future earnings), the earnings figure must be multiplied by a factor to determine its value. Generally, a price/earnings (P/E) multiple is used. For example, if the company is expected to have earnings of $1.5 million in five years and if similar companies are likely to go public at a price to earnings ratio of 10, the company is projected to be worth $15 million five years from now.

The appropriate price-earnings multiple is selected based on norms of the industry and the investment risk. The search for a similar company must be classified in the same industry; the company should share similar markets and have similar products and earnings. A higher multiple is used for a high-risk business and a lower multiple for a low-risk business. Higher multiples are typically applied to companies with higher earnings growth. Growth is directly tied to multiples. Higher growth companies receive higher market multiples (hi-tech, etc.), and lower growth companies or cyclical companies, whose earnings have peaked, typically receive lower multiples (e.g., basic industry or airlines). For example, a low-risk business in an industry with a five times earning multiple would be valued at $7.5 million in the above example.

The P/E ratio is also used to value both publicly traded corporations and privately held companies.[9] To value a private company in a particular industry, research a set of "comparable publicly traded companies" ("comps") to benchmark the private company. Compute the P/E and other valuation ratios for the public comparables. After comparing many financial measures and growth prospects of the private company versus the public company, choose an appropriate P/E multiple based on the public company P/Es. This multiple chosen for the private company is the estimate of the P/E that the market would apply to this company if it were public. This is basically the same process that investment bankers/underwriters undertake for a public company. Also, valuation is determined by dividing the market price of the common stock by the earnings per share. As an example, for a company with 300,000 shares of common stock, trading at $5 per share and net income of $1 share, the P/E would be $5 ($5 divided by $1). In addition, since the company has 300,000 shares of common stock, the valuation of the enterprise would now be $1.5 million (300,000 shares × $5).

When determining valuation of a company that is not publicly held, a market price must be obtained. One method is to use the capitalization rate assumption. For example:

Shares of Common Stock	$100,000
1999 Net Income	$100,000
Assume 15% Capitalization Rate	6.7 price/earnings multiple (derived by dividing 1 into 15)
Price per Share	$6.70
Value of Company ($100,000 × $6.70)	$670,000

Net income for the last year is determined and then capitalized using a P/E multiple. A 15 percent capitalization rate is often used, which is equivalent to a P/E multiple of 6.7 (1 divided by 0.15). If a business has an excellent growth rate, a low capitalization rate can be used, say, 5 percent (a multiple of 20).

In contrast, if the business is stable (low growth rate), a capitalization rate of 10 percent can be used (a multiple of 10). Whichever capitalization rate and multiple are used, the total number of shares outstanding multiplied by the value per share gives the value of the company.

Valuation as stated earlier is a judgmental process involving trial and error. There are several techniques of valuation—no single one can provide the "right" answer. The best, as noted, is a combination of methods that may apply to a given situation.

Fixed Price Example for Two Partners

This approach is used in a buy/sell agreement and is also referred to as a formula approach. Let's assume that two partners equally own a company and 100,000 shares of common stock (a total of 200,000 shares outstanding). The company's net income is $200,000. Here are two basic values to consider calculating a share price:

Example 1:

Assets	$1,000,000
Liabilities	$ 600,000
Net Book Value	400,000
	$1,000,000
Book Value per Share	$2.00
Earnings per Share	$1.00

Example 2:

If we assume a price-earnings multiple of 10 on the earnings per share of $1.00, the value of each share of stock is $10.00. The partners can agree to place a 50 percent weight on the book value per share and 50 percent on the multiple of earnings value. Based on these two assumptions, the weighted value per share would be $6, computed as follows:

Method	Value	Weight	Weighted Value
Book Value	$ 2	50%	$1
Multiple of Earnings	$10	50%	$5
		100%	$6

ASSET VALUATION

Asset valuation[10] is based on the worth of the business's assets. This is a useful starting point for negotiations, for it constitutes the *minimum* value of the business. It would not be appropriate to value most companies using an asset-based approach, especially in the case where the company is a typical earnings-based concern. For example, on average the market valuation of the largest 500 companies in the United States (the S&P 500) is approximately three times their asset value. Shareholders place significant value on so-called intangible assets and other factors. The asset approach is most appropriate when used in a liquidation scenario and/or in valuing an asset-based company such as a real estate holding company or investment holding company. Assets can be valued as follows:

- *Book value*: equals the total net worth or stockholders' equity of the company, as reflected on the balance sheet.
- *Adjusted book value*: adjusts for discrepancies between the stated book value and the actual market value of assets, such as machinery and equipment—which have depreciated; or land—which has appreciated the book value.

● *Liquidation value*: adjusts for the value of assets if the company had to dispose of those assets in a "quick sale." Liquidation value is the amount that can be realized if the company's operations cease and the assets are sold over a reasonable period of time, with the company receiving an auction price for each asset. The first step is to determine the value of the assets and then deduct the liabilities to arrive at the adjusted net assets of the company. The next step is to determine the cost associated with the sale of the assets; legal, accounting, and administrative expenses must be deducted. Let's look at an adjusted book value example, as shown in the following table:

Assets	Book Value	Market Value
Liquid assets	$53,429	$53,429
Receivables	$622,000	$573,983
Inventory	$422,000	$468,184
Equipment/fixtures	$64,255	$94,313
Real property	$250,000	$425,000
Other property	$17,000	$17,000
Liabilities		
Short-term liabilities	$644,140	$644,140
Long-term liabilities	$501,106	$501,106
Net book value	$283,438	
Adjusted book value		$486,663

Now let's look at an example of liquidation value:

Assets	Liquidation	Book Value	Value
Cash	100%	$ 7,000	$ 7,000
Accounts receivable	70	200,000	140,000
Inventories/computers	50	100,000	50,000
Land and buildings	100	250,000	250,000
Equipment	80	100,000	80,000
Other assets	50	80,000	40,000
Total		$ 800,000	$630,000
Less: liabilities			$(400,000)
Cost of liquidation, commissions			$(30,000)
Net liquidation value			$200,000

DISCOUNTED CASH FLOW VALUATION

The real value of any ongoing business is its future earning power.[11] Accordingly, this approach is most often used to value a business. The discounted cash flow method projects future earnings over a three- or five-year period and then calculates their present value using a certain discount or present value rate (e.g., 15 percent). The total of each year's projected earnings is the company's value. The basic principle underlying this method is that a dollar earned in the future is worth less than a dollar earned today. Thus, it is not only the amount of projected income (or net cash flow) that a company is expected to generate that determines its value but also the timing of that income. This method can be used for companies at any stage, but for an early-stage company, where greater uncertainty is attributed to future cash flow forecasts, a higher discount rate is used to account for the larger risk and uncertainty.

In discounted cash flow valuation, the value of a company is the present value of the expected cash flows that will be generated by the company's assets. Every asset has an intrinsic value that can be estimated, based on its characteristics in terms of cash flows, growth, and risk that it can generate.

Information that is needed to use discounted cash flow valuation includes data on the estimated life of the asset, the cash flow forecasts during the life of the asset, and the discount rate to apply to these cash flows. The present value is then calculated according to the following formula.

$$\text{Value} = \sum_{t\,=\,1}^{T\,=\,\text{CF}} \frac{t}{(t + r)t}$$

where CF is the cash flow in period t, r is the discount rate appropriate given the riskiness of the cash flow, and t is the life of the asset. For an asset to have value, the expected cash flows have to be positive some time over the life of the asset. Assets that generate cash flows early in their life will be worth more than assets that generate cash flows later; the latter may, however, have greater growth and higher cash flows to compensate.

The Steps Involved in Discounted Cash Flow

First, estimate the discount rate or rates to use in the valuation. Discount rate can be either a cost of equity (if doing an equity valuation) or a cost of capital (if valuating the firm). Discount rate can be in nominal terms or real terms, depending on whether the cash flows are nominal or real. Discount rate can vary across time. Discounts are higher when there is a greater uncertainty in future cash flows.

Next, estimate the current earnings and cash flows of the company to either equity investors or stakeholders. Estimate the future earnings and cash flows on the asset being valued, generally by estimating an expected growth rate in earnings. Finally, estimate when the firm will reach "stable growth" and what characteristics it will have when it does. Now, calculate and value the discounted cash flow (DCF).

When using this approach in valuing a company, one must decide how to value the cash flows after the forecast period is over. If you were to limit your DCF calculation to just the three or five years in the forecast, you would omit any value that would accrue from year 6 and beyond. The way this "value" is typically captured, as discussed earlier, is by using some P/E to indicate what the selling value of the business would be after year 6, for example.

Let's assume that you will receive $100,000 today and then $100,000 a year over the next four years. What is today's value (present value) of the total $500,000 income stream? To determine the value of the transaction, you must use present value factors. Now let's construct a table that would show you how the total $500,000 payments would be valued today and over the next four years. To compute the value, indicate the amounts by year and apply an 18 percent present value factor to each amount.

Today's Value of Income

Year	Inflow	18% PV Factor	Value Today
Today	$100,000	1.000	$100,000
1	100,000	0.847	84,700
2	100,000	0.718	71,800
3	100,000	0.609	60,900
4	100,000	0.516	51,600
	$500,000	3.690	$369,000

As shown, the total income of $500,000 over five years is worth (today) $369,000. That represents 30 percent less than the $500,000 you thought you were going to receive over the five-year period.

LEARN TO EVALUATE INVESTMENT OPPORTUNITIES: TIME VALUE OF MONEY APPROACHES

In evaluating an investment opportunity, an investor must consider not only how much cash he or she will give out and ultimately receive but also when the cash is received or paid. The *time value of money* approach recognizes that it is better to receive a dollar today than it is to receive a dollar next year or any other time in the future. This is because the dollar received today can be invested so that at the end of the year, it amounts to more than a dollar. It also considers the decrease in the value of a dollar over time due to inflation.

In making an investment, a company invests money today in the hopes of receiving more money in the future. Obviously, a company would not invest money in a project unless it expected the total amount of funds received in the future to exceed the amount of the original investment. But by how much must the future cash flows exceed the original investment? Because money in the future is not equivalent to money today, we must develop a way of converting future dollars into their equivalent current, or present, value.

NET PRESENT VALUE (NPV) METHOD

The net present value (NPV) method is an alternative method[12] for determining whether to make an investment. It is usually applied to later-stage investments or in making investment decisions within a company on whether to undertake a planned project. To illustrate the method, let us evaluate an investment opportunity using the NPV method. A trucking company wants to purchase engine testing equipment. The equipment will have a five-year life. Each year, it will save the company $2,000 in wasted current operation, and it will also reduce labor costs by $20,000. It is estimated that the engine equipment will require maintenance costs of $1,000 per year. The equipment costs $70,000, and it is expected to have a residual value of $5,000 at the end of five years. Management has determined that the rate of return required on any new initiative is 12 percent. Should the company invest in the new equipment?

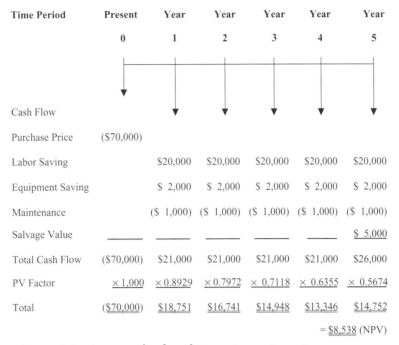

Time Period	Present	Year	Year	Year	Year	Year
	0	**1**	**2**	**3**	**4**	**5**
Cash Flow						
Purchase Price	($70,000)					
Labor Saving		$20,000	$20,000	$20,000	$20,000	$20,000
Equipment Saving		$ 2,000	$ 2,000	$ 2,000	$ 2,000	$ 2,000
Maintenance		($ 1,000)	($ 1,000)	($ 1,000)	($ 1,000)	($ 1,000)
Salvage Value						$ 5,000
Total Cash Flow	($70,000)	$21,000	$21,000	$21,000	$21,000	$26,000
PV Factor	× 1,000	× 0.8929	× 0.7972	× 0.7118	× 0.6355	× 0.5674
Total	($70,000)	$18,751	$16,741	$14,948	$13,346	$14,752

$$= \$8,538 \text{ (NPV)}$$

Figure 6-1   An example of trucking engine equipment.

The Steps Involved in the Net Present Method

The first step in using the net present value method is to identify the amount and time period of each cash flow associated with a potential investment. Investment projects have both cash inflows (which are positive) and cash outflows (which are negative).

The second step is to equate or discount the cash flows to their present values using a required rate of return, which is the minimum return that management wants to earn on investments.

The third and final step is to evaluate the net present value. The sum of the present values of all cash flows (inflows and outflows) is the net present value (NPV) of the investment. If the NPV is zero, the investment is generating a rate of return exactly equal to the required rate of return. Thus, the investment should be undertaken. If the NPV is positive, it should also be undertaken because it is generating a rate of return that is even greater than the required rate of return. Investment opportunities that have a negative NPV are not accepted because their rate of return is less than the required rate of return.

The example presented in Figure 6-1 includes present value (PV) factors for each year's cash flow total. Consider first the $70,000 cash outflow created by purchase of the equipment. Note that the present value factor associated with the $70,000 purchase price is 1.0000. Because this amount is going to be spent immediately, it is already expressed in terms of its present value. Now consider the cash flows in year 1. In this year, the net cash inflow is $21,000. The present value factor for an amount received at the end of year 1 using a 12 percent rate of return is 0.8929 (see Table 6-5, Present Value of $1). Multiplying the present value factor by the cash inflow of $21,000 indicates that the present value of the net cash inflow in year 1 is $18,751. The net present value of the investment in testing engine equipment is found by summing the present values of the cash flows in each year. This amounts

Table 6-5   **Present Value of 1 Due in _n_ Periods.**

	6%	7%	8%	9%	10%	11%	12%	13%	14%	15%	16%	20%	30%
1	0.9434	0.9346	0.9259	0.9174	0.9091	0.9009	0.8929	0.8850	0.8772	0.8696	0.8621	0.8333	0.7692
2	0.8900	0.8734	0.8573	0.8417	0.8264	0.8116	0.7972	0.7831	0.7695	0.7561	0.7432	0.6944	0.5917
3	0.8396	0.8163	0.7938	0.7722	0.7513	0.7312	0.7118	0.6931	0.6750	0.6575	0.6407	0.5787	0.4552
4	0.7921	0.7629	0.7350	0.7084	0.6830	0.6587	0.6355	0.6133	0.5921	0.5718	0.5523	0.4823	0.3501
5	0.7473	0.7130	0.6806	0.6499	0.6309	0.5935	0.5674	0.5428	0.5194	0.4972	0.4761	0.4019	0.2693
6	0.7050	0.6663	0.6302	0.5963	0.5645	0.5346	0.5066	0.4803	0.4556	0.4323	0.4104	0.3349	0.2072
7	0.6651	0.6227	0.5835	0.5470	0.5132	0.4817	0.4523	0.4251	0.3996	0.3759	0.3538	0.2791	0.1594
8	0.6274	0.5820	0.5403	0.5019	0.4665	0.4339	0.4039	0.3762	0.3506	0.3269	0.3050	0.2326	0.1226
9	0.5919	0.5439	0.5002	0.4604	0.4241	0.3909	0.3606	0.3329	0.3075	0.2843	0.2630	0.1938	0.0943
10	0.5584	0.5083	0.4632	0.4224	0.3855	0.3522	0.3220	0.2943	0.2697	0.2472	0.2267	0.1615	0.0725
11	0.5268	0.4751	0.4289	0.3875	0.3505	0.3173	0.2875	0.2607	0.2366	0.2149	0.1954	0.1346	0.0558
12	0.4970	0.4440	0.3971	0.3555	0.3186	0.2858	0.2567	0.2307	0.2076	0.1869	0.1685	0.1122	0.0429
13	0.4688	0.415	0.3677	0.3262	0.2897	0.2575	0.2292	0.2042	0.1821	0.1625	0.1452	0.0935	0.0330
14	0.4423	0.3878	0.3405	0.2992	0.2633	0.2320	0.2046	0.1807	0.1597	0.1413	0.1252	0.0779	0.0254
15	0.4173	0.3624	0.3152	0.2745	0.2394	0.2090	0.1827	0.1599	0.1401	0.1229	0.1079	0.0649	0.0195
16	0.3936	0.3387	0.2919	0.2519	0.2176	0.1883	0.1631	0.1415	0.1229	0.1069	0.0930	0.0541	0.0150
17	0.3714	0.3166	0.2311	0.2311	0.1978	0.1696	0.1456	0.1252	0.1078	0.0929	0.0802	0.0451	0.0116
18	0.3503	0.2959	0.2120	0.2120	0.1799	0.1528	0.1300	0.1108	0.0946	0.0808	0.0691	0.0376	0.0089
19	0.3305	0.2765	0.1945	0.1945	0.1635	0.1377	0.1161	0.0981	0.0829	0.0703	0.0596	0.0313	0.0068
20	0.3118	0.2584	0.2145	0.1784	0.1486	0.1240	0.1037	0.0868	0.0728	0.0611	0.0514	0.0261	0.0053

to $8,538. Because the net present value is positive, the company should go ahead with plans to purchase the equipment.

INTERNAL RATE OF RETURN (IRR)

The internal rate of return (IRR) is the rate of return that equates the present value of future cash flows to the investment outlay. If the IRR of a potential investment is equal to or greater than the required rate of return, the investment should be undertaken. The internal rate of return method is an alternative to net present value for evaluating investment possibilities. Like net present value, it takes into account the time value of money.

Consider a simple case where $100 is invested to yield $60 at the end of year 1 and $60 at the end of year 2. What rate of return equates the two-year, $60 annuity to $100? Recall that when we performed present value analysis for previous annuities, we multiplied a present value factor by the annuity to solve for a present value. That is,

$$\text{Present value} = \text{Present value factors} \times \text{Annuity}$$

In the current case, we set the present value equal to the initial outlay for the investment. Then, we can solve for the present value factor and use it to look up the rate of return implicit in the investment.

$$\text{Present value factor} = \frac{\text{Initial outlay}}{\text{Annuity amount}}$$

Another method to secure capital or debt financing is to structure a strategic partnership that may include an equity investment. When the entrepreneur is rejected from traditional financing methods or is unwilling to accept the equity valuations assigned by potential investors, this option is often used.

With a \$100 cost of the investment and a \$60 annuity, the present value factor is 1.667.

$$1.6667 = \frac{\$100}{\$60}$$

Because the \$60 is to be received in each of two years, we use the annuity table to look up the internal rate of return. In the row for 2 periods in the following table, we find a present value factor of 1.6681 (very close to 1.6667) in the column, for a 13 percent rate of return. Thus, the IRR on this investment is approximately 13 percent. If the required rate of return is 13 percent or less, the investment should be undertaken.

Item	Cash Flow	Present Value Factor	Present Value
Cash flow	\$ 60	1.6681	\$100.09
Initial investment	(\$100)	1.0000	(\$100.00)
		Difference (due to rounding)	\$ 0.09

Strategic Partnerships

Structuring a strategic partnership that includes an equity investment is an excellent alternative for many companies to raise equity funds. This usually occurs when ventures find that they are rejected from traditional financing methods or are unwilling to accept the equity valuations assigned by potential investors. Funding associated with strategic partnerships is usually at a more attractive valuation than it might have been with a traditional financing deal. A strategic partner assigns other nonfinancial values to the transaction that relate to the impact on its own operations and competitive positioning.

Although any financial equity structure is possible, a typical strategic partnership involves the sale of a minority interest in the business to a larger company. In addition to the partner providing equity, the partner may also expect to benefit from the entrepreneurial venture itself. The partner might gain access to technology, add a new product to its product line, or profit from a business opportunity that is identified. From the small company's perspective, such an arrangement can provide access to resources such as development facilities, complementary technologies, fast access to the market, and reputation. An investment from a corporation may make it easier to attract VC funding in parallel.

There may be significant downsides too as the objectives of the small company, the VC investors, and the larger corporation may not coincide.

Here are some points to consider:

- The corporation is usually only seeking access to intellectual property and know-how rather than a direct return on the investment it makes in the entrepreneur's company.
- The corporation may perceive that the small company is financially weak and use this fact to take advantage (refer to the cases on contingent litigation in Chapter 5).
- The relationship may *reduce* the chance of receiving VC funding, particularly if the corporate investor is considered to be a prime target to buy the company later. The value may be depressed as the ability to have an auction to gain the highest price could be compromised.
- Corporations are usually slow in making decisions and may hinder the growth of the smaller firm.
- Corporate management often changes, and the champion supporting the relationship may suddenly disappear or be moved to another position. This can be disastrous for the smaller firm. Always have numerous contact points at different levels to mitigate against this common problem.

On the other hand, many VCs are comfortable with co-investing with a corporate partner, realizing that they can bring value other than just the funding. Balance is required, however, and an entrepreneur should enter into relationships with major corporations being aware of the downside. The best solution is to have a VC lead the investment round, take a board seat, and negotiate the relationship with a known and trusted corporate partner. Many corporate VC funds welcome this arrangement, not wishing to be the "lead investor." Examples include the internal venture funds of Dow Chemical and Intel. Establishing an expression of strategic interest with such a fund may lead to the introduction to VC partnerships with which they have already co-invested.

A minority investment by a larger company is only one way to structure a strategic alliance. Other forms of such alliances include setting up a separate legal entity (joint venture); establishing cooperative arrangements (e.g., to fund research and development or to exploit an idea or strategy); and instituting a variety of cross-licensing or cross-distribution agreements.

Such relationships can ease cash flow constraints and lower the amount of funding the venture must obtain from other sources. Some examples of such relationships are described in Chapter 8.

SUMMARY

Entrepreneurs seeking significant funds for growth may seek out investors who wish to purchase an ownership position in the company. Recognizing that this implies giving up some control in the company, you should not approach investors unless you intend to create a "liquidity event" for them to give a cash return on their investment. Selling equity "dilutes" the ownership of the entrepreneur; combining sale of stock with the bootstrapping and debt financing methods of the previous chapter can reduce the dilution. There are many different types of investors, and they must be carefully matched to the company business, needs, stage of investment, and personal chemistry. The entrepreneur should research sources of funds and only approach investors that are a good fit. Angel investors are typically less demanding than venture capital and other "institutional" professional investors. They are more patient and less demanding as to terms. However, they may not have sufficient funds to take you all the way. Other alternatives include selling stock to accredited investors using a private placement, or attracting corporate partners. In every case, a valuation of the company must be agreed to prior to the investment. This valuation can be calculated in several ways. However, in the end, it comes down to negotiating a satisfactory deal depending on the current investment market for your type of opportunity. Valuation is only one part of the transaction, and often it may be better to accept a lower current valuation in exchange for a better long-term relationship with investors. Investors will undertake detailed "due diligence" prior to making an investment after the terms of a transaction have been agreed to and memorialized in a "term sheet." An entrepreneur should also thoroughly research investors prior to accepting their money.

STUDY QUESTIONS

1. What are various sources of equity investment?
2. What are the main differences between an angel and a VC investor?
3. What are the main ways an entrepreneur can value a business?
4. What guidelines should entrepreneurs follow when they are selecting a venture capitalist?
5. What is a private placement?
6. Why is it important to consider the time value of money when making investments?
7. What is the difference between the earnings valuation approach and the asset valuation approach?

EXERCISES

1. Calculate the net present value using Table 6-5, *Present Value of $1 Due in* n *Periods.* What is the present value of $100 received at the end of seven years if the required return is 12 percent?

2. Examine Table 6-5, *Present Value of $1 Due in* n *Periods.* Discuss why the numbers decrease as you move from left to right and why the numbers decrease as you move from top to bottom in a given column.

3. Assume you will receive $300 per year for the next three years plus an extra $300 payment at the end of the three years. Determine how much this prospect is worth today if the required rate of return is 12 percent.

4. Calculate the internal rate of return. Joe Flicek of SIP Commendations is considering investing $79,137 in a computer storage room. He will rent space to customers and expect to generate $22,500 annually (rental charges less miscellaneous expenses other than depreciation).

   a. Assuming Joe wishes to evaluate the project with a five-year time horizon, what is the internal rate of return of the investment (ignore taxes)?
   b. Should Joe make the investment if his required rate of return is 12 percent?

5. Discounted Cash Flow Valuation. Value a stock in a company of your choice using a discounted cash flow model. List the key drivers of value for the company. (Identify the key assumption or variable that you would focus on in doing a discounted cash flow valuation. Examples would include the growth rate assumption, the growth period assumption, and the net capital expenditure assumption.)

6. Value relative to comparables. Prepare a list of "comparable" companies, using criteria you think are appropriate. Choose a multiple that you will use in comparing firms across the group. (You might have to try out a number of multiples before making this choice.) Evaluate the company against the comparable firms using the multiple that you have chosen for your valuation. Determine if the company is under- or overvalued.

INTERACTIVE LEARNING ON THE WEB

Test your skill-builder knowledge of the chapter using the interactive Web site.

1. Self Assessment:
2. Multiple Choice:
3. Matching of Key Terms:
4. Demonstration:
5. Case:
6. Video:

CASE STUDY: CORETEK, INC.[13]

A physicist by training, Dr. Parviz Tayebati received a B.Sc. with first-class honors from the University of Birmingham, England, in 1982, followed by a Master's degree from the University of Cambridge in theoretical physics and a Ph.D. in quantum electronics from the University of Southern California in 1989. Parviz then joined Foster-Miller, Inc., near Boston, a small firm that in the past had derived much of its revenues by undertaking government-funded research using the SBIR Programs.[14] (See Chapter 5.) While there, Parviz led research in optical computing and, most importantly, learned much about the process for winning technology development awards from the federal government.

Throughout the 1990s, Internet bandwidth and information applications grew dramatically in a kind of "virtuous circle," with more bandwidth making new applications practical and acceptance of these new applications driving demand for even more bandwidth. Recognizing the opportunity to apply his technical and management skills to this area, Parviz formed CoreTek Inc. in 1994 with the vision of developing truly innovative, enabling technologies to support this growth. Continued expansion of the Internet required components and architectures enabling bandwidth to grow faster than costs. CoreTek's tunable laser technology was important because it could address cost growth in two ways: it reduced manufacturing and inventory costs for the source lasers, and it provided an essential element of the wavelength-managed network which promised to reduce costs by dramatically increasing network utilization and efficiency. He initially secured government funds for the development of what was viewed as a speculative technology. Between founding the company and 1998, CoreTek received a total of over $5.5 million in SBIR grants, nine Phase One awards, and five Phase Two awards.

Parviz soon realized that to make his dream come true in this fast-moving field, he would have to accelerate his development program. Therefore, in 1999, CoreTek raised $6 million in an "A" round of preferred stock from a syndicate of three VC firms, led by Adams Capital Management (www.acm.com) valuing the company at $11.5 million prior to the investment. The VCs were attracted by the fact that the company was in a "hot field" and was able to secure significant amounts of government funding. For his part, Parviz chose this investor group not only on the attractive deal that he was offered (in fact, another group of VCs offered a higher valuation), but by witnessing the speed with which they could make decisions and their deep knowledge of the telecommunications industry—the fit was excellent. Parviz and his team were now working 24/7. The development proceeded rapidly, as CoreTek built its first manufacturing line. But the money was still not enough, and only nine months later, the company closed on a "B" round of $20.5 million at a pre-money valuation of over $52.5 million from an extended syndicate of four VC firms. In 2000, a number of the major telecommunication giants expressed an interest in acquiring CoreTek. At that time, the telecommunications industry was anticipating major growth, and technologies such as that developed by CoreTek were seen as vital for them to reach their targets. The oligarchical structure of the industry worked to CoreTek's advantage—a breakthrough in cost/performance in components could radically shift market share. Finally, in June 2001, Nortel Networks purchased CoreTek for $1.35 billion paid in Nortel's publicly traded stock. Parviz joined Nortel as Vice President of Business Development. At that time, Parviz and the other insiders of the company still owned approximately 30 percent of the company.

CASE STUDY QUESTIONS

1. Why did the VC firms like the fact that the company had received significant government grants? Assume that this had not happened and that all the funding for the company had come from VCs. Add an earlier seed round to replace the government funds, and make an estimate of the dilution that Parviz and the founders would have had to take in this case if the VCs were to retain their IRR. Approximately how much less would the founders have in their pocket when the company was sold?

2. Draft a short-term sheet (no more than two pages) for each investment round under the new circumstances of question 1.

3. Give three reasons why Adams Capital Management, the lead VC firm, was a good fit to this opportunity.

ADDITIONAL RESOURCES

Banking References

American Banker's Association (ABA)   1120 Connecticut Avenue, NW, Washington, DC 20036; (800) 338-0626
National Association of Small Business Investment Companies (NASBIC)   666 11th Street, NW, Suite 700, Washington, DC 20001; (202) 628-5055
Annual Statement Studies   Robert Morris Associates, 1650 Market Street, Suite 2300, Philadelphia, PA 19103; (800) 677-7621

Polk World Bank Directory Polk Bank Services   Thompson Financial Services, 1321 Murfreeboro Road, Nashville, TN 37217; (615) 889-3350

Dun & Bradstreet Corp.   3 Silvan Way, Parsippany, NJ 07054; (973) 605-6000; http://www.dbsisna.com

Thompson Bank Directory   Thompson Financial Services, 4709 W. Golf Road, 6th Floor, Shokie, IL 60076-1253; (847) 676-9600

Venture Capital Guides

Accel Partners   One Palmer Square Princeton, NJ 08542; (609) 683-4500

Association of Venture Capital Clubs   P. O. Box 3358, Salt Lake City, UT 84110; (801) 364-1100

The Capital Network, Inc.   3925 West Braker Lane, Suite 406, Austin, TX 78759; (512) 305-0826

National Venture Capital Assoc. (NVCA)   1655 N. Fort Meyer Drive, Suite 400, Arlington, VA 22209; (703) 351-5269

New York Venture Group, Inc.   (212) 832-NYVG

Pratt's Guide to Venture-Capital Sources   Stanley E. Pratt

Venture Economics, Inc.   75 Second Avenue, Suite 700, Needham, MA 02194

Seed-Capital Network, Inc.   8905 Kingston Pike, Suite 12, Knoxville, TN 37923; (423) 573-4655

Web Resources

Companies looking for funding or ways to attract the attention of venture capitalists have plenty of places to look on the Internet. For starters, bookmark these sites:

- **www.vfinance.com**   A comprehensive venture capital resource library
- **www.upside.com**   Electronic site for *Upside* magazine that covers high-tech venture capital networks
- **www.redherring.com**   Site for *Red Herring,* which covers high-tech venture capital network. Online material is tailored toward the venture capital community itself.
- **www.ncva.org**   Headquarters for the National Venture Capital Association
- **www.techcapital.com**   Online magazine dealing with venture capital
- **www.witcapital.com**   Leader among a number of sites creating a market for IPOs
- **www.garage.com**   Assists startups wishing to acquire funding

Networks

Many Angel and VC investors participate in networks. Here are some of them. You can find others through your local chambers of commerce or by searching on the Internet.

The Kauffman Foundation in Kansas City has several programs to help entrepreneurs and also undertakes research on matters affecting startup companies. For example, a 2002 report on Business Angels has valuable information for entrepreneurs seeking angel investments. Web links into the Kauffman Network can be found at www.kauffman.org and www.entreworld.org.

Georgia Capital Network	(404) 894 5344
Investors' Circle	(708) 876 1101
L. A. Venture Network	(310) 450 9544
Mid-Atlantic Investment Network	(301) 681 0162
Northwest Capital Network (only serves businesses located in Oregon)	(503) 282 6273
Pacific Venture Capital Network	(714) 856 8366
Seed Capital Network, Inc.	(615) 573 4655
Technology Capital Network (formerly the Venture Capital Network at MIT)	(617) 253 7163
Texas Capital Network	(512) 794 9398
Venture Capital Network of Minnesota	(612) 223 8663
Venture Line	(518) 486 5438
Washington Investment Network	(206) 389 2559

Venture Clubs

Arizona
Enterprise Network Inc.
Tempe
602-804-0012

California
American Venture Capital
Exchange
San Jose and Bay Area
800-292-1993

Greenhouse Venture Group
Bay Area
415-401-0577

Los Angeles Venture Assoc.
Los Angeles
310-450-9544

MIT Enterprise Forum
San Diego
619-236-9400

No. California Venture Forum
San Francisco
415-296-2519

San Diego Venture Group
San Diego
619-272-1985

Colorado
Rockies Venture Group
Denver
303-831-4174

Connecticut
Connecticut Venture Group
Fairfield
203-333-3284

MIT Enterprise Forum of
Connecticut
Hartford
860-275-0294

Delaware
Delaware Entrepreneurs Forum
Wilmington
302-652-4241

Florida
Central Florida Venture Capital
Network
Orlando
407-277-5411

North Florida Venture Capital
Network
Jacksonville
904-642-4840

Gold Coast Venture Capital Club
Boca Raton
561-488-4505

Hawaii
Hawaii Venture Capital Assoc.
Kailua
802-262-7329

Illinois
Midwest Entrepreneur Forum
Chicago
3312-857-0301

Indiana
Venture Club of Indiana
Indianapolis
317-253-1244

Private Investors Network
Bloomington
812-339-8937

Michiana Venture Network
South Bend
219-282-4350

Kentucky
Kentucky Investment Capital
Network
Frankfort
502-564-2064

Venture Club of Louisville
Louisville
502-589-6868

Massachusetts
Technology Capital Network at
MIT
Cambridge
617-253-2337

Maryland/Virginia/D.C.
Dingman Center for
Entrepreneurship
College Park, MD
301-405-2144

MIT Enterprise Forum of
Baltimore/Washington
Arlington
703-758-4021, www.mitef.org

Michigan
Southeastern Michigan Venture
Club
Southfield
313-884-2727

New Enterprise Forum
Ann Arbor
313-665-4433

Travis Bay Enterprise Forum
Traverse City
616-947-5075

Minnesota
New Venture Collaborative
Minneapolis
612-338-3828

Missouri
Missouri Venture Forum
St. Louis
314-241-2683

Montana
High Plains Venture Group
Great Falls
406-454-1934

New Mexico
New Mexico Private Investors
Albuquerque
505-856-0245

New Jersey
Venture Assoc. of New Jersey
Morristown
973-631-5680

New Jersey Entrepreneurs Forum
Morristown
908-789-3424

New York
Long Island Venture Group
Hempsted
516-463-6326

New York Venture Group
New York City
212-832-6984

Capital Region Tech. Dev.
Albany
518-465-8975

Silicon Alley Breakfast Club
Scarsdale
800-273-2832

Ohio
Ohio Venture Association
Cleveland
216-566-8884

Miami Valley Venture Assoc.
Dayton
937-228-1141

Greater Cincinnati
Venture Association
Cincinnati
513-686-2946

Oregon
Oregon Entrepreneurs Forum
Portland
503-222-2270

Pennsylvania
Greater Philadelphia Venture
Group
Philadelphia
215-790-3660

Texas
MIT Enterprise Forum of Texas
Houston
713-651-5529

MIT Enterprise Forum of Texas
Austin
512-342-0010

Utah
Mountain West Venture Group
Salt Lake City
801-595-1141

Virginia
Charlottesville Venture Group
Charlottesville
804-979-7259

Washington
Northwest Venture Group
Bellevue
425-746-1973

MIT Enterprise Forum of the
Northwest
Seattle
206-283-9595, www.mitwa.org

Wisconsin
Wisconsin Venture Network
Milwaukee
414-224-7070
richard_b_bennett@em.fcnbd.com

Canada-Ontario
MIT Enterprise Forum
Toronto
416-736-5708

APPENDIX 1: DUE DILIGENCE CHECKLIST[15]

Corporate Documents

- Complete record of all charter documents of the company since inception
- Current by-laws of the company
- List of states in which the company is authorized to transact business
- Schedule of all subsidiaries
- Charter and by-laws of all subsidiaries
- List of states in which each subsidiary is authorized to transact business
- Minutes of the proceedings of the stockholders of the company and each subsidiary since inception
- Agreements relating to any acquisition or disposition since inception or which is currently planned

Securities Matters

- List of current stockholders
- Stock books and/or ledger of the company and of each subsidiary since inception (including originals or canceled certificates and copies of outstanding certificates)
- Schedule of outstanding options, warrants, or any other commitments or promises, oral or written with respect to the issuance of the company securities (including where applicable, dates of issuance, exercise price, vesting term, etc.)

- Voting trust agreements, redemption agreements, stockholder agreements, registration rights agreements, restrictive agreements, and other similar agreements, contracts, or commitments
- Agreements for the purchase of shares from the company all private placement memoranda since inception
- Copies of all federal and state securities filings since inception and of all correspondence relating thereto

Financings

- Documents and agreements evidencing borrowings, whether secured or unsecured, other indebtedness (long term or short term), including indentures, credit or loan agreements, commitments letters, etc., relating to any outstanding or available long-term or short-term debt, including amendments thereto and any relating instruments granting security interests
- All documents and agreements evidencing other material financing arrangements, including sale and leaseback arrangements, installment purchases, etc.
- Schedule of all liens and encumbrances against any of the company's assets or stock (whether or not of public record)

Employee Relations

- All employee benefit plans and policies, including salary policies, stock option plans, stock option agreements, stock purchase plans, retirement plans, pension plans, bonus and incentive compensation plans. Please provide details with respect to cost of plans and sources of coverage.
- All audit reports covering retirement, pension, or employee benefit plans of the company and its subsidiaries since inception
- Management, executive, and other employment contracts and agreements not to compete
- Management organization chart, including descriptions of job responsibilities

Management/Directors

- Résumés or detailed biographies for senior management team, including approximate dates of employment
- Reference list for officers
- Social security number and address for officers and permission to do a background check (employment check, record search)
- Description of any outstanding management loans and transactions with affiliates
- Description of director compensation

Insiders

- Details of all board and/or management perquisites and arrangements
- Contracts or agreements (including employment agreements) with or pertaining to the company or any of its subsidiaries and to which directors, officers, stockholders, or any affiliate or the foregoing are parties
- All documents pertaining to any receivables from or payable to any director, officer, stockholder, or affiliate or any affiliate of the foregoing

- Documents relating to any other transactions between the company and directors, officers, stockholders, or any affiliate of the foregoing

Agreements

- Contracts for the sale of the company's products or services
- Licensing agreements
- Product maintenance/warranty/service agreements
- All government contracts
- Supply contracts
- Joint venture and partnership agreements to which the company or any of its subsidiaries is a party
- Equipment leases and other leases
- Any other contracts relating to the products, services, or business of the company

Real Property Matters

- List and descriptions of owned realty
- Deeds and options to purchase or sell real property
- Real property leases (plant and office) in which the company is lessee or lessor
- Easements, licenses, and restrictions on use relating to real property
- Schedule and a copy of title insurance policies
- Copies of any environmental studies relating to property owned/leased by the company or any of its subsidiaries

Sales and Marketing

- Customer list (prior/current) and contacts for reference. List corresponding revenue
- Current customer pipeline/backline
- Copies of marketing material (i.e., brochures)

Trade/Analyst Reports

- Industry information
- Competitor analysis
- Industry analyst name/phone numbers whom you have talked with

Technology Matters

- Schedule of United States and foreign patents, trademarks, service marks, and copyrights, including pending applications of the company and its subsidiaries
- Documents issued by PTO or relative foreign organization
- Licensing agreements to which the company or any subsidiary is a party, whether as licensor or licensee, including research and development, manufacturing, distribution, or marketing agreements
- Copies of all notices and correspondence relating to allegations of infringement of rights of third parties by the company or any subsidiary or of the company's or any subsidiary's rights by third parties

- Copy of the company's policies or written summary or oral policies regarding the protection of trade secret and other proprietary information
- Copy of the company's policies or written summary of oral policies regarding information brought with them by employees from former employers
- Assignment agreements with employees and with other persons, with respect to proprietary information
- Confidentiality/non-disclosure agreements, with employees and with any other persons, with respect to proprietary information
- Agreements with independent contractors for the development of products for use or sale by the company or any of its subsidiaries

Governmental Licenses

- United States federal licenses and permits
- All state, county, city, local licenses, including vendor's and building permits, + environmental-related permits
- Foreign licenses and permits

Insurance

- Copies of all insurance policies
- Schedule and description of all insurance policies

Litigation and Regulatory Compliance

- Schedule and brief description of all pending, potential, threatened or recently resolved legal proceedings or investigations (including claims covered by insurance) to which the company or any subsidiary is subject together, in each case, with the name of the court or agency before which the proceedings are pending, the date instituted, principal parties thereto, a description of factual basis alleged to underlie the proceedings and relief sought, together with copies of all pleadings and other records relating to such proceedings
- Consent decrees, judgments, other decrees or orders, settlement agreements and other agreements to which the company or any subsidiary is a party or is bound, requiring or prohibiting any future activities
- Schedule of contingent liabilities, including any guaranties, indemnification or other agreements whereby the company or any subsidiary is responsible for the obligations of another party
- Copies of all reports, notices or correspondence relating to any violation or infringement of government regulations, and copies of all other correspondence with all federal, state, local or foreign authorities with which the company has filed for approval to transact or conduct its business and with any other federal, state, local or foreign regulatory agency to which the company is subject
- All material correspondence with, reports of or to, filings with, or other material information with respect to any administrative or regulatory bodies which regulate the company's or its subsidiaries' businesses

Tax

- Copies of all federal, state, local, and, if applicable, foreign tax returns for the current and the past three years, together with the most recent Revenue Agent's Report

- Copies of memoranda and other material documentation relating to the company's income or other tax liability or prepared in connection with any tax problems affecting the company, its stockholders or its subsidiaries since inception of which may arise in the future
- Copies of all state sales and use tax reports and returns for the current and the past three years
- A schedule describing any ongoing tax disputes together with copies of reports, correspondence, etc., with respect to pending federal, state, local, or foreign tax proceedings with regard to open years or items

Financial/Accounting

- Audited financials for the last two years
- Copies of operating budget for the current year and estimated operating budget for next year
- Summary of capital expenditures since inception and of anticipated capital expenditures for this year and next
- Accounts receivable and accounts payable agings
- Any internal financial projections and any records regarding any backlog or orders for the company's services, including a list of the backlog of contracts for the company's services
- Historic revenue breakdown by customer
- Monthly financial packages (including management commentary) if any
- Any waivers or agreements canceling claims or rights of substantial value other than in the ordinary course of business or any documents relating to write-downs and write-offs other than in the ordinary course of business
- Auditors' opinions and review letters as to financial statements since inception
- Auditors' *management letters* as to internal controls and related correspondence since inception (annual and updating letters)
- Lawyers' letters to auditors regarding contingent liabilities since inception
- List of accounts payable, exceeding $10,000 each, by age
- Copies of all asset appraisals
- Status of any unreported liabilities (e.g., medical claims, pension, past employment)
- Copies of any analyses pertaining to the potential effects of recent and proposed changes in accounting rules
- Summary of pension fund asset and liability balances and a copy of the most recent actuarial report prepared by the company

Miscellaneous

- Schedule of bank accounts and authorized signatures with respect to each account
- Any other documents or information which in the judgment of officers of the company are significant with respect to the business of the company

APPENDIX 2: MODEL VENTURE CAPITAL TERM SHEET — SERIES A PREFERRED STOCK[16]

(*Note:* This is a checklist for the VC firm to make sure that ALL issues have been considered when drafting a term sheet; in most cases many of its provisions are not included in the actual terms. Nevertheless, the entrepreneur must be prepared to negotiate each term in this list; many of them can be denied, but most VCs will have those that they insist on keeping.)

INVESTORS/AMOUNT OF INVESTMENT

The investor group will purchase__shares at a per-share price of $__, of a new class of securities, Series A Convertible Preferred Stock ("Series A Preferred"). Total investment from all investors ("Investors") will be $__. Pre-money valuation will be $__. The Investors group will own__% of the company, on a fully diluted basis (after all securities, options, warrants, and other rights have been converted or exercised). Funds managed by Acme VC ("AVC"), its affiliates, partners, and/or consultants will own__%. AVC has the right to assign any portion of its investment to its affiliates, partners, and/or consultants.

CLOSING DATE _____

USE OF PROCEEDS/MILESTONES

Describe intended use of proceeds and milestone for investment, if any.

CAPITALIZATION AFTER THE FINANCING

Following the purchase of Series A Preferred, company's equity capitalization shall be:

Owner	Security Type	Shares	Percentage
Founders Shares			
AVC			
Other Series A Investors			
Stock Option Plan			
Warrants (if applicable)			
Total Equity			

Using this capitalization, the post-investment valuation of the company is $__.

OTHER SECURITIES

[Address Warrant coverage, if any, stating percentage of Warrants, exercise price, exercise term and whether common stock or preferred stock.] If debt securities constitute all or part of the investment (including bridge loans), the following terms should be addressed: Term of debt (e.g., Demand Note or fixed payment date or combination): Interest rate: Whether debt is subordinate to third party debt (existing and/or future): Specify what, if any, assets will secure debt (Security Agreement and filing of UCCs): Whether debt may be prepaid (at option of company or Investors): Specify that AVC is agent for lenders and what % of Investors/Lenders may authorize actions or amendments: Events of default (e.g., failure to pay principal or interest, assignment for benefit of creditors, commencement of bankruptcy or insolvency proceedings, assignment of Note by company, failure to perform obligations or breach of a representation or warranty under Loan Agreement, Note or Security Agreement, dissolution of company, etc.): Note assignable by Investor/Lender without consent of company. Warrants, if any.

PROTECTIVE PROVISIONS

The consent of a majority (or___%) of the holders of Series A Preferred, voting separately as a single class, shall be necessary to authorize the following actions (any exceptions should be noted):

1. Any Liquidation Event as described under Liquidation.
2. The alteration of the rights, preferences, or privileges of the Series A Preferred.
3. The creation of a new class of equity or debt having parity, with or preferences over the Series A Preferred.
4. An increase in the authorized number of shares of Series A Preferred or common stock.
5. An increase in the number of shares of common stock or the number of options in the Stock Option Plan.
6. The issuance of debt of more than, singly or in aggregate, $___, *[Optional: other than debt incurred in the normal course of business for the purpose of financing receivables, and financial purchase or lease commitments of greater than $___ that are other than those approved annually by the Board of Directors as part of the annual budget and capital plan],* or the issuance of any debt with equity conversion provisions or warrants, or the guarantee, directly or indirectly, of any indebtedness.
7. Any action that reclassifies any outstanding shares into shares having preferences or priority as to dividend, liquidation, assets, voting or redemption senior to or on a parity with the Series A Preferred.
8. Amend, repeal or waive any provision of the company's Articles of Incorporation or by-laws.
9. The declaration or payment of a dividend on the common stock (other than a dividend payable solely in shares of common stock).
10. Increase or decrease the size of the Board of Directors.
11. Engage in any line of business other than that engaged in by the company on the date of the first sale of Series A Preferred.
12. Redeem or acquire any equity securities of the company other than repurchases from employees, directors and consultants pursuant to agreements where the company has the option of repurchase upon the occurrence of certain events, such as termination of employment.
13. Any material related to third party transactions except as approved by the Board of Directors.
14. The acquisition of stock or assets of any other entity.

INVESTORS RIGHTS

Conversion

The Series A Preferred holders shall have the right to convert, at the then applicable conversion rate, Series A Preferred into shares of common stock at any time and from time to time. Each share of Series A Preferred shall initially be convertible into__share of common stock.

Automatic Conversion

The Series A Preferred will automatically convert into common stock, at the then applicable conversion price, in the event of a consummation of a public offering which results in aggregate gross proceeds to the company in excess of $__, and at a per share price of at least__times the Series A Preferred purchase price. *[Optional: or state specific price per share as adjusted for any subsequent stock dividends, stock splits or recapitalizations.]* Automatic conversion may also be initiated with the consent of __% of the Series A Preferred holders.

Anti-dilution

The Series A Preferred shall have weighted average dilution protection in the event of a financing at an equivalent price per share, adjusted for splits and the like, of less than the original Series A Preferred price. *[Optional: as an alternative to weighted average anti-dilution protection, use full-racket anti-dilution protection.]*

The anti-dilution formula shall have the customary carve-outs for employee stock options and restricted stock grants of up to__shares in the aggregate, shares issued in connection with mergers, stock for stock acquisitions, and an Initial Public Offering (IPO), each of which must be approved by the Board of Directors. *[Optional: carve-outs may also include shares issued in connection with joint ventures, R&D and licensing arrangements and technology transfers approved by the Board of Directors.]*

Redemption

If securities are subject to redemption, the following terms should be addressed:

Whether redemption is optional or mandatory

Time(s) of redemption (5–7 years)

Redemption price

Liquidation

A liquidation event ("Liquidation Event") shall occur in the event (i) that the company is wound up or liquidated, whether voluntarily or otherwise, (ii) of a sale of all or substantially all of the assets or stock of the company, (iii) of a sale of 51% of the company's outstanding stock or assets (by merger, consolidation or otherwise) in a transaction or a series of related transactions, or (iv) of a dissolution of the company.

Upon the occurrence of a Liquidation Event, the holders of Series A Preferred shall receive, in preference to the holders of common stock, $__per share plus all accrued but unpaid dividends.

[Optional: After receiving the liquidation preference, the holders of Series A Preferred shall share proceeds on a pro rata basis with the holders of common stock until the holders of Series A Preferred have received__times the price of the Series A Preferred.]

[Alternative: Upon the occurrence of a Liquidation Event, the holders of Series A Preferred shall receive, in preference to the holders of common stock, an amount equal to__times the price of the Series A Preferred plus all accrued but unpaid dividends.]

Dividends

Series A Preferred shall be entitled to non-cumulative dividends at the rate of __% annually ("Dividends"). Dividends shall have priority over common stock. Dividends shall not have a current pay effect but shall be payable only upon liquidation *[and conversion]*, as described in this Term Sheet. The issuance of Dividends may be delayed or waived, in whole or in part, with the consent of __% of the holders of Series A Preferred.

[Alternative: Dividends shall be cumulative and shall accrue, without interest, from the date of issuance of shares of Series A Preferred.]

[Optional: After the payment of the Dividends to holders of Series A Preferred, for any additional dividend, the Series A Preferred will participate with the common stock on an as-converted basis.]

[Optional: In the event of an IPO or a Liquidation Event, holders of Series A Preferred may elect, in their sole discretion, to be paid any Dividends by accepting shares of common stock whose aggregate value is equivalent to the dollar value of such Dividends. The number of shares of common stock shall be determined by dividing the dollar value of the Dividends by the price per share to be paid in connection with the IPO or Liquidation Event.]

Voting

On all matters submitted to a vote of the common stockholders, the holders of Series A Preferred shall be entitled to vote on an as-converted basis.

Registration

The Series A Preferred shall have the following registration rights:

Demand Registration—If, at any time, after the IPO or __years after the closing, holders of __% or more of the Series A Preferred may request that company file a registration statement for an offering of at least $__, and company shall use its best efforts to cause such shares to be registered. Company shall not be obligated to cause more than two demand registrations and shall be entitled to reduce the number of shares to be registered based on the advice of the underwriters; provided, however, that employees, directors, officers and Founders must be cut back before the holders of registrable securities may be cut back. The company shall not be required to effect more than one demand registration in any 6-month period.

Form S-3 Registration—At any time after company becomes eligible to file a registration statement on Form S-3 (or any successor form relating to secondary offerings), holders of Series A Preferred may request company to effect the registration on Form S-3 (or any successor form) of shares owned by holders of Series A Preferred having an aggregate net offering price of at least $__(based upon the then current market price or fair value). Company will not be required to effect more than one such registration in any six-month period.

Piggyback Registrations—The Series A Preferred holders shall be entitled to unlimited "piggyback" registration rights. Company shall be entitled to limit the number of shares to be registered based on the advice of its underwriters, including exclusion of piggyback registration rights from an IPO; provided, however, that the registration must include at least__% of the shares requested to be included by the holders of registrable securities, *[Optional: and employees, directors, officers and Founders must be cut back before the holders of registrable securities may be cut back.]*

Registration Expenses—The registration expenses, excluding underwriting discounts and commissions, but including a single counsel representing the selling Series A Preferred holders in each of the two demand registrations, and all S-3 and piggyback registrations, shall be borne by company.

Customary Provisions—Customary provisions, including cross-indemnification, push back, underwriting arrangements and the like, shall be included in the Rights Agreement.

Market Stand-off—Each Investor shall upon notice by the company and the managing underwriter, be subject to a 180-day lock-up agreement following the company's IPO, during which period Investor may not sell or transfer shares of the company's stock, other than those registered in such offering, those purchased by the Investor in the IPO and those purchased by the Investor in the open market following the IPO. All officers, directors, Founders and owners of__% or more of the common stock shall be subject to the same lock-up agreement.

Transfer of Rights—The registration rights may be transferred to a transferee who acquires at least__% of the outstanding shares of the preferred stock (or common stock issued upon conversion). Transfer of registration rights to a partner or affiliate of the Investors will be without restrictions as to minimum shareholdings.

Right of First Refusal/Co-Sale/IPO

Company and all common and Series A Preferred holders who own more than__% of company's equity on a fully-diluted basis and future executives who are appointed as corporate officers, will enter into a right of first refusal and co-sale agreement, providing that any of these stockholders (other than Series A Preferred holders) that proposes to sell all or a portion of his shares to a third party must permit the company and then the Series A Preferred holders, at their option (i) to purchase such stock on the same terms as the proposed transferee or (ii) with respect to the holders of Series A Preferred only, to sell a proportionate part of their shares on the same terms offered by the proposed transferee. Series A Preferred holders will be a party to the Agreement but their stock will not be subject to the right of first refusal or co-sale rights.

Right of First Offer

Series A Preferred holders shall have the right, but not the obligation, to participate in subsequent rounds of financing for an amount that will maintain their pro-rata interest in the company, on a fully diluted basis. Failure to exercise this right will not preclude any Series A Preferred holder from participating in future rounds. Such equity shall not include shares issued as part of an approved Stock Option Plan up to an aggregate of__shares, shares issued as part of an acquisition of another company approved by the Board, or shares offered in an approved and underwritten public offering, in each case approved by the Board of Directors.

IPO Participation

The Investors will have a right, subject to compliance with applicable securities laws, to purchase their pro rata share of__% of the shares offered in the company's IPO (to be accomplished through a private offering to the Investors completed, subject to the closing of the IPO, prior to the company's first filing of a registration statement with the SEC).

Information Rights

Series A Preferred holders shall receive the following information:

1. *[For start-up companies with no Business Plan: Business Plan—__months after the closing of this transaction, company shall complete, and have approved by the Board, a business plan that includes a product road map, operating plan, financing plan, marketing plan, and personnel development and recruiting plan that will serve as the basis for the next round of financing.]*

2. Business Plan—Prior to the beginning of each fiscal year, the company shall complete, and have approved by the Board, an annual business plan that includes financial statements on a monthly basis and operating goals for each functional unit.

3. Monthly Unaudited Results—company shall provide either monthly unaudited financial statements or a CEO letter summarizing relevant company developments no later than 30 days after the close of each month.

4. Quarterly Unaudited Results—company shall provide unaudited quarterly financial statements within 45 days after the end of each fiscal quarter.

5. Annual Audited Financial Statements—company shall provide annual audited financial statements within 90 days after the end of each fiscal year *[Optional: to all shareholders]*.

6. An annual budget at least 30 days prior to the end of each fiscal year.

7. Other Management Information—company shall provide other materials customarily made available to Directors.

Qualified Small Business Stock/Parachute Payments

Company shall make reasonable efforts to insure that the Series A Preferred constitutes qualified small business stock within the meaning of Section 1202(c) of the Internal Revenue Code and shall make all filings required under Section 1202(d)(1)(c) of the Internal Revenue Code and related Treasury regulations.

In compliance with "Rule 280G" ("Golden Parachute"), company shall ensure that there is a vote held of the qualified Preferred Stockholders (as defined under Rule 280G) at the time of a change of control or other event that might result in the application of Rule 280G, such that in compliance with Rule 280G a vote of 75% of the qualified shareholders as defined thereunder can alter the applicability of the "golden parachute tax."

BOARD OF DIRECTORS

The company's Articles of Incorporation and bylaws shall provide for a Board of__Directors. The number of directors may not be changed except by amendment.

Upon the closing, the Board shall be composed of__Directors as follows:

Director	Nominated By	Affiliation
	AVC	Series A

All Directors shall be re-elected annually. In addition to the Directors, the Board may elect to have other representatives as observers with the approval of AVC.

Committees

The Board may create committees to conduct such business as may properly come before them. A Director representing AVC shall have the right, but not the obligation, to be elected to any committee constituted by the Board.

Expenses

Company shall reimburse Directors for reasonable out-of-pocket expenses incurred while attending Board meetings, committee meetings or on company-approved business.

OTHER AGREEMENTS

Non-Disclosure and Proprietary Rights

All current and future employees and consultants shall enter into non-disclosure and proprietary rights agreements that are in a form and substance satisfactory to the Investors.

Stock Option Plan

The company's Stock Option Plan shall be in a form and substance satisfactory to Investors. On a fully diluted basis, the Stock Option Plan shall represent__% of company's fully diluted equity at closing. The Board, or a duly constituted Compensation Committee, shall determine the price and other terms of options at the time of award.

All stock and stock equivalents issued after the closing to employees, directors, consultants and any additional new stock options offer to founders, shall be subject to vesting as follows:__% to vest at the end of the__year with the remaining to vest monthly thereafter.

[Optional: Vesting of new employee stock options shall be accelerated by one year upon a change of control.] The Board, or a duly constituted Compensation Committee, shall determine the price and other terms of options at the time of award.

Stock Purchase Agreement

The purchase of Series A Preferred shall be made upon completion of an executed Stock Purchase Agreement which shall contain representations and warranties made by the company as to its assets, liabilities, corporate authority, litigation and similar matters as are customarily given by a seller of securities to a purchaser, including an opinion of company's counsel acceptable to the Series A Preferred Investors.

Founders' Buy Back Agreements

The Buy-Back Agreements shall provide for reverse vesting of__of the Founders' common stock on a__basis over a__year period. The Agreements shall further provide for all remaining unvested shares to vest if a Liquidation Event occurs or if the Founders are terminated without cause during the term of the Agreement. Vesting shall not be accelerated in the event of an IPO.

PRECONDITIONS TO INVESTMENT

Completion of Diligence

The Investors shall complete their due diligence to their individual satisfaction. Such diligence includes, but is not be limited to, the items listed in this section.

Intellectual Property Review

Company will reimburse the investors for the cost of the intellectual property review up to__$. *[Optional: If the investment is not consummated the Investors will pay for the review.]*

Intellectual Property Agreement with XYZ Company (if applicable)

Prior to the closing, the company and __will have entered into a written agreement that in effect transfers the ownership of and the proceeds associated with licensing or commercialization of agreed-upon patents, issued and pending, to the company, on terms acceptable to the Series A Preferred holders.

Corporate and Stockholder Agreements

Company's Articles of Incorporation, Bylaws, Shareholder's Agreements, Intellectual Property Agreements and the like shall be in form and substance satisfactory to the Investors.

Key Manager Insurance

Company shall carry Key Manager Insurance with a value of $_____, payable to company, on_____. The company shall have such policy in place within 45 days of closing.

Opinion of Counsel

Receipt of an opinion of counsel to the company as to customary matters.

Material Changes

Representation by company that no material adverse change in the company's business conditions or prospects from what has been reported to the Investors has occurred.

Directors and Officers Insurance

The company shall maintain Directors and Officers Indemnity Insurance, with a face value of $__and customary terms, in force while it is privately held. The company shall increase the minimum face value of the policy to $__ prior to an IPO.

EXPENSES

Company shall bear its own legal and other expenses with respect to the transaction. The company will pay the investor's reasonable auditing, legal, background check and closing expenses, which shall not exceed a total of $__without company's approval.

PREPARATION OF DOCUMENTS

The operative documents for the Series A Preferred financing shall be prepared by counsel for ACM.

CLOSING

The closing is expected to occur__days after company executes this Term Sheet *[Optional: Additional closings may be held at the option of the Investor Group within__days of the initial closing whereby total proceeds shall not exceed $__ .]*

CONFIDENTIALITY

The company and AVC each agree not to disclose the terms or conditions of this Term Sheet, including the valuation, to a non-affiliated third party other than potential investors in this financing. Notwithstanding the foregoing, the parties hereto may disclose such information to their respective boards of directors, attorneys, accountants and other consultants as part of the due diligence process and the consummation of the financing as may be reasonably required and engage in such other discussions as may be required by law.

STANDSTILL

The company agrees that, upon signing of this Term Sheet, AVC will have__days to complete their diligence and fund the investment as described. The company further agrees that it will use its best efforts to immediately and fully inform AVC if the company is contacted by, or intends to begin negotiations regarding investment in, or acquisition of, the company in whole or part during this period.

[Alternative: The company agrees that it will not solicit, negotiate, or otherwise encourage or accept any other offers to purchase the company's securities (other than employee options) until this transaction is closed unless (i) AVC so consents in writing in advance or (ii) this transaction has not closed on or before___, ___.]

NONBINDING EFFECT

Except for the "Standstill" clause above, this Term Sheet is not intended to create any legally binding obligations on either party, and no such obligation shall be created unless and until the parties enter into definitive documents.

EXPIRATION

This Term Sheet shall expire if not signed by company on or before__.

SIGNATURES

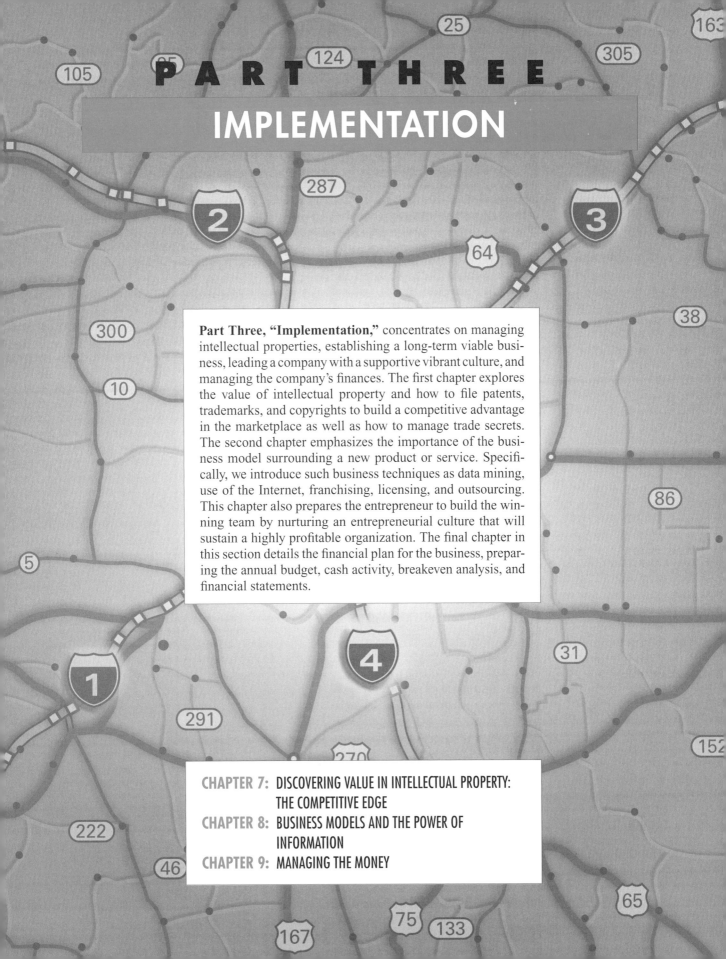

PART THREE

IMPLEMENTATION

Part Three, "Implementation," concentrates on managing intellectual properties, establishing a long-term viable business, leading a company with a supportive vibrant culture, and managing the company's finances. The first chapter explores the value of intellectual property and how to file patents, trademarks, and copyrights to build a competitive advantage in the marketplace as well as how to manage trade secrets. The second chapter emphasizes the importance of the business model surrounding a new product or service. Specifically, we introduce such business techniques as data mining, use of the Internet, franchising, licensing, and outsourcing. This chapter also prepares the entrepreneur to build the winning team by nurturing an entrepreneurial culture that will sustain a highly profitable organization. The final chapter in this section details the financial plan for the business, preparing the annual budget, cash activity, breakeven analysis, and financial statements.

ROADMAP for
PATTERNS OF ENTREPRENEURSHIP
Implementation

- ☑ What Are Trademarks?
- ☑ What Are Copyrights?
- ☑ What Are Patents?
- ☑ What Are the Qualifications for a Patent to Be Granted?
- ☑ How Is Intellectual Property Protected?
- ☑ Documenting the Ideas
- ☑ What Is Prior Art?
- ☑ Using Search Options
- ☑ Progress from Idea to Patent to Enterprise
- ☑ What Are Trade Secrets?
- ☑ Reverse Engineering
- ☐ Definitions in Business Models
- ☐ Capturing Value in the Supply Chain
- ☐ Using Databases to Create Value
- ☐ Locking in Customers
- ☐ Licensing and Franchising
- ☐ Outsourcing
- ☐ Developing a Culture for Innovation
- ☐ Understanding Financial Statements
- ☐ Review and Analysis of the Balance Sheet
- ☐ How to Use Ratios for Financial Analysis
- ☐ The Value of an Income Statement
- ☐ How to Use Ratios for Profitability
- ☐ The Value of the Statement of Cash Flows
- ☐ Understanding Footnotes to Financial Statements
- ☐ Preparing Financial Projections
- ☐ Preparing a Forecast of Cash Flows
- ☐ Preparing a Breakeven Analysis
- ☐ Taxes

CHAPTER 7

DISCOVERING VALUE
IN INTELLECTUAL PROPERTY:
THE COMPETITIVE EDGE

> "Property is an intellectual production. The game requires coolness, right reasoning, promptness, and patience in the players."
>
> RALPH WALDO EMERSON, (1803–1882)

OBJECTIVES

- Know the different forms of intellectual property and how they differ.
- Learn the purpose and value of trademarks, copyrights, and patents.
- Learn how to obtain a copyright.
- Learn the process from creating an idea to patent approval.
- Know the guidelines for selecting professional assistance, such as legal services, in pursuing intellectual property rights.
- Discover the important roles of reverse engineering and trade secrets in intellectual property.
- Be able to apply patent licensing to the venture.

CHAPTER OUTLINE

INTRODUCTION

The realm of intellectual property (IP) deals with a range of usually legally defensible rights conferred upon individuals and companies that have produced original work of some potential value. The work itself may fall in any part of a broad spectrum, including such diverse forms as software processes, oil painting, music composition, and computer chip design. The forms of protection are defined as trademark, copyright, and patent. Yet another form of intellectual property is a trade secret. Trade secrets are not afforded the same assurance of legal protection as their counterparts (laws vary from state to state) but are sometimes a more effective way of securing property rights.

The U.S. Constitution provides specific legal rights for the creators of intellectual property:

> **The Congress shall have the power to ... promote the progress of science and useful arts, by securing for limited times to authors and inventors the exclusive right to their respective writings and discoveries.** — The U.S. Constitution: Article I, Section 8

The importance of intellectual property to the entrepreneur lies in its ability to provide profit or some other form of competitive advantage. Where it is prudent to do so the creator of a piece of intellectual property may wish to share it with his community, whether it is his specific technical community, his country, or the world at large. Sharing means that the creator makes the intellectual property available for public or private use or consumption in some form, usually in a manner that generates profit for the owner of the intellectual property. In exchange, the government will usually confer some form of ownership rights, allowing a possible financial benefit from the sale or use of that creation by others, provided that the creation is properly presented and registered, and meets specific criteria.

This chapter explains these forms of intellectual property (IP) and guides you toward effectively developing, protecting, and promoting your IP. A variety of tools and resources can be found throughout the chapter and in the additional sources offered at the end of this text.

Before going any further, it is important to point out that the laws governing intellectual property are complex and frequently subject to change. It is advised that entrepreneurs pursuing the advancement of their IP consult the appropriate code early in their endeavors to minimize the possibility of wasted time and effort, especially given the importance of timely registration in seeking competitive IP rights. Professional legal advice and assistance may constitute the most appropriate means for efficiently pursuing IP rights for many entrepreneurs.

PROFILE: XEROX CORPORATION

Xerox Corporation is best known for its innovation in the field of document replication and its patents on the exclusive right to use plain copying methods.[1] Xerox invented personal computing and the forerunners of many of its most successful tools. At Xerox's Palo Alto Research Center (PARC), researchers came up with what they called a "personal distributed computing system," which they dubbed the *Alto*. By 1973, the Alto was fully operational. Some readers may remember that

Xerox ran television ads highlighting some of the remarkable new features introduced with the system, among these are the mouse, word processing, laser printing, high-resolution graphics, user friendliness, and port-to-port communications capabilities. The system was a complete original, including novel hardware and software, the first "object-oriented" programming language, and the first local area network, or LAN. Although early PC technology was used successfully in-house at PARC, and executives had some idea that their invention might be successfully marketed, they let external pressures and disorganization cloud their vision and their grasp of a reality that already lay before them. Ultimately, Xerox let the technology go and failed to capitalize on an opportunity that was theirs for the taking, leaving it, instead, to visionaries like Steve Jobs and Bill Gates. To be sure, Xerox is not the first company, nor shall it be the last, to make a blunder of this sort. There is no way to protect the complete potential of any invention until that concept has been put through the gauntlet of tests imposed by time and trial, from the early stages of research and development to the late stages of market. What is certain is that without a belief in and commitment to some concept, an attendant reality can never materialize. Here, the importance of pursuing IP protection is underscored.

WHAT ARE TRADEMARKS?

Trademarks are highly useful tools employed by commercially active entities to distinguish their products and the sources of these products from one another. Trademarks are akin to and in some cases synonymous with "brands." Because of their function, trademarks are one of the most familiar forms of intellectual property.

A trademark can take a number or some combination of forms, including name, symbol, motto, or jingle, just to name a few, and represents a company and/or product with which it is associated.[2] The red triangle on a bottle of Bass Ale is a trademark for the Bass Brewing Company. The slogan "Quality is Job #1" is one of Ford Motorcar Company's trademarks. The three-note call sign of the National Broadcasting Company (NBC) is a well-known example of a trademark in the form of sound.

A lesser-known cousin of the trademark is the *service mark*,[3] which differs only by way of applying to services and their sources rather than to products. Other lesser-known marks include the *collective mark*, which organizations often use to designate membership, but also in commerce, and the *certification mark*, which is used by entities other than the owner of the mark, but with the owner's permission. Because of its association with nonowner entities, the certification mark may be indicative of their identities and the attributes of the products, such as elements of quality and composition.

The following information focuses specifically on trademarks. For additional information on the other marks, consult the proper federal authorities.[4]

ROADMAP	
ACTIONS	Intellectual property is important to the entrepreneur because it can generate profits and create a form of competitive advantage.

What Is the Value of a Trademark?

The key to trademarks is the association they render in the mind of the consumer. They are important forms of intellectual property affecting decisions in the minds of consumers or users. Based on personal experience, word of mouth, advertising, and other means of acquaintance, consumers form impressions about different products or services offered. Those impressions guide the consumer in making decisions about spending time and money when given a choice between competing products or services. Based on these associations, these consumers gain expectations on the products or services they will use. It is specifically the power of the trademark to convey such positive associations that imparts its value.

Even a catchy jingle or attractive design used as a trademark is unlikely to provide a business entity with much value unless that entity takes steps to create the positive associations described. Such associations are initially built with good advertising and promotional trials and are reinforced by such practices as providing good quality, value, user-friendliness, and customer service. In order to achieve the favorable trademark awareness it needs, a business entity will likely have to invest a substantial amount of capital, effort, and time in development. Once a trademark has been reliably established, it can be a highly effective tool for communicating a broad amount of information at a glance and for promoting use among consumers.

How Are Trademarks Registered?

Simply by using a mark in the course of public commerce, the entrepreneur establishes a "common law" right to that mark and may be considered its legal owner. Nonetheless, given the potential for different parties to concurrently use the same or similar mark, the challenge to one's common law right to a mark has the potential to surface and interfere with some or all future rights associated with its use. In order to safeguard one's trademark rights, it is recommended that the user of a mark apply to have it registered with the United States Patent and Trademark Office (USPTO) in Washington, D.C.[5] Figure 7-1 depicts the process involved with filing for a trademark.

Only the owner of a trademark may apply for registration, although an attorney may initiate the application on behalf of an owner. Attorneys are not essential to this process, but they can provide invaluable guidance to the aspiring trademark registrant for avoiding pitfalls and safeguarding the fruit of labor. With or without an attorney, the owner must submit an application along with supporting documentation. If the

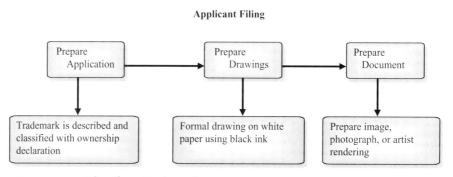

Figure 7-1 **Filing for a Trademark.**

applicant's mark is already in commercial use, you must submit a *use application* that includes a drawing of the trademark on a separate sheet of paper, a filing fee corresponding with the class of product to which the trademark applies, and three specimens of the trademark. Where possible, specimens ought to be actual commercial grade material bearing the trademark. Where specimens are impractically unwieldy, $8\frac{1}{2} \times 11''$ photostats or photographs of actual specimens may be supplied instead.

When an applicant's trademark is not yet in commercial use at the time of application, an *intent-to-use* application must be filed. Submit a drawing of the trademark on a separate sheet of paper with a filing fee corresponding with the class of product to which the trademark applies. Also send either an *amendment to allege use* or a *statement of use*, depending on whether or not the trademark has been published in some form and issued a *notice of allowance* by the USPTO. Owners filing an *amendment to allege use* form must also file an additional *request for an extension of time to file a statement of use* if the trademark is not used within the six months following their submission of application. Failure to make commercial use of the mark without an extension filing will result in the USPTO's disavowal of the application.

Applications should be sent to:

Assistant Commissioner for Trademarks

Box New App/Fee

2900 Crystal Drive

Arlington, VA 22202-3513

Figure 7-2 depicts the actions taken in the Patent Office when registering a trademark.

The USPTO also offers the Trademark Electronic Application System (TEAS) for easy online application printing that can be sent to the above address via mail. For further information, interested parties should start by calling the USPTO's automated message system at (800) 786-9199. Live operators are available if needed.

The USPTO will grant registration approval to the first party to commercially use or file an *intent-to-use* application (see below for more information). Because registration of a trademark with the USPTO confers upon the registrant particular legal privileges, it is recommended that entrepreneurs seek registration as early as possible.

Applicants should expect it to take approximately one year until receiving registration approval for the trademark. During this period, the application is reviewed

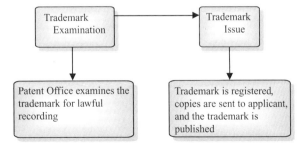

Figure 7-2   Actions Taken in the Patent Office When Registering a Trademark.

by one of the USPTO's trademark attorneys and evaluated for its compliance with regulations and for potential conflict with existing registered marks. Having passed such tests, a trademark will subsequently be published in the USPTO's *Gazette* for review and possible challenge by competitive parties.

Once registration has been achieved, a trademark must remain in commercial use in order for the rights of registration associated with it to remain in force. For newly registered trademarks, a renewal application will need to be filed in order to extend the term of registration (those registered prior to November 16, 1989 need only be registered every 20 years). The only exception to this rule is that in between the fifth and sixth year of initial registration a supplemental affidavit must be filed with the USPTO. Provided that the relevant conditions are met, registered ownership of a trademark can continue indefinitely.

What Are the Benefits of Trademark Registration?

Federal registration of a trademark grants the owner a competitive advantage in the use of the mark.[6] In addition to nationwide public notice of the legal claim being made, the owner has the benefit of legal appeal in federal court concerning matters of dispute and infringement. National evidence of ownership can provide a basis for achieving international registration of the trademark and for preventing importation of international goods, which infringe on the registrant's rights in the United States.

How Are Trademarks Enforced?

Once a trademark is registered with the USPTO, the owner of the mark may use the federal registration symbol® in association with its mark. This will inform others of the exclusive rights afforded by the mark. Until such time as official registration occurs, it is a good idea to use the TM symbol as a way of notifying others that rights are claimed in association with use of your mark. The SM symbol may be used in the case of service marks.

Even when properly registered and kept in constant use, there is no guarantee that others will not infringe on the trademark. Where infringement is deemed to have taken place, the USPTO should be notified. A decision to pursue legal recourse for damages should hinge on the existence of actual or potential financial loss as a result of the infringement, although owners of marks are entitled to file suit even where no such losses are readily apparent.[7] In cases where injury is minimal, it may make more sense simply to notify the infringing party of infringement, providing records of your rights and a request to terminate usage of the mark. Document this action so that you can use it in future prosecution should the infringing party fail to comply. Where compliance is not observed or where significant financial interests are at stake, a qualified attorney should be contracted to perform prosecution.

ROADMAP

ACTIONS   A trademark infringement does not have to be identical to that used by the infringed party. If the trademark is similar and is likely to cause confusion, this is sufficient grounds for infringement.

Until such time as one's trademark can officially be registered with the USPTO, the trademark symbol should be used in conjunction with a mark as a way of notifying others that rights are claimed in association with use of the mark.

The federal registration symbol may be used in association with any mark officially registered with the USPTO. Use of the symbol informs others of the exclusive rights afforded the owner of the registered mark.

Figure 7-3   The Trademark and Registered Symbols.

In order for infringement to exist, a mark need not be identical to that used by the infringed party, only similar enough to be likely to cause confusion. Similar marks are more likely to infringe on one another when used in the same or similar businesses. Furthermore, infringement need not be intentional in order for damages to be awarded. It is the obligation of any party employing a mark to be certain that its use is unrestricted. Nonetheless, determination of intent can strengthen a case against an infringing party and result in the award of greater damages than in cases where intent does not exist.[8] Figure 7-3 depicts the trademark and registered trademark symbols.

Selecting the Right Trademark

Selecting the right trademark can be a useful marketing tool, creating a favorable impression in the minds of target consumers. A good trademark will also serve to distinguish a company and its products from those of competition. Choosing a distinct trademark also helps avoid issues of trademark infringement.

Some general rules of trademark selection are worth following to avoid running into trouble. The first is to avoid using marks similar to those of competitors. Using terms that are descriptive of products or services your company may offer should also be avoided, for they are likely to apply equally to the goods and services of competitors. U.S. law provides for the right to inform customers of such identifying characteristics of products as may be conveyed by descriptive marks, and so the law provides no exclusive protection for use of such marks. An exception to this rule may be made if a descriptive mark has been used for a sufficiently extended period of time to allow consumers to specifically identify a particular company with use of the term. Tasty Baking Company's Tastykake Brand is an example of this exception. Because only the test of time can provide an answer as to whether or not this exception will prove serviceable in any given case, it is an unreliable option for new ventures.

Another association to be avoided is the use of a proper name, such as a family name or the name of a city. Generally speaking, marks employing proper names will only be protected to the extent that they also embody distinct elements making them somewhat unique. Even so, the proper name itself is not protectable and may be used by a competitor to create a trademark virtually identical to an existing mark. The importance of distinction in selecting a trademark in this case should be obvious. In New York City, you might find a Ray's Famous Pizza, a Ray's Original Pizza, and a Ray's Pizza all within a block or two of one another. One would be hard pressed to distinguish between any of them based on name or to extrapolate any valuable information about each company and its products based on the trademarks. Although the long-term use exception described above also applies to use of proper names, such as is the case with the automotive brands Ford and Ferrari, it is, once again, a poor choice for new ventures.

The least desirable of all trademarks are those that employ generic terms. Such terms are afforded no protection whatsoever regardless of time in use. The terms *furniture* in "Swedish Furniture House," and *Auto Parts* in "Bill's Auto Parts" are both unprotectable. One way to partially safeguard a trademark using any of the aforementioned unprotected categories is to fix it in a medium that can convey in a distinct way, such as musically, to a catchy and unique tune, or visually, with distinct graphical representation. Although the terms themselves may not be protectable, repeated use and promotion of marks in this way can strengthen a trademark legally and fix it more firmly and distinctly in the mind of the consumer.

The best trademarks are those that apply unique terms. The ideal mark is one employing a coined term, as *coined* terms are totally novel elements of language, with no meaning other than that which comes to be associated with them through use. An example of a coined term is the Betamax name used by Sony. Coined marks are the least likely to be used by competition and are the easiest to defend based on originality. The *suggestive* mark is a close second to the coined mark in terms of strength. The suggestive term need not be explicitly descriptive in order to impart some valuable association with the company, product, or service it represents, nor does it violate any of the other general restrictions of trademark usage. Pabst's Blue Ribbon beer is an example of a suggestive mark. *Arbitrary* terms are perhaps the next most effective in trademark selection. An arbitrary term will have no particular significance in relation to a specific realm of business endeavor. The *Apple* in Apple Computers is an example of an arbitrary mark.

How Do Entrepreneurs Search for Conflicting Marks?

Though not required, it is highly advisable that an applicant conduct a search of existing marks before submitting an application to reduce the likelihood that the expenditure of work, time, and capital will be in vain.[9] The USPTO will assign the applicant's case to a trademark attorney. Should conflicting marks be discovered, an application may be rejected. In point of fact, simple conflict is not even required; only a great enough similarity to existing marks to cause likelihood of confusion is required. Even the products represented by a trademark can be different when conflict or confusion is found to negate the applicant's registration of a new trademark.

The USPTO does not conduct a search on behalf of an applicant, but it can be helpful in pointing the applicant in the right direction. Interested parties should consult the USPTO Internet site, specifically at http://www.uspto.gov/tmdb/index, or visit the Trademark Public Search Library at 2900 Crystal Drive, 2nd Floor, Arlington, Virginia 22202. Searches at this location are free to the public. Lastly, the Patent and Trademark Depository Libraries offer opportunities for specific searches.

How Are Trademarks Transferred?

Like other forms of intellectual property, the trademark is a transferable asset. When businesses are bought and sold, the trademarks representing their business and products invariably go along with the rest of the property. Trademarks can be licensed or sold by their owners to provide ongoing revenue, such as is the case with franchise income or a profitable exit strategy.

WHAT ARE COPYRIGHTS?

Copyrights are instruments of legal protection given to authors of original works of writing, art, musical composition, photography, and architectural design, to name a few creative areas.[10] In addition to the condition of originality, protected works must be expressed and recorded in a fixed medium, such as in print, by brush stroke, recorded on vinyl disc, and so on. Computer programs may be copyrighted. With rare exceptions, names may not be copyrighted. The same is true of titles, slogans, and short phrases, all of which are potentially protectable by trademark. One exception to this rule is representations of names, titles, and the like presented in a sufficiently original style or manner. Where the name for a band might not be copyrighted (remember that trademark protection is available for such protection), and if that name is rendered in an original manner with sufficient artistic content, for example, it may be copyrighted in that particular form. As is the case with all copyrighted work, it is not the idea per se that is copyrighted but the original expression of that idea. Figure 7-4 depicts the copyright symbol.

How Do Entrepreneurs Obtain a Copyright?

For entrepreneurs holding copyrights, the fundamental importance of the copyright lies in the potential to harvest profit from a marketable copyrighted work.[11] The owner of a copyright generally has the exclusive right to reproduce, distribute, sell, publicly display, and publicly perform (where applicable) his or her protected work, or newer derivative work based on the protected work. Persons other than the owner of a copyright wishing to use the work protected by it in any material way must receive permission from the copyright owner to do so. Unauthorized use may carry stiff penalties under U.S. law. Permitted use of protected work might take the form

ROADMAP

ACTIONS

Entrepreneurs who own a copyright have the exclusive right to reproduce, distribute, sell, and display their protected work. Persons other than the owner of a copyright who want to use the protected work must receive permission from the copyright owner to do so.

Notice of copyright is not required under U.S. law, as ownership rights exist concurrently with creation of a given work. Nevertheless, use of the copyright symbol or the abbreviation "Copr." serves as public notice of the special status afforded a copyrighted work. Furthermore, when proper notice of copyright is given on any work, owners of copyright are entitled to full damages against infringing parties, which might claim innocent infringement for not realizing that the work was copyrighted. Proper copyright notice should include the symbol © or the abbreviation "Copr.," the date of first publication, and the author's' name(s). Example: © 2000 Eric Hirsch.

Figure 7-4 **Copyright Symbol.**

of quoting small portions of a written text and providing proper citation in a new document. The law outlining the boundaries of copyright infringement is specific but complex, and an attorney should be consulted where copyright infringement may be of concern.

One can capitalize on one's copyright by selling copies of the protected work, selling the protected work, or granting the right to reproduce the work in return for a licensing fee. Copying may be redressed in a court of law and may help to obtain damages and attorney fees. As with other forms of intellectual property (IP), ownership of a copyright itself may be transferred via sale or some other mode of transfer. Where significant dollars is at stake, whether negotiating for revenue or suing for infringement, use of a copyright attorney is highly advisable.

The U.S. Copyright Office (USCO) supplies a list of licensing organizations and publication rights clearinghouses on its Web site at www.loc.gov/copyright/. Many of these organizations would be a good starting point for entrepreneurs interested in harvesting the value of copyrighted IP. Figure 7-5 depicts the steps taken in obtaining a copyright.

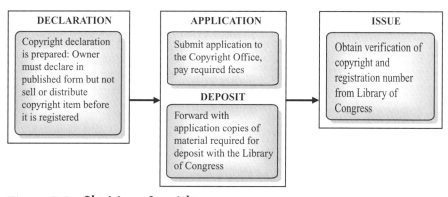

Figure 7-5 **Obtaining a Copyright.**

How Do Entrepreneurs Obtain a Copyright?

In most cases, the author of a work owns the copyright at the moment of its creation. The only exception is in the case of a work made for hire. Work for hire is defined as work not owned by the author or work performed in some other salaried or compensated capacity. An example of a work made for hire could be an article written by an individual author freelancing for a magazine or employed by the same. In the case of a work made for hire, copyright ownership is again present at the moment of a work's creation but is the intellectual property of the party employing or otherwise compensating the actual author.

Because an original work is copyrighted by virtue of its existence and conformity with specific requirements, it need not be registered with the U.S. Copyright Office. Nonetheless, registration is a very good idea where IP value is of potential concern, because registration is necessary before any legal action can be taken against infringement. The U.S. Copyright Office makes it very easy for authors of original works meeting the copyright criteria to register their works federally. A mere $30 must be sent along with a simple application form and nonreturnable copies of the work to be registered. Once registered, an author will receive a certificate of registration for his work; his copyright will be part of the public record and may become part of the collections at the Library of Congress. Registration typically takes approximately eight months but may take as long as a year.[12] Unlike trademarks, copyrights must be renewed to remain in force. The USCO's *Circular 15* and *15a* should be consulted for detailed renewal conditions and benefits. Upon expiration of the copyright, the work becomes a part of the public domain.

To contact the USCO by mail, write to Copyright Office, Library of Congress, 101 Independence Avenue, S.E. Washington, D.C. 20559-6000. By phone: Public Information (202) 707-3000, Application Forms (202) 707-9100.

How Are Copyrights Protected and Enforced?

As mentioned above, original works are considered copyrighted at their moment of creation. Nonetheless, copyright infringement is a widespread problem that has become more complex in recent years owing to the novel nature of electronic forms of authorship found in software and on the Internet and World Wide Web.

To protect their works from copyright infringement, copyright holders must provide a comprehensive notice of their copyright. This notice must include the following, typically in the order listed.

To Protect Work, Provide Notice of Copyright

1. The term *copyright,* or a derivative thereof, such as the abbreviation "copr." or the © symbol. (For original sound recordings, a symbol with a P in a circle is sometimes used instead.)
2. The year of the first production.
3. The name of the author, or copyright owner, if different.

In some countries outside of the United States, including the clause "all rights reserved" may provide additional protection. It should be noted that international copyright protection differs from country to country and may be nonexistent in many.

Another easy step for an author is to send a copy of the copyrighted work to himself or herself via registered mail as early as possible in order to establish a date of earliest production. Once received, the envelopes should be kept sealed in a safe place.

The most formal and important step to take in protecting one's copyrighted IP is to properly register it with the United States Copyright Office as outlined above. Although property rights and ownership exist at the moment of creation, taking steps to register copyrighted material provides stronger legal remedies to owners and makes cases of copyright infringement easier to prove.[13]

Because of the relative ease and cost of registration, it is recommended that all authors take the steps necessary to notice and register their original works with the USCO. Nonetheless, it is recognized that a significant portion of original work is created specifically for private use. For entrepreneurs, the importance of notification and registration increases in relation to the commercial value of any given work of authorship. Similarly, in cases of copyright infringement, the damages afforded in a lawsuit increase in proportion to the value of the copyrighted material and to the actual or potential damages resulting from infringement. Such damages may result even in cases where copyrighted work is reproduced and distributed free of charge, as such infringement can, for example, have a real impact on an author's ability to charge for use of his work in the future.

> "Under copyright law, unless there is permission or a license from the owner, generally it is illegal to copy, reproduce, publish, broadcast, or distribute copyrightable material published on the Internet. Whether a company uses an outside consultant or prepares its Web site in-house, the company ultimately is responsible for compliance with the copyright laws, and the penalties for infringement can be severe."
>
> ROBERT KATZ, ESQ.
> *Cooper and Dunham*

What Is Fair Use of Copyrighted Material?

A fine line exists between what sorts of reproduction and distribution are allowed under U.S. law. Section 107, Title 17, of the U.S. Code stipulates specific conditions of *fair use*, under which copyright infringement is not deemed to take place. According to the code, the issues at hand when determining infringement include:

1. The purpose and character of the use, including whether such use is of a commercial nature or is for nonprofit educational purposes
2. The nature of the copyrighted work
3. The amount and substantiality of the portion used in relation to the copyrighted work as a whole
4. The effect of the use on the potential market for or value of the copyrighted work

Under fair use guidelines, unpublished works are accorded the same protection given published works. Generally speaking, fair use permits limited activity in the realm of editorializing, commentary, and the reporting of news, as well as research and education. Reproduction and distribution of copyrighted material are allowed in some measure but are subject to many restrictions. In spite of the stipulations in Section 107, fair use continues to be a fuzzy area of the law. International rules about fair use and the increased popularity and use of electronic work available on the Internet make fair use an even more complex issue. In recent years, legal decisions have made it clear that great care must be taken to avoid violating the provisions of fair use.

Profile: Nikola Tesla

Nikola Tesla was one of the most prolific inventors of all time, an unknown genius with no business sense. However, for all the innovation he brought to the world, his name is strangely unfamiliar to most of us. While his genius may be virtually unparalleled, his attention to business details almost always took a back seat to the intellectual pursuits of known invention. As a result, Tesla's devotion to invention above business left him virtually penniless in his later years when he could easily have been a wealthy man. Tesla was often without sufficient finances to pursue many of his groundbreaking inventions. Better-financed contemporaries of Tesla, such as Thomas Edison and Marchese Guglielmo Marconi, both of whom had a superb business sense, often impeded Tesla's work and are credited with some innovations that actually belong to Tesla. In fact, Marconi used about seven of Tesla's patents in the pursuit of his own wireless work before being issued a patent by the USPTO in 1904 for the invention of radio. For example, Marconi won the Nobel Prize for inventing the radio. It was this fact that most upset Tesla, but it wasn't until 1943, a few months after his death, that the USPTO reversed its decision and accorded Tesla his due, specifically citing his patent number 645,576. Tesla's genius and devotion to the more intellectual aspects of IP are laudable, but his neglect of business matters provides a tragic example for future entrepreneurs.

WHAT ARE PATENTS?

The U.S. government originally established patents as a way to encourage invention and technological progress by granting inventors rights from which they could gain personally.[14] In exchange for gaining these rights, the inventor is required to disclose to the public the full details of the invention and "teach" anyone with interest how to make the invention work. On this basis, the government encourages the sharing of knowledge for subsequent inventors to build on rather than waste the nation's efforts in "reinventing the wheel." U.S. patents are issued by the United States Patent and Trademark Office (USPTO) in Washington, D.C. In most cases, a patent grants the inventor (or his or her heirs or assignees) specific property rights for a term of 20 years from the date the patent application is filed. In cases where a patent application refers to an earlier filing, the 20-year period shall extend from the date of the earliest referenced filing. The rights granted the inventor apply only within the United States and its territories and possessions. Inventors concerned about securing their rights outside the United States need to file additional foreign patent applications to do so.

In the United States, a patent grants its holder the right to exclude others from making, using, selling, or offering for sale the patented invention. For the value of a patent to be realized, the patent must be exercised to yield the patent holder competitive advantages from which to profit, or present financial compensation for allowing others to participate in the activities otherwise restricted by the patent.

"A patent only enables you to do one thing. You can prevent someone else from practicing what you have claimed in a jurisdiction (country) where you have a valid patent."

ROBERT MYERS
Fairfield Resources Intellectual Property Consulting Firm

What Are the Various Patent Classifications? How Do They Differ?

The following are the various patent classifications available:

1. *Design patents* are issued to individuals who have created a novel ornamental design. A design patent does not include the elements of structure and function.[15]

2. *Plant patents* are issued to individuals who have invented or discovered a novel type of plant and who have been able to reproduce that plant asexually. Plant patents are not issued for either tuber-propagated or uncultivated plant varieties.

3. *Utility patents* are issued to individuals who have invented novel processes, machines, and compositions of concern matter, or improvements thereof. Most of

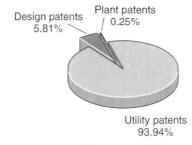

Figure 7-6   **New Patent Applications in the United States, 2001.**

the following discussion concerns utility patents—the most common but most complex of all patents issued.

Figure 7-6 shows the number of new patent applications filed in the United States in 2001. Figure 7-7 charts the amount of new patent activity in the United States in the period 1980–2000.

Anatomy of a Patent

The format and content of a patent are relatively standardized and usually follow this order:

1. A cover sheet that includes a brief abstract of the disclosure or description of the invention, a representative drawing, and other information, such as issue date and identity of the inventor and original owner.
2. One or more pages of drawings of the preferred embodiment of the invention.
3. A brief statement identifying the field of the invention.
4. A background section that states the problem solved by the invention. This may include a description of the prior solutions or attempted solutions and the reasons they were not satisfactory. This section must establish that the invention is indeed novel.
5. A section summarizing the invention, including its key features and advantages.
6. A section providing a brief description of the patent drawings, specifying what is being illustrated in each figure.

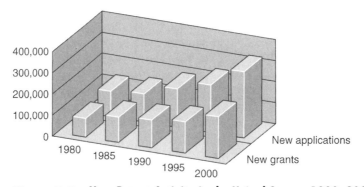

Figure 7-7   **New Patent Activity in the United States, 1980–2000.**

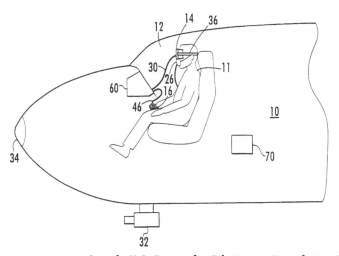

Figure 7-8   **Sample U.S. Patent for Piloting an Aircraft in a Smoke-Filled Cockpit.**

7. A lengthy section setting forth a detailed description of the invention with reference to the drawings. This textual portion of the patent is known as the "specification." The bulk of the "teaching" requirement is found in this section.

8. Finally, the patent concludes with the claims that are the consecutively numbered sentences at the end of the patent.

Figures 7-8 and 7-9 show part of a sample patent granted by the U.S. patent and trademark office.

WHAT ARE THE QUALIFICATIONS FOR A PATENT TO BE GRANTED?

The U.S. patent law has very specific rules for patenting a particular invention. Broadly speaking, all inventions must meet three major categories of requirements if they are to be considered patentable. An invention must have **utility and novelty**, and must be **nonobvious**.

Among the things that may not be patented are naturally occurring objects, entities, laws, and phenomena, as well as abstract ideas. Some types of plant may be patented, but only when the DNA has been genetically manipulated in a unique way, which may yield some novel and useful benefit.

- **Utility**: Nonuseful inventions may not be patented. Any useful machine, process, composition of matter, or improvement on the same may be patented, provided that said machine, process, and so on, is not disclosed in the prior art. The Supreme Court has broadly interpreted the utility requirement to include anything man-made under the sun, including genetically altered cells and animals.

- **Novelty**: For an invention to qualify as novel, a number of very specific conditions must be met. Novelty requires that the original invention predate knowledge and use or sale of the invention by others within the United States or any foreign country. The application must also be submitted within one year of the applicant's patent public use or sale of the invention in the United States.

The Director of the United States Patent and Trademark Office

Has received an application for a patent for a new and useful invention. The title and description of the invention are enclosed. The requirements of law have been complied with, and it has been determined that a patent on the invention shall be granted under the law.

Therefore, this

United States Patent

Grants to the person(s) having title to this patent the right to exclude others from making, using, offering for sale, or selling the invention throughout the United States of America or importing the invention into the United States of America for the term set forth below, subject to the payment of maintenance fees as provided by law.

If this application was filed prior to June 8, 1995, the term of this patent is the longer of seventeen years from the date of grant of this patent or twenty years from the earliest effective U.S. filing date of the application, subject to any statutory extension.

If this application was filed on or after June 8, 1995, the term of this patent is twenty years from the U.S. filing date, subject to any statutory extension. If the application contains a specific reference to an earlier filed application or applications under 35 U.S.C. 120, 121 or 365(c), the term of the patent is twenty years from the date on which the earliest application was filed, subject to any statutory extensions.

Nicholas P. Godici

Acting Director of the United States Patent and Trademark Office

Attest

Figure 7-9 Sample Letter on Receiving a Patent.

- **Non-Obviousness**: If an invention is judged to have been obvious to any person of ordinary skill in the field relating to the invention, it may be barred from receiving patent approval.

Reduction to Practice

At one time, inventors were required to present the USPTO with an actual working model before receiving a patent. Today a *constructive reduction to practice*

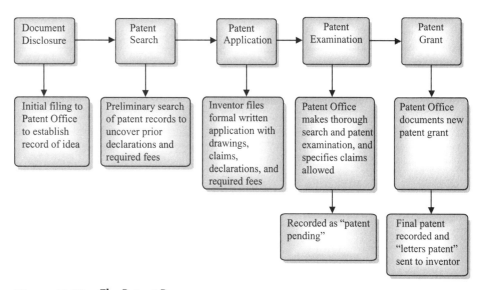

Figure 7-10   **The Patent Process.**

requirement stipulates that only the method of manufacture or effectuation of an invention needs to be made clear (not to the layperson, but to one skilled in the realm of art pertaining to the invention). The method requirement insures that only inventors who can actually deliver on the technological promise of their invention be granted a patent.

Figure 7-10 depicts the patent process from document disclosure to patent grant.

HOW IS INTELLECTUAL PROPERTY PROTECTED?

Many inventors find it useful to begin protecting their IP before applying for a patent. Depending on the sophistication required to both comprehend and copy the ideas, unprotected conversations with other people may or may not constitute a serious threat to security. If an idea truly has potential value, it is important to begin some form of protection and to act with caution. A simple nondisclosure agreement (NDA) or confidentiality agreement (CA) should be drawn up and signed by any person with whom the ideas are discussed, before any substantive conversation takes place.[16] Where the costs of having such an agreement prepared professionally are of concern, the inventor may wish to review some of the popular prepackaged legal software available in stores, or books on the subject for examples on which to base simple CAs (see sample in Chapter 2).

Another step is the protection of working notes and documents. Even simple measures such as using a safe or encrypting computer records could potentially go a long way toward preserving the idea.

What Professional Assistance Is Available?

In order to be certain that adequate background and preparatory work is done in producing an application for submittal, it is advisable that inventors seek the services of a registered patent agent or attorney. These individuals are skilled in carefully addressing the issues that might stand in the way of a successful patent application. Some differences between agents and attorneys are worth discussion.[17]

Registered Patent Agents

Patent agents are not attorneys at law, yet they are specially registered to practice patent law by and before the U.S. Patent and Trademark Office. Although the range of duties these individuals are legally authorized to perform is not as extensive as that of patent attorneys, patent agents are generally equally qualified to perform all of the basic work that many inventors will require in obtaining patents for their inventions. Patent agents generally have an advanced degree or work experience suiting them to their legal function. In addition, any agent who has not served for at least four years as an examiner within the USPTO must pass a special exam given by the USPTO to guarantee competence in the field of work. These individuals do not work for the government but may be found in private organizations, which serve the needs of inventors.

Registered Patent Attorneys

Registered patent attorneys must successfully complete the same exam issued to individuals wishing to become patent agents, but they hold higher credentials that allow them to perform legal services above and beyond those executed by patent agents. Most importantly, patent attorneys, by virtue of their juris doctorates, are authorized to litigate in matters of patent law in any states in which they are licensed to practice law. Having been admitted to the Bar Association, attorneys are bound by a code of ethics. Even if they fail to adhere to the ethics they pledge to uphold, their qualifications also permit them to be sued, should a lawsuit become necessary.

Choosing Your Representative

Generally speaking, one should expect to pay more for the services of a patent attorney, who is licensed to litigate over matters of intellectual property, than for the services of a patent agent, who is not licensed to litigate over such matters. Fees for professional services vary substantially between agents, attorneys, and among the members of the groups themselves. However, considering what many inventors have at stake, the cost of even highly priced professional services may be indispensable. It is advised that total fees be determined before entering into a binding contract with any agent or attorney, because many of the "flat rates" quoted by attorneys and agents do not actually cover work required after submission of an application. For convenience, the accompanying table provides a starting point, with some average figures obtained from a selection of queried professionals. The rates apply to small entities; large corporations will pay much more for comparable services.

Service Description	Agent	Attorney
Initial Consultation	Free	Free
Hourly Rate[18]	$100	$250
Preparation and Submission	$3,000	$4,500
Expected Total Costs	$4,500–7,500	$6,000–10,000

These figures apply most specifically to utility patent applications. Design applications can cost far less, sometimes half the amount of a utility application, and plant patent applications usually cost somewhere between design and utility. Office actions taken by the USPTO require responses from inventors, and rejected applications will require additional capital outlays in order to be disputed. Agents and attorneys may charge for such work by the hour, or these costs may be included in a fixed rate. Many agents and attorneys give inventors the option of paying flat fees, hourly rates, or some combination of the two. Again, the above figures are rough averages only. Inventors can expect to find costs varying considerably, given such factors as the complexity of their inventions.

The most important criterion for selecting a representative will be the relative amount and quality of experience in practicing patent law. You will also want to learn what sorts of activity the representative has regularly engaged in and his or her success. Were any complaints registered? Each of these questions must be answered, and you must weigh your answers carefully in your decision. If you intend to license your inventions to larger corporations as part of your business model (see Chapter 8), it is worthwhile to use an attorney from a larger national firm with a strong litigation department. In this way you are more likely to be taken seriously in any future negotiations.

Whenever possible, use an agent or attorney who specializes or has knowledge in the scientific or technical field pertaining to your invention. You can search the patent database and find patent attorneys who have written strong and important patents in your field. The added insight that comes with such an understanding can be especially helpful in guiding development in the most appropriate manner possible.

Finally, it should be noted that nonregistered agents, attorneys, organizations, and the like do not practice within the USPTO's jurisdiction, and so they fall outside the realm of regulation that the USPTO has over registered professionals. This will be a key consideration to inventors who may have grievances with their attorney, agent, or other representative.

DOCUMENTING THE IDEAS

The U.S. government gives rights to the first person who conceives an idea, provided that it can be proven. Therefore, it is very important to keep a well-documented account of the invention's development wherever possible. This may very well be the most important step an inventor can take in protecting IP rights. As noted earlier, mailing a disclosure of one's work to oneself via registered mail is a useful way to establish a verified date of idea origination for legal purposes. What is not commonly known is that there are more effective methods of establishing the origination of such dates. Some of these methods follow.

The Disclosure Document Program

Send a document disclosing the invention; this document must contain a comprehensive explanation of the invention and how it is produced and used. Where applicable, drawings should be included as well. Furthermore, a disclosure should be made as to the purpose of the invention and what makes it "novel." For the sake of efficiency, the USPTO mandates a specific format for disclosure documents. Contact the USPTO for details on the latest requirements and fees.

The Patent and Trademark Office will keep the disclosure document for a period of two years. During that time, the documents will be considered evidence of the earliest date of conception for the invention. If no official patent application is filed before the end of this initial two-year period, the disclosure documents will be destroyed. It is incumbent upon the inventor to proceed with the patent process in as expeditious a manner as possible to fulfill the intended purpose of safeguarding the origination date of property rights.

Upon receipt of the successfully completed disclosure document, the USPTO will return a receipt form identifying the date of receipt and providing an identification code for the document. Remember that specific reference must be made to the original disclosure document date of receipt and identification number at any such time as further documents, such as an official patent application, are submitted to the USPTO.

Other Options

Another effective way of safeguarding property rights is to maintain a witnessed, permanently bound, page-numbered notebook that records the ideas in an ordered and clearly understandable fashion. This notebook should record as much of the invention's features as possible, including notes as to the novel and useful distinctions and advancements over any existing similar art. Every time new material is added to this record, an objective witness should sign and date said additions as soon as possible. Forms of notarized records other than the bound book may also be kept.

WHAT IS PRIOR ART?

Before beginning the often lengthy and expensive campaign to get one's idea or invention patented, it is highly advisable that one conduct a search for prior art. The term *prior art* refers to all subjects that do not meet the condition of novelty, as explained earlier in the section on patent qualifications.

The USPTO examiner's first step in evaluating a patent application is to review the prior art. Discovery of the existence of prior art will immediately nullify any possibility of the application's approval. Consequently, it ought to be clear that beginning the patent process without having conducted a prior art search may very well be an exercise in futility.

USING SEARCH OPTIONS

Since professionals usually charge between $500 and $1,000 for a simple prior art search, most inventors should initially explore prior art on their own. While there's no way one can be sure how long the search may take, it is easily possible that their invention may be already disclosed in the prior art within just the first few minutes of searching. A variety of tools, including the Internet, can help the inventor discover the prior art status.

Internet Searching

The most easily accessible tool is the World Wide Web. By performing even simple searches on Internet search engines, the inventor will find hundreds of sites devoted to intellectual property, ranging from university programs to home pages for law firms. For best results, you should try using search terms related to your topic such as "intellectual property" and "patent." The USPTO's own home page, located at www.uspto.gov, is perhaps the most indispensable Internet site, replete with all of the information needed to successfully patent a qualifying invention. The additional sources appended to this chapter present numerous other sites worth visiting.

Agencies and Organizations

In addition to the Internet, several public and private agencies may assist the inventor in discovering prior art. The costs of employing them can vary considerably, but so does the effectiveness of each organization's searching capabilities. Inventors choosing to use professional assistance should research the firms, agents, and attorneys that they're dealing with before entering into any binding agreements. Look for a track record of success, among other things.

Government Resources

The United States Patent and Trademark Office

Crystal Plaza 3

2021 Jefferson Davis Hwy.

Arlington, VA 20231

The USPTO provides physical facilities that the general public can use in pursuing intellectual property research.

Independent Resources

Independent search firms will often employ the same computer databases available through the USPTO site. Whether paying an hourly rate or a fixed sum, inventors are likely to spend several hundred dollars for search services. Although some firms possess technical expertise in prior art search, there is no guarantee that the patent examiner will not repeat the process. Another factor is that some firms average four to six weeks to return the results of the prior art searches, though services may usually be expedited if a fee is paid for express service. The high cost of employing expert services this early in the patent process may be unwarranted given the complexity of many inventions. This matter calls for consideration on the part of the individual inventor.

Other Resources

In addition to the independent search firms, patent agents, and attorneys offering search services, a variety of other organizations offer various forms of service. These services may also be available through some of the aforementioned firms, agents, and attorneys.

Typically, an inventor can find both local and national inventors' organizations offering a broad range of services that can be equally helpful to both the novice working on the first invention and the veteran with one or more patents. Some of these organizations are nonprofit, and many require no fees or only moderate fees to join. In addition to being a valuable resource, organizations are often good launching pads for inventors looking for other resources such as journals, magazines, and other organizations. The World Wide Web and the local Yellow Pages are good places to start when seeking such organizations. For some additional information consult the additional sources at the end of this chapter.

Some Words of Caution

Before using the services of any organizations, check with the local Better Business Bureau to see if any complaints have been lodged. Be particularly wary of services that ask for up-front fees to promote your invention. The USPTO issues a warning on its Web site about "inventor services." It states that "there are many firms who prey on small inventors"; they essentially start with a small fee and grossly escalate charges while providing little in the way of substantive assistance. The Federal Trade Commission (FTC) is currently conducting an operation investigating such companies. Any inventor considering using an unfamiliar firm should contact the FTC for more information. Should an inventor already be mired in a troublesome relationship, it is wise to seek assistance from the FTC. Poor quality of work done for the inventor can actually do more harm than good to the long-term intellectual property rights. This is not to say that all such firms are untrustworthy, but forewarned is forearmed.

What Is the Patent Application Process?

Generally, only the inventor himself may apply for a patent.[19] In cases where more than one inventor are responsible for generating the idea, inventors must file jointly. Only in cases of insanity or death may another person legally apply instead of the inventor. Exceptions are when an inventor declines to apply or is unable to apply, in which case some person with an exclusive interest in the intellectual property may apply on an inventor's behalf.

The USPTO offers a choice of two patent applications, depending on what state of development an inventor's subject is in at the time application is made. Essentially, the inventor with a complete concept who is fully prepared to submit a comprehensive "case" for patentability will submit a *nonprovisional* application. Inventors who want to establish a filing date, but are not prepared, can file a *provisional* application giving them one full year from the date of filing to complete development of the invention. Concerns regarding marketability, licensing, capital requirements, and the like, should also be included. Only inventors seeking design patents are limited to use of the nonprovisional application form. Inventors seeking utility or plant patents may use either form.

Provisional Application

Provisional applications serve to establish an official date of filing with the USPTO. These applications are not as complete as the nonprovisional applications and must be succeeded within 12 months of initial filing in order for the formal patentability review process to follow.

The provisional patent application must include the following:

1. A cover sheet consisting of:

(a) a statement that identifies the application as provisional

(b) the inventor name(s)

(c) the inventor residence(s)

(d) the title given to the invention

(e) the correspondence address

(f) identification of any U.S. government agency with a property interest in the IP

(g) the name and registration number of any attorney(s) or agent(s) involved

(h) the docket number (if applicable)

2. A partial specification: this sort of specification may simply be an adequate description of the invention. No specific claims are necessary.

3. A drawing in cases where it is necessary.

4. A fee (consult the USPTO for fees, for they change annually).

Nonprovisional Application

The nonprovisional application is the more complete of the two application forms offered by the USPTO. Submission of a nonprovisional application will initiate the process of examination leading to a USPTO judgment on patentability.

The nonprovisional patent application must include the following:

1. A specification—a written description of the invention that makes at least one specific claim.

2. An oath or declaration.

3. A drawing in cases where it is necessary.

4. A fee (consult the USPTO or updated fee schedule for current fees).

The claims must be as comprehensive as possible. They will form the basis for an invention's patentability and serve to settle legal considerations concerning infringement after such time as a patent might be issued.

How Are Claims Drawn?

Claims are the most important element of the patent application. They officially designate the property boundaries of the invention. In a very real sense, the claim defines the intellectual property. If the claim is too broad, it may be invalid, and if the claim is too narrow, it may be infringed by a copier. Drafting claims is where patent lawyers earn their fees.

The Patent Review Process

Once the completed nonprovisional application has been filed with the USPTO, it will be assigned to a specific examination group knowledgeable in the realm of technology where the invention falls. From within this group, a particular examiner will take up the review. Reviews are conducted in the order in which patents are filed, or as otherwise prescribed by the commissioner of Patents and Trademarks. Inventors who wish to make a case for special consideration, including early review, must have appeals approved directly by the commissioner.

What Does "Patent Pending" Mean?

Inventors who want to engage in the production and/or sale of any article for which they've already submitted an application for patent may elect to mark these articles with the term *Patent Pending*. Doing so will serve notice to others that they may be in violation of patent infringement should they choose to engage in competitive production or sale of such articles or those that are substantially similar. No actual infringement can occur unless patent status has already been granted. Hence, the "Patent Pending" mark carries no legal weight. Nonetheless, the term may prove an effective deterrent to potential competitors. If, for no other reason, it might be used on this merit. The "Patent Pending" mark may appear on the article itself, its packaging, in materials promoting the article, or in any other appropriate and relevant way.

What Financial Considerations Should Entrepreneurs Keep in Mind?

Although receiving a patent is an accomplishment, it is worthless if it is not used. A patent simply gives its holder a "negative right" to prevent others from using the idea or infringing on rights in some other way. In order to make the patent and its related work and costs worthwhile, you must capitalize on the opportunity the patent presents. Doing so need not entail actually taking the idea and putting it into practice, although this is the option of choice for many entrepreneurs. As the owner of a patent, you may choose for a variety of reasons to employ any number of different avenues to realize some of the potential rewards available. Your decision either to start a business or use the competitive benefits offered by the patent to sell or license will include your risk preference, personal and professional constraints, as well as money consideration.

How Are Patents Licensed?

To license a patent, the owner authorizes a person or business to engage in activity that would otherwise infringe on the patent. In consideration for this benefit, the licensee will typically pay some kind of up-front fee, ongoing royalty, or both, to the owner of the patent. The decision to license one's patent for use by another need not exclude the owner of the patent from using it independently. Some inventors prefer simply to create and to leave more commercial endeavors to others. Having a revenue stream from up-front fees and ongoing royalties can help to finance the development and patenting of future inventions. Others simply don't have the time or finances to start a business built on the inventions. Even where time and finances might not be of concern, the licensing option can be a highly attractive alternative.

The subject of licensing is dealt with in more detail in Chapter 8 in the context of using it as an ingredient of a business model.

PROGRESS FROM IDEA TO PATENT TO ENTERPRISE

The following are the steps entrepreneurs must take to go from idea to patent enterprise.

1. Conceive an idea and perform a preliminary analysis of the market and patent potential. Take preparatory steps to protect your idea, limiting exposure and documenting carefully.

2. Document a brief, descriptive record of the idea. Define what is being protected. There are numerous forms of protection, and each may vary from a single attribute or range of services. Product features or an entire line of products may be included.

3. Select an intellectual property law firm. Consider the firm's success in handling applications and its experience with the technology related to the patent. Visit the firm for an initial consultation, which is usually provided free of charge. It might be helpful to compare the services and costs of using registered agents and attorneys.

4. Conduct preliminary research. Depending on your financial position, you or your attorney should perform the initial prior art search. This search may be done using the online resources of the USPTO or with on-site computers dedicated for this purpose. Attorneys and agents will have their own resources with which to perform this search. If no prior art is discovered, you may proceed to the next step.

5. Perform a detailed search. Conduct an in-depth review to identify and review related patents. This research must be disclosed to the patent office. If there are no conflicting patents, you can proceed to the next step.

6. Prepare the patent application using diagrams and flow charts. File the patent with a law firm and receive filing data from the patent office.

7. Expect a waiting period. It takes approximately 9 to 12 months to get a response from the patent office in the form of an Office Action letter. More than one such letter may require a response.

8. Respond to the Office Action letter. This is your opportunity to address any objections or issues raised by the USPTO with regard to the application.

9. Wait some more. For the next four to six months, wait to hear if the patent is accepted or rejected. It may happen that only part of the patent or claims is accepted. If you and your representatives have done a good job, however, the entire application will be approved.

10. Look for notice that the patent is accepted and that a patent number has been issued.

11. Embark on your new enterprise. Options may include licensing the patent for use by others. Ultimately, an exit strategy involving the sale of the patent can also be considered.

12. Maintain vigilance and safeguard your rights by searching for patent infringement and prosecuting appropriately.

WHAT ARE TRADE SECRETS?

In the realm of intellectual property, at times information is best left undisclosed, even if disclosure and registration with the federal government would afford a measure of legal protection. Vital information not shared with the general public, but valuable to the success of an entrepreneurial entity, may fall within the realm of trade secrets.

What Are Trade Secrets?

Modern trade secret law dates back to the Industrial Revolution in England, but its precedent goes back much farther: to ancient Roman law, which imposed punishment for persons found guilty of impelling others to disclose secrets of trade. In the United States, the Uniform Trade Secrets Act (UTSA) was drafted by the National Conference of Commissioners on Uniform State Laws. Because the protection of trade secrets differs from state to state, entrepreneurs need to familiarize themselves fully to best safeguard trade secrets.

Broadly speaking, a trade secret may constitute any manner or form of information that, by way of its secrecy, yields its user potential or actual economic value and economic and/or competitive advantage over others. In order for a trade secret to be legally defended as such, its "owner" must take reasonable steps to ensure its secrecy. Information subject to common knowledge may not be protected as a trade secret, but trade secrets needn't be complex or novel in order to qualify as such. Among the many forms a trade secret may take are those of formula, pattern, device, and process. Even a customer list may serve as a trade secret when meeting the above requirements. In some cases, such trade secrets are more appropriately referred to as *business secrets*.

What Are the Advantages and Disadvantages of Trade Secrets?

The trade secret's greatest advantage over other forms of intellectual property may be in the potentially limitless duration of its value and service to its owner. Coca-Cola is an oft-quoted example of a company that has maintained a trade secret for over 100 years and continues to enjoy the economic benefit of such.[20] Coke claims that it has been successful in keeping the formula for its popular soft-drink secure from outside discovery. However, this trade secret could probably be broken using the most modern methods of chemical analysis, but it would be to little avail. The years of withholding the recipe allowed the company to build such a powerful brand that, even if you could duplicate the product, no one would accept that it was identical!

There is a danger, however, in relying totally on trade secrets. Any formulation, process, or other form of IP maintained as a trade secret by one party can be lawfully employed by an outside party if development is done independently and without any infringement. Because the value of a trade secret may be compromised even under the best cases of internal protection, the decision to maintain some IP as a trade secret rather than filing and registering for a patent, for instance, must be weighed carefully. To help make such a decision, consider whether disclosing the details in a patent or just making it public would give your competitors a valuable head-start to develop a competing idea. Also, if you patent a process, for example, way to mix paints, it may not be possible to determine if the paint on sale was actually mixed the same way. In fact, in this case, it may be impossible to "police" whether someone else is using your invention. This is not true for a physical product, say a new type of pen, for this can readily be detected as soon as it is offered for sale. For this reason, many companies do not patent processes, but take careful steps to retain them as secrets.

You must also consider whether the value of some intellectual property might be reasonably expected to endure beyond the period of protection afforded by a patent. If only 5 to 10 years of real value are expected, a patent may be the way to go, because patents provide a more guaranteed form of protection. On the other hand, filing for, registering, and defending patents can often be far more costly than maintaining trade secrecy. Having a patent and yet no money to defend against an alleged infringer is the same as not having the patent. Here a cost/benefit analysis must be employed.[21]

What Is Trade Secret Licensing?

As with other forms of IP, licensing can be a viable business option for owners of trade secrets. Trade secret licensing is remarkable, however, because it may present the most interesting example of intellectual property longevity yet. Although the value of a trade secret may be compromised in the event that independent discovery of its fundamental aspects occurs, once a trade secret has been licensed under specific terms, that license remains inviolate regardless of what kind of information falls into the hands of the general public. Only the licensing party has the authority to amend the terms of a licensing agreement, should such amendment be requested on the part of the licensee. Even if the licensed IP becomes less valuable to the licensee, or to the licenser for its own use, the licensing fees and other financial provisions of a licensed trade secret may be enforced for as long as a trade secret license remains in force.

How Are Trade Secrets Protected?

The first step in protecting a trade secret lies in its identification as such. It is important that the entrepreneur or business entity engaging in competitive commerce inventory its portfolio of knowledge to determine whether trade secrets exist. Once identified, the trade secret must be actively protected. Failure to take clear and decisive precautions in this regard can lead to the loss of a valuable trade secret.

One of the most effective ways of maintaining a trade secret is to limit disclosure. The smaller the number of persons exposed to a trade secret, the lower the likelihood that it will fall into the hands of competition. Where possible, it is a good idea to expose only part of a trade secret to any given individual in whom some trust must be placed (such as a worker required for completing only part of a process).

An even more important consideration than the number of persons exposed is the *nature* of the persons exposed. It is better to place faith in a large number of individuals who can be relied upon to maintain the secrecy of some information than in just one who cannot. Members of a venture who have a vested interest in maintaining trade secrecy are naturally more likely to be reliable in terms of not disclosing key knowledge. Keep the trade secret disclosure on a need-to-know basis, and in all cases make sure that some form of CA, NDA, or other employment agreement is filled out and kept safe as early as possible.

Special attention is called for in cases where an employee, partner, or other individual may be leaving a venture. In such cases, filing a *noncompete agreement* would also be advisable. Agreements should also be made with entities working outside of the venture itself, such as venture capitalists, attorneys, engineers, suppliers, vendors, and other business partners. The company must also clearly demonstrate that it values its trade secrets. All visitors should be signed in and only allowed to visit "nonsecret" areas with the entrances secure at all times.

Any proprietary information fundamental to the ongoing success of a venture should be considered worthy of protection. Whether it takes the form of a supplier list or a supplier's price list, sensitive financial information, computer programming code, a manufacturing process, recipe, or marketing strategy, information that yields competitive and economic advantage must be safeguarded.

REVERSE ENGINEERING

What Is Reverse Engineering?

Reverse engineering is a process whereby an existing system of structure, design, code, or otherwise is analyzed and broken down with the purpose of understanding the system and how it functions, and it is then reproduced or improved upon. Commercially, reverse engineering is used principally in the study of high-tech systems such as those found in software and robotics.

How Can Reverse Engineering Benefit the Entrepreneur?

Provided that IP protection regarding patents, trademarks, and copyrights is not violated, this method can be a highly effective tool in building improved products. Given the enormous costs and great deal of time often required to bring new and competitive products to market, the advantages of reverse engineering should not be overlooked. However, reverse engineering can be an extremely expensive undertaking. Conditions such as market maturity, demand, product lifespan, and consumer loyalty (to existing competitors' products) should all be carefully weighed in any decision to reverse engineer, for they will factor strongly in the profitability of any reverse engineering venture.

How Can Entrepreneurs Avoid Intellectual Property Infringement in Reverse Engineering?

The issue of patent and copyright infringement has received growing attention, particularly in the software and communications global market. The software object code may receive protection under both copyright and patent law. However, the protection of the software code has differed with regard to the reverse engineering process. In order to circumvent infringement, entrepreneurs engaging in reverse engineering should observe the following steps:

1. Legally acquire a copy of the copyrighted or patented work.
2. Apply the reverse engineering to the work and develop an understanding.
3. Determine what aspects of the work are unprotected.
4. Incorporate only unprotected elements of the work into the new product.

These guidelines constitute only the barest of conditions one must comply with in conducting reverse engineering for commercial gain. This domain of intellectual property law is by far one of the most complex and least intuitive. Because of the highly complex nature of this realm of inquiry, inventors and entrepreneurs are strongly advised to consult legal aid in dealing with these issues.

SUMMARY

The United States and most foreign governments make provisions for protecting intellectual property. Among these provisions are copyright, trademark, patent, and trade secret. The government's purpose in granting protection for IP is to encourage the advancement of "science and the useful arts" by offering rewards to those who make such advancements. Intellectual property is important to the entrepreneur because it provides profit or other form of competitive advantage. Intellectual property possesses many of the same characteristics as other forms of property. It may be used, bought and sold, licensed, or otherwise transferred.

The development and protection of intellectual property can be a painstaking and costly process. Many tools exist to assist entrepreneurs in pursuing IP rights, some of which can add significantly to the costs involved, but which can prove invaluable to doing the job right. The government agencies responsible for the oversight and administration of IP matters are among the most accessible, inexpensive, and useful resources available to entrepreneurs. In addition, a variety of public and private organizations are available for hire in pursuing IP rights. Registered patent agents and attorneys may be the most qualified to help entrepreneurs. In spite of the higher fees charged by agents and attorneys, their qualifications and expertise can help overcome the complex hurdles encountered in the pursuit of IP rights.

Each form of IP offers different levels of legal protection by the federal government. Protection for IP differs widely internationally and in the case of trade secrets may even vary from state to state within the United States. Promoting and protecting IP is an active process. Specific steps can, and should, be taken to achieve these ends. It is equally important to defend one's IP as it is to avoid infringing on another's. Particular care should be given to avoid infringement in reverse engineering. Infringement can be extremely costly and may prove the downfall of even the most well-planned venture. However, if done right, reverse engineering can prove instrumental in advancing an endeavor. If you are involved in IP infringement, a cost-benefit analysis should be employed in determining what legal remedies, if any, to employ. The costs of prosecution can be daunting and may not prove worthwhile unless real financial gain is at stake. Where significant value may be in jeopardy, it is recommended that entrepreneurs engage legal counsel.

The field of law pertaining to intellectual property is complex and in constant flux. Recent developments in technology have only added to the complexity of IP law. It is recommended that the entrepreneur stay abreast of current developments and consult early with professionals in the field. The way entrepreneurs handle the development, protection, enforcement, and prosecution of intellectual property can make or break any enterprise. It also can be of particular consequence to startup companies with less experience and fewer resources. Conscientious attention to detail and commitment to one's project are vital to ensuring the success of an IP-based enterprise.

INTERNET IP SOURCE SITES

- U.S. Patent and Trademark Office: www.uspto.gov
- U.S. Copyright Office: www.loc.gov/copyright
- Delphion Intellectual Property Network: www.delphion.com
- IPWorldwide: www.ipworldwide.com
- Inventors Resource Homepage: www.gibbsgroup.com
- Derwent-Thomson Scientific: www.derwent.com
- Hoover's Corporate Information: www.hoovers.com
- Thomas Register of American Manufacturers: www.thomasregister.com
- Licensing Executives Society: www.les.org
- Everything You Want to Know about SEC Filings: www.10Kwizard.com
- American Intellectual Property Law Association: www.aipla.org
- Franklin Pierce Law Center: www.fplc.edu
- Inventors' Alliance: www.inventorsalliance.org
- Patent Café: www.patentcafe.com
- Inventors' Digest: www.inventorsdigest.com
- ABOUT.COM Inventors' Page: www.investors.tqn.com

STUDY QUESTIONS

1. What are the different forms of intellectual property, and how do they differ?
2. What is the purpose of trademarks, and how are they registered and protected?
3. What is the copyright process, and why is it important?
4. What are the various forms of patents, and what is the patent application process?
5. What qualifications must be met for a patent to be granted?
6. When does an idea need to be protected?
7. What steps would you take to choose a patent attorney?
8. What is the disclosure document, and how is prior art defined in the patent process?
9. What are the 12 steps to create a patent from idea to completion?
10. What are the advantages and disadvantages of trade secrets?

MINI EXERCISES

Case: The Use of Trademarks for a New Venture

Kurt Jones formed a new venture to design, track, and manage databases for retailers located in the Midwest region. The name selected—*Track and Monitor, Inc.*—was approved by the Corporations Department of the Secretary of State for their state in Denver, Colorado. Kurt wants to use the corporate trade name as a trademark to market the services nationally.

Question: Can Kurt safely use the name to market the services without conflicting with others and possibly change the name at a later date?

Case: The Use of a Service Mark

The first user of a mark doesn't register it. Later, a second user of the identical mark does register it.

For 20 years Charlie has conducted a furniture assembly kit business under the trade Name "*Build-Right*." Charlie has a large shop and sells building kits and unfinished furniture to customers in wide areas of Minnesota, Iowa, and Wisconsin under the *Build-Right* name (that is, he uses his trade name as a trademark and as a service mark). One day Charlie receives a stiff letter from a New York attorney informing him that five years ago the attorney's client placed the mark *"Build-Right"* on the federal trademark register as the name of a computerized block game, and that Charlie must cease and desist from further use of the name.

Question: Does Charlie, as the first user of the mark, have to stop using his mark just because someone else got it on the Federal Register?

Case: Project Name of Business to Be Marked on a National Basis

Rebecca plans to open an expensive Italian restaurant named *Ospettini*, in Boulder, Colorado, a university town visited by travelers and tourists. She wants to market the restaurant nationally and internationally through reviews in food magazines, guide books, travel and sports magazines, and food columns in newspapers, such as the *New York Times, Washington Post, Chicago Tribune*, and *L.A. Times*.

Question: Can Rebecca protect this name outside the state of Colorado?

INTERACTIVE LEARNING ON THE WEB

Test your skill-builder knowledge of the chapter using the interactive Web site.

1. Self Assessment:
2. Multiple Choice:
3. Matching of Key Terms:
4. Demonstration:
5. Case:
6. Video:

CASE STUDY: DATAMARK PATENT

EXAMPLE: HOW TO READ BUT NOT TO WRITE A PATENT

The way a patent is written can be extremely important in protecting a company's intellectual property. This case will show you how to read a patent and test whether you can find a way to get around the claims.

BACKGROUND

Datamark's original business idea was to create a new credit card format that would allow a consumer the benefit of only having to carry one credit card rather than the pocketful with which we are all burdened. In order to get into this business, one of Datacard's employees, Doug Taylor, filed a patent to cover the concept using a well-known firm of patent attorneys. It was recognized that without a patent, once the idea was known, any of the large banks or credit card companies could copy the idea and put small Datamark out of business.

PATENT FILING

The patent was filed in February 1995 and issued in November 1996, U.S. patent number 5,578,808. Go to the U.S. patent site, www.uspto.gov, and find this patent. Briefly scan it. Note the following points. After the abstract, you will find the list of prior knowledge and then the claims. After the claims, the patent gives the background to the invention including a discussion of "prior art"—that is, what is already known and the benefits. The inventor must demonstrate a need and a uniqueness beyond what anyone else has done. The next section tells the reader how the invention can actually be made. Again, to get a patent, the inventor must describe the "how-to." This is because patents are granted in order to increase the spread of ideas for the benefit of all; the trade-off for the inventor is therefore between publishing know-how against gaining a market monopoly for many years.

CASE STUDY QUESTION

Now turn to the claims and note the following points:

● There are only four claims, and three of them depend on the first claim. Usually there are more claims than this, in a patent including more "primary claims." Check out some other patents to see how many claims they have.
● The first claim begins with the words "A smart card...."
● The fourth claim lists four groups of applications that can be carried out by the card.

  It should not be too difficult for you to see how to get around these claims. Focus on claims 1 and 4 and see if you can think of a card format that would meet the original concept for "one card does all" but is NOT covered by Datamark's claims.

ADDITIONAL RESOURCES

Avoiding Patent, Trademark, and Copyright Problems   U.S. Small Business Administration SBA Publications, P.O. Box 30, Denver, CO 80201-0030

The Complete Copyright Protection Kit   Intellain, Inc., 1992, P.O. Box 6492, Denver, CO 80206

Inventors Clubs of America   Alexander T. Marinaccio, P.O. Box 450621, Atlanta, GA 31145-0261 (800) 336-0169

The Inventor's Notebook, 2nd Edition   Fred Grissom and David Pressman, Nolo Press, 950 Parker Street, Berkley, CA 94710 (800) 955-4775 or (510) 549-1976

Licensing Industry Merchandisers' Association   350 5th Avenue, Suite 2309, New York, NY 10118 (212) 244-1944

NASA Tech Briefs   Associated Business Publications, Inc., 317 Madison Avenue, New York, NY 10017 (212) 490-3999

National Technical Information Service Center   Center for Utilization of Federal Technology, U.S. Department of Commerce, 5285 Court Royal Road, P.O. Box 1423, Springfield, VA 22151 (703) 487-4600

Patent It Yourself   David Pressman, Nolo Press, 950 Parker Street, Berkley, CA 94710 (800) 955-4775 or (510) 549-1976

ROADMAP for
PATTERNS OF ENTREPRENEURSHIP
Implementation

☐ What Are Trademarks?
☐ What Are Copyrights?
☐ What Are Patents?
☐ What are the Qualifications for a Patent to Be Granted?
☐ How Is Intellectual Property Protected?
☐ Documenting the Ideas
☐ What Is Prior Art?
☐ Using Search Options
☐ Progress from Idea to Patent to Enterprise
☐ What Are Trade Secrets?
☐ Reverse Engineering
☑ **Definition of Business Models**
☑ **Capturing Value in the Supply Chain**
☑ **Using Databases to Create Value**
☑ **Locking in Customers**
☑ **Licensing and Franchising**
☑ **Outsourcing**
☑ **Developing a Culture for Innovation**
☐ Understanding Financial Statements
☐ Review and Analysis of the Balance Sheet
☐ How to Use Ratios for Financial Analysis
☐ The Value of an Income Statement
☐ How to Use Ratios for Profitability
☐ The Value of the Statement of Cash Flows
☐ Understanding Footnotes to Financial Statements
☐ Preparing Financial Projections
☐ Preparing a Forecast of Cash Flows
☐ Preparing a Breakeven Analysis
☐ Taxes

CHAPTER 8

BUSINESS MODELS AND THE POWER OF INFORMATION

"Some day, on the corporate balance sheet, there will be an entry
which reads, 'Information'; for in most cases, the information is
more valuable than the hardware which processes it."

GRACE MURRAY HOPPER

OBJECTIVES

- Learn the importance of business models.
- Understand the five components of innovative business models.
- Uncover value in supply chains.
- Use databases to engage and lock in customers.
- Compare licensing and franchising.
- Learn about outsource services.
- Learn how to build an innovative culture.

CHAPTER OUTLINE

INTRODUCTION

As we saw in Chapter 2, the environment in which a new company finds itself is increasingly competitive, with pressures not only from local firms but from overseas competitors as well. Moreover, technological advances are accelerating, customers are becoming more informed, and new products and services are being generated at a breathtaking pace. No longer is it sufficient to build a company around just one new product or service idea. Something more is needed if profits are to be sustained. As your company grows, you will need to explore ways to retain its competitive position against challenges from existing and new market entrants. The frameworks in which a sustainable high-profit company are constructed are called *business models*. This chapter explores this relatively new way of thinking about how companies are "designed" using innovations not just in the products and services that are sold but in the *way* they are offered.

A new company will start with an initial concept of how it will be structured to serve its customers, work with suppliers, and how it will evolve. As the company begins to grow, the entrepreneur will uncover knowledge about the company's environment that may not have been obvious at the outset. This new information must be fed into the company's plans to stimulate innovation not just in products and services but in the very fabric of how the company will operate within a unique "business model."

Creation of a powerful business model, as we shall see, requires blending all the aspects of the business into an integrated operating "system" where manufacturing, marketing, information, suppliers and customers, product development, and so on become one. This is not easy and requires you to build a way of thinking into your company—its culture—so that continuous innovation becomes a daily routine.

This chapter covers a number of topics related to business model design and implementation. We rely heavily on examples to help you understand what is meant by an innovative business model. Because there are almost as many novel business models as companies, rather than try to catalog them, we will present examples that will stimulate you as you plan your own company for growth. We will introduce different ideas that can be incorporated into a business model such as using information to lock in customers, learning how to capture value from your suppliers, deciding when to use licensing or franchising, and recognizing when to outsource activities to consultants or other companies.

Before defining a business model, we will present a well-known example that will help to introduce the topic.

Example: The Dell Business Model

Michael Dell became interested in computers at the age of 15 when he took apart an Apple computer and rebuilt it as a personal challenge. In 1984, while an undergraduate at the University of Texas, he formed a company called PC's Limited and started selling IBM-compatible computers assembled from standard components.

In 1985, PC's Limited made its first in-house designed computer using an Intel 8088-compatible processor running at 8MHz. These "Turbo PC's" were sold directly to customers via advertising in computer magazines. Each computer was custom built from a selection of options, thus providing a combination of prices lower then retail brands, yet with greater convenience than assembling from kits. Dell dropped out of school to run the business full-time; he made over $6 million in sales the first year.

In 1987, PC's Limited set up its first service programs to cover for the lack of local retailers willing to help. In 1988, the company was renamed Dell Computer Corporation, and in 1992, *Fortune* magazine included Dell Computer Corporation in its list of the world's 500 largest companies.

In 1999, Dell overtook Compaq to become the largest seller of personal computers in the United States. In 2002, Dell temporarily lost this position to

Hewlett-Packard when HP acquired Compaq but regained the lead in 2003. Dell has managed to grow rapidly as its profitability has grown, while its major competitors, such as HP/Compaq, Sony, and IBM have been unable to compete without sustaining major losses. IBM recently gave up the fight by selling its PC business to Lenovo in China. In its fiscal year ended January 28, 2005, Dell made a net profit of $3.32 billion on revenue of $49.2 billion. These figures represent 26 percent and 19 percent growth, respectively, over the previous fiscal year. After just 20 years, Michael Dell's "direct model" had created a company worth $105 billion.

Dell's ability to succeed while others have failed is a result of its powerful business model and the company's passion in execution of the model—not its ability to conceive and develop novel products.

According to Michael Dell, "Our direct model starts and ends with our customers. With the power of this model and our team of talented people, we are able to provide customers with superb value; high-quality, relevant technology; customized systems; superior service and support; and products and services that are easy to buy and use."[1]

With its singular focus on the customer, the model takes four basic concepts and creates a unique way of building and selling electronic products. This not only sets Dell apart from its competitors, but it means that the customer experience is revolutionary.

The four concepts behind the "direct model" which enables Dell to remain the low-cost quality provider are:

- **One-to-one customer contact.** Dell believes that the most efficient path to the customer is through a direct relationship, with no intermediaries to add confusion and cost. The company is organized around groups of customers with similar needs, removing inefficient translation of customers' requirements by resellers. This approach also reduces the costs to the customer by taking out at least one level of distribution expenditure, which can amount to up to 30 percent of the retail price.

- **Accountability.** Dell recognizes that technology can be complex. By making the company the single point of accountability, resources necessary to meet customer needs can be easily marshaled in support of complex challenges.

- **Made-to-Order.** Dell provides customers exactly what they want in their computer systems through easy custom configuration and ordering. "Build-to-order" means that Dell need not hold months of aging and expensive inventory. This concept is deeply embodied within the day-to-day operations of the company, with sometimes surprising innovations. For example, Dell does not take ownership of microprocessors until just before they are inserted into the circuit boards; they remain the property of their suppliers, such as Intel, right up to this moment. This reduces not only Dell's inventory costs, but also insurance and quality management expenses. If components are shipped by plane from Asia, the suppliers must provide their own transportation on a regular "just-in-time" schedule at their own cost. The supply of parts is so "lean" at Dell that the company pays for its inventory *after* the customer has actually purchased the product, thereby removing the need to have cash reserves to hold inventory. If the inventory on hand does not align precisely with demand, then Dell is ready with special-offer advertising programs that immediately redress the balance. Dell also allows customers to configure their own product at their Web site. The real-time data collected from this site feed directly into the supply chain information system that communicates directly with

Dell's component suppliers. It also reduces the cost of selling by removing labor costs of salespersons. Everyone at Dell is looking to improve on these ideas every day they go to work.

- **Non-unique products.** Dell uses standard technology as a key to providing customers with relevant, high-value products and services. Focusing on standards gives customers the benefit of extensive research and development not only from Dell but an entire industry. Unlike proprietary technologies, standards give customers flexibility and choice. This concept also reduces Dell's research expenditures well below those of any of its competitors. Unique "first-to-market" products are not the reason for Dell's success but a rigorous focus on the "direct business model.

The Dell business model seems so obvious and easy to replicate, so why have the competitors not been able to follow? First, the "old model" of selling through distributors and retail outlets was established by Compaq and IBM before Dell came on the scene. In order for these competitors to switch to a direct model, they would have to tear down their existing distribution network. This cannot be done overnight, and setting up a direct sales channel would compete directly with their existing resellers. This action might prompt a mass exodus of these independent partners, say to a competitor's products, destroying overnight the major sales capability before a direct sales model could be built up. Customers would also be confused by two price levels for the same product and where they would go for customer support. A local distributor would hardly welcome customers asking for support after they had purchased their computer online at a lower price. The difficulty of switching from a "legacy" retail distribution model to a direct model is a major reason for the inability of the competitors to follow Dell. Also, Dell has a "monoculture" built around its business model; every employee and partner is focused on its execution and continual improvement. The competitors, caught between conflicting business models, are unable to perform either one effectively to compete in a very cost-conscious market.

DEFINITION OF BUSINESS MODELS

A business model provides a framework in which entrepreneurs can examine their business plan and explore alternative ways for the company to function and grow profitably while building barriers to ward off competitors. It is more than a business strategy, for it describes how the different functions within a company work harmoniously together to build "more than the sum of the parts." The following definition captures the meaning: "A business model is a description of how your company intends to create value in the marketplace. It includes that unique combination of products, services, image, and distribution that your company carries forward. It also includes the underlying organization of people, and the operational infrastructure that they use to accomplish their work."[2] If you read the Dell example again, you will see how all of these factors work together to construct the unique Dell business.

A more concise summary definition can be stated as follows: "A business model is the way a company applies knowledge to capture value."[3] Note the emphasis on *capturing value*. Establishing value for your customers, and suppliers, too, and building a company that can hold onto this value are key to optimizing your business model. The greatest inventions may not be able to retain the value that they can provide. For example, imagine that you have invented a simple instrument, costing less than a thousand dollars, to detect the early stages of Alzheimer's disease, long before symptoms are detectable. Your test can enable preventive medication to be used to delay major patient needs for care and support for up to 10 years. The value of this is clearly enormous, not only in financial terms but in social benefits, too. Ten years of *not* requiring full support could easily add up to several hundred thousand dollars. Yet, who will pay you for your invention at a price that will reflect a major part of the value you are promising: patients, doctors, pharmaceutical companies, family members, health insurers, the government? None of these potential customers has a way of paying you for the value you can provide, and it requires a really novel business model to do so. Perhaps you have some ideas on how to do this. When you review the examples in this chapter, think about how the companies have designed their business to both capture value and protect themselves against competitive attacks.

Analyzing five vital components helps us construct a unique business model.[4]

- Articulate the *value proposition*, that is, the value created for the user of the product or service. Sometimes the value may not be created for the most obvious user. For example, the value of the Alzheimer's test may be for the health insurers rather than the patients or their caregivers. Such insights can trigger ideas for business models. Also, the value may not be obvious; talking to different users may highlight hidden values (see the DBI and Greif cases later in this chapter).

- Identify a *market segment*, that is, users to whom the product of service is useful and for what purpose; specify how this will generate revenues for the firm. This will help you focus your marketing messages and sales resources so that they deliver the highest and most profitable sales. This focus is particularly important during the early stage of building a company when resources are limited.

- Define the structure of the *value chain* in which the firm operates, and define the assets that are needed for the firm to function in this environment. Dell provides value to its direct customers and its suppliers. The Greif case presented in Chapter 2 illustrates how value can be created in several parts of a *value* or *supply* chain. Suppliers, customers, and other stakeholders operate more and more in *value networks*. Competitors may also be customers. The more you understand where your company fits in these networks, the better you can create a viable business model.

- Estimate the *cost structure* and *profit potential* of delivering the product or service given the value proposition and value chain. Having great products and services in a fast-growing firm, yet selling them at a loss, does not constitute a sustainable business model.

- Formulate the *competitive strategy* by which the innovating firm will gain and hold advantage over rivals. This summarizes how all the other attributes fit together in a model that both captures value and builds competitive barriers.

The rest of the chapter relies heavily on examples of different business models. In each case, you should analyze the models using these five attributes. In this way, you will gain valuable insights into how sustainable business models are constructed and followed. In particular, note how in most cases, they are innovative and not immediately obvious. Innovation in business models is becoming a key skill in the entrepreneur's toolkit. The following sections describe business models built around supply chains, databases, customer lock-in, licensing and franchising, and outsourcing. These examples can be applied individually or in combination to design your own unique business model.

ACTIONS

Every business exists within a network of suppliers, customers, competitors, and other companies, all vying to capture as much value as possible. Ask how you can capture some of the value that they currently provide, or add more value for your customers through innovation.

CAPTURING VALUE IN THE SUPPLY CHAIN

Any company finds itself in a so-called supply chain. No company undertakes all of the functions required to deliver an end product from "soup to nuts." Intel, for example, does not mine and refine the sand for making the silicon wafers for microprocessors. Rather, it purchases raw materials and manufacturing equipment from other firms, and it does not sell computers or other electronic products. It focuses on what it does best: developing new silicon integrated circuits for use in the products of other companies such as Dell. Intel relies on other companies in the supply chain and focuses on extracting value from microprocessors, leaving the computer value to companies such as Dell. Intel's business model is structured to maximize its retention of value in what it offers in this supply chain. If you are opening a restaurant, you will require fresh ingredients from the markets, tableware and kitchen equipment, staff, and perhaps a chef with years of experience. All these are components of your supply chain. You will also have to advertise, create promotional programs, and the like, all of which are your bought-in services. Every business is continually trying to maximize the value it can command and retain in its own supply chain or network. Sometimes the business model to achieve this goal is not obvious. Turn to the Greif example in Chapter 2 and think about the move from being a commodity supplier of metal drums to a value-added service provider of "trip-leasing."

USING DATABASES TO CREATE VALUE

Examples: Selling snow-blowers is a tough business. The majority of blowers are bought on impulse a day or two before a major snowstorm lands. And these storms are difficult to forecast. Competing for a last-minute sale of a snow-blower requires that a potential customer has *your* product in mind when she goes to the store—and just before the snow hits. Toro greatly improved its efficiency in this regard

We live in the information age. Data are being collected daily about nearly everything. Much of these data are freely available. Think how you can use data combinations creatively to generate greater value for your customers, and sustain your competitive position. How much of these data must you generate yourself, and how much are free?

by building a software program that took into account several independent weather forecasts, had local advertisements ready to go into local press and radio media, and tied its own supply network and dealers together so that they could get products into local outlets. This innovative combination of externally and internally created data helped the company capture greater market share from its competitors and reduce its cost of inventory that sat in stores where the sun was shining. Or consider Wal-Mart's vaunted supply chain software system which detected a sudden upsurge in the sale of flags on September 12, 2001. Its purchasing department immediately contacted its suppliers and tied up nearly all of the short-term supply of U.S. flags worldwide enabling Wal-Mart to be the "sole source" of flags for the next few weeks, bringing more customers into its stores.

The fall in price of computers and data storage devices, coupled with the Internet, have made the use of digital information as a competitive weapon no longer just the domain of larger companies. Startup companies can now harvest information technology to provide their customers with greater value and to create subtle barriers to competition. Indeed, this new low-cost digital freedom may even give smaller companies advantages over larger firms which are encumbered by "legacy" data systems and cultures freezing them in outdated business models. It was, after all, Amazon and eBay that created online bookstores and auctions rather than Barnes & Noble and Sotheby's.

Capturing data on customer requirements and using it to create unique services or products can be a powerful way of adding value and keeping out competitors. Recall the case of Netflix in Chapter 2, which has changed the way consumers rent movies. The power of the Netflix business model derives not only from the convenience but also the ability to "mine the data" obtained by combining information from ALL customers nationwide. This enables the company to make suggestions on what you might like to rent based on not only your past rentals but on matching your behavior with others with similar tastes. This ability is termed *collaborative filtering*. In addition, by getting instant feedback from their database (customers provide long lists of future wants), Netflix can balance its inventory centrally to meet both current and anticipated customer requirements, something that cannot be done on a local basis. Using this novel database structure, Netflix is able to provide its customers with a convenient personalized service, as it continually optimizes its own supply chain.

Example: DBI Services Corporation

When Neal and Paul DeAngelo left school in 1978, they decided to start their own company. Using a truck bought for them by their father and some standard mowing equipment, the two brothers provided services in "vegetation management" to businesses rather than homeowners. This choice of customer segment turned out to be the right one; businesses were more stable, and, as the company, DBI Services,[5] soon learned by listening carefully to them, businesses have greater and more complex needs than homeowners. For example, "Class I" railroads are regulated by the federal government on the amount of vegetation that may grow on their rights of way. This, for example, mitigates against fire hazards and ensures a clear line of sight at crossings for safety. DBI realized that the *value proposition* for these customers was not focused on low cost but on the reliability and speed with which a service provider could treat the vegetation growing along the tracks. If any equipment breaks down on the railroad, the loss of income from trains not being able to run will greatly surpass any small cost savings for the service.

Understanding the customers' true needs has enabled DBI to build a dominant position in this sector by designing and building its own vegetation treatment road/rail vehicles. These vehicles rapidly mount the track and detect the location and type of vegetation along the line, mix optimized herbicides in real time, and spot-spray using robot arms on the truck. This minimizes the amount of chemical carried and used, limiting any environmental damage and coincidentally reducing the time needed to refill the containers with herbicides. By mapping the exact location of every plant using on-board GPS technology, the company ensures that its next service run can be accomplished in minimum time, with highly efficient utilization of chemicals and equipment. The proprietary data that the company collects on its clients' unique situations are a major competitive advantage, making it exceedingly difficult for a competitor to bid accurately on a contract and to compete in service. DBI has no patents but protects its know-how and data through trade secrets and works with universities to augment its own science and technology. Neal and Paul have now "bootstrapped" their business to over $80 million in sales, using only bank loans to finance the growth. Their business model is based on the principles of providing business customers with reliable and customized services supported with proprietary information systems. Many students earn summer money by cutting grass; few grow a large and successful company from such a humble start.

LOCKING IN CUSTOMERS

Netflix and the DeAngelo brothers use customer data to provide superior services, making them tough competitors. This can be taken a step further. Information can be shared between customers and suppliers, so that the one is closely locked into the other as business partners. A business model based on information sharing can provide high barriers against competitors because the costs involved in integrating incompatible data and computer systems can be prohibitive. On the other hand, the entrepreneur must be aware of becoming too dependent on one supplier or customer when the "lock-in" can become disadvantageous. A sound business model using data lock-in will have multiple partners so that the dependence on one partner is reduced.

AOL has retained many of its earlier customers, even though its monthly fee is considerably higher than that of other Internet service providers. This is due to the "inertia" that results from the amount of personal convenience and data that AOL manages for its customers, making a change to a new service bothersome. Similar "data lock-ins" inhibiting a move to a competitor can be found in banking, insurance, and health-care services. Such lock-ins can also occur between businesses.

Gaining customers costs five times as much as retaining them. What information can you share with your customers that would provide benefit to both of you? Will this bind you together such that it would be difficult for your customer to change suppliers? In so doing, can you perform higher value services that would make it even more difficult for a split?

Example: General Fasteners

For years, suppliers of components to the major automotive companies have been squeezed more and more on price as the global competition in this sector has become increasingly tough. Even if a supplier has some proprietary technology, the large buyers such as GM and Ford are so powerful that they insist that their suppliers share their unique know-how so that they can play off multiple competing suppliers against each other. Life is particularly tough when the component is simple to make, the product is not proprietary, and there is an oversupply. Faced with these daunting pressures on profits, General Fasteners (GF),[6] a manufacturer of bolts and other metal fasteners for the automotive industry, looked for an innovative business model to change its competitive status. It started by undertaking the engineering design for new car "platforms," taking responsibility for how the car would be reliably assembled. This requires special, hard-to-come-by engineering skills. GF then contracted to supply the car company with just-in-time components directly to the production lines, with 100 percent quality inspection and guarantees. GF either uses fasteners that are made in its own plants or purchases them from other suppliers. It manages an integrated supply chain from design to final assembly. This requires GF's computer systems to seamlessly integrate with car plants exchanging data in real time. They are "locked in" to their customers in both design and operations, making it difficult for competitors to displace them. They provide both products and services. In addition, by taking over the front-end skilled design work, their customers have no need to retain these expensive skills in-house for occasional use, and therefore become more dependent on their supplier when they are ready to design a new family of cars.

LICENSING AND FRANCHISING

Licensing and franchising can be valuable components of a business model. They are often confused. This section describes their similarities and differences and explores when they are best employed as the basis or as a part of a business model.

Licensing and franchising refer to types of contracts between an "issuing" entity—the licensor or franchisor—and a "receiving" entity—the licensee or

Sharing your business with others can accelerate your own growth pathway and reduce your need for cash. Rather than selling part of the company to stockholders, you can use licensing or franchising. Is your idea a match to these methods either as a part or even the core of your business model?

franchisee. These contracts grant the receivers certain rights to access certain "intellectual properties" such as patents, trademarks, trade secrets, and copyrights, as discussed in Chapter 7.

The License Agreement and How to Use It

A license agreement allows a licensee to use intellectual property under certain conditions as spelled out in the agreement. A license agreement usually includes the following key topics:[7]

- The licensor and licensee are identified together on the basis of their reasons for entering into the agreement. This helps ensure that there are no misunderstandings between the two parties.
- The licensed intellectual property (IP) is precisely defined. This may give patent numbers, trademarks, and lists of trade secrets, together with a description of the products, services, and processes covered by the IP. The agreement also clearly states whether the licensor and licensee have any rights to improvements that either of them makes in the future. It is usual for the licensor to have rights to any improvements made by the licensee; if not, then the licensor could find itself blocked by new inventions made by the licensee.
- The granted rights to the IP are carefully defined. Licensees may have a great deal of freedom, or they may be limited to selling products, making and not selling, and so on. Any limitations to rights are also stated here. For example, if the licensee is not allowed to further license the IP (referred to as sublicensing), this requirement is clearly stated. On the other hand, if sublicensing is allowed, then the terms of this stipulation must be clearly defined.
- The "territory" allowed for practice of the rights is defined. For example, if a licensee only has a marketing presence in one country, then the territories can be divided among several licensees. The Dyson case presented in Chapter 5 illustrates how breaking IP into territories can be used to bootstrap financing creatively. The company sold rights to regions where it had no presence in order to finance the home markets. Only later did Dyson repurchase these rights. If the IP covers several different applications, then an entrepreneur can license rights in market sectors where it does *not* intend to operate, using the proceeds to fund its core business.
- The level of exclusivity is defined. An exclusive license provides just one licensee the rights stated in the agreement. Of course, if there are licensees for different products, territories, or markets, each of these may or may not be exclusive. A nonexclusive license means that the licensor can enter into as many licenses as it wishes even if the rights are identical. For example, when you use Microsoft software, you are actually doing so under a license agreement. You do not expect this right to be exclusive, and Microsoft issues unlimited licenses to its products. It is also possible to offer limited exclusivity. For a small company, it is important to examine the advantages of these different strategies. Giving one large company exclusive rights to an important piece of intellectual property may give too much control to a powerful outsider. On the other hand, granting unlimited licenses provides little competitive advantage to any one licensee. This should only be considered if the license is to the ultimate "end user" as is the case for the Mi-

crosoft Office™ suite of software. We usually recommend that a small company restrict the number of licenses it issues to two or three competitors. In this way, each has some advantages and yet not too much control is taken away from the entrepreneur.

- In exchange for gaining certain rights, the licensee pays fees to the licensor. These fees can be of several types. An *up-front* fee may be paid to initiate the contract. This fee can be very helpful to an early-stage company as a form of bootstrap funding. *Running royalties* are paid as a percentage of net sales of products or services. The percentage rate can range from 1 percent in the case of a simple product to 10 percent for a pharmaceutical formula once it has been approved for sale. *Advances* or *minimums* may be paid periodically to maintain the rights before royalty income is received. Minimums may prevent a licensee from just sitting on the rights and not trying to generate sales.

- Other terms include such items as term of the agreement, treatment of confidentiality, payment scheduling and licensor's ability to audit sales, treatment of breaches of contract, any warranties, liabilities, and indemnifications offered by either party, and other general legal requirements.

Licenses can be a key component of a business model. For example, an entrepreneur could license the rights to *market and sell* its products in certain markets, while restricting any manufacturing. This strategy provides several benefits: the company needs less cash to develop its sales organization; partnering with a larger company can provide reputation and customer confidence, which is invaluable to an unknown company; and the income from the license can be used to fund other development activity. The Ultrafast case on the Web site associated with this book describes how a small company supplying the car industry used licensing of non-core products to develop foreign markets, gain reputation, and provide early-stage, nonequity financing.

At the other end of the spectrum, some companies base their business model entirely on licensing and have no intention to produce or sell any product. For example, Intertrust Inc. in California[8] owns 32 patents with another 100 filed worldwide in the field of digital rights management, or DRM. DRM is software that protects the copyrights of composers, writers, film-makers, and software producers when the results of their efforts are transmitted electronically over the Internet. Intertrust recognized early on that this would be an important area for creating patents, which was borne out by the developments of such companies as Napster and the emergence of a number of high-profile lawsuits between copyright producers and users of their output. Intertrust's business model is to "stake out" the field by acquiring or developing a large portfolio of patents and then requiring purveyors of digital media to license these if they wish to continue to operate using technology and processes covered by the patents. License fees in this area can top $1 million up-front, with continuing royalties based on sales.

Other companies use a business model in which more than just rights to IP are provided to their licensees. For example, Amberwave Inc.[9] New Hampshire has developed a way of greatly improving the performance of the microprocessors found in every personal computer by modifying the properties of the basic silicon semiconductor "wafer" that are the foundation of most integrated circuits. Amberwave was started by Dr. Gene Fitzgerald, a professor at MIT. He undertook the original research there, and, in fact, the company initially licensed technology *from* MIT before developing the concepts further. Amberwave now owns or has exclusive rights to over 100 patents issued or filed in the area of so-called *strained silicon*. The company offers its licensees much more than just rights to these patents. Amberwave has invested heavily in developing the processes for using its IP, including building a complete semiconductor processing plant. This has created vast amounts of detailed "know-how" or "trade secrets" that would take any licensee many years and considerable investment to replicate. Amberwave therefore offers as part of its license agreements a program of "technology transfer" in which the licensee is taught the know-how existing within Amberwave and how to apply it to its own processes and products.

The Franchise Agreement and How to Use It

A franchise[10] is defined as a "legal and commercial relationship between the owner ('franchisor') of a trademark, service mark, trade name, or advertising symbol and an individual or group ('franchisee') wishing to use that identification in a business." In this case, the franchisor is viewed as providing a "starting-kit" for a new business, which enables the franchisee to create a new business with lower risk and costs than developing a business from scratch. Franchisors can grow their businesses into many locations without needing to raise the cash to do so, giving up total ownership of all the opportunity, while gaining some revenue in the form of fees to compensate giving up this "upside." In exchange for lowering risk, the franchisee pays some profits to the franchisor but gains from national advertising, centralized product/service development, and reputation derived from a national or even an international reputation and image.

Probably the best known franchise organization is McDonald's™. Each location is owned by a franchisee committed to funding the facility and startup costs but benefiting from a large and powerful central resource and strong brand. The franchisor has strict requirements regarding menus, quality, training, hygiene, facility design, and the like because any single bad franchise can seriously damage the value of all other local franchise holders. Such items as opening hours may also be required but may be left to the local owner. However, there are many other franchised organizations, and you can see the enormous variety at such Web sites as www.franchiseworks.com, where many new franchise opportunities are offered.

An entrepreneur should not seek to be a franchisee or build a business as a franchisor without taking competent legal advice. The field is littered with embittered partners, which can lead to expensive legal cases for resolution. These cases often arise because local conditions are highly diverse, whereas the franchise is based on creating uniformity across markets. Thus, a hair-dressing franchisor may spend a lot on advertising the latest "chic short-haired styles from Europe," which may play well in New York or San Francisco but perhaps not so well in the Midwest. Sales in one location may fall, and rise in another, leading to obvious concerns on fair use of fees. In contrast to licensing agreements, the federal government has issued regulations that require franchisors to prepare an extensive disclosure document called the Uniform Franchise Offering Circular (UFOC).[11] A copy of this document must be given to any prospective franchise purchaser before he or she buys a franchise. This law arose partly because of the concern that many potential franchisees did not understand the complexities and dangers of a franchise agreement, which ultimately led to legal wrangling and personal bankruptcies.

The franchise agreement allows a franchisee to participate in building a business together with other franchisees, under the rules stipulated by the franchisor and under certain conditions spelled out in the agreement. The agreement usually includes the following key topics:

- The franchisor and franchisee are defined together for the reason that they are entering into the agreement.
- The business of the franchise is stated, and the deliverables that the franchisor must provide to the franchisee are specified. These deliverables may vary considerably depending on the business type. They may include use of intellectual property, trademarks and names, recipes, formulas, training and training manuals, design rules for facilities, promotional materials, operations manuals, forms of advertising, products or ingredients that must or may be bought from the franchisee, identification of a suitable site, and so on. It is important that these specifications be as complete as possible to avoid future disagreements. The limitations of the franchisee's business are defined. Usually this entails a location or region of activities. There may be "area development rights," which are optional rights to develop multiple individual franchises in a specific geographic area.

The limitations may also spell out precisely what the franchisee may offer to its customers. Significant problems may arise in this area. For example, a restaurant franchisor based in California may stipulate that only organic health products are used in the foods sold; a franchisee in West Texas may find little market for this locally and wish to add barbecued meat products into the menu. The franchisor will argue that this devalues the franchise for everyone else by diluting the brand message, whereas the franchisee will claim that she cannot prosper when there is little market for organic health foods locally.

- The franchisor may offer to fund part or all of the startup costs. This may be an option or mandatory. Usually, the franchisee must show that it has access to a sufficient amount of cash to fund the startup.
- The commitments of the franchisee are defined. Again these may be very broad and include such items as the minimum investment in the business, local advertising expenditures, meeting quality requirements, purchasing from approved suppliers, sharing new ideas with the franchisor, and using common software systems.
- In exchange for entering into the agreement and receiving support from the franchisor, the franchisee pays fees to the franchisor. These fees can be of several types. An *up-front* fee may be paid to initiate the contract. There is usually an advertising fee of up to 3 percent of net sales due to the franchisor and then a royalty on net sales of several percent. The franchisee may also be obligated to purchase certain supplies from the franchisor or from "designated suppliers."
- There may also be items stating under what terms a franchisee can sell its business, including, for example, an option for the franchisor to purchase the business and make it a franchise-owned property. In this way, an entrepreneur can view franchising as an alternative route to building a large wholly owned company using franchisees' funds for the growth phase. Franchisees may welcome this built-in "exit strategy," giving them a fair return on their own investment and efforts.
- Other terms include such items as length of the agreement and conditions for renewal (the initial period agreed upon is typically around seven years), treatment of confidentiality, payment scheduling, and franchisor's ability to audit sales, treatment of breaches of contract, any warranties, liabilities and indemnifications

offered by either party, and other general legal requirements, including a noncompete stipulation.

Unlike licensing, which is often only a small, if important, part of a business model, franchising is usually the core of a business model. However, even within the confines of a standard franchise agreement, entrepreneurs have managed to innovate powerful new business models.

Example: ChemStation's Franchise Model

George Homan founded ChemStation[12] in 1983 after he had spent some years as a distributor of industrial cleaning chemicals. His close contact to customers led him to recognize that businesses do not want to handle bulky containers of cleaning chemicals. George saw an opportunity to provide a better service by offering custom-formulated, environmentally friendly industrial cleaning and process chemicals delivered to proprietary refillable containers, which are placed free of charge at customer facilities. ChemStation has used a franchise business model to expand rapidly nationally without the need for the founding entrepreneur to raise any external capital. ChemStation has used its franchisee network very effectively to get tremendous reach within the U.S. market. The first franchise was given in 1985, and since then 48 franchises have been awarded. Today there are 50 units operating in the United States, of which only two are company owned. George's elegant business model is depicted in Figure 8-1.

The franchisor's headquarters are based in Ohio, which also serves some local customers and uses its buying power to purchase cleaning chemicals at a lower price than small competitors. The headquarters also holds the secure and coded database of proprietary cleaning formulas for specific customer needs, whether to clean egg-packing equipment or the floors of a car-assembly plant. A franchisee is granted a region to service and funds the local marketing, sales, and delivery services after paying an entry fee of about $1 million to ChemStation. In exchange, the franchisee gets access to the database on demand when a customer need is defined. This provides the formula for the optimum cleaner components and the usage instructions. In this

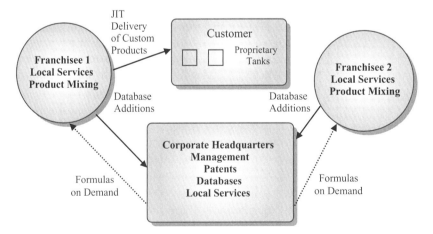

Figure 8-1 **ChemStation's Unique Business Model.**

way, the franchisee can provide customers with an immediate, proven solution to their cleaning problems.

In addition, if a major national company, for example, a rental car firm, would like every car to be cleaned the same way and have a distinctive brand-building aroma, ChemStation can provide the formula to every franchisee for delivery to local offices. A small local firm is unable to guarantee this service. In the event that no solution can be found in the database for a customer's new problem, and the franchisee develops the answer, then the franchise agreement commits them to submit the answer to the central database, where it becomes available to all franchisees and adds to ChemStation's intellectual assets. In this way, the franchise model is enhanced by the continual building of a proprietary database of customer solutions, adding greater value to both the franchisor and franchisees.

Whatever problems are solved at a franchisee's location are fed into the software package that has been devised by ChemStation, and the new solution now becomes an integral part of the ChemStation database. The sharing of such information by the franchisees with the HQ is mandated by a written agreement between ChemStation and its franchisees. The database is a key asset for ChemStation, and it has the necessary software and framework in place to interpret the results and distribute the data. The database also builds barriers against competition. For example ChemStation solved a cleaning problem at a Harley Davidson plant within its shock absorbers manufacturing division, which resulted in using one cleaning solution on one line and another solution for the adjacent sister line. This subtle know-how becomes part of ChemStation's data bank. Such captured knowledge helps to lock in customers and prevents competitors from gaining the account. Since its founding, ChemStation has captured, in less than 10 years, around 25 percent of the $300 million U.S. industrial cleaner market from local "mom 'n' pop" suppliers. It has done so by providing customized cleaning solutions in an innovative business model, which includes elements of franchising, data mining of customer information, and customer lock-in.

OUTSOURCING RESOURCES

Every company, large or small, is now contemplating "outsourcing" some and even most of its functions, for several reasons.[13,14]

- The costs associated with certain activities are much lower in certain parts of the world than in others. This is particularly true for the manufacture of high-volume consumer products and garments, staffing of call centers, and more recently, software production.

- Certain functions may not be core to the business, and experts that focus on just one thing, say Web site design, can usually be more effective as a supplier to you than you performing this function in-house, particularly if you only need these resources for a certain time.

- Some routine activities such as payroll management, Internet services, and healthcare management need either large investments in hardware or very specialized databases. By outsourcing such functions, a company can gain from economies of scale without having to make a large investment. The third-party investment is spread over many customers.

ACTIONS

Startup companies are strapped for resources. If there is someone who can do something better and faster than you can and it is not core to the company's business, then you should seriously consider outsourcing the work.

- Small companies are always short of management time and skills. These should not be wasted on noncore functions.
- Knowledge is becoming more specialized. Even large companies cannot afford to have a very narrow, yet deeply knowledgeable, expert sitting around waiting for the day that her know-how will be needed.

Outsourcing can be a viable option for everything from payroll, accounting, manufacturing, and delivery to customer service, employee training, property management, and computer services. The key advantage of outsourcing is that it enables you to invest your resources in more profitable activities. Companies, however, should be careful not to outsource functions that appear negligible but that are actually essential, such as customer service operations in a small business that wishes to build rapport and a loyal customer base.

Outsourcing functions range from use of individual specialist consultants and focused service providers to full manufacturing facilities and large software program developers. Small companies, in particular, are nearly always stretched for resources, and careful use of outsourcing should be part of their business model. Use the following checklist to test whether you should outsource a task:

- Is the activity central to the company's success? (E.g., will you lose close contact with your customers, or will you not be able to control later versions of your products?)
- Can the outsourcing lead to a loss of intellectual property rights or leakage of valuable trade secrets to competitors of their suppliers? (E.g., outsourcing the engineering of a piece of manufacturing equipment tailored to your proprietary products might leak to a competitor using the same engineering contractor, providing valuable knowledge about your business.)
- Is the task routine and wasteful of your staff's time? (E.g., payroll tax calculations, payments of regular bills.)
- Is this a one-off or periodical need? (E.g., building a stand for a trade fair or managing relationships with the media.)
- Is it less expensive to have an outsider do it rather than in-house? (E.g., writing routine software, or staffing a call center.)
- Alternatively, will the task cost less in-house BUT use resources that are more valuable elsewhere? (E.g., building 10 extra prototypes of a new product for customer trials when you need your designers to work on the *next* product.)
- Is the skill so specialized that it's impractical to have a full-time employee provide the best input? (E.g., you need to know how to do accelerated sunlight aging tests on a new fabric you plan to use in a planned range of women's coats. Don't balk

at paying a high fee for the best consultant. One full day's briefing from an expert, even if it costs you $5,000, can save you many times that by avoiding mistakes.)

If none of these questions elicits concern, you should consider outsourcing the task. Here are some tips for finding and working with an external consultant or company.

- Ask around in your field for recommendations on good outsourcing firms or consultants. Search the Internet to expand the list. Ask the companies or consultants to give you references, and interview their clients to find out how reliable and flexible service providers are or how knowledgeable the expert consultants were. Unless the references are stellar, do not proceed. This is a case of "when in doubt, don't." A small company does not have the luxury of making a bad decision. You must feel entirely comfortable with the provider.

- Choose a company that understands *your* needs and can meet them. Devise a contract that allows you to adjust the terms of the agreement to suit unpredictable changes. An arrangement that's satisfactory now may not work in the future as your company expands or competition increases. For example, Intuitive Controls, described in Chapter 2, outsources all of its manufacturing to a small firm that has been very supportive, including being accommodating in demanding payments when Intuitive Controls has been short of cash. Now that sales are accelerating, a concern is whether the outsource manufacturer can expand fast enough to meet new demand. The companies meet regularly to make sure that they can resolve these issues as they arise and modify their contract accordingly.

- Outsourcing implies loss of direct control and supervision, so communicate clearly the performance standards you expect. Record these standards in the contract in detail, include a "right to inspect" clause, and check up periodically to make sure your standards are being met.

- Schedule regular meetings with your staff member who is managing the outsourcing and discuss any day-to-day problems encountered. Staying abreast of what's going on will prevent potential problems from getting out of hand.

- Always make sure you have a backup in place in the event that the outsourcing company cannot complete its tasks. A call center, for example, should provide you with a regular electronic log of all calls; a manufacturer should provide a copy of drawings of any equipment made for your project, together with an operating manual, quality control (QC) procedures and data, and these should be kept in a secure location.

Example: Outsourcing Application Service Providers

Entrepreneurs can outsource critical software applications rather than deploy them in-house. Using an application service provider (ASP) to host an application can save time and money, especially if the business does not have the necessary technical expertise. An ASP is any company that remotely hosts a software application on a recurring fee basis. ASPs are often able to provide entrepreneurs with software tools that are equal or even better than those that have been developed in-house by large corporations. ASPs provide a number of advantages:

1. Applications can be up and running quickly with low up-front costs.
2. Ongoing operational, maintenance, and continual product improvement headaches are removed from the company.

3. Outsourcing frees capital and personnel resources that can be used for more important tasks.

For example, Schoolwires Inc.[15] hosts Internet portal software for school districts. This enables students, teachers, parents, and the community to interact on the Internet without the schools having to develop their own software or in-house skills for managing their Web site. Schoolwires is an ASP serving the education sector. The company uses two sales channels for its products and services. It maintains a direct salesforce for certain regions as the company wishes to hear directly from customers about new features they are seeking. These ideas are vital to the company as it continually enhances its products. However, developing a national salesforce would be too costly for the company; therefore, it also works through re-sellers in many of its markets. Efficiently managing such a complex sales distribution network also requires specialist software. Therefore, Schoolwires itself purchases this function from another ASP, www.salesforce.com, preferring to devote its in-house computer experts to building its own proprietary software.

ROADMAP

ACTIONS

Companies do not succeed unless they have an internal culture that is fully aligned with the firm's mission and allows the organization to respond rapidly to external changes. Cultures are easier to build starting from scratch. Learn the leadership skills to build the right culture for your company.

DEVELOPING A CULTURE FOR INNOVATION

A successful entrepreneur must demonstrate strong leadership skills and the ability to engage everyone in pulling together toward a single defined goal. As we have seen, innovation, not only in products and services, but in the all-encompassing business model, is an important factor for success. Companies with seemingly identical financial assets, products, brand recognition, and the like may perform entirely differently—one is highly successful, the other gradually declines. The successful one is judged as innovative, the other dull or unable to get its innovative ideas executed smoothly. Why is this? Michael Dell was not the first person to experiment with the "direct model" for computers. Why did he succeed where others failed? We believe that the ability to lead an organization on a mission where everyone is involved every day in moving forward toward clearly defined goals makes the difference between success and failure.

Much research has been done in this area, and many business books have been written about the field. On one point at least there seems to be consensus. A culture for innovation requires leadership from the very top of an enterprise. It is never too early to start, and this section will guide you in shaping a winning culture for your company. Getting it right from the start is *much* easier than trying to change an old, unsuitable, and deeply embedded culture.

We have narrowed the leadership attributes down to 10 factors, which should be practiced and demonstrated by your leadership style. We have tried to make these factors largely independent of each other so that you can identify areas where you

Table 8-1   **Cultural Attributes of a Successful Innovative Company**[16]

Attribute	Definition	Example Statements
Honesty	The degree to which each employee has total confidence in the integrity, ability, good character of others, and the organization, regardless of role	"I trust the people I work with; I find it easy to be open and honest with people from other departments."
Alignment	The degree to which the interests and actions of each employee support the clearly stated and communicated key goals of the organization	"We have clear aims and objectives which everyone understands; we build consensus around key objectives; we recognize and reward loyalty."
Risk	The degree to which the organization, employees, and managers take risks	"I am encouraged to experiment; we take calculated risks; we encourage trial and error."
Teams	The degree to which team performance is emphasized over individual performance	"We promote teamwork; it is the center of everything that we do; there are usually people from other departments in my team; we have both problem-solvers and 'out-of-the-box' thinkers in our teams."
Empowerment	The degree to which each employee feels empowered by managers and the organization	"As a manager, I am expected to delegate; we have a 'no-blame' culture; we allow staff to make decisions."
Freedom	The degree to which self-initiated and unofficial activities are tolerated and approved throughout the organization	"I am allowed to do my own thing; we encourage people to take initiatives; we recognize the individual."
Support	The degree to which new ideas are welcomed from all sources and responded to promptly and appropriately	"We encourage fresh ideas and new approaches; we reward innovative individuals; we reward innovative teams."
Engagement	The degree to which all levels of the organization are engaged with the customer and the operations of the organization	"Management understands the operations of the company; I can share problems with my managers; I know why my job is important."
Stimuli	The degree to which it is understood that unrelated knowledge can impact product, service, and operations improvements	"I am encouraged to search externally for information and obtain data from many sources; we listen to suppliers' suggestions."
Communication	The degree to which there is both planned and random interaction between functions and divisions at all levels of the organization	"I am kept in the picture on how we are performing; we have excellent formal channels of communications; we use best practice knowledge transfer between departments; we actively manage our intellectual assets."

can improve your management style, without too much concern that changes in one area will create other problems.

Table 8-1 provides definitions of these ten cultural attributes, together with illustrative statements that might be casually overheard within a company. We suggest that you review these factors and ask yourself whether your leadership style exhibits these attributes. Imagine what you might hear if you could be a fly on the wall in the offices of a company you are leading. If you cannot imagine hearing these statements, start modifying your behavior and adopt a leadership style in which such factors would become more evident. This will help you build a flexible, innovative organization where everyone is valued and is able to contribute to innovation daily.

It is easy to imagine successful entrepreneurs encouraging these behaviors. When you next see or read an interview with a successful entrepreneur, you will not find it difficult to imagine how she would have run her own organization along the lines of these attributes.

SUMMARY

In today's increasingly complex world, a new product or service idea is unlikely to be sufficient to grow a successful new company that can sustain good profits over a long time. Increasingly, innovation must be invested in the *way* of doing business to capture value from your efforts and prevent competitors from eroding your position. These ways are called business models. There are many different types of such models, and this chapter described several that will help you create your own versions. As a company evolves, its business model may change, and a successful entrepreneur will continually learn from customers, suppliers, and other sources so that the company can "move with the times." It is important that, as a leader, the entrepreneur builds an organization that involves everyone in the day-to-day process of driving the company toward its stated goals and innovating where appropriate to do so. The earlier the right culture is created, the more successful the company will be.

STUDY QUESTIONS

1. What definition of business model do you find most useful, and why? What are the four basic components of Dell's business model?
2. What are the five factors to consider when analyzing a business model?
3. Refer to the Greif case in Chapter 2. Why was Greif able to capture more of the value in the supply chain? Where did the extra value come from, and were there others who lost the value they were selling?
4. What is digital collaborative filtering? Name three companies that are successfully using this technique in their business model. Can you think of other businesses that might employ this technique in their business models? (*Hint:* Think of media companies and retail stores.)
5. What do you find most innovative about the DBI business model? Can you think of similar examples where these concepts might be used?
6. Name three similarities and three differences between a franchise and a license.
7. Name six factors that make outsourcing attractive.

EXERCISES

1. Why do you think Dell was successful when other companies trying the same model failed?

2. Turn to Table 8-1 and grade yourself on a 1–5 scale on each attribute (5 being the highest). If you started a company, what three things would you do to improve your leadership style?

3. Think of a possible idea for a franchise business model. You can search the Internet for ideas if you wish. In this case, would you rather be the franchisee or the franchisor? Why?

INTERACTIVE LEARNING ON THE WEB

Videos: Go back and read the DBI case and then watch the four video sequences of Neal DeAngelo. Visit the company's Web site. Consider the following questions:

1. Do you feel that Neal has a "passion" for what he and his brother are building? Are you willing to work as hard in the early years and take the personal risks?

2. DBI serves both private and government clients. In some cases, customers are mandated by law to take the lowest bid. How does DBI manage this situation? What sort of relationships does DBI have with its customers? How do these relationships shape the company's business model?

3. DBI has grown rapidly and has several locations. Does Neal think about forming a unique culture for the company, and, if so, how can this be accomplished? Do you think the company has a clear plan?

4. DBI is still owned by the DeAngelo family members. Is the company a lifestyle company? What specific issues does this private family-owned structure raise with regard to financing growth, management succession, and eventual "cashing-out" of the value that has been built?

5. Why does DBI outsource for some research tasks to universities? What are the dangers in doing so?

CASE STUDY: ULTRAFAST

We have created a case study for this chapter on the book Web site. It concerns a company started and grown by an entrepreneur after recognizing a "point of pain" when working for a larger company. The founder used licensing and government grants to bootstrap the company, retaining control before the company actually went bankrupt—however, not before building a complete manufacturing plant to supply the car industry. We chose this case because failures often provide insights that are not seen in stories of success. Go to the book Web site at www.wiley.com/college/kaplan and watch the video sequence on the Ultrafast case related by one of the authors.

1. Describe how the company used licensing to accelerate its development. What advantages and disadvantages did this strategy have for the company in the short and long term, and for the tool licensees, Bosch and Atlas Copco?

2. Draw a diagram of all different types of companies in the supply chain that Ultrafast found itself, including bolt manufacturers, suppliers of automatic assembly equipment, hand tools used in repair workshops, companies that chemically treat car components, and the car manufacturers themselves. How do these relate to each other? What value did each of these supply to their customers *before* Ultrafast came on the scene? How is the value distribution changed when the Ultrafast method is proven and enters the market? Which companies can gain most from Ultrafast, and which can suffer? Is the business model followed by the company the best one for capturing the value from the invention?

3. Using licenses and government grants to bootstrap the company, the founding entrepreneur managed to retain full control of the company right to the end. Was this ultimately the best thing for him or the company? If not, why not? What lessons on ownership and personal ambitions can you gain from this example?

4. Imagine that you had started this company. What would you have done differently?

ADDITIONAL RESOURCES

The Licensing Executive Society, LES, is a professional organization for those practicing licensing and technology transfer. Their Web site (www.usa-canada.les.org/) provides information about licensing and has many links to other sites of interest on this topic.

For access to articles and advice on franchising, visit www.franchisefoundations.com/. Although this is a commercial site offering consulting advice to potential franchisors and franchisees, there are excellent references and links to a number of valuable articles and learning tools.

To access a number of articles and cases on building organizational culture, refer to www.business.com/directory/management/organization_development/corporate_culture/.

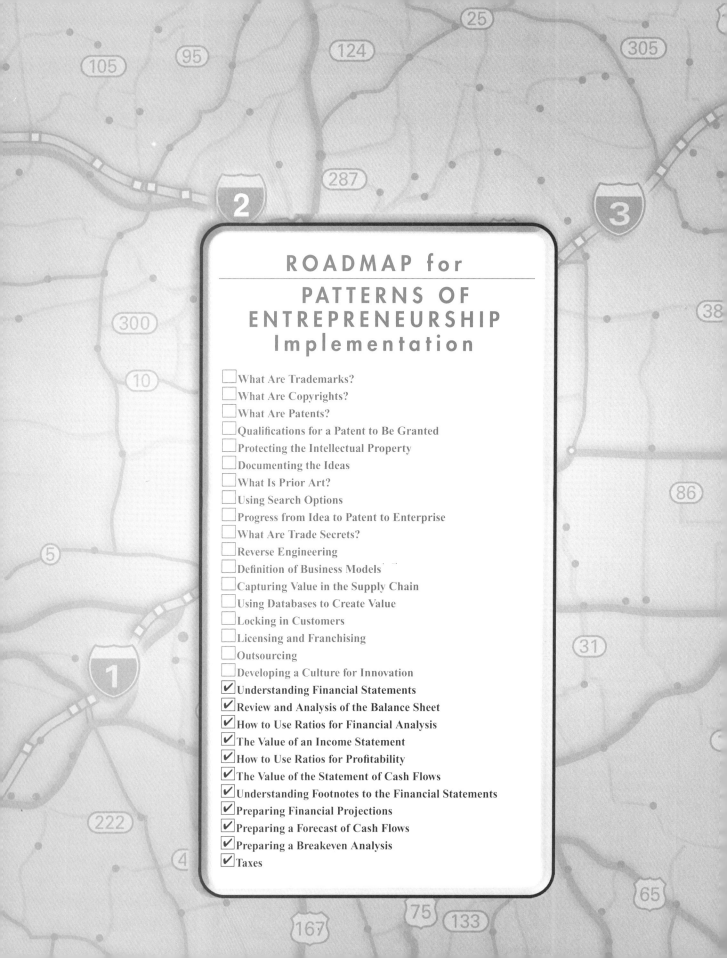

ROADMAP for

PATTERNS OF ENTREPRENEURSHIP
Implementation

- ☐ What Are Trademarks?
- ☐ What Are Copyrights?
- ☐ What Are Patents?
- ☐ Qualifications for a Patent to Be Granted
- ☐ Protecting the Intellectual Property
- ☐ Documenting the Ideas
- ☐ What Is Prior Art?
- ☐ Using Search Options
- ☐ Progress from Idea to Patent to Enterprise
- ☐ What Are Trade Secrets?
- ☐ Reverse Engineering
- ☐ Definition of Business Models
- ☐ Capturing Value in the Supply Chain
- ☐ Using Databases to Create Value
- ☐ Locking in Customers
- ☐ Licensing and Franchising
- ☐ Outsourcing
- ☐ Developing a Culture for Innovation
- ☑ **Understanding Financial Statements**
- ☑ **Review and Analysis of the Balance Sheet**
- ☑ **How to Use Ratios for Financial Analysis**
- ☑ **The Value of an Income Statement**
- ☑ **How to Use Ratios for Profitability**
- ☑ **The Value of the Statement of Cash Flows**
- ☑ **Understanding Footnotes to the Financial Statements**
- ☑ **Preparing Financial Projections**
- ☑ **Preparing a Forecast of Cash Flows**
- ☑ **Preparing a Breakeven Analysis**
- ☑ **Taxes**

CHAPTER 9

MANAGING THE MONEY

"The secret of success in life is known only to those who have not succeeded."

J. CHURTON COLLINS

OBJECTIVES

- Understand financial statements, including burn rate, balance sheet, and income and cash flow statements.
- Use ratios to calculate solvency and profitability.
- Prepare financial projections such as the budget, cash flow forecast, burn rate, and runway.
- Calculate and interpret return on investment.
- Prepare a breakeven analysis.
- Calculate the lifetime value of a customer.

CHAPTER OUTLINE

INTRODUCTION

Being able to understand financial statements, analyze them, and then prepare budgets and cash flow forecasts will contribute to the success of the entrepreneurial business. This chapter provides you the tools to analyze a company's performance, to manage the day-to-day activities, and to prepare financial statements for investors and lenders.

We begin with one of the most important measures of financial performance, namely the company's "burn rate." The burn rate is important for two reasons:

1. It provides the business manager with a financial picture of where the company is going and what needs to be done *before* cash becomes a problem.
2. It allows management to dynamically analyze the financial position of the business and determine how long the business can operate if changes are not made to its operations.

The "Burn Rate," or "How Long Can the Entrepreneur Keep It Going?"

The burn rate is the rate at which a new company uses up its cash to finance overhead before generating positive cash flow from operations. In other words, it's a measure of negative cash flow. Burn rate is usually quoted in terms of cash spent per month.

$$(COH + I)/BR = MO$$

where COH is cash on hand, I is income from all sources, BR is monthly burn rate, and MO is remaining months of operation.

COH is the cash in all bank accounts *plus* expected cash from customers, suppliers, and other accounts. If the business intends to borrow to access cash (e.g., bank credit line or revolver), be sure to include the cost of this debt in the burn rate. Additional considerations include quarterly or semiannual payments, such as tax installments or advertising. Include a pro rata of these expenses in the calculation. The burn rate is determined by looking at the cash flow statement. The cash flow statement reports the *change* in the firm's cash position from one period to the next by accounting for the cash flows from operations, investment activities, and financing activities. Compared to the amount of cash a company has on hand, the burn rate gives investors a sense of how much time is left before the company runs out of cash—assuming no change in the burn rate. This time period is called the "runway."

Time left before cash runs out = Cash reserves/Burn rate

If you want to know if a company is really in trouble, compare its burn rate with the working capital measured over the same time period:

Example of Measuring Burn Rate

Refer to the cash flow forecast in Figure 9-1. Net cash from operating activities was $(382,771) for the year ended. This means that the core business operations burned cash at a rate of about $31,898 per month, largely due to continuing net losses.

The net cash flow from investing was also negative, owing primarily to purchases of certificates of deposit (CDs). The negative cash flow was $309,158, which represents another big use of cash. Indeed, the net cash burned by operations and investing amounted to over $691,934—a burn rate of over $57,661 per month.

Finally, the cash flow from financing was positive, but it was due primarily to the issuance of $2,500,000 worth of preferred stock.

Statement of Cash Flows
Year Ended December 31, 2000

Cash Flows from Operating Activities	
Net income (loss)	($262,381)
Adjustments to reconcile net income (loss to net)	
Cash provided by (used in) operating activities	
Depreciation	99,182
Issuance of common stock in lieu of compensation	0
Bad debts	14,875
Deferred taxes	(241,800)
	(390,124)
Changes in Operating Assets and Liabilities	
Accounts receivable	(12,387)
Loan receivable, employee	0
Prepaid expenses and other current assets	(32,213)
Accounts payable and accrued expenses	56,845
Income taxes payable	(4,892)
Net Cash Provided by (Used in) Operating Activities	(382,771)
Cash Flows from Investing Activities	
Purchases of certificates of deposit	(250,000)
Purchases of property and equipment	(59,158)
Net Cash Used in Investing Activities	(309,158)
Cash Flows from Financing Activities	
Repayment of loan	(14,644)
Issuance of common stock	6,423
Issuance of preferred stock	2,500,000
Acquisition of treasury stock	(363,398)
Net Cash Provided by (Used in) Financing Activities	2,128,381
Net Increase (or Decrease) in Cash	1,436,452
Cash, beginning of period	48,021
Cash, End of Year	$1,484,473
Supplemental Disclosures of Cash Flow Information	
Cash paid during the period for:	
Interest	$380
Income taxes	$0

Figure 9-1   **A Typical Cash Flow Statement.**

This illustration demonstrates the primary importance of knowing a company's burn rate. The bottom line: is the company staying in business because it's "burning cash," that is, using debt and shareholder equity to remain viable, or is the company generating enough cash from operations to sustain its expense structure?

The various financial metrics and exhibits introduced in this chapter are designed to optimize learning. It is important to develop a comfortable working knowledge of financial statement analysis, for these skills are a critical tool for the successful entrepreneur. We recommend a three-step approach to the study of financial analysis: (1) skim the chapter for a quick overview; (2) read the chapter carefully and pay attention to the formulas and statement analysis; and (3) test your knowledge using the interactive Web site to practice reviewing financial operations.

UNDERSTANDING FINANCIAL STATEMENTS

The financial statements are the tools through which the company communicates its financial condition to others. Financial statements include the balance sheet, financial performance for a given period (income statement and statement of cash flow), and supplemental financial information.

Financial statements should reflect the operation of the business in the same way that management views its business. When these statements are used to forecast what the business would look like given certain events, they are referred to as "pro forma statements."[1]

PRO FORMA

A Latin term that translates into "for the sake of form." In the investing world, the term describes a method of calculating financial results in order to emphasize either current or projected figures.

Pro forma financial statements could be designed to reflect a proposed change, such as a merger or acquisition, or to emphasize certain figures when a company issues an earnings announcement to the public.

Investors should heed caution when reading a company's pro forma financial statements, because the figures may not comply with generally accepted accounting principles (GAAP). In some cases, the pro forma figures may differ greatly from those derived from GAAP.[2]

Most businesses use the following basic financial documents:

1. The balance sheet (also called the statement of financial position)
2. An income statement or profit-and-loss (P&L) statement
3. The statement of cash flows (also called source and use of funds)

The Value of the Balance Sheet

The balance sheet provides a picture of the business's financial position at a particular point in time—generally at the end of a financial period (e.g., month, quarter, or year). It is essentially a snapshot of a company's resulting financial position, encompassing everything the company owns (assets) or owes (liabilities), as well as the investments into the company by its owners and the accumulated earnings or losses of the company (equity).

The balance sheet equation is:

$$\text{Assets} = \text{Liabilities} + \text{Shareholder equity}$$

Assets are current if they can be converted into cash within one year; liabilities are current if they must be paid off within one year; otherwise they are considered long term. Inventory is considered current because it is sold within one year from date of receipt; however, certain business inventories can be further segregated into work-in-process (WIP), raw materials, or finished goods inventories.

This sample pro forma balance sheet in Figure 9-2 shows shareholders' equity, or the net worth of the company projected to be $182,200 in Year 1 and 462,600 by

Pro Forma	Year 1	Year 2	Year 3	Year 4	Year 5	Comments
Balance sheet						
Assets						
Cash	$ 33.0	$ 39.9	$ 47.9	$ 57.5	$ 69.0	% of Sales
Accounts receivable	180.7	174.2	209.1	250.9	301.1	% of Sales
Inventories	168.6	158.6	190.3	228.3	274.0	% of CoGS
Current assets	382.3	372.7	447.3	536.7	644.1	
Net fixed assets	107.6	130.1	156.1	187.3	248.8	% of CoGS
Other	16.1	18.2	21.8	26.1	31.4	% of Sales
Total assets	$ 506.0	$ 521.0	$ 625.2	$ 750.2	$ 900.2	
Liabilities & Net worth						
Notes payable, banks	$ 209.7	$ 169.0	$ 202.0	$ 237.0	$ 281.0	% increase in NP
Accounts payable	53.7	61.0	73.2	87.8	105.4	% of CoGS
Accrued expenses	24.4	28.5	34.2	41.0	49.2	% of CoGS
Current portion, LTD	1.0	1.0	1.0	1.0	1.0	
Current liabilities	288.8	259.4	310.3	366.8	436.6	
Long-term debt	5.0	4.0	3.0	2.0	1.0	
Convertible debt	30.0	30.0	30.0	-	-	
Net worth	182.2	227.5	281.8	381.4	462.6	

Figure 9-2   Sample Pro Forma Balance Sheet.

Year 5. Equity is calculated by subtracting the total liabilities of $323,800 (Year 1) from the total assets of $506,000 (Year 1).

REVIEW AND ANALYSIS OF THE BALANCE SHEET

When analyzing a company's balance sheet, managers and investors alike must view it in terms of its type of business. For example, one would expect to see that fixed assets accounted for a greater percentage of total assets in a manufacturing operation as opposed to a distributor or professional services company. In addition, the balance sheet should be analyzed with respect to the volume of the company's business. For instance, receivables should be compared to sales to determine how quickly the company collects its cash, or current liabilities compared to expenses to see if the company is paying its short-term obligations in a timely fashion.

Book Value

Book value is derived through an analysis of the *balance sheet*: totaling up the tangible assets, then subtracting all the liabilities. Whatever is left is the book value. Divide the book value by the number of shares outstanding, and you'll know the value each share would have were the company to go out of business. Some companies such as Amazon.com have negative book value—and can be risky investment propositions. But if a company is trading for less than its book value, its stock might be a bargain for an acquirer or an investor. Book value does not include intangible assets such as patents and intellectual property, and it does not take into account the value of a company's business relationships, or *going-concern value*.

When a firm is acquired, the difference between its book value and its going-concern value is called *goodwill*. Goodwill includes factors that add value but cannot be easily liquidated or sold, such as brand, market share, the "learning curve," and human capital.

Note: The Financial Accounting Standards Board (FASB) Rule 142 of 2001 changed the GAAP treatment of "goodwill." It is no longer amortized; rather, it is written down when "impaired." FASB issued SFAS 142, *Goodwill and Other Intangible Assets*, in June 2001.

The New Accounting Treatment of Goodwill

SFAS 142 made two major changes to goodwill accounting:

- Amortization of *all* goodwill ceased, regardless of when it originated. Goodwill is now carried as an asset without reduction for periodic amortization.
- Companies are to assess goodwill for impairment at least annually. If goodwill is impaired, its carrying amount is reduced and an impairment loss is recognized.

Effect on Valuations

Ending amortization while keeping other factors constant will increase earnings and decrease price-to-earnings (P/E) ratios.

Although the company does not have a great deal of cash, the fact that its current assets are well in excess of its current liabilities (Year 1: 382.3; 288.8) indicates its ability to meet current obligations. The fact that the company's total debt is more than its fixed assets means it is likely that the debt was used to finance operations rather than equipment purchases. Its positive retained earnings indicate overall profitability.

ROADMAP

ACTIONS   The entrepreneur must be able to apply financial ratios to address its financial condition. Ratios can also be used to analyze a balance sheet. *Current Ratio* is the total current asset divided by the total current liabilities. *Quick Ratio* or *acid-test ratio*, is very similar to the current ratio except that it includes only these current assets—cash and accounts receivable.

HOW TO USE RATIOS FOR FINANCIAL ANALYSIS

Ratios can also be used to analyze a balance sheet. The following solvency ratios are the most commonly used by entrepreneurs for financial analysis.[3]

Current Ratio

This is the total current asset divided by the total current liabilities. Current assets and liabilities are those items expected to generate cash or require the disbursement of cash within the next year. The current ratio indicates the company's ability to meet its obligations for the next year. The higher the ratio, the greater the liquidity. A low ratio indicates a lack of liquidity and a potential problem in meeting maturing obligations. Figure 9-3 shows a list of current ratios by industry.

Current Ratios by Industry			
Construction	1.5	Manufacturing:	
Finance (banks)	0.9	Food and retail	1.1
Services (hotels)	0.8	Apparel	1.9
(personal)	1.9	Printing and publishing	1.3
Retail (restaurants)	1.0	Motor vehicles	0.9
General merchandise	1.4	Grocery stores	1.2
Furniture	1.9	Insurance agents	1.3

Source: BizStats.com.

Figure 9-3   **Ratios by Industry.**

Quick Ratio

Also called the *acid-test ratio*, this ratio is very similar to the current ratio except that it includes only those current assets—cash and accounts receivable—that can be most readily used to pay bills today. The quick ratio excludes inventory, which must first be sold and the cash collected before it can be used to pay liabilities. It also excludes current assets such as prepaid expenses, which are never converted to cash (they are simply assets paid for in advance). As a result, the quick ratio is a good indication of how well the company is able to meet current liabilities in a crunch situation. In general, the entrepreneur should try to maintain a quick ratio of 1:1, which means that $1 worth of cash and accounts receivable is on hand for every $1 of total current liabilities.[4]

Rules and Examples

Although a satisfactory value for a current ratio varies from industry to industry, a general rule of thumb is that a current ratio of 2:1 or greater is fairly healthy. In terms of dollars, a 2:1 ratio means that there exists $2 of current assets from which to pay every $1 of current bills. A smaller current ratio may mean that the company has successfully negotiated to pay its suppliers later than the usual 30 days, which essentially gives the company an interest-free source of cash. Let's say current assets are $15,000 and current liabilities are $10,000, yielding a current ratio of 1.5:1. In this scenario, the entrepreneur could improve the current ratio to 2:1 by paying $5,000 of the current liabilities with the current assets, thereby reducing both by $5,000 (i.e., $10,000 divided by $5,000 = 2:1). If, however, the suppliers were willing to wait for payment without charging interest, this would probably be a bad idea (unless a financing agreement required the company to maintain a current ratio of 2:1).

Solvency Ratios

Debt management ratios can help the entrepreneur evaluate the business liabilities. Since debt is associated with risk, the greater the debt, the higher the return rate will be. If the liabilities are large compared to equity or assets, potential lenders and investors may feel that the company is already too indebted and is not a good investment risk. Other solvency ratios include:

- Current liabilities to net worth
- Total liabilities to net worth
- Fixed assets to net worth

Current Liabilities to Net Worth Ratio

The current liabilities to net worth ratio is calculated by dividing current liabilities by net worth.

What Does It Mean?

The current liabilities to net worth ratio contrasts the funds that creditors are temporarily risking with the funds invested by the stockholders or owners. The smaller the ratio, the more secure the creditors.

Total Liabilities to Net Worth (Debt-to-Equity) Ratio

The total liabilities to net worth ratio is calculated by dividing total liabilities by net worth.

What Does It Mean?

Total liabilities to net worth ratio (debt to equity) expresses the relationship between capital contributed by creditors and capital contributed by owners. It expresses the degree of protection provided the creditors by the owners. The higher the ratio, the higher the risk being borne by the creditors.

A business with low debt equity ratios usually has more borrowing power and longer term financial security. The ratio indicates how highly leveraged the business is. Lower is usually better.

Fixed Assets to Net Worth Ratio

The fixed assets to net worth ratio is calculated by dividing fixed assets by net worth.

What Does It Mean?

The fixed assets to net worth ratio shows to what extent the owner's equity has been invested in fixed assets. Lower ratios show a proportionately smaller investment in fixed assets in relation to net worth. A lower ratio indicates that the business has a better cushion for short-term cash needs or in case of a sudden liquidation. A high ratio indicates that the business may be too heavily invested in fixed assets (plant, equipment, autos, etc.) and may be strangling its supply of working capital.

Debt-to-Worth Ratio

The debt-to-worth ratio is calculated by dividing total liabilities by net worth. Also called debt to owners' equity, this ratio compares the total liabilities of the business to the total owners' equity or net worth (the value of the total assets minus the total liabilities from the balance sheet). This ratio gives insight into whether the company's previous finding has been through equity (sales of stock) or debt. The higher the ratio, the higher the risk borne by creditors. A low debt ratio usually means more borrowing power and financial security.

This discussion of ratios is not meant to be all-inclusive. Each industry and business will have a set of ratios that is especially pertinent. The point to remember is that ratios are nothing more than a comparison of two numbers. So, if the entrepreneur finds a particular ratio that is helpful in the financial management of the firm, then, by all means, it should be used.[5]

ROADMAP	
ACTIONS	The entrepreneur should also use the income statement to evaluate its financial condition. The income statement shows how the business made a profit by displaying how much money it generated in sales and how much money it cost to run the business.

THE VALUE OF AN INCOME STATEMENT

The statement of operations, also known as income statement, profit-and-loss statement, or P&L statement, summarizes the revenue (or income) and expenses of a company on a monthly basis for one year, or on an annual basis for several years. It divides expenses into broad categories, such as cost of goods sold and operating expenses. The cost of goods sold would represent the resources that went into production of the products ultimately recognized as sales. These costs would include materials, labor, and manufacturing expenses. Two more terms for costs of goods sold are:

1. *Inventory costs*—costs that are assigned to inventory before being sold
2. *Production costs*—costs that are identified with the product

Operating expenses are costs that are not identified with the product. The major categories include research and development, sales and marketing, general and administration (otherwise known as SG&A), and financial expenses.

The income statement in Figure 9-4 shows how the business made a profit by displaying how much money it generated in sales and how much money it cost to run the business. The equation used to determine net profit or loss is:

$$\text{Net profit (or loss)} = \text{Gross sales} - \text{Total expenses}$$

The entrepreneur should be aware that operating income is not the same as net profit. Operating income is determined by subtracting costs from sales and does not include taxes or interest charges. Operating income is the amount the business earns **after** expenses but **before** taxes and other income and taxes. It is sometimes referred to

Pro Forma Income Statement	Year 1	Year 2	Year 3	Year 4	Year 5	Comments
Sales	$ 605.0	$ 726.0	$ 871.2	$ 1,045.4	$ 1,254.5	% increase in Sales
Cost of goods sold	349.5	406.6	487.9	585.4	702.5	% of Sales
Gross profit	255.5	319.4	383.3	460.0	552.0	
Research & development	100.4	108.9	130.7	156.8	188.2	% of Sales
General & administration	106.9	123.4	148.1	177.7	213.3	% of Sales
Income from operations	48.2	87.1	104.5	125.5	150.5	
Interest expense	19.7	19.0	20.0	21.0	23.0	% of Debt
Profit before taxes	28.5	68.1	84.5	104.5	127.5	
Taxes	10.0	23.8	29.6	36.6	44.6	Income Tax Rate

Figure 9-4   **Income Statement Pro Forma.**

as EBIT (earnings before interest or taxes). The ratio of EBIT to interest is used to show how many times earnings cover interest.

The EBIT to interest ratio is calculated as follows:

$$\frac{\text{EBIT}}{\text{Interest}}$$

For example, if operating profits were \$10,000 and interest was \$10,000 the business would breakeven. This is risky, as a slight downturn in sales or an increase in interest rate would cause losses.

A Rule of Thumb

The ratio should be at least 3:1. Monthly trends might fluctuate (building up inventory for seasonal fluctuations, awaiting payment on large receivable, etc.), but in the long term it is important that this ratio hover in the 2.5+ range.

HOW TO USE RATIOS FOR PROFITABILITY

When analyzing the income statement, the entrepreneur must view it in terms of the type of business and how long the company has been involved in its current operations. Many companies change their type of business over time through acquisitions, divestitures, or diversification. Ratios can also be used to analyze the statement of operations. Four of the more commonly used ones are as follows.

1. **Return on Investment (ROI).** This ratio compares the net profit of the business to the investment (net worth) of the business. It is calculated as net income after taxes (from the income statement) divided by total owner's equity (from the balance sheet).

$$\text{Return on investment} = \frac{\text{Net income}}{\text{Shareholders'equity}}$$

To relate return on investment to the debt-to-worth ratio, remember that given a fixed total asset figure, the greater the debt, the lower the net worth. Therefore, given two companies of identical asset size and profitability, the company with the higher debt-to-worth ratio will also have a higher return on equity ratio. When potential leaders and investors consider the risk of investing in the business, they will look at the return on equity ratio.

2. **Level of Reliability of ROI.** Return on investment is not a totally reliable measure of financial performance for the following reasons:

- Returns are examined without the risk factors of the business.
- The assessment is measured in an annual time frame, and long-term decisions may not be reflected.
- Book value is used for shareholders' equity rather than market value.

Therefore, return on investment should be examined in relationship to the business and environment rather than just mechanically.

3. **Return on Total Assets**. This measures how efficiently the business is using the assets in negotiating net income. This is calculated as the net income after taxes (from the income statement) divided by the total assets (from the balance sheet). Assets are used to generate profits. Therefore, the return on total assets is a measure of how effectively the entrepreneur is employing the assets of the business.

Understanding the Terms *Gross Profit Margin, Operating Profit Margin, and Net Profit Margin*

Gross profit margin (or percentage) is the ratio of gross profit (gross sales minus the cost of goods sold) divided by gross sales, expressed as percentages. High gross margins are usually a sign that the company is in a strong competitive position. As a benchmark, venture capital investors may look for high gross margins projections (60 percent or above) when investing so that they can create a high valuation when it's time to "exit" the investment. All three percentages should usually be included on the income statements. To analyze the profitability, compare these percentages to the industry's averages or those of the immediate competitors (if this information can be obtained). Of course, the entrepreneur will always want to compare the current year's profitability percentages to the percentages from the company's previous years in order to determine the progress of the company.

ROADMAP

ACTIONS

When analyzing cash flows, the entrepreneur needs to determine if the numbers are positive or negative. Examine the relationship between cash available through operations and cash from investment. Examine whether growth in receivables is due to increased sales or poor collection results. Is an increase in debt matched with fixed assets, or is the debt being used to fund operations? The statement of cash flows is usually overlooked by investors, but it can frequently disclose information about how a company manages its cash.

THE VALUE OF THE STATEMENT OF CASH FLOWS

The statement of cash flows (SCF) summarizes where cash comes from and how it is used over a period of time. The SCF is divided into three parts: Cash from Operations, Cash from Financing Activities, and Cash from Investing Activities. The SCF begins with the net income sourced from the income statement. It then shows adjustments for items that do not involve cash (such as payables and depreciation); other nonoperational sources; and uses of cash (such as fixed asset purchases, financing proceeds, and vendor payments). Finally, the increase or decrease in net cash balance is calculated. The statement shows the movement of funds through a business over time. The format used in the Figure 9-5 shows how the sources of funds are accumulated. This includes changes in operations, new sources of capital such as debt and equity, the sale of fixed assets, and all the uses of the company's funds. The bottom line is the net change in working capital.

Year Ended December 31, 2000	
Cash Flows from Operating Activities	
Net income (loss)	($262,381)
Adjustments to reconcile net income (loss to net)	
Cash provided by (used in) operating activities	
Depreciation	99,182
Issuance of common stock in lieu of compensation	0
Bad debts	14,875
Deferred taxes	(241,800)
	(390,124)
Changes in Operating Assets and Liabilities	
Accounts receivable	(12,387)
Loan receivable, employee	0
Prepaid expenses and other current assets	(32,213)
Accounts payable and accrued expenses	56,845
Income taxes payable	(4,892)
Net Cash Provided by (Used in) Operating Activities	(382,771)
Cash Flows from Investing Activities	
Purchases of certificates of deposit	(250,000)
Purchases of property and equipment	(59,158)
Net Cash Used in Investing Activities	(309,158)
Cash Flows from Financing Activities	
Repayment of loan	(14,644)
Issuance of common stock	6,423
Issuance of preferred stock	2,500,000
Acquisition of treasury stock	(363,398)
Net Cash Provided by (Used in) Financing Activities	2,128,381
Net Increase (or Decrease) in Cash	1,436,452
Cash, beginning of period	48,021
Cash, End of Year	$1,484,473
Supplemental Disclosures of Cash Flow Information	
Cash paid during the period for:	
Interest	$380
Income taxes	$0

Figure 9-5   **Statement of Cash Flows.**

UNDERSTANDING FOOTNOTES TO THE FINANCIAL STATEMENTS

Financial statements are usually accompanied by footnotes. Like the statement of cash flows, these footnotes are often overlooked but contain valuable information. Certain footnotes are especially important, as shown by the following six.[6]

General Description of Business. The first footnote usually includes a general description of the company's business and a recent history, usually detailing any events that have a material impact on the company's current financial statements, such as an acquisition, or increased competition.

Acquisitions and Divestitures/Discontinued Operations. If the company has acquired or sold either the assets or stock of a company, the details of the transactions will be included in this footnote. In addition, if a company has discontinued a material segment of its business, the details of the discontinuance will be included.

Intangible Assets. This footnote details any intangible assets the company has on the balance sheet, such as goodwill, capitalized patents, or capitalized research and development. The viewer should make note of how much the company capitalized during the year and how quickly it is being amortized.

Debt. The debt footnote will classify the debt on the balance sheet by loan instrument and by the bank. It will also include the current interest rates and may disclose how much financing is available in the future as well as the payoff schedule of the company's present debt.

Legal Proceedings. This footnote must disclose any material legal proceedings either by or against the company. This should always be reviewed to determine if any legal proceedings could significantly affect the company's financial viability.

Subsequent Events. This footnote details any unusual and material events that have occurred after the date of the financial statement, but before the issuance of the financial statement.

PREPARING FINANCIAL PROJECTIONS

Entrepreneurs need to be able to plan operations and evaluate decisions using financial accounting information. Budgets, cash flow forecasts, and breakeven analyses are not only important management tools, but are usually required information for potential investors or lenders.

One of the first steps in any business is to establish a financial plan to measure financial performance. There are three widely used methods of measuring financial performance.

1. **Measuring sales volume.** The first perspective is to view performance in terms of sales, such as percentage of increased sales or new business. Many Internet companies measure success in terms of increased sales volume. However, if the expectation is that additional sales mean higher profits, which may not always be the case, certainly increasing sales is a part of the financial plan. But to stop at that point is shortsighted.

2. **Measuring profits.** The second perspective is to measure profits, that is, the difference between revenues and expenses as reported in the income statements. Sales must be profitable for the business to succeed. A firm can determine the profitability of either products or customers. It can also provide incentives to its salesforce to encourage more profitable sales.

3. **Measuring cash generated.** Just because a company has an income statement that shows it is profitable does not necessarily mean it is generating cash. If the company uses accrual accounting, a sale is recognized when, as an example, a customer takes title to the product, even though the cash may not be collected for some time. Accrual accounting does not recognize that cash may have been required to purchase materials, labor, and other resources in advance of the sale.

Frequently, businesses, though profitable, may run out of cash because when a sale occurs, the cash from the sale is not collected until a later date. It is important, especially for undercapitalized companies, to project cash flow and to note any periods where it will have inadequate cash, so that the company can secure outside financing; otherwise the company may be forced into bankruptcy. Poor cash management is a major cause of failure of startup companies rather than lack of customers willing to pay.

These financial methods give the entrepreneur an idea of the nature of financial goals that may be set for her company. Obviously, how high the goals are set depends on the nature of the business, the opportunities available, and management's decisions.

How to Prepare an Annual Budget

The annual budget presents a month-by-month projection of revenues and expenses over a one-year period. The budget is the foundation for projecting the other financial statements. It presents a more detailed accounting of expenses than does the income statement. In a budget, expense details are usually grouped by department or functional area, such as general, administrative, and research and development. The details of a standard budget are divided into 11 major categories:[7]

1. **Sales.** The budget detail should include all or some of the following: sales by product line and sales by customer, geographical region, and goals for each sales representative.

2. **Cost of Goods Sold.** The detail should include both material and shipping costs, as well as any allocated overhead if the company is a manufacturer. If sales are identified by product line, the cost of goods sold for each product line should be calculated in order to determine gross profit by product line.

3. **Gross Profit.** The detail should include, where possible, the gross profit by whatever categories the sales are classified (e.g., product line, geographical region). Gross profit is defined as sales, less those costs directly incurred in order to achieve the sales (such as component pieces and assembly labor in the sale of a computer).

4. **Operating Expenses.** The detail should classify expenses by research and development, sales and marketing, and general administrative. Within these categories the detail should reflect the budgeted expenses by category, such as salary, benefits, rent, and telephone. Some expenses should be further categorized by such items as salary by employee and allocation of rent expenses.

5. **Operating Profit/Loss.** If operating expenses can be identified by sales category, an operating profit/loss for each sales category should be calculated.

6. **Other Income and Expenses.** This category usually includes interest expense, which should be detailed by each type of debt (e.g., leases for computers, and copying equipment, lines of personal credit, and bank loans) and other income and expenses not related to the normal operations of the business, such as a legal settlement or loss due to fire.

7. **Pretax Income.** Income before taxes is calculated by taking operating profit and factoring in other income and expenses. It denotes the income that will be subject to corporate income tax.

8. **Income Taxes.** This is management's estimate of what taxes will be owed on its earnings. Detail should reflect amounts owed for federal and state taxes.

9. **Net Income.** This is the amount available for dividends or reinvestment in the company.

10. **EBIT.** This is the earnings (net income) before interest expense, interest income, and income taxes. It measures the profitability of the company's current operations as if it had no debt or investments.

11. **EBITDA.** This is the earnings before interest expense, interest income, income taxes, depreciation, and amortization. It measures the profitability of a company's operations without the impact of its debt, investments, and long-term assets.

The sample budget in Figure 9-6 shows a projection of the first five months of the company's fiscal year. An actual budget would include all 12 months and a column totaling the months. It could also include a column after the total column showing the previous year's activity for comparison purposes.

PREPARING A CASH FLOW FORECAST

Reasons to Prepare a Cash Flow Forecast

As stated earlier, one of the major problems that startup companies face is cash flow. Lack of cash is one reason that profitable companies fail. Cash managers can anticipate temporary cash shortfalls and have sufficient time to arrange short-term loans if needed.

A cash flow forecast shows the amount of cash coming in (receivables) and cash going out (payables) during a certain month. The forecast also shows a bank loan officer (or the entrepreneur) what additional working capital, if any, the business may need. In addition, it provides evidence that there will be sufficient cash on hand to make the interest payments on a revolving line of credit or to cover the shortfalls when payables exceed receivables.

Computer spreadsheet programs such as Microsoft Excel or any variety of full-faceted business software can be very useful for generating a cash flow worksheet. Reliable cash flow projections can bring a sense of order, well-being, and security to a business. The most important tool that owners and/or managers have available to control the financial liquidity of their business is the cash flow worksheet.

Getting Started

Step One: Consider Cash Flow Revenues
Find a realistic basis for estimating sales each month. For a startup company, the basis can be the average monthly sales of a similarly sized competitor's operations, which is operating in a similar market. Be sure to reduce your figures by a startup year factor of about 50 percent a month for the startup months. Libraries and bookstores offer publications that discuss methods of sales forecasting.

For an existing company, sales revenues from the same month in the previous year make a good basis for forecasting sales for that month in the succeeding year. For example, if the trend in the industry predicts a general growth of 4 percent for the next year, it will be entirely acceptable to show each month's projected sales at 4 percent higher than the actual sales the previous year. Include notes to the cash flow to explain any unusual variations from the previous year's numbers.

Step Two: Consider Cash Flow Disbursements
Project each of the various expense categories (normally shown in your ledger) beginning with a summary for each month of the cash payments to suppliers as well as wages, rent, and equipment costs (accounts payable).

Five Months Sample

Company X
Budget for 2006

	January	February	March	April	May
Income Statement					
Sales					
Product A	1,000,000	1,040,000	1,080,000	1,120,000	1,160,000
Product B	525,000	565,000	605,000	645,000	685,000
Product C	300,000	340,000	380,000	420,000	460,000
Total Sales	1,825,000	1,945,000	2,065,000	2,185,000	2,305,000
Cost of Goods Sold					
Product A	500,000	520,000	540,000	560,000	580,000
Product B	262,500	282,500	302,500	322,500	342,500
Product C	150,000	170,000	190,000	210,000	230,000
Total Cost of Goods Sold	912,500	972,500	1,032,500	1,092,500	1,152,500
Gross Profit					
Product A—Profit	500,000	520,000	540,000	560,000	580,000
Product A—Margin	50.0%	50.0%	50.0%	50.0%	50.0%
Product B—Profit	262,500	282,500	302,500	322,500	342,500
Product B—Margin	50.0%	50.0%	50.0%	50.0%	50.0%
Product C—Profit	150,000	170,000	190,000	210,000	230,000
Product C—Margin	50.0%	50.0%	50.0%	50.0%	50.0%
Total Gross Profit	912,500	972,500	1,032,500	1,092,500	1,152,500
Total Gross Margin	50.0%	50.0%	50.0%	50.0%	50.0%
Operating Expenses					
Research and Development	90,000	90,000	90,000	90,000	90,000
Sales and Marketing	125,000	125,000	125,000	125,000	125,000
General and Administrative	215,000	215,000	215,000	215,000	215,000
Total Operating Expenses	430,000	430,000	430,000	430,000	430,000
Operating Profit	482,500	542,500	602,500	662,500	722,500
Operating Margin	26.4%	27.9%	29.2%	30.3%	31.3%
Other Expense					
Interest Expense	40,000	37,500	35,000	32,500	30,000
Total Expense	40,000	37,500	35,000	32,500	30,000
Income before Income Tax	442,500	505,000	567,500	630,000	692,500
Provision for Income Taxes					
Federal	177,000	202,000	227,000	252,000	277,000
State	44,250	50,500	56,750	63,000	69,250
Total Taxes	221,250	252,500	283,750	315,000	346,250
Net Income	221,250	252,500	283,750	315,000	346,250
Sales Detail					
Product A					
Eastern Region	400,000	425,000	450,000	475,000	500,000
Central Region	320,000	325,000	330,000	335,000	340,000
Western Region	280,000	290,000	300,000	310,000	320,000
Total Sales of Product A	1,000,000	1,040,000	1,080,000	1,120,000	1,160,000
Product B					
Eastern Region	105,000	120,000	135,000	150,000	165,000
Central Region	320,000	340,000	360,000	380,000	400,000
Western Region	100,000	105,000	110,000	115,000	120,000
Total Sales of Product B	525,000	565,000	605,000	645,000	685,000

Figure 9-6   Preparing Budget Projections.

(*continues*)

Product C					
Eastern Region	110,000	125,000	140,000	155,000	170,000
Central Region	30,000	40,000	50,000	60,000	70,000
Western Region	160,000	175,000	190,000	205,000	220,000
Total Sales of Product C	300,000	340,000	380,000	420,000	460,000
Costs of Goods Sold Detail					
Product A					
Parts	200,000	208,000	216,000	224,000	232,000
Assembly Labor	200,000	208,000	216,000	224,000	232,000
Factory Overhead	100,000	104,000	108,000	112,000	116,000
Total COGS Product A	500,000	520,000	540,000	560,000	580,000
Product B					
Parts	105,000	113,000	121,000	129,000	137,000
Assembly Labor	105,000	113,000	121,000	129,000	137,000
Factory Overhead	52,500	56,500	60,500	64,500	68,500
Total COGS Product B	262,500	282,500	302,500	322,500	342,500
Product C					
Parts	60,000	68,000	76,000	84,000	92,000
Assembly Labor	60,000	68,000	76,000	84,000	92,000
Factory Overhead	30,000	34,000	38,000	42,000	46,000
Total COGS Product C	150,000	170,000	190,000	210,000	230,000
Operating Expenses Detail					
Research and Development					
Salary and Payroll Tax	33,000	33,000	33,000	33,000	33,000
Benefits	7,000	7,000	7,000	7,000	7,000
Rent	12,000	12,000	12,000	12,000	12,000
Office Expense	5,000	5,000	5,000	5,000	5,000
Telephone	10,000	10,000	10,000	10,000	10,000
Consulting	15,000	15,000	15,000	15,000	15,000
Insurance	7,000	7,000	7,000	7,000	7,000
Miscellaneous	1,000	1,000	1,000	1,000	1,000
Total R & D	90,000	90,000	90,000	90,000	90,000
Selling and Marketing					
Salary and Payroll Tax	42,000	42,000	42,000	42,000	42,000
Benefits	10,000	10,000	10,000	10,000	10,000
Rent	15,000	15,000	15,000	15,000	15,000
Office Expense	7,500	7,500	7,500	7,500	7,500
Telephone	14,500	14,500	14,500	14,500	14,500
Commissions	25,000	25,000	25,000	25,000	25,000
Insurance	9,000	9,000	9,000	9,000	9,000
Miscellaneous	2,000	2,000	2,000	2,000	2,000
Total S & M	125,000	125,000	125,000	125,000	125,000
General and Administrative					
Salary and Payroll Tax	65,000	65,000	65,000	65,000	65,000
Benefits	20,000	20,000	20,000	20,000	20,000
Rent	25,000	25,000	25,000	25,000	25,000
Office Expense	10,000	10,000	10,000	10,000	10,000
Telephone	20,000	20,000	20,000	20,000	20,000
Legal	55,000	55,000	55,000	55,000	55,000
Insurance	15,000	15,000	15,000	15,000	15,000
Miscellaneous	5,000	5,000	5,000	5,000	5,000
Total G & A	215,000	215,000	215,000	215,000	215,000

Figure 9-6 **(Continued)**

Each month shows only the cash that is expected to be paid that month to the suppliers. For example, if suppliers' invoices are paid in 30 days, the cash payoffs for January's purchases will be shown in February. If longer terms are obtained for trade credit, then cash outlays will appear two or even three months after the stock purchase has been received and invoiced.

An example of a different type of expense is insurance expenditure. Commercial insurance premiums may be $2,400 annually. Normally, this would be treated as a $200 monthly expense. However, it will not be recorded this way on the cash flow statement. Rather, the cash flow records show how it will be paid. If it is to be paid in two installments, $1,200 in January and $1,200 in July, then that is how it must be entered on the cash flow worksheet. The same principle applies to all cash flow expense items.

Step Three: Reconcile the Revenues and Disbursements

The reconciliation section of the cash flow worksheet begins by showing the balance carried over from the previous month's operations. To this, the net inflows/outflows or current month's receipts and disbursements will be added. This adjusted balance will be carried forward to the first line of the reconciliation portion of the next month's entry to become the base to which the next month's cash flow activity will be added or subtracted.

Making the Best Use of the Cash Flow Statement

Cash flow statements must constantly be modified as new things are learned about the business and paying vendors. Since this cash flow forecast will be used regularly to compare each month's projected figures with each month's actual performance figures, it will be useful to have a second column for the actual performance figures alongside each of the 'planned' columns in the each flow worksheet. Look for significant discrepancies between the planned and actual figures.

For example, if the business's actual figures are failing to meet cash receipt projections over a three-month period, this is a signal that it is time to revise the year's projections. It may be necessary to apply to the bank to increase the upper limit of a revolving line of credit. Approaching the bank to increase an operating loan should be done well in advance of the date when the additional funds are required. Do not leave cash inflow to chance.

Designing a Cash Flow Worksheet

A cash flow forecast can be presented in a variety of ways. The best way is to show only revenues from operations and the proceeds from sales.

The format should be a double-width column along the left side of the page for the account headings, then two side-by-side vertical columns for each month of the year, beginning from the planned opening month (e.g., the first dual column might be labeled April Planned and April Actual). (See Figure 9-7.)

From there, the cash flow worksheet is divided into three distinctive sections. The first section (at the top left portion of the worksheet, starting below and to the left of the month names) is headed Cash revenues (or cash in). The second section, just below it, is headed Cash disbursements (or cash out). The final section below that is headed Reconciliation of cash flow.

Item	April Planned	April Actual	May Planned	May Actual
Cash revenues/cash in	$22,000	$18,500	$24,000	$22,500
Cash disbursements/cash out				
Wages	$10,000	$11,500	$11,000	$12,000
Commissions	$ 2,000	$ 1,500	$ 2,000	$ 2,000
Rent	$ 3,500	$ 3,500	$ 3,500	$ 3,500
Equipment payment/computers	$12,000	$12,000	$12,000	$12,000
Total cash out	$27,500	$28,500	$28,500	$29,500
Reconciliation of cash flow				
Opening cash balance	$ 5,000	$ 5,000	($500)	($5,000)
Add: Total cash revenues in	$22,000	$18,500	$24,000	$22,500
Deduct: Total cash disbursements out	$27,500	$28,500	$28,500	$29,500
Closing cash balance				
(Carry forward to next month)	($500)	($5,000)	($5,000)	($12,000)

Figure 9-7   **Sample Cash Flow—Planned versus Actual.**

ACTIONS

The entrepreneur should use the breakeven technique as a decision-making model to determine whether a certain volume of output will result in a profit or loss and to measure the profit associated with a given level of output. To use this technique, you need only three types of information: fixed costs of operation, variable costs of production, and price per unit.

PREPARING A BREAKEVEN ANALYSIS

The breakeven technique is a decision-making model that helps the entrepreneur determine whether a certain volume of output will result in a profit or loss. The point at which breaking even occurs is the volume of output at which total revenues equals total costs. The technique can be further used to answer the question, "What is the profit associated with a given level of output?" To use this technique, you need only know the fixed costs of operation, variable costs of production, and price per unit.

Fixed costs are expenses that do not change in the short run, no matter what the level of production and sales. Variable costs differ according to the volume produced; they are usually expressed in terms of per-unit variable costs. Total costs are the sum of fixed and variable costs. Price is the total amount received from the sale of one unit of the product. Multiplying the price by the number of units sold yields the amount, which are revenues. Profit is what remains when the total costs are subtracted from the total revenues. The breakeven point is the level of output or sales at which total profit is zero—in other words, where total revenues equals costs.

Example 1

Suppose the company spent $10,250 of variable material cost and $20,000 of variable labor cost in the prior month when the company sold 10,000 units. How much variable cost should the company plan on for the current month if it is expected to increase by 20 percent? Assume costs change in proportion to changes in activity.

Note that although the total variable cost increases from $30,250 to $36,300 when production changes from 10,000 to 12,000 units, the variable cost per unit

	Prior Month		Current Month	
Units	10,000	Per Unit	12,000	Per Unit
Variable costs				
Direct material	$10,250	$1.025	$12,300	$1.025
Direct labor	20,000	2.000	24,000	2.000
Total variable costs	$30,250	$3.025	$36,300	$3.025

does not change. It remains $3.02 per unit. With variable cost of $3.02 per unit, variable cost increases by $6,050 (i.e., $3.025 × 2,000) when production increases by 2,000 units.

Example 2

Suppose that in the prior month the company incurred $22,500 of fixed costs, including $10,000 of depreciation, $7,500 of rent, and $5,000 of other fixed costs. If the company increases production to 12,000 in the current month, the levels of depreciation, rent, and other fixed cost incurred should remain the same as when it was only 10,000 units. However, with fixed costs, the cost per unit does change when there are changes. When production increases, the constant amount of fixed cost is spread over a larger number of units. This drives down the fixed cost per unit. With an increase in production from 10,000 to 12,000 units, total fixed cost remains at $22,500. Note, however, that fixed cost per unit decreases from $2.250 per unit to $1.874 per unit.

Month	Prior Month		Current Month	
Units	10,000	Per Unit	12,000	Per Unit
Fixed costs				
Depreciation	$10,000	$1.000	$12,300	$0.833
Rent	7,500	0.750	7,500	0.625
Direct labor	5,000	0.500	5,000	0.416
Total variable costs	$22,500	$2.250	$22,500	$1.874

Using the Breakeven Formula

A quick way to calculate the breakeven point is to use the following formula. The price per unit (P) multiplied by the number of units sold (X) is equal to the fixed costs (F) plus the variable costs (V) multiplied by the number of units produced expressed as the following formula:

$$P(X) = F + V(X)$$

As an example, if fixed costs (F) are $40,000, the variable costs per unit (V) are $15, and the price per unit (P) is $20, the breakeven point (X) can be calculated by plugging these values into the equation:

$$20(X) = 40,000 + 15(X)$$
$$20X - 15X = 40,000$$
$$5X = 40,000$$
$$X = 8,000 \text{ units}$$

The breakeven point is one measurement of your business's "time to profitability." This measure can be used in different ways, for example, the startup phase or the expansion phase. What if the business wants to expand its production? We can readily calculate the additional capital needed to fund this expansion, but a very important question must be asked, "Are the customers there, and what will it cost me to capture them?" "If I can capture these new customers, will it be profitable?" These questions can be answered by employing a second measurement of viability—the lifetime value of a customer (LVC).

The LVC is the net profit customers generate over their *Lifecycle*. You should not spend more to get a customer than their lifetime value, or you might lose money.

Example

When many businesses look at a customer, they see the value of the first sale. If Jeffrey bought a product worth $99, many companies would see Jeffrey as being worth $99 in revenue. Then if, and only if, later on Jeffrey buys another $99 product from you will he be seen as worth $198 in revenue. Let's assume X Company looks at customer value this way.

A better approach would be to let the above model also reflect the element of the time value of money. The true value of Jeffrey is the value of all the purchases he has made plus the value of all the purchases he is likely to make in the future (*discounted to the present*). This is called the lifetime value (LTV).

Do not be afraid to spend more than the profit on the first sale to acquire a customer, however. As long as your cash flow is healthy enough to support it, spend whatever you need to acquire that customer, as long as it is less than the average lifetime profit plus your current customer acquisition cost.

Increasing the lifetime value of your customers comes down to three objectives; increasing the length of time a customer buys from you, increasing the amount customers spend on each purchase, and decreasing the time between purchases.

EVALUATING COMPANY STATEMENTS

The Securities and Exchange Commission (SEC) requires already public companies, or those applying to go public, to file a variety of forms quarterly, annually, or on an as-needed basis. The SEC also requires independent audits of companies' financial statements. Learn how to determine a business's basic financial health by reviewing some of the following documents which can be accessed on the Internet.[8]

- *S-1: The Prospectus*. Companies must file this form before selling shares to the public. It contains details of the company's operations, including recent quarterly results. Check the "Competitors" section as well as "Risk Factors" to determine the risks.

EVALUATING COMPANY STATEMENTS (cont.)

- *10-Q: The Quarterly Report*. This contains a company's balance sheet, its income statement, and an accounting of its cash flow. Check the "Management Discussion" section for developments such as acquisitions, new customers, or unexpected losses.
- *10-K: The Annual Report*. Current shareholders receive this report by mail. The 10-K includes employment details and credit and lease agreements, and often lists pending legal actions.
- *8-K: The Current Report*. Companies have filed more of these forms as a result of the SEC's Regulation FD (fair disclosure). The regulation requires that companies reveal any material information to all investors simultaneously, instead of feeding it first to Wall Street analysts.
- *144: Insider Trades*. When officers, board members, or major shareholders want to buy or sell its stock, they must first register their intent with the SEC under Form 144.
- *13D: Beneficial Ownership*. Any individual or company that acquires more than 5 percent of another company's shares is required to report this fact to the SEC.
- *DEF-14A: Proxy Statement*. This document, issued before a company's annual meeting, details a directors' compensation and insiders' shareholdings as well as proposed changes in corporate governance.

SOURCES OF INFORMATION

The original source for public U.S. corporations' financial documents is the SEC's electronic data gathering, analysis, and retrieval system, also known as EDGAR. Its site is edgar.sec.gov. Other sites that have licensed EDGAR data include:

- FreeEDGAR (www.freeedgar.com)—clean look and straightforward index.
- EDGAR Online (www.edgaronline.com)—subscription service with annotated and filtered searches.
- 10K Wizard (www.10kwizard.com)—filings search site with a friendly interface.

FINANCIAL ACCOUNTING STANDARDS BOARD

The FASB is a powerful institution, even though, as a nongovernmental, not-for-profit body, it doesn't wield the might of the SEC. By defining generally accepted accounting principles (GAAP), the FASB plays a big part in making sure the numbers companies report accurately reflect their business performance.[9]

TAXES

The entrepreneur is required to withhold federal and state taxes from employees. Each month or quarter (depending on the size of the payroll), deposits or payments need to be made for funds withheld from wages. Generally, federal taxes, state taxes, Social Security, and Medicare are withheld from employees' salaries and are deposited later. If payments are late, high interest and penalties will be assessed. In addition to withholding taxes, the company may be required to pay a number of taxes, such as state and federal unemployment taxes, a matching FICA and Medicare tax, and other business taxes. These taxes will need to be part of the plan since they will affect cash flow and profits.

The federal and state governments also require the company to file end-of-year returns of the business, regardless of whether it earned a profit. A tax accountant should be consulted for advice on handling these expenses. The accountant can also assist in planning or budgeting appropriate funds to meet any of these expenses.[10]

SUMMARY

Financial statements that can help analyze and monitor overall performance should be examined, including the balance sheet, profit and loss statement, and cash flows. These important accounting statements show the company's financial picture either at a given time or for a given period. The balance sheet itemizes assets, liabilities, and shareholders' equity at a given time and gives a detailed picture of where a company stands at a particular time. The income statement is an itemized statement of revenues and expenses during an accounting period. It basically shows revenues, minus expenditures, resulting in income or loss. The cash flow statement is an itemized statement of receipts and expenditures, resulting in increased or decreased cash. Both the income and cash flow statements uncover important trends and overall performance, giving management direction as to what adjustments need to be made to the business's operations.

Another effective approach for checking overall performance is the use of financial ratios. Ratios indicate strengths and weaknesses in the business expectations. Entrepreneurs must also value different groups of customers to determine how much should be invested in procuring and managing them over time. Financial management is a key attribute of an entrepreneur and one that is often underestimated. Too many good companies fail because the founding entrepreneur was not adequately concerned with managing cash, assets, and profits. Budgets, projections of cash flow, and breakeven analysis must be monitored on a regular basis and evaluated when changes occur.

Launching a successful business requires an entrepreneur to create a solid financial plan. Such a plan is not only an important tool in raising the capital needed to get a company off the ground, but also an essential ingredient in managing a growing business.

STUDY QUESTIONS

1. What financial measurements should be prepared to measure performance?

2. What are the categories and steps in preparing a financial budget?

3. What are the major categories and steps in preparing the projected cash activity?

4. What is the difference between quick ratio, debit ratio, and current ratio?

5. Describe the breakeven technique in the decision-making model to determine profit and loss.

6. Why are some customers more valuable than others. How can these differences be measured and used for decision making?

EXERCISES

1. List four items that entrepreneurial companies should show on a balance sheet.

2. Ratios are important in analyzing a balance sheet; list those most commonly used by entrepreneurs for financial analysis.

3. Prepare a breakeven analysis for the following example. David Falk, the Vice President of Business Development, wants to determine the breakeven point for the company's gift card product. The analysis will help David determine the possibility of incurring a loss for the product. The company will sell the product for $200 per customer. Variable costs are estimated at $185,000 per month, composed of $95,000 for producing the product and $65,000 for fixed selling and administrative costs. How many units must be sold to break even?

4. Calculate the Pre-tax Income and the Return on Investment (ROI) for a company with sales and expenses as follows:

Sales	$40,000,000
Cost of Goods Sold	25,000,000
Selling and Administrative expense	5,000,000
Interest expense	1,000,000
Income taxes	5,850,000

Assume the current shareholders' equity is $800,000.

5. Comment on the company's profitability.

 **INTERACTIVE LEARNING ON THE WEB**

Test your skill-builder knowledge of the chapter using the interactive Web site.

CASE STUDY: PETSMART.COM

This case was prepared by Jeffery Barach, Columbia EMBA 2005, under the supervision of Professor Jack M. Kaplan as the basis for class discussion on the subject of initial financing and continuing capital needs. Copyright © 2005.

BACKGROUND

The purpose of this case is to determine the cash flow needs of the company as it begins its life and garners traction in the marketplace. The startup phase requires investment in technology as well as marketing efforts for customer acquisition. A key feature of the business will be its success in negotiating exclusive lockup contracts with state agencies. As this will take time, startup costs will be financed by founders' capital as well as "friends of the family" investors.

When will the company turn cash positive or "run out of money"?

PetSmart.com was founded in 2005 by three Columbia EMBA classmates. As they brainstormed for an idea for their entrepreneurial management class project, two of the members were struck by the presentation a week before concerning SmartCard technology. That same day, during a break for lunch, a news story appeared highlighting the prior failure of a service that would have linked people's health records with SmartCards. They later found out that the "failure" was due not to the technology to be employed but to the privacy laws associated with people's health records and the medical industry's reluctance to participate.

Later that day, the three founding members came up with an idea to marry the SmartCard technology with the need to bring standardization, portability, and convenience to another huge "health market"—that of the pet industry! They decided to create a pet licensing and health records business. (The key is that there are no restrictions on the health records privacy of nonhumans.)

FIRST THINGS FIRST

Is it a business or just an idea? They decided to test the market for size, availability and segmentation dynamics. Their research concluded that there are approximately 63 million dog owners in the United States, of which 12 million are licensed.

Dog Market

States	Population— July 2004 (U.S. Census)	No. of Households	No. of Households with Dogs	No. of Dogs	No. of Dog Licenses	Potential Revenue: Dog Licensing
Total U.S.	293,655,404	109,983,297	39,703,970	63,570,346	12,714,069	$19,071,104

Assumptions: 2.67 members per household, 3% households have dogs, 57% households have multiple dogs, 20% of all dogs are presently paper licensed, 1.50 per e-licensing as fee to us.

The business will initially focus on acquiring customers within the tristate area (New York, New Jersey, and Connecticut). The marketing research indicates the following.

Market Potential: Tristate Area (NY, NJ, CT) by County

New York County	Population— 2000 Census	No. of Households	No. of Households with Dogs	No. of Dogs	No. of Dog licenses	Potential Revenue: Dog Licensing
Totals	18,976,457	7,107,287	2,565,731	4,108,012	821,602	$1,232,404
New Jersey County						
Totals	8,414,350	3,151,442	1,137,671	1,821,533	364,307	$546,460
Connecticut County						
Totals	3,405,565	1,275,493	460,453	737,235	147,447	$221,170

Using a conservative conversion rate of 20 percent will provide revenue of $ 2,018,034 in year 1. Setting this against the first year's expenses and startup costs shows the following:

Startup Costs

Development:		
Database Design	$ 50,000	
Smart Card Technology	$ 20,000	
Web Development/Graphics	$ 10,000	
Security Software	$ 2,000	
Tag Development	$ 12,000	$ 94,000
SG&A		$ 73,400
Total		$ 167,400

Therefore, all the founders' efforts will go to designing a revenue model that minimizes startup expenses as much as possible. The revenue model is as follows:

	Yr 1	<=== Pre-Launch Activity ===>		
PetSmart.com	Q1	Q2 Q3	Q4	Total
No. of Licensing Transactions				–
No. of New Subscription Conversions				–
No. of New Direct Subscribers				–
No. of Renewal Subscribers				–
Total Subscribers				–
Revenue				
Licensing Transactions				$ –
New Subscriptions				$ –
Subscription Renewals				$ –
Total Revenue				$ –
Cost of Revenue				
Licensing Transactions				$ –
New Subscriptions				$ –
Subscription Renewals				$ –
Total Cost of Revenue				$ –
Gross Margin			$ –	$ –
			0.0%	0.0%
Operating Expenses				
Sales, General & Administrative		$ 17,500	$ 55,900	$ 73,400
Development		$ 47,000	$ 47,000	$ 94,000
Total Operating Expenses		$ 64,500	$ 102,900	$ 167,400
Earnings before Interest & Taxes		$ (64,500)	$ (102,900)	$ (167,400)
Interest				$ –
Earnings before Taxes		$ (64,500)	$ (102,900)	$ (167,400)
Taxes (ignores NOLs)	35%	$ –	$ –	$ –
Net Income		$ (64,500)	$ (102,900)	$ (167,400)

| | Year 2 | | | | | |
	Q1	Q2	Q3	Q4	Total	Yr 3
No. of Licensing Transactions	50,000	50,000	50,000	50,000	200,000	400,000
No. of New Subscription Conversions	2,500	2,500	2,500	2,500	10,000	20,000
No. of New Direct Subscribers			—	—	—	100,000
No. of Renewal Subscribers						2,000
No. of total Subscribers	2,500	2,500	2,500	2,500	10,000	122,000
Revenue						
Licensing Transactions	$ 75,000	$ 75,000	$ 75,000	$ 75,000	$ 300,000	$ 600,000
New Subscriptions	$ 62,475	$ 62,475	$ 62,475	$ 62,475	$ 249,900	$ 2,998,800
Subscription Renewals	$ —	$ —	$ —	$ —	$ —	$ 29,980
Total Revenue	$ 137,475	$ 137,475	$ 137,475	$ 137,475	$ 549,900	$ 3,628,780
Cost of Revenue						
Licensing Transactions	$ 33,750	$ 33,750	$ 33,750	$ 33,750	$ 135,000	$270,000
New Subscriptions	$ 43,733	$ 43,733	$ 43,733	$ 43,733	$ 174,930	$ 2,099,160
Subscription Renewals	$ —	$ —	$ —	$ —	$ —	$ 11,992
Total Cost of Revenue	$ 77,483	77,483	$ 77,483	$ 77,483	$ 309,930	$ 2,381,152
Gross Margin	$ 59,993	$ 59,993	$ 59,993	$ 59,993	$ 239,970	$ 1,247,628
	43.6%	43.6%	43.6%	43.6%	43.6%	34.4%
Operating Expenses						
Sales, General & Administrative	$ 141,100	$ 141,100	$ 141,100	$ 141,100	$ 564,400	$ 630,688
Development					$ —	$ 20,000
Total Operating Expenses	$ 141,100	$ 141,100	$ 141,100	$ 141,100	$ 564,400	$ 650,688
Earnings before Interest & Taxes	$ (81,108)	$ (81,108)	$ (81,108)	$ (81,108)	$ (324,430)	$ 596,940
	−59.0%	−59.0%	−59.0%	−59.0%	−59.0%	16.5%
Interest					$ —	
Earnings before Taxes	$ (81,108)	$ (81,108)	$ (81,108)	$ (81,108)	$ (324,430)	$ 596,940
Taxes (ignores NOLs)	$ —	$ —	$ —	$ —	$ —	$ (208,929)
Net Income	$ (81,108)	$ (81,108)	$ (81,108)	$ (81,108)	$ (324,430)	$ (388,011)

The business is projected to be net cash flow positive in Year 3. Initial startup capital required:

Startup costs	$ (167,400)
WC to cash position	$ (251,569)
Cash from Founders	$ 50,000
Additional Capital Req'd	**$ 368,969**

CASE STUDY QUESTIONS

1. When will the Company turn cash positive?
2. When will the Company run out of money?
3. Is the initial start-up capital estimated correctly?

ADDITIONAL RESOURCES

- **Dunn and Bradstreet Information Services**   www.dbisna.com
- **Hoover's Corporate Information**   www.hoovers.com
- **NASDAQ**   www.nasdaq.com
- **Small Business Advisor**   www.openmarket.com/leqis-nexis
- **Thomas Register of American Manufacturers**   www.thomasregister.com

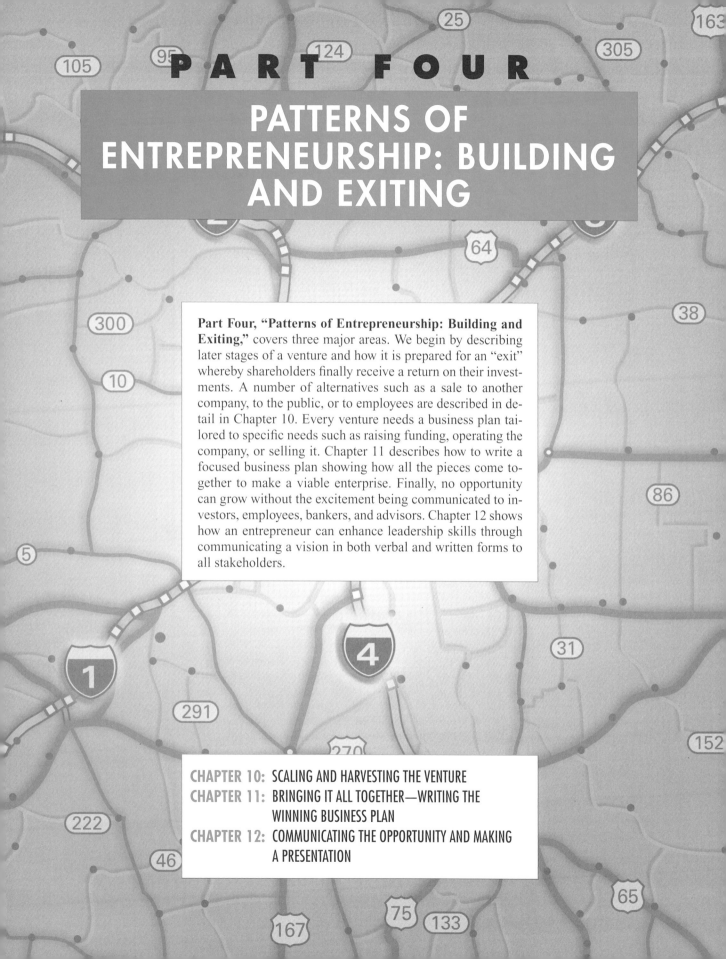

PART FOUR

PATTERNS OF ENTREPRENEURSHIP: BUILDING AND EXITING

Part Four, "Patterns of Entrepreneurship: Building and Exiting," covers three major areas. We begin by describing later stages of a venture and how it is prepared for an "exit" whereby shareholders finally receive a return on their investments. A number of alternatives such as a sale to another company, to the public, or to employees are described in detail in Chapter 10. Every venture needs a business plan tailored to specific needs such as raising funding, operating the company, or selling it. Chapter 11 describes how to write a focused business plan showing how all the pieces come together to make a viable enterprise. Finally, no opportunity can grow without the excitement being communicated to investors, employees, bankers, and advisors. Chapter 12 shows how an entrepreneur can enhance leadership skills through communicating a vision in both verbal and written forms to all stakeholders.

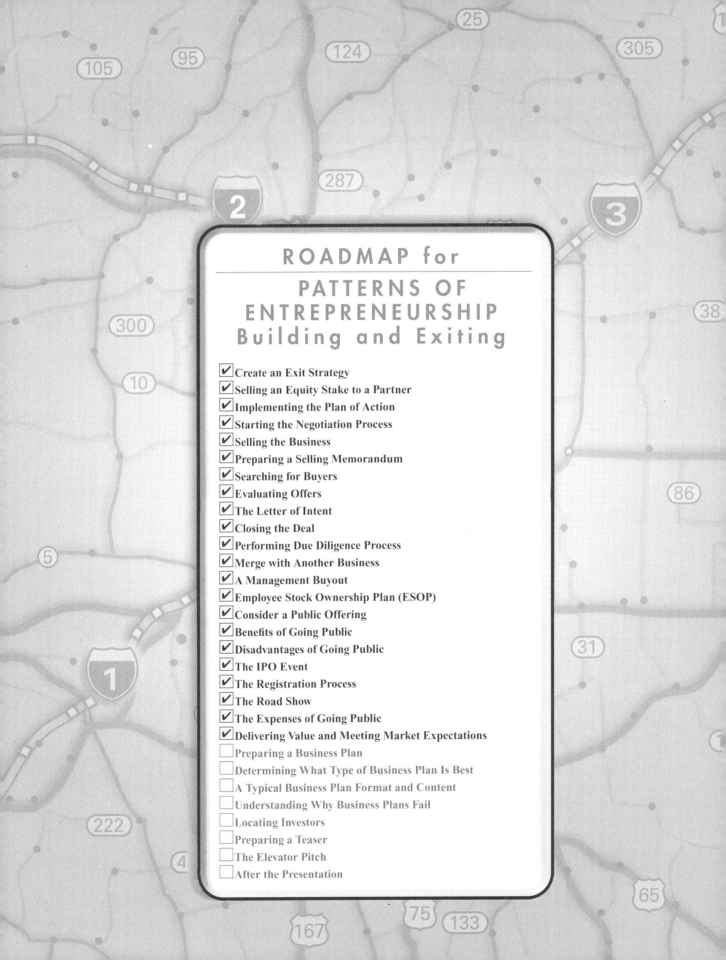

ROADMAP for

PATTERNS OF ENTREPRENEURSHIP
Building and Exiting

- ✔ Create an Exit Strategy
- ✔ Selling an Equity Stake to a Partner
- ✔ Implementing the Plan of Action
- ✔ Starting the Negotiation Process
- ✔ Selling the Business
- ✔ Preparing a Selling Memorandum
- ✔ Searching for Buyers
- ✔ Evaluating Offers
- ✔ The Letter of Intent
- ✔ Closing the Deal
- ✔ Performing Due Diligence Process
- ✔ Merge with Another Business
- ✔ A Management Buyout
- ✔ Employee Stock Ownership Plan (ESOP)
- ✔ Consider a Public Offering
- ✔ Benefits of Going Public
- ✔ Disadvantages of Going Public
- ✔ The IPO Event
- ✔ The Registration Process
- ✔ The Road Show
- ✔ The Expenses of Going Public
- ✔ Delivering Value and Meeting Market Expectations
- ☐ Preparing a Business Plan
- ☐ Determining What Type of Business Plan Is Best
- ☐ A Typical Business Plan Format and Content
- ☐ Understanding Why Business Plans Fail
- ☐ Locating Investors
- ☐ Preparing a Teaser
- ☐ The Elevator Pitch
- ☐ After the Presentation

CHAPTER 10

SCALING AND HARVESTING THE VENTURE

> "Think of yourself as on the threshold of unparalleled success, a whole clear life lies before you. Achieve. Achieve."
>
> ANDREW CARNEGIE

OBJECTIVES

- Learn how to use alliances to sell an equity stake in the venture.
- Identify the various sources to develop an exit strategy.
- List the exit options available for entrepreneurs.
- Describe the process and sequence of events in selling a business.
- Describe the selling memorandum and its contents for selling the business.
- Learn the process of launching an initial public offering (IPO).
- Understand the advantages and disadvantages of going public.

CHAPTER OUTLINE

Introduction

Create an Exit Strategy

Selling an Equity Stake to a Partner

Profile: Navin Chaddha

Implementing the Plan of Action

Selling the Business

Preparing a Selling Memorandum

Searching for Buyers

Evaluating Offers

Merge with Another Business

A Management Buyout Agreement (MBO)

Consider an Employee Stock Ownership Plan

Consider a Public Offering as a Harvest Option

Profile: Alan Trefler

Determining the Benefits of Going Public

Profile: Melissa Craig

Determining the Disadvantages of Going Public

Managing the IPO Event

Completing the Registration Process

Presenting a Road Show

The Expenses of Going Public

Delivering Value and Meeting Market Expectations

Summary

Study Questions

Exercises

Interactive Learning on the Web

Additional Resources

INTRODUCTION

This chapter provides the knowledge to identify the best exit plan for the entrepreneur and the venture's shareholders, and how to be in the strongest position to manage the process. Not until the shares of the company are purchased by a third party, can investors sell their ownership position and "cash-out," hopefully at a profit. This is called a "liquidity event."

A number of techniques and strategies can help the entrepreneur develop an exit plan. The chapter highlights the methodology, procedures, and options available for entrepreneurs when considering an exit strategy. There are several ways a company can realize an exit plan from the value it has created. Described in the chapter are the most common methods, namely, to sell an equity stake to a partner, sell the business, merge with another company, or implement a leveraged buyout. We also discuss the planning for a public offering (IPO) that offers an option to sell a portion of the venture and to scale the business for growth.

CREATE AN EXIT STRATEGY

Entrepreneurs spend so much time creating a business that many do not plan for a successful exit. The entrepreneur often sees selling the company as "selling out" and in most cases not meeting the expectations of investors or the management team. This situation can occur when new technologies are introduced and they impact the current product revenues in declining sales, or when competitors are gaining in market share and the company is losing its market position.

Usually the entrepreneur begins to develop reasons for exiting the business, including the stress level of managing the business and not finding enough time for the company because of family commitments. The opposite may also occur: the entrepreneur spends so much time on the venture that his or her family commitments suffer. Another first sign, which usually occurs in the early stages of growth, is the struggle for the company to stay alive. Therefore, it is important to prepare the exit plan early in the business cycle and at the right time. As discussed in Chapters 6 and 11, any entrepreneur seeking equity funding for growth must have plans for an exit prior to accepting external investors. There are several ways a company can realize an exit from the value it has created; the most common follow.

ACTIONS   Entrepreneurs may want to exit the business by establishing a strategic alliance and selling an equity stake in the business. An effective equity alliance can substantially increase the value of the venture and offer an exit option at a later date.

SELLING AN EQUITY STAKE TO A PARTNER

Selling an equity stake in the business to a strategic partner can substantially increase the value of the venture and offer an exit option to the entrepreneur. However, it takes research and due diligence to sell a minority or major equity interest in the venture to a strategic partner. Just picking up the phone and calling as many "big players" as possible in the hopes that they will want to buy an interest will generate

> "Although selling an equity stake of a business is financially attractive, entrepreneurs must consider where they are in regard to their personal plan and at what point they are willing to give up control of their business. For many entrepreneurs, the control issue is as important if not more important than the financial gain."
>
> LIZ ELTING
> *President and CEO*
> *Transperfect Translations, Inc.*

lots of effort but few results.[1] A well-researched and targeted effort is needed to determine why an alliance partner should purchase a majority or minority stake and the reasons and justification for the sale. Usually, for the entrepreneur to sell an equity position, the partnership must be beneficial to all parties. In most cases, an exploratory alliance is formed first. After measuring the success of the relationship, an equity position is negotiated to sell out completely or receive a minority stake in the venture. As an example, to initiate the alliance the entrepreneur can offer the company licenses to patents, copyrights, or trade secrets, and the other company can bring a stronger marketing organization with an eye toward growing the business. When the companies have complementary skills, the alliance can accomplish tasks that neither party could do alone. This positions the relationship for equity participation. The parties can also share customer relationships and costs, and reduce their individual exposure to risk. The alliance can be mutually beneficial by obtaining additional revenue from existing products, limiting the amount of capital to invest in needed capacity, and avoiding the need to add personnel. Additional benefits can increase the chances of getting into the market faster or obtaining first mover advantage and possibly gaining exclusive access or license to a product. Success in any or all of these factors of strategic alliances develops the relationship for the partners to purchase an equity stake in the venture.

PROFILE: NAVIN CHADDHA OF RIVIO

In 1999, a 28-year-old immigrant from India designed a software that bundled together all of the administrative tasks for a small-business owner. His name: Navin Chaddha. His company: Rivio. Chaddha's software allows payroll, time and attendance cards, accounting, and online banking to be handled on a single Web site. But how would he market the program? A Rivio board member called a friend, a senior executive of Bank of America, which has 1.7 million small-business customers. Bank of America didn't want its entrepreneurial clients to defect to "do it yourself" Web service providers. So Bank of America struck a deal with Rivio in May 2000 to create a partnership that included about $3 million for the Web-marketing budget. Bank of America has extended the partnership and is now one of Rivio's largest funders, contributing $50 million along with BellSouth and FleetBoston.

Today Rivio has 80 alliances, including Automatic Data Processing, InterPay, Microsoft, UPS, and OfficeMax. Each integrates its service with Rivio's application platform. The platform is also distributed by the channel partners—like BellSouth, FleetBoston, Bank of America, and Verizon—through their small-business services. The platform has access to 15 million small-business owners.[2]

IMPLEMENTING THE PLAN OF ACTION

The first principle in positioning the alliance partner to acquire an equity stake is to know what value the partner sees in the business.[3] The most common value for most alliances is increasing the revenue or decreasing the costs of operation. Before any serious negotiation, however, this value needs to be determined, and both sides require an evaluation to quantify the present and potential market opportunities. Also, the entrepreneur needs to identify what the alliance will cost in time and money. For example, a relationship with a partner may limit the chances of selling the venture to the company's competitors. The following actions serve as a guide for establishing an alliance:

- Identify the objective of a proposed alliance. The entrepreneur should determine the time requirements and the expectations of the parties involved in the process.
- Build a target list of possible candidate companies. It is best to go after more than one possible partner—also, a mixture of size and scope is important. Although it might be exciting to go after a global brand, in some instances (especially on the support and development side) finding a possible partner of like size, and/or with existing industry experience and a regional player, is a smarter move. The parties will be more interested in partnering and making the relationship work.
- Research the candidates and examine the Web sites and press releases. Determine who is in charge of business development—the CEO or the president. Look at information and articles they placed. The key is to find out their mission and focus. Build a document on each target—including contact information and phone numbers.
- Present the finding on each target to the key members of the areas that will be impacted by the relationship (i.e., if it is software development, IT, marketing, sales) and gather their input, concerns, and interests.
- Develop a nonconfidential introduction kit and cover letter to send to possible alliance partners. (This could be an e-mail with attached document/PDF). (More about creating such a document is covered in Chapter 12.) The letter should be short and to the point, highlighting why the relationship would be of value to the partner. The goal should be an in-person meeting. It is best that the first meeting be on the potential alliance partner's terms and location. In this way you can make an on-site inspection, and they will be more comfortable and more likely to know that you are showing commitment. A sample meeting agenda should be prepared as follows.

MEETING AGENDA

- Prepare an agenda, with names, titles, and contact information.
- State the goals and desired outcomes of the meetings.
- Prepare an overview of the business and role (have hard copies, including additional ones).
- Review the specific reason for the meeting and the driving reason for an alliance.
- Prepare a general business overview.
- Conduct a walk-through and tour (no matter how small an office, walk the floor and talk with people, get a sense of the environment and the culture).
- Review the level of interest and get ideas on how the two businesses would work together.
- Agree on the relationship, timing, next steps, action, and who will be the responsible persons on each side.[4]

Making an alliance work requires constant involvement and communication. The companies need to stay connected and be in constant communication. Because of this time commitment and effort, the company should target only a few key alliances.

The entrepreneur should also prepare, as a follow-up, a single-page, one-sided document developed and ready to review. This document is called an **Alliance Value Statement** and is divided into two halves. The top half states the value and positioning of the alliance, whereas the bottom half attempts to define the values and points on behalf of the potential partner. The document should be updated regularly and shared with all members of both businesses.

Otherwise the alliances will die off, and the cost of time, legal, and emotional investments will never be recouped.[5]

Starting the Negotiation Process

When the negotiating starts, both companies should use their best efforts to make it work. The parties should establish a relationship with the highest officers and decision makers. The entrepreneur should make sure he is kept informed and does not entrust the fate of the partnership to a lower level person. To determine the price or value as part of the negotiation, the outline of the selling memorandum on the following page will assist in maximizing efficiencies: When the contract is prepared, keep in mind that the best results for a successful alliance are the responsibility of both parties.

SELLING THE BUSINESS

Selling the business is another option in the entrepreneur's exit plan. However, in a weak economy selling a business seems a risky option to the entrepreneur. The best plan is to build valuable assets and identify them in the selling process. The obvious assets are inventory, receivables, equipment, and real estate. If the business is a service company, the entrepreneur must become more inventive. The entrepreneur should plan to arrange long-term employment deals with his staff or sign extended contracts with customers or key suppliers. This plan can be very time consuming and be an emotionally charged experience, as it is typically one of the most significant events in an entrepreneur's business life. If you have outside investors and have added experienced board members, they can be extremely valuable in preparing and structuring a sale of the company.

After the initial assessment to sell the business, a preliminary calculation of the company's value should be determined. Selling a company is time consuming, and you will not want to proceed unless the company's value meets your own and your shareholders' expectations. However, in a tight money environment it can take a lot of give-and-take to close a deal. Sellers may have to agree to a long-term payment for part or all of the transaction or lease high-priced equipment to the buyer.

Along with determining an acceptable price, the entrepreneur should think about what kind of compensation or payment is acceptable. Cash only? Earn-out agreements based on reaching agreed earnings? Stock? What form of seller employment agreements and noncompete clauses? Or is he or she willing to help the buyer finance the purchase? Although these decisions do not have to be made immediately, the entrepreneur should start to consider the alternatives. The sellers who thrive are

An independent advisor can also assist the entrepreneur with all the steps of selling. He or she should look for experienced advisors who can add value to the process and supplement the skills of the management team.

those who are flexible in their strategies and actions, capable of moving quickly, and adapting to change.

PREPARING A SELLING MEMORANDUM

Entrepreneurs should use the business plan as a marketing tool to help sell the company. In this context, the revised plan becomes the "selling memorandum." The information in the business plan will be the basis for the buyer's preliminary evaluation of the company.

A selling memorandum normally includes information about the company's history, the market in which the company competes, the company's products, its operations, and its strengths. The memorandum should be a very comprehensive document because it reflects the quality of the organization. Once the selling memorandum is completed, the company is in a good position to refine the preliminary valuation and begin determining an appropriate range of selling prices.[6]

OUTLINE OF A SELLING MEMORANDUM

EXECUTIVE SUMMARY

The executive summary should explain the purpose of the memorandum and describe all the key elements of the memorandum in just a few pages. A well-written summary should convince the prospective buyer to continue reading. The summary has another important use. It can be sent separately to people who may not be serious buyers. If after reviewing the summary they are still interested in seeing the whole plan, the entrepreneur can release it to them after they sign a confidentiality agreement drafted by an attorney. This should help protect the confidential details of the memorandum.

PRODUCTS AND SERVICES

The memorandum should describe the company's products and services. How are they different from others on the market? Are they patented? Are there follow-on products? What R&D is required, and what technological risks exist? Include any product literature that is available.

MARKETING

Describe the market for the products and services. Explain the dynamics of the market, market size, market trends, growth potential, user demographics, and so on. What are the company's marketing strategies, pricing strategies, penetration targets, and advertising and promotional plans? Include a competitive analysis,

OUTLINE OF A SELLING MEMORANDUM (cont.)

listing direct competitors, their strengths and weaknesses, their market share, financial information, and the like.

MANUFACTURING

How are the products manufactured? How will the resources be used? Describe required raw materials and their sources. Are there second sources for all critical items? Describe production facilities and capacity requirements and constraints. What warranties do the products carry, and how is this service provided?

MANAGEMENT

Describe the current organization. List key personnel who will be staying with the company and describe their positions and experience. Do not disclose their compensation, however, since this could provide recruiting information to competitors.

EMPLOYEES

Describe how the employees are compensated. What major benefits are provided? Does a union represent them? If so, what are the significant terms of the contract? How have relations been with the union?

HISTORICAL FINANCIAL STATEMENTS

Present financial statements for the most recent interim periods, including comparisons with prior years' results and with budgets. Also include statements for the last three fiscal years, including auditors' reports, if any.

FINANCIAL PROJECTIONS

Prepare financial projections for the next three to five years. Some sellers include their projections, and the assumptions underlying the projections, in the selling memorandum.[7]

SEARCHING FOR BUYERS

When the selling memorandum is complete, a search for potential buyers begins. Who might be interested in purchasing the company? The potential list that is prepared can include individual investors or entrepreneurs, existing management, other employee groups, competitors, customers, vendors, investment groups, and foreign investors. Each of these groups has different motivations to buy, and depending on the company's situation, some groups may be more appropriate than others as potential buyers.

ROADMAP

ACTIONS

The most desirable way for the entrepreneur to find the right buyer is to have a file of prospective buyers who have contacted the company. In addition to personal contacts, other sources of potential buyers include trade associations, investment bankers, lawyers, bankers, and accountants.

Several types of professional intermediaries are available to help identify potential buyers:

- The major investment banking firms have mergers and acquisitions departments that specialize in providing a wide range of services for these types of transactions. These firms are probably the most sophisticated and generally focus on transactions where the purchase price is $25 million or more.
- Commercial banks recently have developed affiliates that provide services similar to the services of investment banking firms. As affiliates of banks, they have information about and access to the bank's client companies.
- Finally, smaller independent firms that specialize in these areas can be highly qualified intermediaries. These intermediaries participate in a range of transactions from small ones to those of about $5 million, with the majority on the smaller side. There are also some intermediaries who can generate a list of sales prospectuses and the placing of newspaper ads.

The intermediary's key role is to identify potential candidates and assist both parties throughout the entire process to consummate the sale. This task is usually undertaken on an exclusive basis. Fees for bringing together the buyers and sellers are generally guaranteed by the seller, who provides an up-front retainer and a substantial amount contingent upon completion of the transaction. The total fee is often based on the "Lehman formula," which calls for fees of 5 percent of the first $1 million of purchase price, 4 percent of the second million, 3 percent of the third, 2 percent of the fourth, and 1 percent of amounts in excess of $4 million. Variations of the Lehman formula usually work well for midsize transactions. However, a different arrangement may be negotiated for very small and very large transactions.

EVALUATING OFFERS

In evaluating prospective offers, sellers should investigate the prospective buyer's (1) credentials and track record, (2) creditworthiness, especially if a portion of the purchase price is deferred or is paid in notes or stock, (3) management style, and (4) integrity.

The investigation may uncover some hidden problems with the buyer's company. The information gathered may indicate that the timing of the sale is inappropriate for business or personal reasons. More important, the research may prove that the buyer is simply the wrong party to make the purchase for any number of reasons. Discussions with some of the companies the buyer has already acquired might yield further insights.

After potential buyers are identified, the entrepreneur must determine which ones are financially capable of purchasing the business. The seller business contacts, credit bureaus, and trade journals can be used to rule out buyers who cannot afford the asking price. Next, determine which prospects are most likely to be interested in the company. Look at the business from each of the prospective buyers' standpoints, and determine why each one might be interested in the business.

Holding the Initial Meeting

One of the most critical steps in effecting the sale of a company is the initial meeting between the buyer and seller. Both buyer and seller will have certain objectives. The

The letter of intent is an agreement by the parties to negotiate in good faith and contains the terms of a definitive contract. The letter of intent is only an expression of intention, has escape clauses, and is usually not binding. It allows both parties the opportunity to withdraw from the deal at any point.

buyer will want to know the seller's motives for selling the company and how serious the seller is, as well as more detailed information about the business. The seller will also want to know how serious the buyer is, if the buyer has the financial resources necessary to purchase the company, and whether the buyer is the type of person to whom he or she wants to sell the company.

If the results of the initial meeting warrant further consideration of the deal, the buyer will next begin to evaluate the company and develop a financial structure for the proposed purchase. The buyer should hold preliminary discussions of the proposed financial structure with specific lenders and any investors to get their thoughts on the viability of the deal. As in the initial meeting with the seller, the buyer should avoid the tendency to negotiate the specific points of investor agreements and should instead concentrate on whether there is an appropriate degree of interest in the transaction.

Negotiating

Negotiations play a key role throughout the acquisition process. There is no single session of negotiations in this type of transaction; rather, negotiations will be made at every step of the process as new information becomes available and additional analyses are performed.

Volumes have been written on the art of negotiating. The key to successful negotiation is an understanding of the objectives, needs, strengths, and weaknesses and those of the other party. In a successful negotiation, both sides feel they have won. Give-and-take is inherent in the negotiating process. Both the buyer and the seller need to be flexible and to understand which bargaining points are important to win and where compromises can be reached. The buyer should consult with key advisors to develop a negotiating strategy and should keep those people involved throughout the process.

Create the Letter of Intent

Before investing the time and money needed to thoroughly evaluate the target company, the buyer will want to know that the seller is interested in continuing the process. A letter of intent is often written to confirm the interests of the two parties and to outline the basic terms that have been agreed upon in the initial phase of negotiation. The letter of intent is, in many ways, similar to the "term sheet" for venture investments discussed in detail in Chapter 6.

The letter of intent is an agreement by the parties to continue to negotiate in good faith. Generally, it contains provisions that the terms are subject to a definitive contract and proclaims the document to be only an expression of intention. The letter of intent will have many escape clauses in it to allow both parties the opportunity to withdraw from the deal at any point. Such clauses may include requirements for approval by the Board of Directors or by the stockholders. Certain issues related to the transaction are normally addressed at this stage, and the preliminary resolution of these issues will be contained in the letter of intent:[8]

- *The Purchase Price*. This is either its amount or an agreed-upon formula for its computation.
- *What Is Being Purchased?* The general categories of assets, liabilities, and operations that are being transferred to the buyer and those being retained by the seller should be identified.
- *The Structure*. The parties need to agree about whether the sale will be a sale of assets, a sale of stock, a merger, or some other structure.
- *The Payout or Types of Compensation*. Will it be cash, notes, equity, or some combination of these?
- *Escrow for Contingencies*. The buyer may want to establish an escrow account into which a portion of the purchase price will be deposited. This escrow might cover such items as unrecorded liabilities that later surface or recorded items that are only estimates (e.g., the allowance for uncollectable accounts).
- *Other Significant Terms*. These include contingent payments, covenants not to compete, and employment contracts.
- *Other Required Agreements*. These include renegotiated leases and long-term purchase contracts.
- *The Purchase Agreement*. What is the expected timing for preparing the purchase agreement? Who will draft it? Typically, the buyer's counsel will be the drafter.
- *Due Diligence*. What are the timing and extent? What are the buyer's expectations for documentation? Are management personnel and records available? (See Chapter 6 for a complete due diligence checklist for investment and purchase transactions.)
- *Professional Fees*. Who will be responsible for the various related fees, including fees for attorneys, accountants, appraisers, and investment bankers?
- *Exclusivity Agreement*. A buyer will want to negotiate with the seller on an exclusive basis. The seller will usually grant such a right for a defined period, such as 90 or 120 days.
- *"Bust-Up Fees."* It has become fairly common for the buyer to want a provision for bust-up fees if the company is ultimately sold to another bidder. The buyer will argue that, by putting the company "in play" (i.e., performing a valuation and beginning negotiations so that other companies are aware the target company is seriously for sale), the buyer has added value to the target company. If another buyer then outbids the original buyer, the original buyer should receive a portion of the increased price as compensation for this value added. Sellers, of course, will try to avoid such a fee.

Other Conditions

The following conditions for closing will also be included in the letter of interim:

- *Applicable Law*. If the transaction involves parties located in different states, it is common to identify which state laws will govern the agreements.

- *Adjustments of Purchase Price for Interim Results.* A purchase price is usually negotiated based in part on historical financial information. The price may be adjusted for any income or losses that occur through the actual closing date.

Performing Due Diligence

Both the buyer and the seller will have to perform legal due diligence. The seller and advisors will review and prepare the disclosure schedules of information that are requested by the buyer to investigate the affairs of the company. They will also perform a legal "audit" in order to render an opinion on legal contingencies and other legal issues as of the closing.[9]

The typical information requested includes all corporate records (articles of incorporation, by-laws, minutes, stock records, etc.), material contracts, loan agreements, pending or threatened litigation, royalty agreements, labor agreements, leases, commitments, employment contracts, and stockholder agreements. An increasingly important area is environmental liability, as current owners of businesses may be held responsible for cleaning up toxic chemicals left by prior owners. Also, the need for regulatory clearance relating to restriction of trade concerns may have to be identified and obtained. The seller's counsel will issue a legal opinion at the closing that generally covers (1) the legality of the transaction (i.e., the company is authorized to do it and has all the requisite approvals), (2) confirmation of capital stock information, (3) the validity and enforceability of all material contracts, and (4) knowledge and status of pending or threatened litigation.

Preparing the Purchase Agreement

As the buyer's team begins its detailed evaluation of the company, the attorneys will be preparing the purchase agreements. The drafting of the documents will give rise to rounds of negotiations to resolve some of the obstacles deferred earlier in the process and to renegotiate issues previously agreed upon but modified because of information that has come to light in the evaluation process.

The purchaser's attorney usually drafts the purchase agreement. Although the letter of intent will serve as the outline for this agreement, the final document will generally be quite lengthy. New issues often arise as a result of the due diligence process, and much time is spent in drafting the representations and warranties of both the buyer and the seller, as well as in drafting the indemnification provisions.

Closing the Deal

Once all these issues have been resolved and the financing commitments have been received, the deal is in condition to close—all the documents are signed, the stock or assets are transferred, and the consideration exchanges hands.

Often, certain time-consuming procedures such as obtaining a tax ruling, receiving an audited balance sheet, or perfecting the title on assets are a prerequisite to consummating the deal. Rather than wait until everything is done, the parties will agree to a deferred closing. The purchase agreement may be signed and the consideration may change hands, but the actual passage of title may occur at a later date. "Conditions" are obligations that must be met in order for the deal to legally close. Typical conditions include fulfillment of key employment agreements, delivery of financial statements, maintenance of minimum net worth requirements, provision of accountants' comfort letters and legal opinions, and, if applicable, gaining third-party consent on the transfer of material agreements, licenses, or rights.

MERGE WITH ANOTHER BUSINESS

A merger is a transaction between two companies, and is an alternative to selling the business or selling an equity stake to a strategic partner. Why should an entrepreneur consider a merger? The chart below indicates several reasons. A merger between two businesses ranges from survival to value-added services for the growth of the new venture. When a company loses its competitive advantage in the marketplace, a merger may be the only path left to follow.

On creating a merger, the entrepreneur should identify areas of similarity and differences and then define the capability that shows the value of each company.

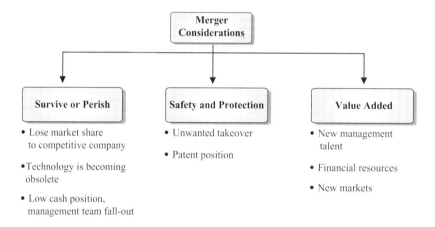

Planning a merger requires calculating the value of both the business and all existing resources. (Use Chapter 6 to determine which valuation methods are best and how to evaluate the other company's management and capabilities.) The benefits of a merger can be the route to instant product diversification and quick completion of product lines. It also can provide technical know-how, greater executive depth, economies of scale, improved access to financing, entry into otherwise closed markets, vertical integration of manufacturing operations, and new marketing strength.

A MANAGEMENT BUYOUT AGREEMENT (MBO)

A management buyout occurs when the founder sells the business to its partners or management team. If the business has a positive cash flow or assets, the financing can be accomplished via banks, insurance companies, and financial institutions. The problem is that the managers or partners who want to buy out the owners usually do not have sufficient capital. The buyer must have the cash up front or the sale can be very fragile, and full realization of a gain is questionable. Most buyers require the seller to take a limited amount of cash up front and a note for the balance of the purchase price over several years. If the purchase price is tied to the profitability of the business, the seller is totally dependent on the buyer's ability to manage the business so that it can generate sufficient cash to buy the business over time. In this case, the seller will end up on the short end of the deal.

CONSIDER AN EMPLOYEE STOCK OWNERSHIP PLAN

An ESOP, or Employee Stock Ownership Plan, is a mechanism by which the founding entrepreneurs can sell the company over time to key employees. This alternative is usually considered when there is no immediate requirement to provide a major liquidity event to external shareholders, the founder(s) do not need immediate cash, they wish to retain the culture of the company and incentivize key employees to remain with the company and continue the legacy built by the founder. ESOP's are therefore most often used by privately held companies that do not have family members available to continue managing the company. Paul Silvis at Restek (see Chapter 5) selected an ESOP for his company because he wished to continue as part of the management team, gradually phasing out his involvement. He believed that, slowly transferring ownership to the employees was the best way to retain the unique "family" culture he had created and would ensure the continuing success of the plan. An ESOP could also be considered later by the DeAngelo brothers, although as the interview with Neal showed (see Chapter 8), it is too early to make plans in this regard. Because tax advantages can be gained using an ESOP structure, the rules are rather stringent and any entrepreneur considering this route to "cash-out" should take appropriate advice from someone practiced in setting up such plans.

CONSIDER A PUBLIC OFFERING AS A HARVEST OPTION

"Perhaps the most critical decision entrepreneurs face as they develop their dreams from an idea to a sustainable growth company is whether to do an IPO. Once they are willing to sacrifice their privacy, certain personal freedoms, and oftentimes control, entrepreneurs will begin this next chapter in their lives by learning to manage the expectations of their new shareholders, namely their stockholders. The benefits of going public frequently outweigh the costs and sacrifices along the way. An IPO provides the necessary capital to make acquisitions, attract talent, and develop strategic partnerships that help companies get to the next level of growth."

S. BRIAN WILSON
Former Vice President of Global Sales NASDAQ

Entrepreneurs can realize a harvest from the value they have created by considering a public offering. In deciding whether to go ahead with a public offering, it is important that entrepreneurs remember that the initial offering (IPO) is neither more nor less important than any of the exit options we have discussed. It is usually one that a company may undertake over time. An important consideration for an IPO is the timing of the transaction, as the demand for newly issued stock can be extremely volatile. In deciding whether to do an IPO, it is always advisable to proceed with a backup plan. Even if the company is well prepared and the market is favorable, the economy can change by the date of the IPO.[10] Going public represents a rite of passage for a company and provides both benefits and obligations that should be carefully considered. The IPO process is difficult, the pitfalls are numerous, and stakes are high. Poor market timing and inadequate planning can jeopardize an IPO. Despite initial positive performance after the offering, many companies discover that the values recede soon after going public and the company underperforms in both profits and share price.

The following questions need to be addressed in making an IPO decision:

- Are you ready to share the ownership of your company with the public?
- Are you prepared to disclose your company's most closely held secrets?
- Can you live with the continued scrutiny of investors and market analysts?
- Can you devote the 100 percent required of your time for six to eight months and pay the substantial fees that it takes for a typical IPO?
- Are you prepared to take on the issues, challenges, and responsibility to go public?

PROFILE: ALAN TREFLER

Then: Owner of a large amount of stock of a private company
Now: Owner of a large amount of stock of a public company
Alan Trefler has done something every entrepreneur dreams of but few accomplish: he took his company public and retained more than 70 percent of equity. Trefler founded Pegasystems Inc. in 1983. The Massachusetts-based business creates software that wades through databases to help corporations capture useful information about their customers. Back in the late 1970s, Trefler offered to create software for his previous employers at Citibank, but they turned him down. Ironically, the bank signed on as one of Pegasytems' first customers. Through the 1980s Trefler bootstrapped the business completely, never seeking or accepting a dime of venture capital. In 1996 he took the company public, and because so few people owned equity, he was free to keep a huge chunk of stock for himself. Pegasystems has grown to $76 million in revenues and a market capitalization of $318 million since then, leaving Trefler with a considerable fortune.[11]

DETERMINING THE BENEFITS OF GOING PUBLIC

The benefits of going public are many and diverse. To determine whether they outweigh the drawbacks, you must evaluate them in the context of personal, shareholder, and corporate objectives. Some of the most attractive benefits include the following:[12]

Improved financial condition. Selling shares to the public brings equity money that does not have to be repaid, immediately improving the company's financial condition.

Benefits to the shareholder/investor. Going public offers liquidity to existing investors despite the sales restrictions imposed on the major investors and officers and directors of the company. Underwriters will restrict founding stockholders and management from selling their sales through "lock-up" agreements (normally 180 days) for a specific period of time; eventually they can convert their shares into cash. The value of the stock may increase remarkably, starting with the initial offering. Shares that are publicly traded generally command higher prices than those that are not. Investors are usually willing to pay more for public companies because of (1) the marketability of the shares, (2) the maturity/sophistication attributed to public companies, and (3) the availability of more information.

Diversification of shareholder portfolios. Going public makes it possible for shareholders to diversify their investment portfolios. IPOs often include a secondary offering (shares owned by existing shareholders) in addition to a primary offering (previously unissued shares). The entrepreneur must ensure that potential investors and shareholders do not perceive the secondary offerings as a bailout for shareholders. Underwriters frequently restrict the number of shares that can be sold by existing shareholders in a secondary offering.

Access to capital. Accessing the public equity markets enables you to attract better valuations, accept less dilution of ownership, and raise more money. The money from an IPO can repay debt, fund special projects, and be used for acquisitions. For example, it can use the proceeds to acquire other businesses, repay debt, finance research and development projects, and acquire or modernize production facilities. Another plus is that raising equity capital through a public offering often results in a higher valuation for your company, through a higher multiple of earnings (or price-earnings ratio), as compared with many types of private financing. Thus, it often results in less dilution of ownership than with some other financing alternatives, such as venture capital. Raising capital in this way also avoids the interest costs and cash drain of debt financing.

Management and employee incentives. The company can issue stock options to management and employees. This can be more motivating and rewarding to employees than issuing illiquid stock and will attract and retain the key executives.

Enhanced corporate reputation. The company's public status and listing on a national exchange can provide a competitive advantage over other companies in the same industry by providing greater visibility and enhanced corporate image. This can lead to increased sales, reduced pricing from vendors, and improved service from suppliers.

Improved opportunities for future financing. By going public, an entrepreneurial venture usually improves its net worth and builds a larger and broader equity base. The improved debt-to-equity ratio will help the company borrow additional funds as needed or reduce the current cost of borrowing. If the stock performs well in the continuing aftermarket, the company is more likely to be able to raise additional equity capital on favorable terms. With an established market for the stock, the entrepreneur will have the flexibility to offer future investors a whole new range of securities with liquidity and an ascertainable market value.

A path to acquisitions. Private companies often lack the financial connections and resources to assume an aggressive role in acquisitions. Well-conceived acquisitions can play a big part in corporate survival and success. Going public enhances a company's financing alternatives for acquisitions by adding two vital components to its financial resources: (1) cash derived from the IPO and (2) unissued equity shares that have a ready market. Public companies often issue stock (instead of paying cash) to acquire other businesses. The owners of an acquisition target may be more willing to accept a company's stock if it is publicly traded. The liquidity provided by the public market affords greater flexibility and ease in selling shares using shares as collateral for loans.

PROFILE: MELISSA CRAIG

Then: Early-stage international wholesale telephone operations
Now: Instead of an IPO, the company was acquired.

Melissa Craig, CEO of General Telecom, embodies the spirit of a new-age entrepreneur: see the problem, create the solution, and execute it better than anyone else. Originally founded in 1990, General Telecom operated as a reseller of used Northern Telecom switches being disposed of by merging U.S.-based carriers. With the deregulation of the telephone industry in the early 1990s, Melissa and her partners at General Telecom, Tom Tilton and Jeanne Swanke, saw an opportunity and seized it. New international wholesale telephone operations were cropping up everywhere, buying service from major carriers to resell to consumers at below-retail rates. These operators needed to lease a portion of a switch from an existing phone company to connect calls, monitor their customers' traffic, and prepare bills. Melissa and her partners decided that they would not resell their used telephone switches, and instead they set up the first and only Independent Gateway Service Provider. General Telecom is not a carrier but a service provider, and it is never in conflict with its customers. As the industry has evolved, so has General Telecom; it currently operates as a support center for its customers, consulting on how carriers can implement different value-added services. Melissa Craig and General Telecom considered an IPO but were not prepared for all the risks and issues they would face. Instead, the company was sold.[13]

DETERMINING THE DISADVANTAGES OF GOING PUBLIC

The benefits of going public must be weighed against its drawbacks. Here again, the entrepreneur must view the possible drawbacks in the context of personal, company, and shareholder objectives. In many cases, the impact of these drawbacks can be minimized through thoughtful planning backed by the help of outside advisors.[14]

Loss of control. Depending on the proportion of shares sold to the public, the entrepreneur may be at risk of losing control of the company now or in the future. Retaining at least 51 percent of the shares will ensure control for now, but subsequent offerings and acquisitions may dilute control. However, if the stock is widely distributed, management usually can retain control even if it holds less than 50 percent of the shares. To retain voting control, it is possible to have a new class of common stock with limited voting rights. However, such stock may have limited appeal to investors and may therefore sell for less than ordinary common stock.

Sharing the success. Investors share the risks and successes of the new venture to which they contribute capital. If the entrepreneur realistically anticipates unusually high earnings in the next two or three years and can obtain bank or other financing, he or she may wish to temporarily defer a public offering. Then, when the company does go public, the shares will, most likely, command a higher price.

Loss of privacy. Of all the changes that result when a company goes public, perhaps none is more troublesome than the loss of privacy. When a company becomes publicly held, the Securities and Exchange Commission (SEC) requires disclosure of much information about the company—information that private companies don't ordinarily disclose. Some of those disclosures contain highly sensitive information such as compensation paid to key executives and directors, special incentives for management, and many of the plans and strategies that underlie the company's operations. These disclosures rarely harm the business. For the most part, employee compensation, and the price paid for materials and received for the products, are governed by market forces—not by the disclosed financial results.

Limits on management's freedom to act. By going public, management surrenders some degree of freedom. While the management of a privately held company generally is free to act by itself, the management of a public company must obtain the approval of the Board of Directors on certain major matters; on special matters, it must even seek the consent of the shareholders. The Board of Directors, if kept informed on a timely basis, can usually be counted on to understand management's needs, offer support, and grant much of the desired flexibility.

Demands of periodic reporting. Management is required to comply with SEC regulations and reporting requirements. These requirements include quarterly financial reporting (Form 10Q), annual financial reporting (Form 10-K), and reporting of current material events (Form 8-K). Reporting the requirements of a registrant demands significant time and financial commitments. Securities analysts will also demand management's time. Recently, the additional costs and personal burdens imposed by the Sarbanes-Oxley legislation for financial reporting have become a further concern to senior management.

Initial and outgoing expenses. Going public can be costly and will result in a tremendous commitment of management's time and energy. The largest single cost in an IPO ordinarily is the underwriter's discount or commission, which generally ranges from 6 to 10 percent of the offering price. In addition, legal and accounting fees, printing costs, the underwriter's out-of-pocket expenses (generally not included in the commission), filing fees, as well as registrar and transfer agent fees can typically add another $300,000 to $500,000.

New fiduciary responsibilities. As the owner of a private business, the money invested and risked is the owner's. However, as the manager of a public company, the money invested and risked belongs to the shareholders. The entrepreneur is accountable to them, so he or she must approach potential conflicts of interest with the utmost caution. It also will be necessary to work with the Board of Directors to help them discharge their fiduciary responsibilities when acting on corporate matters.

MANAGING THE IPO EVENT

The IPO event follows many months of careful preparation.[15] During the IPO, the president/CEO will serve as the company's major representative, delivering the company's story to the financial market. The CEO will be involved in setting the strategic direction for the SEC Registration Statement.

The IPO event usually lasts between 90 and 120 days, but some take up to six months.[16] It includes preparing and filing the Registration Statement (and one to three amendments—responding to comments from the SEC), going on the road show, and the closing and buying of the company stock by the Underwriting Syndicate. Other events will include the first periodic reports, proxy solicitation, and dealing with restricted stock.

Example of Timetable for an IPO[17]

Day 1	First meeting ("all hands")
Day 45	Draft of registration statement
Day 55	Second meeting—revisions and agreement
Day 60	Filing of registration statement with the SEC
Day 90	Receipt of SEC comment letter
Day 70–100	The road show
Day 90–110	Revisions and pricing
Day 115	Effective date
Day 120	Closing

COMPLETING THE REGISTRATION PROCESS

The registration process begins when the entrepreneur has reached an understanding with an underwriter on the proposed public offering. From this point on, he or she becomes subject to SEC regulations on what may or may not be done to promote your company. The center of the process is preparing the Registration Statement (S1), which includes a complete description of the company, its business, the market for its products, and the regulatory environment in which it operates. This entails establishing the appropriate internal accounting policies for the business, systems, and management, and preparing the required financial data, including highlights and timing. The financial statements must be audited and should reflect income statements for the preceding three years, balance sheets for the prior two years, and interim financial statements for the applicable periods. The Statement also lists the company's officers and directors, biographies, compensation, and stock ownership. Other factors to consider are employment contracts, compensation, and the Board of Directors.

The first step in preparing the Registration Statement is the initial meeting or "all hands," which includes company executives, attorneys, auditors, underwriters, and underwriters' attorneys. At this meeting, responsibility is assigned for gathering information and for preparing the various parts of the Registration Statement. Typically, the attorneys play a coordinating role in directing this team effort.[18]

The Registration Statement is usually approved by company counsel and has comments from the underwriter, management, and company accountants. The prospectus, which is a part of the Registration Statement, becomes the marketing document for the IPO.

THE REGISTRATION PROCESS

Example of an IPO prospectus cover.

Initial Public Offering Prospectus

TECH-DATA INCORPORATED

10,000,000 Shares of Common Stock

$5.25 per share

TECH-DATA, INC.	We sell enterprise software to companies in the United States and Canada.	
Per share price $5.25	Total $52,500,000	This is the initial public offering, and no public market currently exists for the shares.
Less Discounts	$0.525 $5,250,000	
Proceeds	$4.725 $47,250,000	

Proposed Trading Symbols:

The Nasdaq SmallCap Market™—DII

This investment involves a high degree of risk. You should purchase shares only if you can afford a complete loss. See "Risk Factors."

Neither the Securities and Exchange Commission nor any state securities commission has approved or disapproved these securities or determined if this Prospectus is truthful or complete. Any representation to the contrary is a criminal offense.

LEAD UNDERWRITERS, INC.

Initial Public Offering Prospectus.

Filing the Registration Statement

When outstanding issues have been resolved and the company officers and majority of the Board of Directors have signed the Registration Statement, it is filed with the SEC (normally electronically) on the SEC's EDGAR system. In addition to filing with the SEC, the statement is also filed with any state in which the securities will be offered and with the National Association of Securities Dealers. At closing, documents are executed and stock certificates are exchanged. Usually company officers, counsel, transfer agent, and managing underwriters attend the final closing. The rules also require that a final prospectus be delivered to all purchasers of the company stock.

Waiting During the Quiet Period

The SEC places restrictions on what a company can do while "in registration." These restrictions apply during the "quiet period"—from the date and understanding with the managing underwriters are agreed to until 25 days after the securities are offered to the public (90 days for securities not listed on a national exchange or quote) on Nasdaq. During the quiet period, any publicity release can raise questions or concerns about whether the publicity is part of the selling efforts—even if the publicity does not specifically mention the public offering.[19] However, this does not preclude the normal ongoing disclosure of factual information about the company. The SEC encourages companies to continue product advertising campaigns, periodic reporting to shareholders, and press announcements on factual business and financial developments, such as new contracts and plant openings.

The company, however, can publish a limited notice of the offering, including the amount of the offering, the name of the company, and a description of the security, the offering price, and the names of the underwriters. Known as "tombstone ads" because of their stark appearance, these notices are typically published in newspapers shortly after the initial filing of the registration statement and are not considered sales literature. The accompanying exhibit shows a tombstone ad for a company's IPO.

This announcement is neither an offer to sell nor a solicitation to buy these securities.

The offering is made only by the prospectus.

New Issue **February 15, 2001**

10,000,000 Shares

TECH-DATA, INCORPORATED

Common Stock
Price $5.25 per Share

Copies of the Prospectus may be obtained in any State in which this Announcement is circulated from only such of the undersigned or other Dealers or brokers as may lawfully offer these securities in such State.

PRESENTING A ROAD SHOW

After the Registration Statement has been filed, the underwriters generally will take representatives of the company on a traveling road show, also referred to as a "dog-and-pony show." These meetings give prospective members of the underwriting

The road show presents the opportunity to tell the company's story to the people who will help sell the securities and influence potential investors. It will also allow the CEO to meet many of the people who will follow the company after the public offering. The show is so challenging that no one can ever be completely prepared. The plan is to present a balanced view of the business, market, and competition, and why the company will be a huge success.

syndicate, institutional investors, and industry analysts an opportunity to meet the company's management team and ask questions about the offering and the company.

The participants probably will be the company's chief executive officer and chief financial officer whose major task will be to generate interest in the investors, and the investment bankers, who will manage the tour and monitor the book, or computerized log of orders. Typically, the road show consists of five to seven back-to-back meetings every day for two weeks. The question-and-answer period is equally important and requires extensive preparation. If the entrepreneur can anticipate the most challenging questions and welcome them, he or she will have a chance to turn what might have been an issue into a nonissue.

THE PREPARATION OF THE ROAD SHOW TO INTERESTED INVESTORS SHOULD INCLUDE:

- Development of a precise, 20- to 25-minute slide presentation. Detail the company's business, strategy, financial history, management, growth prospects, market, and regulatory environment.
- Determination of which management personnel will present material and field questions
- Education of the underwriters' team
- Dry run of the road show presentation before institutional sales and corporate finance presentations are given at selected locations

Selecting the Underwriter

The underwriter that manages the offering plays a critical role in the success of the IPO. The role is to prepare the company's Registration Statement and sell the company's securities. In selecting an underwriter, the following factors are important:

1. *Experienced Industry Analyst.* The underwriter should have an experienced analyst in IPOs and the industry you are in.
2. *Synergy.* The company should feel comfortable with the individual bankers. The right synergy between the bankers and management is important.
3. *Distribution.* The investment bank should have the resources of a retail salesforce to sell the stock.

4. *Post-IPO Support.* The underwriter should have a strong record of the post-IPO price performance of companies it has recently taken public. A solid track record will indicate how well the investment bank priced recent transactions.

THE EXPENSES OF GOING PUBLIC

Underwriters' Compensation

The underwriters will receive a discount (spread) between the price at which they buy stock and the price at which the underwriters sell the same stock to the public. The amount of the spread is negotiated based on the size and risk of the offering. A typical firm commitment–offering discount is approximately 7 percent of the public offering price of the stock.

Underwriters may also be granted warrants as partial compensation for an offering. Other compensation may include reimbursement of expenses and rights of first refusal on future underwriting, directorships, and consulting arrangements.

Accounting and Legal Fees

The lawyers' and accountants' fees depend on the amount of work involved in preparing the Registration Statement and reviewing the financial statements and other financial data. The company should endeavor to do as much of the work of preparing the Registration Statement as possible in order to cut costs.

Directors' and Officers' Insurance

Before going public, a company needs to take out a personal liability insurance policy that will protect the officers and directors from being held personally liable if a shareholder suit is brought based on incorrect information in the Registration Statement.

DELIVERING VALUE AND MEETING MARKET EXPECTATIONS

When the IPO is completed and finalized, the entrepreneur and the management team must begin meeting the shareholders and Board of Directors. Investors and shareholders are very well informed, and if the company misses earnings projections by even a small amount, the stock price can drop 10 percent or more the next day. It has been said that it can take six quarters of on-target performance to win the market back. The challenge after the IPO is to deliver the value that the company promised to deliver in the business plan and offering memorandum. Delivering the value is a balancing act that involves meeting and exceeding the expectations of the market and all the stakeholders while the company implements the strategic initiatives on time and on budget.

For the entrepreneur/CEO of a public company, credibility is important. Yet many elements cannot be controlled such as the fluctuations of the industry, the stock market, and national and world economics. Nevertheless, the entrepreneur should continue to provide strong leadership by delivering the growth that is promised and by communicating to the stakeholders.

Meeting Expectations

The pressure most public companies face is to maintain short-term earnings growth. The financial markets generally react adversely to reports of lower earnings, even if the long-term strategic decisions from which they result are sound. Consequently, companies are often tempted to maintain share prices by sacrificing long-term profitability and growth for short-term earnings. The entrepreneur must plan and implement a business strategy that is balanced between short- and long-term needs and communicate the plan to shareholders and the financial community.

SUMMARY

It is important to prepare a harvest and exit plan for the business to be executed at the right time. A company can realize the value it has created in several ways. The most common are selling an equity stake to a strategic partner, selling the business, merging with another business, considering a buyout agreement, using an ESOP, and employing a public offering. Selling an equity stake to a strategic partner can attract needed capital interested in their technology and can lead to completely selling the business at a later time. Selling the business is another option but in a weak economy may be risky. Entrepreneurs may have to agree to long-term payment plans that include a stock-for-stock exchange that may result in stock price declines. Merging with another company involves a transaction between two companies and is an alternative to growing a business. When a company loses its competitive advantage in the marketplace, this alternative can be an option to follow. The founders can also sell the company, usually over time, to the management team (an MBO) or to a broader group of employees through an ESOP. The entrepreneur can also obtain a harvest option by going public. This option can be the most profitable strategy for the entrepreneur, but it has the disadvantages of costing a great deal of time and money and demanding significant financial commitments. Securities analysts will also demand management's time. The advantages from an IPO can repay debt, fund special projects, and be used for acquisitions.

STUDY QUESTIONS

1. What are the various options to establish a harvest strategy?

2. Briefly describe the procedures in selling a business.

3. List the major pitfalls in creating an alliance.

4. Describe the methods that make alliances successful.

5. Why should the venture consider an IPO?

EXERCISES

Develop an Exit Strategy

1. Prepare and list an entrepreneur's reasons for developing an exit strategy:

Reason for an Exit Strategy	Importance (1–10)	Company/Strength/Weaknesses		
		Low	Average	High
1.				
2.				
3.				
4.				
5.				

2. When does an alliance start and end in selling an equity stake?

3. Describe a scenario in which an equity alliance will succeed.

Alliance Analysis

List the types of alliances and complete the table with descriptions and figures:

Name	Approx. Sales	Target Market	Type of Alliance
1.			
2.			
3.			
4.			
5.			

Selling a Company

Complete the following table by describing the company's exposure to the risks listed on the left and the company's planned response to an exit strategy:

Area of Potential Risk	Company Exposure	Exit Strategy
Industry growth		
Product technology or liability		
Financial		
Management changes		

INTERACTIVE LEARNING ON THE WEB

Test your skill-builder knowledge of the chapter using the interactive Web site.

       1. Self Assessment:

       2. Multiple Choice:

       3. Matching of Key Terms:

       4. Demonstration:

       5. Case:

       6. Video

ADDITIONAL RESOURCES

- **AllianceStrategy.com**   www.alliancestrategy.com
- **Association of Strategic Alliance Professionals**   www.strategic-alliances.org
- **KPMG Alliances Home Page**   www.kpmg.nl/alliances
- **ReCapIT**   www.recapit.com
- **Smart Alliances**   www.smartalliances.co

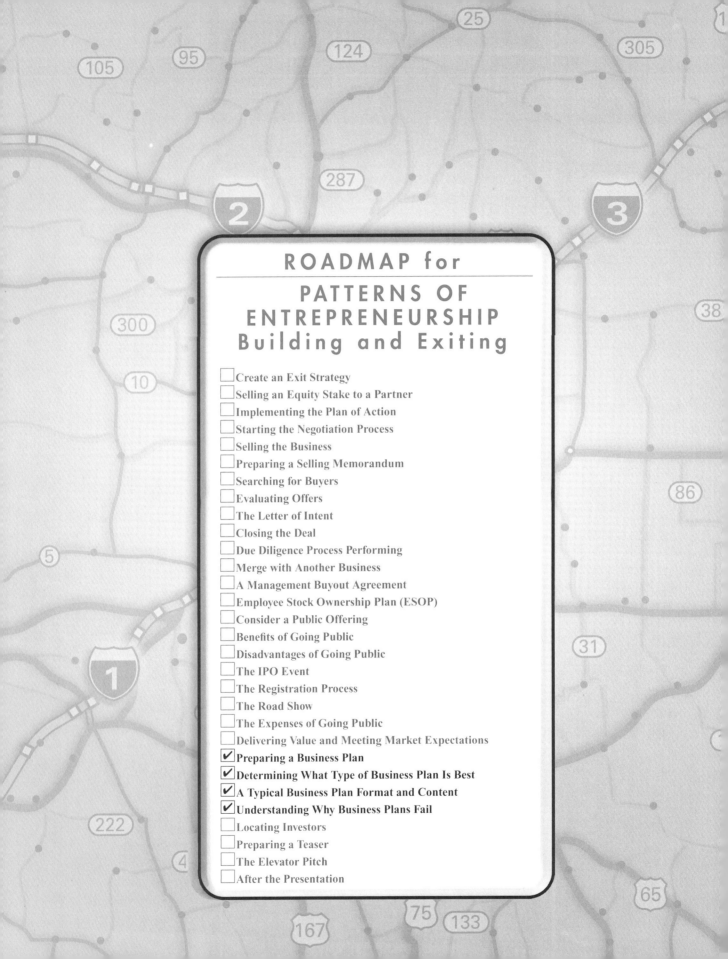

ROADMAP for

PATTERNS OF ENTREPRENEURSHIP
Building and Exiting

BRINGING IT ALL TOGETHER—WRITING THE WINNING BUSINESS PLAN

"The best business plans are straightforward documents that spell out the
who, what, where, why, and how much."
MICHAEL BUCHEIT, ASSOCIATE, W.R. HAMBRECHT, INVESTMENT BANKERS

OBJECTIVES

- Understand the value of writing a business plan.
- Explain how a business plan serves as a blueprint for building a company.
- Know the steps toward completing a business plan.
- Learn the detailed components of a business plan.
- Understand how to write a business plan so that it targets investors.

CHAPTER OUTLINE

INTRODUCTION

Smart entrepreneurs recognize the value of a business plan for securing capital and
growing their businesses. Business plans are the preferred mode of communication
between entrepreneurs and potential investors. In addition, entrepreneurs often find

that developing a business plan forces them to introduce discipline and a logical thought process into all of their planning activities. Additionally, a properly prepared business plan will help entrepreneurs consistently establish and meet goals and objectives for their employees, investors, and management.

In this chapter, we'll establish the value of a business plan and lay out a step-by-step procedure entrepreneurs can follow to create one. We'll also discuss why certain information is required in a business plan as well as how it should be presented.

Once you decide to start a business you understandably should have a plan to produce products or supply services, and to attract the optimum marketing, operations, management team, and financing in order to get the business off to a "good start."

It is important to realize and deal with the various "interest groups" that will be crucial to your success. Each group wants to hear something from your story that provides a comfort factor. For example:

- Financial interests want to know the risk/reward "formula" and the future "cash out/in" possibilities associated with your new venture.
- Employees want to feel secure in knowing they not only have a job with your company but a possible career.
- Marketers need to know the product/service, pricing, placement, and positioning, ("4 P's").
- Vendors, suppliers, and associates need to know what your operations will look like so they can plan to be part of your supply chain.
- Your partners (if any) need to codify their legal and fiduciary rights and responsibilities for their own protection and growth.
- The entrepreneur needs to place his or her ideas beside a companion roadmap in order to compare and contrast "where the business is going to where it was supposed to go."

How do you accomplish all of the above in a professional and concise manner?

PREPARING A BUSINESS PLAN

In this chapter, we establish the value of a business plan and lay out a step-by-step procedure entrepreneurs can follow to create one. We also discuss why certain information is required in a business plan as well as how it should be presented. Let's begin our discussion with a look at one entrepreneur whose winning business plan helped her achieve her business goals.

PROFILE: BARBARA K. KAVOVIT

Barbara K. Kavovit of Barbara K! Enterprises is a former New York City general contractor who used her apartment as her first office. Barbara's vision and determination helped her land her first corporate client, IBM. She was also IBM's first-ever female contractor. Soon after, she attracted clients such as Carnegie Hall, iVillage, and Polo Ralph Lauren. Her work in construction led Barbara to the realization that tools made for men were intimidating for women to use—she had observed a "point of pain." This was the motivation for starting barbara k!. She designed and launched her initial product line of high-quality tools, toolkits, and accessories in May 2003. Since that time, barbara k! has grown and expanded to other categories, including automotive, craft, college market, and apparel.

"My true desire is to inspire women to become more self-reliant and confident in their own abilities. We all have 'it' within ourselves to do things that we never imagined we could. All it takes is a little motivation, a little know how, and the right 'tools', for every woman to achieve a more independent lifestyle."[1]

ROADMAP

ACTIONS

The term *business plan* means the development of a written document that spells out like a roadmap where you are, where you want to be, and how you want to get there.

What Is a Business Plan?

A business plan is a 25- to 40-page written document that describes where a business is heading, how it hopes to achieve its goals and objectives, who is involved with the venture, why its product(s) or service(s) are needed in the marketplace, and what it will take to accomplish the business aims.

There are three essential reasons to prepare a business plan:

1. Entrepreneurs reap benefits from the planning activity itself.
2. The plan provides a basis for measuring actual performance against expected performance.
3. The plan acts as a vehicle for communicating to others what it is that the business is trying to accomplish.

"Business plans should be taken very seriously. Entrepreneurial waters are far too wide and deep to not spend earnest investigation and personal time developing a legitimate business plan."

ROBERT F. CHELLE
Director for the Center for Entrepreneurial Leadership, University of Ohio, Dayton

Setting Goals and Objectives

A business plan serves as a blueprint for building a company. It is a vehicle for describing the goals of the business and how these goals can be reached over the coming years. A business plan provides a means to:

- determine whether the business is viable
- raise capital for the business
- project sales, expenses, and cash flows for the business
- explain to employees their responsibilities as well as company expectations
- improve and assess company performance
- plan for a new product/service development.

ROADMAP

ACTIONS

The biggest problem most business plans have is that they don't include a clear description of the market, competition, and customers. Most plans spend too much time describing the features and capabilities of the new idea rather than how this approach will be better than the current solution.

However, *the single most important reason for preparing a business plan is to secure capital*. Investors agree that an effectively prepared business plan is a requisite for obtaining funding for any business, whether it is a new business seeking startup capital or an existing business seeking financing for expansion.[2]

The bottom line—Business plans help to define **the who, what, why, when, and how of the business.**

Investors need to know parameters, timetables, and expected future revenue streams. Thus, the business plan needs to set goals, but it must to be realistic in doing so.

A business plan is a first attempt at strategic planning. The entrepreneur should use it as a tool for establishing the direction of the company and for establishing the action steps that will guide the company through the startup period.

Many entrepreneurs say that the pressure of the day-to-day management of a company leaves them little time for planning. However, without a business plan, managers run the risk of proceeding blindly through a rapidly changing business environment.

Writing a business plan does not guarantee that problems will not come up. Managers who have a well-thought-out process in place will be better able to anticipate and handle any problems that occur. In addition, a well-constructed business plan can help managers avoid certain problems altogether. This is especially true for entrepreneurs and startup companies.[3]

Setting Performance Benchmarks

Entrepreneurs can also use a business plan to establish goals and document milestones along the business's path to success. Entrepreneurs often find that it is difficult for them to look objectively at the business's day-to-day performance. A business plan provides an objective basis for determining whether the business is viable and can meet established goals and objectives.[4]

STARTING THE PROCESS TO WRITE THE PLAN: FIVE STEPS

As entrepreneurs are bound to discover, they must tell and retell their business's story countless times to prospective investors, new employees, outside advisors, and potential customers. The most important part of the business's story is the part about its future—the part featured in a business plan. Thus, the business plan should show how all the pieces of the company fit together to create a viable organization capable of meeting its goals and objectives. The business plan must also communicate the company's distinctive competence to anyone who might have an interest. But how do entrepreneurs write a business plan that accomplishes these goals? Let's look at the five steps involved in this process.

Step 1: Identify the Objectives

Determine who your audience is, what they want to know, and how they will use the information you are imparting to them. For example, if the business plan's audience is a group of investors, they will review the plan to gain a better understanding of the business objectives and to determine whether an investment is worth the risk. Entrepreneurs should use the business plan as an opportunity to develop as managers.

As they create the business plan, they should think about competitive conditions, new opportunities, and situations that are advantageous to the business. The plan is also an important tool entrepreneurs can use to familiarize sales reps, suppliers, and others with the company's operational goals.

Step 2: Draft the Outline

Once the objectives have been identified, the entrepreneur must prepare an outline for the business plan. The outline should provide enough detail so that it is useful to both the entrepreneur and his or her audience. A sample business plan outline is listed later in this chapter in the section, "The Roadmap Guide for Writing a Business Plan." The information shown is included in most effective business plans.

Step 3: Review the Outline

Next, the entrepreneur should review the outline to identify areas that should be presented in even greater detail. While doing the draft outline, follow up with research on areas for which you did not have sufficient information. Detailed support for any assumptions and assertions made in the business plan should also be available.

Step 4: Draft the Plan

Entrepreneurs will probably need to conduct a great deal of research before they have enough information to start drafting the business plan. Most entrepreneurs begin by collecting historical financial information about their company and/or industry and by conducting market research (refer to Chapter 3). After they have completed their initial research, they prepare initial drafts of proposed financial statements and projections. By preparing these statements, the entrepreneur will know which strategies will work from a financial perspective before investing many hours in writing a detailed description.

In the financial section of the business plan, entrepreneurs demonstrate the viability of their business; the plan should show first-year projections by each month and quarterly projections for the next two to three years. According to Ralph Subbinono, partner at Ernst & Young, the biggest problem with most business plans is that they contain unrealistic financial projections. Thus, entrepreneurs should carefully rethink their projected performance and make necessary changes before passing on the plan to others. Entrepreneurs should also keep detailed notes on the assumptions being made in the business plan draft so that they can later add footnotes to accompany the statements.

The last element to be prepared is the *executive summary*. Since this is a summary of the entire business plan, its contents are contingent on the rest of the document; thus, it cannot be finished until the other components of the plan are essentially complete. As each section is written, entrepreneurs should refer to the detailed outline included later in this chapter to make sure they have covered each area adequately.

The executive summary consists of:

1. **Business Concept.** This section describes the business, its products or services, and the market it will serve. It should point out exactly what will be sold, to whom, and why the business will have a competitive advantage.

2. **Success Factors.** This section details any developments within the company that are essential to its success. It includes patents, prototypes, location of a facility, any crucial contracts that need to be in place for product or service development, and results from any test marketing that has been conducted.

3. **Current Position.** This section supplies relevant information about the company, its legal form of operation, the year it was formed, the principal owners, and key personnel.

4. **Financial Features.** This section highlights the important financial information about the business, including its sales, profits, cash flow, and return on investment. (Refer to Chapter 9 for more details.)

Step 5: Have the Plan Reviewed and Updated

Once the entrepreneur has completed a draft of the business plan, he or she should have an independent professional review it for completeness and effectiveness. The plan must then be updated at least every six months and as objectives change. A business plan is not a static document that will sit on your shelf, but one that is continually reviewed and updated. In fact, it is rare that the original plan used to start the business is the one eventually followed. However, without a sound starting plan an entrepreneur will be unable to acquire a bank loan, or any equity investors, or have a template against which deviations, both internally or externally from the plan, can be judged and taken into account.

DETERMINING WHAT TYPE OF BUSINESS PLAN IS BEST

"When I judge the business plan competition at Columbia Business School, I first read the executive summary followed by the financial section. Only if the concept is intriguing will I spend more time reading the entire plan. We perpetually review about 100 plans and it's quite difficult to read them all. For those plans that capture my attention to receive funding, usually about 5 percent, there is a well-conceived detailed plan."

CLIFFORD SCHORER
Entrepreneur in Residence, The Eugene Lang Center for Entrepreneurship, Columbia University Business School

What type of plan should entrepreneurs prepare to meet their requirements? Three major types of plans exist:[5]

Full Business Plan

An entrepreneur should use a full business plan when he or she needs to describe the business in detail in order to attract potential investors, strategic partners, or buyers.

Executive Summary Plan

An executive business plan is a two- to five-page document that contains the most important information about the business and its direction. It is often used to gauge investor interest and to find strategic partners. It can also be used to attract key employees and to persuade friends to invest in the business.

Action Plan

An implementation or action plan is a document the management team uses to implement the plan. It consists of a timetable and a list of tasks that should be accomplished within a certain time frame.

Targeting the Plan to Selected Groups

A business plan could be the perfect tool to reach the following target groups.[6] Some investors invest only in certain types of businesses, such as technology, health care, or financial services. Therefore, entrepreneurs must consider which investors or groups are relevant to their needs and send a plan only to the appropriate groups. These can include:

- Bankers—to provide loans for expansion and equipment purchases
- Business brokers—to sell the business
- New and potential employees—to learn about the company
- Investors—to invest in the company
- The Small Business Administration (SBA)—to approve business loans
- Investment bankers—to prepare a prospectus for an IPO
- Suppliers—to establish credit for purchases.

How Long Will the Preparation Take?

A general rule of thumb is that it takes twice as long to write a good plan as foreseen. A useful benchmark is that it will take at least 200 hours of dedicated effort to produce a good plan. The best way to reduce this burden is to begin drafting out initial ideas, sections where you have some good input, background information, and so on, before there is an urgent need for a full plan to present to outsiders. This is much easier than sitting down with the aim of writing a full plan in a short period, say two weeks, that you have allotted to the task. Our experience with many entrepreneurs indicates that a sound, well-thought-through and researched plan that can be defended under intense questioning will take at least 8 to 12 weeks to produce. This assumes that the writing is not continuous, but time is allotted for thinking, discussing alternatives with advisors, and obtaining missing information. Sometimes entrepreneurs use consultants to help write the plan. While this can be of value and reduce the personal load, particularly for the first attempt, remember that the plan is yours and not the consultants. If you cannot fully identify with the plan and defend each and every point and claim in the due diligence process, this will be detected by bankers and investors, who will then doubt your ability to lead the venture.

Writing the Business Plan

An effective and complete business plan should answer the following questions:

1. What is the primary product or service?
2. Is there a market for the product or service? Has the opportunity been well defined?
3. Who are the target customers for the product or service and what value do you provide them?

4. What is the pricing structure?
5. Who is the competition, and what are the barriers to entry?
6. What risks and market constraints are involved?
7. What sales distribution channels will be needed to sell the product or service?
8. Who is the management team, and what are their specific talents?
9. What is the current financial cash flow and breakeven plan?
10. What are the immediate financial needs of the business?
11. What are the future financial goals for the business and its founder?

A TYPICAL BUSINESS PLAN FORMAT AND CONTENT

Examples of business plans and executive summaries can be found on the book Web site.

Title Page

Creating the Title Page and Table of Contents

The title page includes the name, address, and phone number of the company and the CEO. The table of contents provides a sequential list of the business plan sections as well as their corresponding pages.

Executive Summary

I. Writing the Executive Summary

As we noted earlier, the executive summary must be able to stand on its own. It should serve as a synopsis of the business plan. Investors may read only the executive summary; therefore, it must be comprehensive and well written in order to gain the investors' confidence.

　　The executive summary should be no more than two to three pages long and should convince the reader that the business will succeed. An example of a targeted executive summary can be found for "Leafbusters Inc." in Chapter 12.

Overview

II. Writing the Overview of the Company, Industry, Products, and Services

The company description provides an overview of how all of the elements of the business fit together. This section should not go into detail, however, since most of the subjects will be covered in depth elsewhere.

　　The section begins with a general description of the legal form of the company, which should take no more than one paragraph. It should present the fundamental activities and nature of the business. This section addresses questions such as: What is the business? What customers will it serve? Where is it located, and where will it do business?

　　Some further insight should also be offered as to what stage the company has reached. Is it a "seed"-stage company without a fully developed product line? Has it developed a product line but not yet begun to market it? Or is it already marketing its products and anxious to expand its scale of activity?

Market Analysis

III. Compiling the Marketing Analysis

The marketing analysis section should describe how the business will react to market conditions and generate sales to ensure its success, and should explain why the business is a good investment. Keep in mind that overcoming marketing challenges is critical to a company's success. Therefore, potential investors pay a lot of attention to the marketing analysis section. In fact, venture capitalists say that the most important criteria for predicting the success of a new company are those factors that establish the demand for the product or service. If a real market need is not presented, all of the talent and financing in the world will not make a company successful.

Some of the most important issues to address in the marketing analysis section include:

Market Opportunity: The marketing section must establish a demand or need for the product or service and should define both the market and opportunity. The secondary target market should also be addressed. You should also quantify the size of the market. Investors like to see a large "Total Available Market" (TAM) which is the size in dollars if you were able to capture 100 percent of the opportunity.

Competition: The marketing section should describe the market conditions that exist in the business, including the degree of competition and what impact this competition is likely to have on the business. It is also important to address other forces, such as government regulations and outside influences.

Marketing Strategy: The marketing section should define how the business will use its marketing tools. This can include factors such as distribution, advertising and promotion, pricing, and selling incentives. The mission and vision will vary depending on the stage of development.

Market Research: The marketing section should document market research as a part of the marketing plan or in a section by itself. Of most value are data obtained from primary market research, for this is the best evidence showing that, if the venture can offer a product of service at the price used in the financial projections, then there are actual customers who will buy from the company. Bankers and investors like to talk to potential customers when undertaking due diligence, and positive responses go a long way to establishing confidence in the business.

Sales Forecasts: Usually, financial projections are presented in the financial section of a business plan. However, it is useful to present sales projections in the marketing section. These forecasts might include projected sales growth, market share, and sales by customer.

Support Material: Include in the appendix materials that will make the plan more credible, such as industry studies, letters of support, brochures, and reviews or articles related to the product or service.

While there is a great deal of flexibility in the writing of the marketing section, the plan should be focused to fit the characteristics of the proposed business.

The *products and services* section of the business plan describes the characteristics and appeal of the products or services. This section may include a prototype, sample, or demonstration of how the products work. The section should include the following:

A Physical Description: A description of the physical characteristics of a product usually includes photographs, drawings, or brochures. In the case of a service, a diagram sometimes helps to convey what service is providing the business.

A Statement Regarding Use and Appeal: The entrepreneur should comment on the nature of the product or the service's various uses and what constitutes its appeal. This is an opportunity to emphasize the unique features of the product or service, the value proposition to customers, and thereby establish the potential of the business.

A Statement Regarding Stage of Development: This is a description of the stage of development (prototype design, quality testing, implementation, and so on) of the product or service that the entrepreneur plans to introduce into the marketplace.

Testimonials: Entrepreneurs can include a list of experts or prior users who are familiar with the products or services and who will comment favorably on them. Such testimonials may be included in letter or report form in an appendix.

The company description should describe the objectives of the business opportunity. Perhaps the business is seeking a certain level of sales or geographic distribution. Will it become a publicly traded company in a few years when revenues reach a certain level, or will it become an attractive acquisition candidate? A statement of such objectives is important and may succeed in generating significant interest.

Marketing and Sales Plan

IV. Describing the Marketing and Sales Plans

The marketing and sales strategy section of the business plan describes how the business will implement the marketing plan to achieve expected sales performance. This analysis will guide the entrepreneur in establishing pricing, distribution, and promotional strategies that will enable the company to become profitable within a competitive environment.

Pricing Strategy and Plan

As we mentioned earlier in the book, pricing is an important element in the marketing strategy because it has a direct impact on the business's success. The marketing and sales strategy section of the business plan should address policies regarding discounting and price changes as well as their impact on gross profit (revenue less cost of goods sold). When considering what price to charge, it is important to realize that price should not be based entirely on cost plus some profit. Consider these pricing methods to generate the necessary profits for the business.

Cost-Plus Pricing: All costs, both fixed and variable, are included, and a profit percentage is added on.

Demand Pricing: The business sells the products or services based on demand, or whatever the market will bear.

Value Pricing: The business sells its product/services to capture a major part of the overall value that is created for the customer.

Competitive Pricing: The company enters a market where there is an established price and where it is difficult to differentiate one product from another. In this situation, there is limited flexibility to make price adjustments.

Markup Pricing: The price is calculated by adding the estimated profit to the cost of the product. In some industries, such as cosmetics and health care, profit levels may be higher than in others, such as automotive components.

Entrepreneurs should analyze competitors' distribution channels before deciding to use similar channels or alternatives. Distribution channels include:

Direct Sales: Products and services are sold directly to the end user. This is the most effective distribution channel.

Original Equipment Manufacturer (OEM) Sales: An OEM will often bundle or promote its products with yours or pay a royalty on each product sold.

Manufacturer's Representatives: These individuals handle an assortment of products and divide their time based on the products that sell the best.

Brokers: These individuals buy products, often overseas, directly from the distributor and sell them to retailers or end users.

Web E-Commerce: Products and services are sold through a Web site or through Internet partner alliances.

Advertising, Public Relations, and Promotion Strategies

The purpose of this section in the plan is to describe how you will tell potential customers that you have a product or service that can satisfy their demands, to convince those customers to buy from you, and to successfully compete with similar businesses.

Many startup companies feel they are unable to pursue advertising, public relations, or promotion strategies until they are more established and have generated significant revenues. However, public relations companies are becoming more willing to partner with startup companies. Instead of the usual retainer that public relations firms request, they are willing to work on an hourly or budget basis.

Other Elements

The marketing and sales strategy section should also include PowerPoint pie charts, graphs, tables, and other graphics that effectively show how the marketing effort will be organized and business resources will be allocated among various marketing tools. "A picture is worth more than a thousand words" also applies to business plans.

Operations

V. Describing Operations

The operations section of the business plan provides a detailed, in-depth operational plan. Creating this part of the plan gives entrepreneurs an opportunity to work out potential problems on paper before beginning operations. The importance of creating an operations plan will depend on the nature of the business. An e-commerce production site will probably require significant attention to operational issues. In contrast, most retail businesses and some service businesses will probably have less operational complexity. Issues addressed in this section of the business plan include:

Product/Service Development It is not unusual to prepare a business plan before a business's full range of products and services is developed. This is especially true of startup companies. Even after the product has been developed, it is often necessary to continue developing it to maintain a competitive position. It is usually worthwhile to present a summary of the development activities that the company will undertake.

Manufacturing In the case of a production facility, it is important to discuss the process by which a company will manufacture its products. This usually involves some description of the plant, equipment, material, and labor requirements.

Entrepreneurs should also include a description of the techniques they may employ in combining these resources, including assembly lines and robotics, as well as the capability of the business in terms of production rates and constraints on production capabilities. If some or all of the operations will be outsourced, then details of the subcontractors should be supplied.

Maintenance and Support The plan should address the level of support a company will provide after a customer has purchased a product or service. This is particularly important in the case of a software or technical product.

Management Team

VI. Describing the Management Team

The management team's talents and skills should be detailed in the management team section of the business plan. If the business plan is being used to attract investors, this section should emphasize the management's talents and indicate why management will help the company have a distinctive competitive advantage. Entrepreneurs should keep in mind that individuals invest in people, not ideas. Issues that should be addressed in this section include:

Management Talent and Skills Detail the expertise, skills, and related work experience of the proposed management team and the backgrounds of those individuals expected to play key roles in the venture. These include investors, members of the Board of Directors, key employees, advisors, and strategic partners.

Organizational Chart After introducing the key participants, it is appropriate to offer an organizational chart that presents the relationships and divisions of responsibility within the organization. In some instances, a brief narrative instead of, or in addition to, a chart may be helpful in providing further detail.

Policy and Strategy for Employees Include a statement as to how employees will be selected, trained, and rewarded. Such background can be important for investors to give them a feel for the company's culture. A brief reference to the type of benefits and incentives planned may further help define the company's spirit.

Board of Directors and Advisory Board Describe the number of directors that will comprise the Board of Directors for the company. The directors can be founders of the company, individuals, or venture capitalists who invested financially or who bring specific business experience to the management team.

Financial Plan

VII. Describing the Financial Plan

The financial plan section of the business plan should formulate a credible, comprehensive set of projections reflecting the business's anticipated financial performance. If these projections are carefully prepared and convincingly supported, they become one of the most critical yardsticks by which the business's attractiveness is measured.[7]

While the overall business plan communicates a basic understanding of the nature of the business, projected financial performance directly addresses bottom-line interests. This is where the investor discovers the return on investment, performance measures, and exit plans.

The financial plan is the least flexible part of a business plan in terms of format. While actual numbers will vary, each plan should contain similar statements—or schedules—and each statement should be presented in a conventional manner. There should be enough information in these statistics to know not only the business but also how it relates to similar businesses. In general, the following information should be presented.

Set of Assumptions: The set of assumptions on which projections are based should be clearly and concisely presented. Numbers without these assumptions will have little meaning. Only after carefully considering such assumptions can investors assess the validity of financial projections.

Projected Income Statements: These statements most often reflect at least quarterly performance for the first year, while annual statements are provided for years 2 through 5.

Projected Cash Flow Statements: Such statements should be developed in as great a level of detail as possible for the first two years. Quarterly or annual cash flows, corresponding to the period used for the income statements, are sufficient for years 3 through 5.

Current Balance Sheet: This should reflect the company's financial position at its inception. Projected year-end balance sheets, typically for two years, should also be included.

Other Financial Projections: This may include a breakeven analysis that will demonstrate the level of sales required to break even at a given time.

This section should not contain every line item in the financial pro formas; these are better confined to an appendix. Judicial use of charts and graphs can make this section easier to read.

Financial Requirements

VIII. Establishing the Amount of Funds Required

The funds required and uses section of the business plan should describe how much money is required to finance the business, where these funds will be spent, and when they will be needed. To determine financing requirements, entrepreneurs must evaluate and estimate the funds needed for (but not limited to) research and development, purchases of equipment and assets, and working capital. For example, to finance research and development of a product, entrepreneurs might experience a long delay between incurring research expenses and actually generating sales. Thus, it may be appropriate to fund these expenses with long-term financing.[8]

Exhibits (Typical)

Census data and other population statistics

Market potential

Process flow (operations)

Detailed financials

ACTIONS   Visit the book's Web site to view sample business plans in different markets.

UNDERSTANDING WHY BUSINESS PLANS FAIL

The authors have reviewed hundreds of business plans from entrepreneurs seeking advice or funding and, in so doing, have compiled the following list of the factors that differentiate a successful plan from those that fail to attract investments or loans, and ultimately either do not get off the ground or do not fulfill the entrepreneur's dream. Remember that there are far more inadequate business plans floating around than good business opportunities. Therefore, any reviewer will try to find a quick reason *not* to read your plan, but to reject it. You have to find a way to sustain interest and to get your plan to the top of the reviewer's pile. Any one of the following factors is likely to trigger a "no-thanks" note from a banker, angel, or VC investor or a corporate partner.[9]

- The executive summary is unclear, not concise, and not specifically targeted to the intended audience.
- The basic concept of the business has not been researched and validated.
- The business is "so unique that there are no competitors." There are always competitors. They may not be obvious, but they are waiting out there to attack your business.
- The entrepreneur has never spoken to a potential customer. "I will build a new mouse-trap and they will come."
- The financial projections are far too optimistic. Sales and cash flow follow a "hockey-stick" curve, with the company turning cash positive after 18 months of operations and growing at an annual rate of 200 percent thereafter.
- There is no discussion of either how a loan will be repaid or how an investor will get his cash out with a satisfactory return.
- The entrepreneur signals that she wants to remain in control come whatever. One indicator of this is not mentioning how a board will be constructed with "arms-length" experts that may challenge the entrepreneur.
- The stated valuation of the company is outrageously high and unrealistic.
- If the company depends on intellectual property to retain its competitiveness, there is no mention of any IP search showing that there is no conflict with other companies or inventors.
- The management section refers to a group of resumés that turn out to be friends or merely acquaintances who are not really suitable for the positions but have been included because this is required in the plan. Often these resumés are barely readable and are in different formats. It is better to be open about the positions that will need to be filled and how this will be accomplished.[10]
- The financials are heavy on irrelevant details such as weekly postage costs each month for 10 years, but have fundamental flaws in the most important assumptions such as sales and distribution costs or overly high compensation for the founder.

ROADMAP

ACTIONS

Investors will ask the following questions: Will I get my money back before the entrepreneur? Will I have the right to invest in future rounds? What role will I play in the company?

- There is a fact in the plan that can easily be checked independently and it turns out that the entrepreneur has not been completely honest in the document. Nobody wants to invest in, lend to, or partner with someone they cannot fully trust.

SUMMARY

This chapter has established the value of a business plan and the step-by-step procedure involved in its preparation. A startup company's business plan is usually its first attempt at strategic planning. Entrepreneurs can use the business plan as a guide for establishing the direction of the company and the action steps needed in obtaining funding.

Before drafting the plan, the entrepreneur will need to collect information on the market and manufacturing operations as well as financial estimates. This information should be evaluated based on the goals and objectives of the company, which provide a framework for writing the plan. The executive summary, a part of the business plan, must be able to stand on its own. It should describe the customers, financial requirements, and the expected payback.

The marketing section of the business plan must establish the demand for the product or service and the potential for the business. This section typically includes a summary of the business's growth potential, the sources of demand, and the ways in which the demand is satisfied.

The company description section of the business plan begins with a brief, general description of the company. This section should present the fundamental activities and nature of the company. A fine level of detail is not appropriate in this section because it is included in other sections.

The marketing and sales strategy section of the business plan describes how the business will implement the marketing plan to achieve expected sales performance. In this section, the entrepreneur establishes pricing, distribution, and promotional strategies that will allow the business to succeed in a competitive environment.

The operations section of the business plan presents the potential problems and the ways in which these problems can be resolved. The importance of creating an operations plan will depend on the nature of the business. An e-commerce production site will probably require significant attention to operational issues. In contrast, most retail businesses and some service businesses will probably have less operational complexity.

The management team section of the business plan details the management team's talents and skills. If the business plan is being used to attract investors, this section should emphasize the management's talents and indicate why they will help the company have a distinctive competitive advantage. Investors always look for a strong management team before making investments. Many businesses fail because the proper talent has not been assembled. This issue is addressed by describing the objective assessment of the team's strengths and weaknesses as well as the company's requirements for growth. It includes how employees are selected, trained, and rewarded.

The financial plan section of the business plan should formulate a credible, comprehensive set of projections reflecting the business's anticipated financial performance. If these projections are carefully prepared and convincingly supported, they become one of the most critical yardsticks by which the business's attractiveness is measured.

As is often the case in the preparation of a business plan, the quality of information included is dependent on the amount of energy devoted to gathering it. Good sources for such data include trade associations, trade literature, industry studies, and industry experts. Your business plan will be competing with many others to get attention from bankers, investors, partners, suppliers, customers, and employees, so the document must be clear, concise, reasonable, realistic, honest, and compelling.

The business plan is essential in launching a new business. The product of many hours of preparation will be a concise, yet comprehensive, well-written, well-organized, and attractive document that will serve as a guide and an instrument for the entrepreneur to raise necessary capital and funding.

STUDY QUESTIONS

1. What are the benefits of preparing a written business plan?

2. What are the components of a business plan?

3. How long does it take to write a business plan?

4. Why do business plans fail?

5. Why should the executive summary be written last?

EXERCISES

Please circle the correct answer, either True (T) or False (F) for each question. Visit the book's Web site to review your answers.

1. Many small companies do not prepare a formal business plan because: The major benefit of a business plan is the discussions that occur during its preparation. Therefore, in the absence of adequate resources or time, an oral plan is adequate. T ( ) or F ( ).

2. The business plan's primary purpose is to:

    (a) develop new technologies. T ( ) or F ( ).

    (b) guide the entrepreneur. T ( ) or F ( ).

    (c) avoid competitors in the market. T ( ) or F ( ).

    (d) provide a historical perspective of the business. T ( ) or F ( ).

3. Business plans are planning documents. As a result, they are frequently optimistic and should not be used to assist management in operating the business, nor should they be used as the basis for performance evaluation. T ( ) or F ( ).

4. Companies need NOT produce a business plan if:

    (a) they lack the necessary planning department. T ( ) or F ( ).

    (b) there is insufficient time and money to develop a meaningful plan. T ( ) or F ( ).

    (c) management does not know how to prepare a plan and is not aware of the benefits that can be derived from it. T ( ) or F ( ).

    (d) annual sales are less than $50 million. T ( ) or F ( ).

5. Financial statements are an important part of the business planning process because:

    (a) the planning process relates primarily to the financial function of the company. T ( ) or F ( ).

    (b) after completing the business plan, the next step is to develop financial projections. T ( ) or F ( ).

    (c) financial statements are commonly used to express business expectations and results of performance. T ( ) or F ( ).

6. Business planning is primarily a financial activity; therefore, top managers from departments other than finance need not be involved in the preparation of the business plan. T ( ) or F ( ).

7. Because an outsider would be unfamiliar with a given business, entrepreneurs should not expect a business plan to be meaningful to such outsiders. T ( ) or F ( ).

INTERACTIVE LEARNING ON THE WEB

Test your knowledge of the chapter material using the book's interactive Web site.

CASE STUDY: SURFPARKS LLC

This business plan case study was prepared by James Meiselman, Columbia M.B.A. 2002, under the supervision of Professor Jack M. Kaplan as the basis for class discussion on the subject of business plans. Copyright © 2002 by the Lang Center for Entrepreneurship, Graduate School of Business, Columbia University, 317 Uris Hall, 3022 Broadway, New York, NY 10027.
Note: For competitive reasons, some financial figures—specifically, financial costs and marketing figures—have been altered or fabricated.

INTRODUCTION

The purpose of this case study is to evaluate the business plan of Surfparks LLC. The mission of the venture is to create and operate/franchise the world's first surfing-specific wave pools, targeted primarily at the rapidly growing surfer population. Read the case carefully and then prepare answers to the following questions:

1. Does the executive summary describe key elements of marketing, company services, current position, and financial features?

2. Is the proposed offer well written and concise, and are key data included?

3. Where would you place the technology overview section?

4. Are the sections in the business plan listed in the right order?

5. What are the important marketing issues and competitive advantages that should be described in the marketing section?

6. Does the financing section address the funding requirements and how the capital will be used?

7. What are your recommendations for revising the plan to attract needed capital?

EXECUTIVE SUMMARY

The World's First Surf Pools

Surfparks LLC was formed to market and manage a global franchise of surfing-specific wave pools. While crude technology to generate surfing waves in a large pool has existed for nearly 20 years, stand-alone Surf Pools were considered infeasible due to high energy costs, slow wave intervals, and poor wave quality.

Surfparks' innovative business model, combined with newly patented technology in both wave generation and pool shape, has now made the perfect surfing wave both technically feasible and economically viable. The new technology generates perfect waves up to 8 feet high with rides up to 75 yards long. Wave height and shape have near infinite variability due to a computer-controlled wave-making system and a padded adjustable "reef" lining the pool floor.

Surfparks LLC has formalized a partnership with the developers of this technology: Aquatic Development Group (ADG) and ASR Ltd. (ASR). The partnership grants Surfparks exclusive license and preferential pricing on their current and future Surf Pool technology.

The Pilot Surfpark Facility

Surfparks LLC is currently seeking partners to finance construction of the pilot Surfpark. Total required startup capital ranges from $6 to 8 million, depending on land costs and the extent of site preparation. Surfparks has already secured financing for an aggressive prelaunch marketing campaign for this facility. Surfparks LLC will manage and market this facility for its owners in exchange for a management fee and/or share of ownership.

Optimal sites for a pilot Surfpark include Orange County, California; Brevard County, Florida; and Monmouth County, New Jersey. Appropriate sites have been found in each location. Each of these selected locations combines a large existing surfer population with poor and/or terribly overcrowded natural surfing conditions, making them ideal candidates for a Surfpark.

In addition to the large Surf Pool, the pilot Surfpark will include a small "training pool" for beginner lessons, a Wahoo's Fish Taco restaurant, a full-service surf shop, a board demo/rental center, party rooms, and shower/changing facilities. The marketing plan includes an aggressive member acquisition strategy utilizing highly targeted direct mailings (via merging of *Surfer Magazine/Surfing Magazine* and Surfline/SWELL.com's subscriber database), surf-shop sponsored trips, and a national/regional PR and advertising campaign. Regularly scheduled contests, lessons, camps, and other special events encourage customer retention.

Market Demand

A rapidly increasing global surfer population, combined with a severe shortage of high-quality natural surfing venues, has raised demand for supplemental surfing facilities to a critical level. **The active U.S. surfer population, currently at 2.25 million, is increasing at a rate of over 20 percent per year.** (*Source:* American Sports Data.) Global surfer population (currently 17 million) is rising at similar or even higher rates. At this point, the surfing community is not asking *if* surf pools will be built, they are asking *how soon* they will be built and *who* will build them.

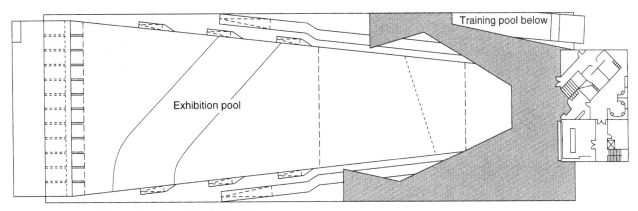

Figure 11-1   **Planned Surfpark Facilities Diagram.**

Specific market research reinforces that this demand exists. A recent Surfparks-sponsored Web survey of 2,200 surfers gauged price sensitivity and interest in a surf pool. At the proposed session price of $25 for 20 waves, **nearly 50 percent of the respondents said they would use a Surfpark at least once per week, and 91 percent said they would use it at least once per month.**

Surfpark Pro Forma Highlights

The breakeven point to achieve positive cash flow is between 10 and 15 percent utilization of pool users. This translates to about 25,000 individual pool uses per year, or 69 visitors per day, based on 360 operating days per year. This is the equivalent to filling approximately two full 36-surfer sessions per day. By contrast, 100 percent utilization of the big pool equals approximately 214,000 individual visits per year, or 594 visitors per day. Revenue at 100 percent utilization would exceed $10 million, with earnings before interest, taxes, depreciation allowances (EBITDA) over $5 million and investors recouping their full investment in less than two years. At a more conservative utilization of 35 percent, investors will recoup their full investment in three to four years.

Expansion Plans

An aggressive global rollout of Surfpark franchises is planned. Based on existing Web and print PR, Surfparks is already receiving multiple inquiries per week from parties around the world interested in operating a Surfpark facility. Hundreds of suitable locations, both coastal and inland, have been identified for continued growth. With proximity to the ocean no longer a requirement, a Surfpark brings the wave-riding experience to a huge, currently untapped inland market. Investors in the pilot facility will have preferential rights to invest in these future facilities. Figure 11-1 shows a Surfpark diagram of a planned franchise.

The Surfparks Team

Management Team
James A Meiselman: Founder, Chairman, & CEO

- 10+ years action sports (surf, skateboard, snowboard) sales and product management experience

- Managing Editor, *TransWorld Snowboarding*, *Snowboarding Business*, *Skateboarding Business* magazines
- General Manager, Generics & Blax Snowboarding, USA
- Category Manager, Boots, Burton Snowboards
- B.A. Dartmouth College; M.B.A. (Finance, Entrepreneurship) Columbia University *XXXX XXXX: Founding Partner, CMO*
- Director, New Media, National Basketball Association
- Director Business Development, *Sports Illustrated*
- VP Business Development ESPN.com
- B.A. Connecticut College; M.B.A. NYU Stern School of Business
XXXX XXXX: Partner, Director of Development
- Co-Owner, Del Rey Properties (commercial/residential developer, manager, construction company)
- Owns/manages LA Equestrian Center, 350,000 square feet of commercial space and 300 multi-family housing units
- Del Rey has built over $100 million in commercial real estate projects
XXXX XXXX: East Coast Marketing/Promotions
- 15-year director, East Coast Marketing/Promotions, Quiksilver Inc.
- Producer, Quiksilver East Coast Surf Camps and "King of the Peak" pro surf contest
- Owner, Kechele Surfboards and X-Trak promotions

SECTION 2
THE SURFPARK CONCEPT

Market Opportunity

All surfers dream of riding a perfect wave. Unfortunately, the perfect surfing wave requires a precise mix of wind, swell, tide, and sea-floor contour; and these elements can be found in only a handful of locations around the world. In spite of its elusive playing field, surfing has undergone explosive growth in the last decade. With participation rates increasing at over 20 percent per year for the past three years, there are now an estimated 2.25 million surfers in the United States, and 17 million surfers in the world. Currently, all but the most remote world-class surf breaks are dangerously overcrowded. It is not uncommon to see over 100 surfers at a single surf spot.

This capacity problem, coupled with inconvenient ocean access for inlanders and the intimidating ocean environment, has actually restrained the potential growth and size of the surfing population. The mass appeal of the surfing lifestyle is well documented in mainstream media and proven by the fact that the surf *clothing* industry is over 10 times the size of the surf *equipment* industry.

The Solution

A solution to this surf scarcity is to create artificial waves. Artificial reefs have recently been designed and installed in select locations, but these reefs still rely on the presence of optimal swell, wind, and tide to break suitably. For reliable wave quality, a safe learning environment, and increased access for inlanders, all of these factors must be controlled. This is the idea behind Surfparks: **perfect surfing waves in a controlled pool environment.**

Hundreds of wave pools exist in the world today, but every one of those pools has been built as an extension of a waterpark or resort, targeted for casual recreational use. As a result, the wave quality in these pools has been designed for safety and maximum capacity. While crude technology to generate surfing waves in a large pool has existed for nearly 20 years, stand-alone Surf Pools were considered infeasible due to high energy costs, slow wave intervals, and poor wave quality.

Surfparks LLC's unique business model, combined with newly patented technology in both wave generation and pool shape, has now made the perfect surfing wave technically feasible and economically viable.

The Surfpark can be an indoor or outdoor facility, depending on climate. The centerpiece of each Surfpark facility is the full-sized Surf Pool, suitable for intermediate to pro-level surfers and bodyboarders. In addition to the big pool, each facility includes a small "training pool" for beginner lessons, a Wahoo's Fish Taco restaurant, a full-service surf shop, a board demo/rental center, a board shaping/glassing facility, party rooms, and shower/changing facilities.

Competition and Market Positioning

Since no surf-specific pools have ever been built, Surfparks' only direct competitor is the ocean. On its best days, the ocean is a tough competitor, but 99 days out of 100, waves at a Surfpark are superior to those in the ocean. In addition, the structured operating model at a Surfpark ensures that each surfer rides a wave alone, removing the common frustration of being cut off or outmaneuvered by aggressive or inexperienced surfers.

Surfparks understands that no matter how good the wave, surfing in a pool can never replace the benefits of the ocean. It is not our intention to make ocean surfing obsolete. Rather, we aim to be an enjoyable, productive supplement to the natural surfing experience. A Surfpark acts as a consistent, entertaining training facility, much like a golf driving range complements a golf course. With this in mind, we target locations with sub-par, non-existent, or overcrowded occur wave conditions where surfers have a difficult time logging quality water time.

Surfparks aims to make this surf experience affordable, variable, and exciting enough to warrant frequent return visits. To keep the experience fresh, the wave generator can produce a wide range of wave heights, and the pool has a computer-controlled reef that allows wave shape, peeling speed, and direction (left/right) to be altered at frequent intervals. Salt water will be used to simulate the buoyancy, smell, and feel of ocean water.

Competitive Insulation

Armed with proprietary technology, perpetual R&D resources, and an optimized business model, Surfparks aims to establish the first and dominant global brand of wave-riding facilities. We will develop a captive customer base through our membership program. Surfpark members will have privileges at an ever-increasing network of franchised facilities, increasing loyalty and raising switching costs.

High upfront capital costs and a captive Surfpark membership base will discourage potential competitors from entering the marketplace.

Surfparks franchises will benefit from a global brand marketing campaign, constant improvement in operational efficiency, and access to continual technological innovation from the R&D team. The R&D focuses on improvement in both product quality and operational efficiency. Our current technology is by far the most efficient method of creating a high-quality 8-foot surfing wave in a pool, and Surfparks will strive to maintain its lead in quality, efficiency, and intellectual property.

SECTION 3
TECHNOLOGY OVERVIEW

Existing Wave-Generation Technology

There are two commercialized technologies used to create artificial waves: pneumatic and hydraulic. Pneumatic systems utilize large fans to create small (up to 6-foot) energy-efficient, high-frequency waves. Such pneumatic systems are used in the majority of recreational wave pools. Hydraulic systems drop a large quantity of water into the back end of the pool, displacing the pool water into a large (up to 8-foot) moving linear swell. Disney World's Typhoon Lagoon, for example, uses a hydraulic system and is thus suitable for surfing. However, the Typhoon Lagoon system is capable of producing only one wave every 90 seconds. Similar to a toilet, large storage tanks must refill before a new wave can be produced. Higher wave frequency from such a system would require additional horsepower to pump water into the chambers at a faster rate, crippling the energy efficiency of the equipment.

Surfparks' Wave-Generation Technology

At Surfparks' request, WaveTek engineers have developed a new wave-generation system that combines the frequency/efficiency of pneumatic systems with the wave quality of hydraulic systems. This wave-generation system is capable of producing up to 8-foot waves in 6- to 30-second intervals. Wave size is adjustable, from 3 to 8 feet, via computer interface.

WaveTek wave-generation machines have proven to be reliable in over 350 installations worldwide. The machines require no significant maintenance and are backed up with 24-hour technical support. The partnership agreement with ADG/WaveTek grants Surfparks global exclusivity and preferred pricing for this technology.

Pool/Reef Design

Once a swell has been generated, its breaking characteristics are determined by the pool shape and pool floor contour. Surfparks partner ASR has developed a patent pending pool/reef design that maximizes ride length, wave quality, safety, and operational efficiency in a minimum pool area. The pool design simulates a wide channel with converging walls (like a tapered pant leg). Waves are generated in the wide end of the pool, and they travel down the length of the pool, maintaining size, shape, and energy as the converging walls compact the swell. Salt water will be used in the pool to mimic the buoyancy and feel of ocean water.

To maintain variety in the surfing experience, ASR and WaveTek have developed a computer-controlled modular reef system. The shape of the pool bottom can be changed by raising or lowering padded reef sections via computer-controlled winches. Entirely new breaks can be created in a few minutes with the press of a button. ASR has charted the reef/bottom contour of over 40 of the world's best surfing breaks. With this database, it is possible to re-create world-class breaks in the Surfparks pool. Enticing promotions like "Malibu Mondays" or "Teahupo'o Tuesdays" can offer challenge and variety to all skill levels and ensure regular visits.

SECTION 4
SURFPARK BUSINESS MODEL

Facility operations are divided into two basic processes: the registration process and the actual surf-session pool operation. Surfparks encourages repeat usage via a membership model. Membership benefits include reduced-rate waves, express check-in, priority reservation status, and surf shop discounts.

Registration Process

Entering the front door in street clothes, members and non-members with reservations proceed directly to the clothes/board checkroom. A self-service kiosk allows members to swipe their card through a magnetic reader, which dispenses a barcoded, waterproof wristband. The barcode contains information regarding their session time and the number of waves remaining in their account. Non-members with reservations receive this wristband from the check-in personnel at the clothes/board checkroom. Non-members without reservations must check in at the front desk to sign waivers and receive their wristband before proceeding to the clothes/board checkroom.

Once they have received their wristband, customers hand their board (if they brought one) to the clothes/board checkroom attendant, and the attendant will hand them a clothes bin and direct them to the changing room. Customers then change into their swimsuits, return their clothes/valuables to the attendant, and receive their board back. The attendant stores the clothes and valuables safely behind the counter and marks the customer's bin number on their wristband. If the customers did not bring their own board, they can proceed to the board rental/demo center to choose an appropriate board. Once the customer is changed into his or her swimsuit, has a wristband, and has a board, he or she proceeds to the Surf Pool area. Showers are located near the "beach" area, where surfers can rinse off before and after surfing.

Pool Operations

Surf sessions are booked in two-hour increments, and beginners/novices are segregated from intermediates/experts. In an "intermediate" or "expert" session, surfers wait in a queue on the side of the deep end of the pool. During a 15-second lull in wave action, a group of six surfers enters the pool via a stairway. As surfers enter the pool, a staff-member scans their bar-coded wristband, deducting one wave from each surfer's account. After the 15-second lull, a set of six waves comes in 9-second intervals. Each of the six surfers takes a wave to himself or herself. The surfer rides toward the shoreward end of the pool until the wave "closes out" for a final move at the end of the pool. If any surfer fails to catch his/her allocated wave, he or she remains in the pool and gets a second chance during the next set.

The wave generator and reef design are flexible enough to host advanced and intermediate surfers in the same session. Scale model tests show a single reef design capable of producing an 8-foot tubing wave for experts and a slower, 4-foot wave for intermediates/novices. In this arrangement, advanced surfers queue at the stairs closest to the back of the pool and intermediate surfers queue at the stairs 40 feet closer to the front.

A complete ride takes approximately 10 to 15 seconds, depending on wave size (bigger waves move faster). From the zero-depth "beach," the surfer can exit the pool and walk back to the queue, or paddle back in a current-assisted "lazy river" that runs parallel to the pool. Each surfer will ride 10 to 20 waves in this two-hour period.

ADDITIONAL FACILITIES

Mexican Restaurant/Observation Deck

To increase revenue and desirability of the wave pool, an informal southern California-style Mexican restaurant will be positioned on the second floor of the main building and will have an "observation deck" view of the entire pool. Wooden support pilings will extend downward from the deck to create a pierlike effect. The restaurant serves pool patrons but will also be marketed to the general public, who will be attracted to the unique "surfside" views and elusive southern California fish tacos. The restaurant/observation deck is designed to be a comfortable place for surfers to relax before or after a session or for friends and family to watch the action in the pool.

Surfparks has secured a commitment from **Wahoo's Fish Taco** to lease the restaurant space in all facilities. Wahoo's will serve breakfast, lunch, dinner, snacks, soft drinks, and beer. For authenticity, exotic beers will be imported from various famous surf locations, including Mexico, Indonesia, Costa Rica, Tahiti, and Australia. This atmosphere will provide a perfect complement to the surf theme.

Pro Shop

A proshop, located in the reception area, will be the source for last-minute surf accessories (wax, leashes, traction pads, fins, swimsuits, rash guards, and so on) and will stock a large selection of surf and bodyboards. It is not our intention to be a direct competitor with local surf shops, as these surf shops will act as our best promoters, organizing group trips and funneling lessons to the Surfparks facility. To maintain this symbiotic relationship with all surf shops, Surfparks must carry a strategic product mix and create an atmosphere that enhances sales at *all* surf shops.

"Pay-Per-Wave" Membership/Pricing Structure

1. Surfers pay a yearly membership fee in 12 monthly installments (billed automatically to a credit card).

2. Four membership levels are available: Platinum, Gold, Silver, and Bronze.

3. Members receive a specified number of "waves" in their account. A wave is deducted each time a surfer enters the pool. The exact number of waves deducted depends on whether the session was standard, peak, or off-peak.

4. All waves in account expire one year from sign-up date.

5. Nonmembers purchase lower-quantity bunches of waves at higher rates.

A summary of the membership levels and pricing structure is as follows:

Membership Level	Monthly Installment	Waves/Year	Avg. $ Per Wave
Platinum	$200	2,400	$1.00
Gold	$150	1,440	$1.25
Silver	$100	800	$1.50
Bronze	$ 50	300	$2.00

Non-Members	Cost Per Bunch		Avg. $ Per Wave
100 Waves	$225		$2.25
20 Waves	$ 50		$2.50

SECTION 5
SURF MARKET ANALYSIS

The following are highlights of demographic research conducted for Surfparks LLC:

- American Sports Data claims there were 2.25 million "active" surfers in the United States in 2000, a 25 percent increase from 1999. One million of these surfers are based on the East Coast, 1 million on the West Coast, and 250,000 in Hawaii.

- Based on surf shop and magazine distribution, approximately 750,000 surfers live in southern California (San Diego–Santa Barbara).

- Of the 1 million East Coast surfers, half live between North Carolina and Maine; half live between South Carolina and Florida.

- American Sports Data defines "very active" (significantly more than four surfs per year) surf population as 20 percent of the above figures. Using the 20 percent formula, adjusted numbers would be 200,000 "very active" surfers on the East Coast.

SURFPARK COMPARABLES

Disney World's Typhoon Lagoon Wave Pool

Surfers will pay a premium to ride a decent wave, especially when conditions in their region don't cooperate. An example of this demand is seen at Typhoon Lagoon, the wave pool in Disney World in Orlando, Florida. For the past decade, Disney has been renting the pool to private parties before and after regular park hours. The wave was designed for recreational use and is judged by surfers as mediocre at best, but is often the only alternative to the flat conditions on Florida's Atlantic and Gulf coasts (about an hour drive in either direction from Orlando).

Current pool rental rates are between $1,000 to $1,500 for 100 waves. Thus, each individual in a group of 10 surfers pays $100 to $150 to ride 10 short waves. This kind of expense is for the seriously wave-deprived and can be justified only a few times per year. Interestingly enough, the sea of desperation is pretty large, as the pool is booked solid up to six months in advance, attracting users from as far as New Jersey.

Vans Skateparks

Action Sports footwear company Vans, Inc., is operating skateparks in 11 locations throughout the United States. The skateparks act as a facility for Vans' target market to practice this sport in a safe facility. From a marketing perspective, the parks are a vehicle to incubate, maintain, and foster growth of this target market.

The Vans Skateparks are also an important revenue source. The parks have construction costs of about $3 million each. Yearly membership fees are $50, with session fees (for two-hour sessions) ranging from $7 to $9 for members and $11 to $14 for non-members. Park capacity is approximately 200 people per two-hour session.

Each park has operating costs of approximately $700,000 per year and revenue of approximately $3.3 million per year. Retail and concessions make up nearly half the park revenue. Approximately 10 percent of the park's customers visit more than once per week. Each park sells approximately 120,000 sessions per year. The Vans Skateparks customer (10- to 20-year-old male) is almost identical to the younger Surfparks customer, an indication of customers' financial resources and willingness to spend these resources on their favorite pastime.

Golf Domes

Another operation worth examining is the Golden Bear Golf Dome near Albany, New York. The privately owned Golf Dome has a nearly identical physical structure to the proposed Surfparks facility. A large air-supported dome houses an indoor driving range, and an attached permanent structure contains a restaurant, pro shop, and rest rooms. The Golf Dome currently attracts 700 to 800 customers on weekdays and 1,300 to 1,400 customers on weekends. There are several dozen "Golf Dome" type facilities in the northern United States and Canada. The success of Golf Domes displays the viability of the dome-type structure. Air domes have proven themselves the most cost-effective and aesthetically pleasing structure for indoor sports.

Marketing Plan

The goal of the Surfparks Marketing Plan is simple: to establish Surfparks as a viable and enjoyable supplement to the ocean wave-riding experience. There are several strategies to achieve this goal:

- Gain allegiance to Surfparks with the core target market (current active surfers/bodyboarders).
- Establish legitimacy of Surfparks through pro surfer endorsements.
- Foster development of new surfboard/bodyboard customers.
- Optimize access to a Surfparks facility, especially for younger (<17) customers.
- Promote the membership program.
- Maximize global exposure of Surfparks through a multi-channel PR campaign.
- Gain global exposure to ready future markets for expansion.

An essential component to the marketing plan is Surfpark LLC's marketing partnership with the leading U.S. Surfing media properties: *Surfer Magazine*, *Surfing Magazine*, and Surfline/SWELL.com. This partnership gives Surfparks access to a highly targeted database of subscribers/Swell customers, exceeding 250,000 U.S. surfers.

As a part of this partnership, these media partners will provide a variety of marketing tools, including Internet and subscriber mailings for the Surfparks membership drive, ongoing Internet/mail/editorial promotions, and Web site hosting and design.

The marketing plan is divided into two parts: pre-launch and ongoing. The following is a summary of key components.

PRE-LAUNCH MARKETING ACTIVITIES

ISO "Initial Surf Offering"

When the first shovel hits the dirt, an ISO (Initial Surf Offering) pamphlet will be sent out to a group of several thousand surf VIPs (Surfrider Foundation Members, Surf Shop Owners/Employees, Magazine Subscribers). The pamphlet will present a thorough explanation of Surfparks and offer discounted memberships for those who sign up before the grand opening. The early membership also allows an individual to reserve optimum pool-space before the general public gets a chance. There is no risk to ISO members. They will not pay membership dues until the park opens, and there is a satisfaction guarantee on the wave quality. Once the Surfparks opens, they will be billed monthly for their membership dues. The purpose of the ISO is to ensure that Surfparks is operating as close to capacity as possible from opening day onward.

Web Site/Construction Cam

To ensure customers that Surfparks is not a "Pipe Dream," a construction cam on the Surfparks Web site will monitor the progress of park construction. Customers can watch from their computers as the park takes shape. The Web site will also allow users to make online reservations and purchase a membership. The site will provide a full explanation of the Surfparks concept, updated news stories, an e-mail/phone contact for further information, and a chat room to monitor public discussion and sentiment about the project.

Advertising

A kickoff advertising campaign will begin approximately two months after the ISO and four months before the grand opening. The campaign will run in all national surfing/bodyboarding magazines (*Surfing Magazine/Surfer Magazine/ Bodyboarding Magazine/TWSurf Magazine*) in addition to the more specifically targeted *Eastern Surf Magazine*. Ads will also appear in more popular surf-related Web sites (SWELL.com, Surfinfo.com, Surfline.com). Poster-style ads will also appear in all surf shops within a 300-mile radius of the park. The ads will encourage membership, foster interaction via the Web site/cam, and promote the grand opening contest/party.

Press Conference

A press conference will be held prior to the grand opening at a major national surf trade show. Ideally, the conference will include a live-remote hookup to the pool (via web or "staged" videotape) with pro surfers in action. This builds credibility of Surfparks with the surf industry, increases media exposure, and establishes momentum for the grand opening contest/party.

Media Sneak Previews

To increase media exposure and buildup, select surf and mainstream media will be allowed to shoot photos and write "sneak preview" stories before the official park opening. Action Sports TV shows will also be contacted for the opportunity to film pre-opening activities.

Web Site

Integrated into SWELL.com, the Surfparks Web site will continue to offer a live pool-cam so surf sessions can be viewed remotely. The site will also offer a monthly calendar, listing special events and operation hours. Reservations can also be made online.

Possible humorous Web site features include a "Surf Forecast" (which is always the same, since it's a wave pool) and the ability to place bets (for fun) on the surfers. The best surfer in a session gets a "Web Surf Contest Winner" T-shirt or the like. Surfers could tell their friends/family that they'll be surfing at X o'clock, and they can log on, watch the action, and score their favorite surfer. Camera-shy surfers may also request the Web-cam to be turned off.

To increase Web site traffic, links to popular surf/sports-related Web sites (SWELL.com, Surfline.com, Surfinfo.com) will be purchased or traded.

Regional radio advertisements will also be scheduled, with an on-air "surf report" a possibility to promote Surfparks.

Lessons

To attract new customers and increase retention, surfing and bodyboarding lessons will be available to all ability levels. Resident pros will teach private and group lessons. In addition, "guest pros" will also teach lessons during scheduled promotions. The lessons will be promoted through area surf shops and Surfparks' magazine/Web/local newspaper/radio advertising. The pool will have regularly scheduled "lesson blocks" used exclusively for lessons. Board rental and video analysis will be included as part of the program. A partnership with renowned women's surf instruction company, "Surf Divas," is also being discussed, where a Surf Divas affiliate would be based at Surfparks.

SECTION 6
STARTUP COSTS

The largest capital expenditures for a Surfparks facility will be for installation of the pool, reef, and wave-generation equipment. Wave machine/pool/filtration construction would comprise approximately two-thirds of the startup costs. As an equity holder in Surfparks LLC, ADG/WaveTek is providing wave-related equipment at a small margin above cost and giving Surfparks exclusive rights to the technology.

Research on land and building costs has been conducted as well. Several specific properties, with favorable zoning and town/county support, have been identified in all three pilot locations. Land costs range from $125,000 to $850,000. Total startup construction costs are highly dependent on how much utility, site work, and other infrastructure preparation would be required. For example, building the facility next to an existing waterpark, ski area, or other recreational facility could reduce startup costs by up to $3 million compared to a stand-alone facility. Start-to-finish construction time would be approximately six months. A late spring/early summer opening would be preferred. Complete startup capital requirements are outlined below. More specific costing data is available in the Pro Forma Appendices.

Construction	In $
Land Acquisition (Incl. Legal/Permits)	500,000
Architecture & Engineering	250,000
General Conditions	180,620
Sitework	524,475
Landscape/Irrigation	50,000
Electric	286,500
Utilities	162,500
Parking Lot/Driveways	118,750
Fencing/Barriers	65,750
Wave Pool/Equipment Buildings	1,606,700
Wave-Generation Equipment	1,160,000
Filtration/Misc.	255,000
Dome/Shelter*	800,000
Variable Reef/Wall Padding	920,000
Main Building (Inc. Pier)	576,000
FF&E	250,000
Contingency	300,000
Total Startup Construction	**$8,006,295**

These figures represent the estimate for a stand-alone facility requiring a significant amount of site work, utility, and infrastructure installation.

Surfparks LLC has secured financing to cover an aggressive marketing campaign leading up to the opening of the pilot facility.

SECTION 7
POOL USAGE AND CASH FLOW FORECAST

Based on the established pricing/membership structures, we have assembled a model to demonstrate the earnings before interest, taxes, and depreciation allowances (EBITDA) from the pool in a fiscal year at a Surfparks facility. Since members pay as low as $1 per wave and non-members pay as much as $2.50 per wave, revenue forecasts are highly dependent on the ratio of member uses to non-member uses. Below is a sensitivity table that shows the forecast Year 1 (for the EBITDA) based on pool utilization ranging from 10 percent to 100 percent and average pool-revenue per customer (20 waves) of $37.50. This analysis also includes additional capacity gained from a waterpark location, where waterpark customers can purchase shorter half-hour sessions for $20.

Sensitivity Analysis

Pool Utilization	Year 1 EBITDA	Total Visits	Visits per Day
10%	(184,536)	21,384	59
15%	111,552	32,076	89
20%	407,639	42,768	119
25%	703,727	53,460	149
30%	999,814	64,152	178
35%	1,295,902	74,844	208
40%	1,591,989	85,536	238
45%	1,888,077	96,228	267
50%	2,184,164	106,920	297
55%	2,480,252	117,612	327
60%	2,776,339	128,304	356
65%	3,072,427	138,996	386
70%	3,368,514	149,688	416
75%	3,664,602	160,380	446
80%	3,960,689	171,072	475
85%	4,256,777	181,764	505
90%	4,552,865	192,456	535
95%	4,848,952	203,148	564
100%	5,145,040	213,840	594

As the table indicates, the EBITDA breakeven point lies between 10 percent and 15 percent utilization of the pool. This translates to about 25,000 individual pool uses per year, or 69 visits per day, based on 360 operating days per year. This is the equivalent to filling less than two full 36-surfer sessions per day. This attendance level is the equivalent of 1 in 30 southern California surfers attending one time per year.

By contrast, 100 percent utilization of the pool equals approximately 214,000 individual visits per year, or 594 visitors per day. Keep in mind that at full capacity, only 1 in 3 southern California surfers would need to attend once per year. Recall that Surfparks' market research revealed that 51 percent of the surveyed surfers would use a Surfpark once *per week*.

APPENDIX: THE ROADMAP GUIDE FOR WRITING A BUSINESS PLAN

The roadmap guide leads you through a detailed table of contents for preparing a business plan and a framework, which provides the guidelines for writing the sections in the plan. This business plan table of contents was developed at Columbia Business School's Eugene M. Lang Center for Entrepreneurship by Clifford Schorer. Schorer has over 15 years of experience working with students and venture capitalists in evaluating business plans. There is no one way to write a business plan, and there are many ways to approach the preparation for and the writing of a business plan. Entrepreneurs will probably find it necessary to research many areas before they have enough information to start writing. Most begin by collecting historical financial information about their company and/or industry and completing their market research before beginning to write any one part.

Initial drafts of proposed financial statements and projections are often prepared next, after the basic market research and analysis are completed. By preparing these statements, the entrepreneur knows which strategies will work from a financial perspective before investing many hours in writing a detailed description. Entrepreneurs should keep detailed notes on their assumptions so that later they can include footnotes with their statements.

The business plan framework provides a three-step process to help identify ideas, issues, and research needed to complete the eight sections included in a business plan. The guide is based on the five-phase opportunity analysis described in Chapter 2 and assumes that you have completed preparing the marketing analysis and competition section in Chapter 3.

The following is a sample table of contents that details the eight sections for the business plan.

Business Plan

Table of Contents

Section I. Executive Summary (usually 1–2 pages)

A. The Business Opportunity and Vision
B. The Market and Projections
C. The Competitive Advantages
D. The Management Team
E. The Offering

Section II. The Company, Industry, and Product(s) or Service(s)

A. The Company
B. The Industry
C. The Product(s) and Service(s)
D. Growth Plan

Section III. Market Analysis

A. Market Size and Trends
B. Target Customers
C. Competition

Section IV. Marketing and Sales Plan

A. Marketing Strategy
B. Pricing
C. Sales Plan
D. Advertising and Promotion
E. Channels of Distribution
F. Operations Plan

Section V. Operating Plan

A. Product Development

B. Manufacturing Plan

C. Maintenance and Support

Section VI. Management Team

A. Organization Chart

B. Key Management Personnel

C. Policy and Strategy for Employees

D. Board of Directors

E. Advisory Board

Section VII. The Financial Plan

A. Actual Income Statements and Balance Sheets

B. Pro Forma Income Statements

C. Pro Forma Balance Sheets

D. Pro Forma Cash Flow Analysis

Section VIII. Funds Required and Uses

A. Financial Required

B. Amounts, Timing, and Terms

C. Use of Funds—Capital Expenditures, Working Capital

Appendixes

Financial Data Assumptions

Exhibits and Appendices

Business Plan Framework

The following framework and worksheets will assist entrepreneurs in preparing and writing the business plan by helping them gather their ideas and list the research needed, and issues and questions they must address in the key sections in the plan.

Step 1. BUSINESS PLAN PREPARATION
Step 2. BUSINESS PLAN WORKSHEET
Step 3. BUSINESS PLAN FINANCIAL PLANNING

The worksheets can also be downloaded from the Web site www.wiley.com/college/kaplan. Entrepreneurs can review the business plans on the Web site to determine the worksheet that best fits their individual needs.

Step 1. Business Plan Preparation
The business plan preparation framework identifies the market need, competitive advantages, management team, and growth guidelines that should be emphasized in the plan.

Guidelines	List	Questions

1. Focus on Market-Driven Opportunities

- Demonstrate how product/service meets market needs for the venture.
- Establish the size of the market for the product or service and define the specific buyers.
- Analyze the competition and the competitive environment.

2. Stress Competitive Advantages

- Demonstrate the distinct competence that the business will provide.
- How substantial is your advantage in the marketplace?

3. Describe the Management Team

- List the talent, skills, and experience of the management team.
- List how the team will be retained and what incentives will be provided for employees.

Step 1. Business Plan Preparation (*Continued*)

Guidelines	List	Questions

4. Support Projections for Growth
- Analyze the market structure and industry.
- Identify the growth rate for the product or service.
- Validate the results of your research by showing the total revenue expended for the business and the total number of current and potential customers.

Step 2. Business Plan Worksheet

The business worksheet details helpful tips, research needed, and further questions that need to be addressed in the sections. The following are tips to help the entrepreneur get started and make the writing of the business plan easier:

Guidelines	List	Questions

1. Executive Summary

- Make sure that the executive summary isn't more than three pages long.
- Make sure that the executive summary captures the reader's interest.
- Quickly and concisely establish what, how, why, where, when, and so on.
- Complete the executive summary after all other sections have been written.

2. Company Overview Section

- Describe the business's name.
- Include background of the industry as well as a brief history of the company.
- Define the potential of the new venture and list key customers, major products, and applications.
- Spell out any unique or distinctive features of the venture.

3. Marketing Analyze Section

- Convince investors that sales projections can be met.
- Use and disclose market studies.
- Identify a target market and market share.
- Evaluate all competition and specifically explain why and how this business will be better than the competition.
- Describe the pricing strategy that will be used to penetrate and maintain a market share.
- Identify advertising plans with cost estimates to validate the proposed strategy.

4. Marketing and Sales Plan Section

- Describe the feature and benefits of the services or products.
- Describe in detail the current stage of development.

Step 2. Business Plan Worksheet (*Continued*)

Guidelines	List	Questions

5. Research, Design, and Development Segment Section
- State the costs involved in research, testing, and development.
- Explain carefully what has already been accomplished (prototype, lab testing, early development, and so on).
- Mention any research or technical assistance that has been provided.

6. Operations Segment Section
- Describe the advantages of the business's location (such as zoning, tax laws, and wage rates).
- List the production needs in terms of facilities (plant, storage, office space) and equipment (machinery, furnishings, supplies).
- Describe the access to transportation (for shipping and receiving).
- Explain the proximity to the business's suppliers.
- Describe the availability of labor in the business's location.

7. Management Section
- Provide résumés or curricula vitae of all key management personnel.
- Carefully describe the legal structure (sole proprietorship, partnership, S-Corporation, LLC, or C-Corporation) of the business.
- Describe any expected added assistance by advisors, consultants, and directors.
- Provide information on current ownership and options for an exit strategy such as selling the business or going public.

Step 3. Business Plan Financial Planning

Guidelines	List	Questions

8. Financial Section
- Convince investors that the business makes sense from a financial standpoint.
- Prepare three- to five-year financial projections.
- Prepare first-year projections by month.
- Prepare second-year projections by quarter.
- Include an income statement and balance sheet.
- Include a cash flow statement for years 1 and 2.
- Include a three-year annual forecast.

9. Selling the Plan
- Prepare financial presentation.
- Seek assistance of OUTSIDE experts.
- Identify funding sources.
- Schedule meeting for funding.
- Get started and introductions.

ADDITIONAL RESOURCES

- **Biz Plan Software**   www.jian.com
- **Biz Women**   www.bizwomen.com
- **Business Plans**   www.bplans.com
- **Business Plans Made Easy**   www.entrepreneur.com
- **Entreworld**   www.entreworld.org
- **Small Business Advancement National Center**   www.sbanet.uuca.edu

www.wiley.com/college/kaplan

ROADMAP for

PATTERNS OF ENTREPRENEURSHIP
Building and Exiting

CHAPTER 12

COMMUNICATING THE OPPORTUNITY AND MAKING A PRESENTATION

"I have made this letter a rather long one, only because I didn't have the leisure to make it shorter"

BLAISE PASCAL (1623–1662), FRENCH MATHEMATICIAN

OBJECTIVES

- Understand how to target the business plan to investors.
- Prepare oral and visual presentations to investors.
- Learn the investor evaluation process.
- Commence negotiations with an investor.
- Prepare the investor presentation.

CHAPTER OUTLINE

INTRODUCTION

No idea, however good it is, will attract resources to help a company grow unless the entrepreneur can communicate the opportunity clearly to potential stakeholders whether they be investors, bank loan officers, or corporate partners. (In this chapter we use the term *investors* broadly to encompass other stakeholders that may provide resources to help the company grow.) Communication skills are therefore key to successful entrepreneurship. This chapter will help you gain those skills.

ACTIONS

Entrepreneurs need several prepared documents and verbal presentations to communicate their opportunity to interested parties. These are an executive summary, a full business plan, and both a short and long presentation. All of these must be adjusted to take into account the specific needs of the audience.

Any communication whether verbal or written must be customized to the target audience. One message does not fit all. For example, when seeking a bank loan entrepreneurs have to show how the risk is minimized for the lender, whereas, if talking with a venture capitalist, the entrepreneur will need to show how the business fits with their investment profile, how it can grow quickly, and how an "exit" for the investors will be created.

Any commitment from an investor will not come quickly. There has to be an exploratory period during which the two parties get to know one another. This "dating" period requires different levels and types of communications as the process proceeds. The first communication should be in the form of an "executive summary," or "teaser." The purpose of this short document is merely to gain the attention of the targeted audience. Most investors receive a torrent of business plans and teasers, so it is important that their attention is grabbed quickly.

The verbal equivalent of the teaser is the so-called elevator pitch. The name describes an imaginary situation in which an entrepreneur finds him or herself by chance in an elevator with a potential investor/lender and has her ear for just the length of the elevator ride. In the minute or two available a crisp compelling message that engages the recipient must be conveyed.

If the teaser or elevator pitch is successful, it is likely that a full business plan will be requested for review. If this plan continues to appeal to the investor, the next step is usually an invitation to give a full "investors' " presentation.[1]

Think of these stages of more and more engagement with potential investors as similar to trout fishing. A good angler will choose his bait carefully to match what he thinks the fish are feeding on at that moment. After setting the appropriate bait, and the fish takes it, the angler "plays" the fish, gradually bringing it closer and making sure that nothing happens to allow the fish to get off the hook.

Chapter 11 has already shown you how to produce a winning business plan. Now is the time to get it in front of the right stakeholders and convince them to participate in your venture. In this chapter you will learn how to approach stakeholders, prepare the appropriate documents and presentations, and move toward closing a negotiation.

LOCATING INVESTORS

Once the entrepreneur has prepared a business plan, a presentation that contains 10 to 16 slides (see later), and an executive summary, it is time to contact potential stakeholders to see if they may be interested in funding the business.

Investors are busy people, and it is important that the entrepreneur only contact those who are likely to be interested in their opportunity. This requires some research before making an approach. One way to do this is to speak with other entrepreneurs in similar business fields who have been successful in getting investment, closing loans or entering into a corporate partnership. The Internet is valuable here in locating and learning about the interests for different investors and finding the correct contact.

To locate active investors, one should first look within the industry where the business is focused. Investors prefer involvement in a business they know this will require less explaining or selling the concept. Locating the right investor can add value in a number of ways, besides investment. This can include identifying and helping to recruit key management team members, and providing key industry and professional contacts. The investor can serve as a mentor, confidant, and sounding board for ideas and plans to solve problems. In some cases, the investor helps to establish relationships with key customers, suppliers, and potential corporate partners.

Another less obvious alternative to finding active investors is to pursue passive or "arms-length" investors, who will have little or no involvement in the business. This could include companies that wish to diversify or groups of investors formed for tax advantage reasons. In general, this route is not recommended. "Smart money" brings not only funding but knowledge, help, and contacts and is far more valuable. Entrepreneurs may feel that "hands-off" funding is preferable as they won't have interference in their business while growing it. This thinking is misguided, and finding sources of funding coupled with real help is *always* the best choice.

The initial conversation with the investor is to present a summary of the plan describing the business and the type of financing needed. The entrepreneur should also prepare a list of potential investors and phone them for an interview. If an investor asks for a business plan, one should explain that a meeting is preferred before handing over a formal plan. Investors invest in people, not plans. The entrepreneur should arrange to send the business plan or preferably only the executive summary prior to requesting a face-to-face meeting. Send the plan or summary with a cover letter. One should try to be as specific as possible in the letter and refer to matters discussed in the initial telephone conversation so that the letter is not perceived as a mass mailing. A follow-up call in two weeks should be made to answer any questions.

Here are some tips on finding the right contact:

- If an entrepreneur thinks that the opportunity is best fitted to an angel investor or angel investor group, go to any local entrepreneurs' networking function. Often Angels go to these meetings to seek out new deals. Many local angel groups now have Web sites where your opportunities can be listed; these sites can easily be found by Web searching. There may be someone in the local community who has been successful in a similar field whether in retail, software, construction, or

ROADMAP

ACTIONS   Entrepreneurs should use a "rifle" rather than a "shot-gun" strategy for engaging with potential investors. Imagine that there are only 20 *people* (not just organizations) that might have interest. Research them and contact them after knowing precisely what is likely to interest them. Blasting your idea out to everyone wastes time and devalues your opportunity.

technology. He or she may be investing privately in new opportunities, or know individuals who are—they are often willing to make introductions. Introductions can also be made through accountants and lawyers. As entrepreneurs build their businesses, they will need such services, and it is wise to choose professional service firms that are able to access strong local networks. Chapter 6 lists several useful places to enter the Angel networks.

- If the target is a VC firm, then it is important to narrow down the targets to just a few. VC firms are usually very focused and do not look at opportunities that do not pass through their tight filter. The filters usually have the following important categories:
  - *Stage of company.* Taking an early-stage company opportunity to an expansion stage investor is futile.
  - *Domain or field.* Many VCs invest only in businesses that sell to other businesses (B2B); others focus on retail opportunities. Others may prefer technology-based businesses, software companies, or franchises.
  - *Size of investment.* If $250 thousand is sought, there is no point in talking to a firm that only invests upwards of $5 million.
  - *Location.* The majority of VC firms have a bias to invest in a local region which they can reach within a three-hour drive, say.
  - *Stage of fund.* VCs usually have a 10-year horizon to invest their money. If it is getting near to the end of their fund, it is unlikely that they will invest in a biotech firm that will take seven to eight years to mature to an exit.

A match can be found by first accessing "Pratt's Guide to Venture Capital"[2] online or at a local library. Once a short list of potential VC firms has been made, each can be researched in greater detail by visiting its Web site. VC firms are looking for matching deals and therefore are usually very clear in their communications as to what they are looking for. In addition, their past investments ("portfolio") will be listed on their Web site. Reviewing these will determine whether there is a good fit with your company. Calling the CEOs of the portfolio companies most closely aligned with the new opportunity can provide more insight and may lead to a personal introduction, which always helps. Venture capitalists are much more likely to review an opportunity that is referred to them by someone already in their network rather than looking at unsolicited business plans.

- If a small-business loan is sought, then there are probably several local banks that seek such opportunities. Calling them and asking if they have a small-business loan officer can start the conversation. They may participate in the federal lending programs to support small companies.

> "If an entrepreneur cannot locate me, and send me a compelling executive summary that is a close fit to what I am looking for, then they have already failed the first test of being an entrepreneur!"[3]
>
> BILL FREZZA
> *Partner, Adams Capital Management (www.acm.com)*

PREPARING A TEASER

Once a target has been identified and researched, the bait needs to be set. This requires a well-written executive summary or "teaser." This document must be impeccable in its appearance, short and to the point, clear both in the description of the opportunity and what benefit is offered to the targeted investor or partner.

Writing a clear, concise, elegant, and engaging short document is extremely difficult and requires considerable practice. Although everyone has a personal

ACTIONS	Writing a compelling "teaser" can take an experienced entrepreneur a full day. Do not underestimate either the importance or difficulty of this task. You will need help and practice.

approach to writing, we find that it is best to create a draft rather quickly and then wait a couple of days before going back and reading it critically *as if you were the recipient*. Edit this document to a second draft, and again wait. This is a good time to have someone not closely involved in the company, but with business experience, read the document and provide criticisms and suggestions for improvement. It must read logically, smoothly, with every sentence carefully constructed and grammatically correct; there must be no typos or spelling errors. Avoid repetition, long sentences, jargon, and short forms. Avoid "woolly" words such as "hopefully," and "maybe" and the conditional verb forms. Finally, go through the document with a fine tooth-comb and be ruthless in removing every word that is not absolutely necessary and could be seen as padding.

Teaser Example: LeafBusters Inc.

The idea for this new business was triggered by an entrepreneur reading an article about how farmers in the Midwest do not own their own combine harvesters, but use crews with their own equipment to take in the wheat crop. These crews move from north of the Canadian border and follow the harvest time southward as the climate changes. This makes sense for the farmers who cannot justify the high cost of a combine, or have the skilled labor available for just a short harvest period. For the crews, the cost of the equipment can be justified much more easily as it is in use two to three months a year, not just two weeks. The entrepreneur recognized that leaf collection has much the same issues, and so she conceived a company to provide leaf-collecting services to local municipalities. After researching the opportunity and creating a business plan, the entrepreneur decided that the $3 million required to fully finance the startup should come from two sources. Since half of the money would be for leaf-collecting equipment, a bank loan could be used for the purchases as there would be "hard assets" with which to secure the loan. The rest of the money would be best raised from Angel investors. This size of investment would most likely require more than one Angel, so an Angel's network was sought—one that was local to the region where the Entrepreneur lived. After meeting one of the Angel Group members at a local networking meeting, the following "teaser" was supplied to the Angel Group for discussion.[4]

EXECUTIVE SUMMARY

THE OPPORTUNITY

LeafBusters Inc. offers leaf collection services to municipalities in the Northeast region with a significant cost savings over their current operations. Our research has shown that municipalities use their own workforce and equipment, spending as

EXECUTIVE SUMMARY (cont.)

much as $1 million per year to perform this service for residents. We estimate that our service will be able to offer municipalities a 10 to 20 percent cost reduction. Our business model has tremendous growth potential since we will be able to perform this service at a 30–40% lower cost than the municipalities can for themselves.

THE MARKET

Leaf collection is a major activity performed 10 to 12 weeks every fall in virtually every town and city in the United States with hardwood trees. Municipal employees normally perform this activity with a variety of leaf collection equipment owned by the municipalities. Our research estimates the expenditures on leaf collection to be $250–500 million/year throughout the United States and southern Canada. Budgets for leaf collection range from $100,000/year for small towns to $1 million/year for large suburban counties.

Municipalities are under significant pressure to reduce costs. Outsourcing of the leaf collection process will provide them with a very attractive cost-cutting solution to their budget pressures.

THE COMPETITION

We are surprised to find that no significant business competition currently exists for this activity. Individual municipalities perform an estimated 98 percent of the leaf collection in this market, with no significant sharing of resources. Small local subcontractors perform the remaining leaf collection primarily for business properties. Although we do expect our success to draw the attention of potential entrants, our business model should provide us with the flexibility and economies of scale to remain the consolidated market leader.

BUSINESS MODEL

LeafBusters Inc. intends to become the premier supplier of seasonal curbside leaf collection services throughout the United States and Canada. All contract services will be provided from regional service centers, with more efficient collection cycles than those currently available from local municipalities. Shorter collection times will allow LeafBusters Inc. to cover more areas, with less equipment and staff than is currently used. Our business model will create an outstanding opportunity for investors such as the NEtwork Angel Group. Based on our projections, we believe that we can capture 20 percent of the market within the first five years of operations.

LeafBusters Inc. will provide the staff and equipment necessary to perform those services currently provided by local governments for curbside leaf collections. While the length of annual leaf collection programs varies (depending on weather and the volume of leaves), the normal program length is 10 to 12 weeks. Our business model involves moving leaf collection equipment and

EXECUTIVE SUMMARY (cont.)

operations from north to south, following the leaf fall patterns, which will allow us to expand the collection season. For example, the first regional rollout will begin in New England and end in North Carolina, with a total collection period of at least 14 to 16 weeks. Instead of the usual 8 to 10 hour/day staffing by most municipalities, LeafBusters Inc. will operate for approximately 20 hours each day. The goal is to use less equipment and staff to cover more areas by migrating them based on schedule collections. While the transportation of equipment is extremely important, particular care will be taken in recruiting and retaining seasonal staff. Transportation and accommodations will be provided, as well as a competitive hourly pay rate and per diem.

The collected leaves will be turned over to local recycling and composting facilities in an effort to assist communities achieve their solid waste reduction goals.

Some optional services available from LeafBusters Inc. are scheduling services, communications services (to notify home owners of collection days and times), and compost distribution services.

OPERATING SUMMARY

During its first year of operations, LeafBusters Inc. will focus on acquiring equipment and on obtaining at least 30 contract awards for leaf collection in its first targeted region. In each ensuing year, one additional region will be added to operations, until all four are operational.

The regional rollout of services will be the Northeastern states, the Midwestern states, and the West Coast, with final expansion into Canada. This approach will allow LeafBusters Inc. to properly manage growth while providing a high level of service to customers. In addition, proving our concept in stages will allow us to deliver success stories as a part of the bid submission process. We already have two orders from municipalities that we will service as soon as our financing is in place.

Although the focus during the first regional rollout will be on those municipalities that currently offer leaf collection programs, those that do not do so will be targeted during the next phase. We intend to offer our services as a means for municipalities to save money on solid waste removal efforts and to improve their recycling efforts.

In addition, each rollout phase will include the exploration of additional lines of business such as tree trimming services, street sweeping, solid waste removal, and composting facilities. These additional services will allow us to further utilize our seasonal staff and equipment, keeping our staff employed and improving our return on assets.

PRELIMINARY FINANCIAL SUMMARY

The following table summarizes the preliminary five-year forecast of revenue, expense and net income for LeafBusters Inc.

EXECUTIVE SUMMARY (cont.)

**ProForma Income Statement
LeafBusters Inc.**

(in thousand USD)

For the Year Ending Dec. 31,

	2003	2004	2005	2006	2007	2008
Revenues	$0	$6,075	$13,669	$30,755	$69,198	$107,001
Direct Labor	0	1,519	3,417	7,689	15,224	23,540
Gross Profit	0	4,556	10,252	23,066	53,974	83,461
SG&A	500	2,126	4,784	10,764	22,143	34,240
Other Expenses		911	2,050	4,613	10,380	16,050
EBIT	(500)	1,519	3,417	7,689	21,451	33,170
EBIT Margin		25.0%	25.0%	25.0%	31.0%	31.0%
Net Income	($600)	$1,063	$2,392	$5,075	$14,158	$21,892
Profit Margin		18%	18%	17%	20%	20%
Cumulative Income/(Loss)	($600)	$463	$2,855	$7,930	$22,088	$43,980

FUNDING REQUIREMENTS

LeafBusters Inc. is seeking initial financing of $2.5 million, of which $1.5 million will be a bank loan secured against equipment and $1 million as equity in the form of preferred stock from angel investors. These funds are sufficient to initiate the establishment of a leaf collection fleet and begin operations. These funds will finance the equipment, marketing activities, labor expenses, organizational costs, and working capital for the first year. Since we expect that contracts will be in place for the fall 2004 season with the profitability shown above, no additional external funding will be needed after the 2005 season.

EXIT STRATEGY

There are several possible exit strategies. The most attractive option will likely be selling the business to a major municipal service company such as a solid waste removal company after three to four years of operations. We anticipate providing our first-round investors with an internal rate of return exceeding 40 percent.

For further information contact:
LeafBusters Inc.
Main Street
Anytown, USA   www.leafbuster.com   1-800-Leafbust

Normally, the document would be provided with a short personal cover letter highlighting the opportunity and expected outcome. Note the following points in this document:

● The Summary has a clear identity and image. It looks like something from a company and not an individual. The company has a name, relating directly to the opportunity.

- The opportunity, market size, and the customer "value proposition" are spelled out clearly at the outset.
- Competition, business model, and how the company will be operated are described.
- Six-year financial projections are summarized.
- Expectations from investors, including the expected payback and the method of achieving liquidity are all stated unequivocally. There are no "woolly" terms like "might," "hopefully," and "could." Such words convey doubt and hence high risk; edit them out.

Anything beyond this content detracts from its impact. Keep it brief and to the point.

THE ELEVATOR PITCH

An elevator pitch is essentially a verbal version of the teaser. For an example of an actual elevator pitch visit www.wiley.com/college/kaplan where Ankit Patel pitches an idea for how to reduce the operating costs of major U.S. freight railroads. Again, making all the points in a one- to two-minute presentation is extremely difficult. Elevator pitches must be rehearsed, first alone and then in front of an audience. Pay attention to the following factors:

- Speak clearly, do not mumble, and do not rush. Modulate your voice and make the presentation pleasant and engaging.
- Get the audience involved and interested as early as possible. A good way of doing this is to relate your opportunity to something that the audience already knows. This is particularly important if your idea is rather obscure or highly technical.
- Be enthusiastic. If you are not excited about the opportunity, how can you expect someone else to be?
- Enthusiasm is also reflected in body language. You should be comfortable with your posture, but hands in pockets, masking your face, or other involuntary movements detract highly from the impact.
- Do not be overanxious or overact. Take some deep breaths before starting and be determined to enjoy the experience yourself. Avoid theatricals.
- Finish on an up-note and let your closure focus on the next actions.

Get into the habit of watching professional presentations and analyzing what is powerful, natural, and engaging about them.

Investors' Presentation
Preparation for the Meeting

After reviewing the executive summary, or hearing the elevator pitch, the investors, if interested, will ask for a copy of the business plan. Follow up with a phone call a few days after submitting the plan to test reactions and to deal with any immediate questions. In reality, most investors do not read business plans in detail, but just enough to determine whether they wish to go to the next step.

NOTE ON CONFIDENTIALITY

Most investors will not sign a confidentiality agreement at this stage. Only put in the plan materials that are not considered proprietary. If the business is based on new technical inventions, the inventors are justifiably concerned about disclosing proprietary information. Indeed, so doing can jeopardize the patent filing process. On the other hand, we find that scientists and engineers are only too eager to disclose their invention in looking for professional recognition or kudos from "their baby." Remember: investors are interested in the *business* opportunity, not the invention itself. Therefore, the entrepreneur only has to state *what the invention can do*, not *how it does it*. For example, "I have invented a new fuel injector for cars that increases the efficiency of existing gasoline engines by up to 7 percent. It has been tested at an independent test facility, and I can share the results with you. The market for such a product is $900 million annually. I am willing to disclose the details of the invention with you under a confidential agreement at a later date should you choose to enter into full due diligence for making an investment in my company." This statement does not threaten the proprietary nature of the invention, yet it gives the potential investors comfort that, should they proceed in detail, they will learn more but under a full confidentiality agreement.

A further intermediate step can be taken to protect both parties. They can agree to let an independent third party review the invention and comment on its status, viability, originality, and so on, but not disclose the invention to the investors. This is called "escrowing the IP" and is often used when investors want to get an opinion that the invention is likely to be patentable. No details are provided to the investors, only an opinion on status and likelihood of success in getting patents granted.

If the investors wish to proceed after a review of the plan, they will usually require the entrepreneur to make an oral presentation. This is an important event. This presentation is more formal than the teaser or elevator pitch and it is normally made to a group of "investors," perhaps the senior partners of a VC firm, an Angel investment board, two or three loan officers at a bank, directors of a local enterprise development board, a road show before an IPO, or several executives within a corporation deciding whether to become a partner with your company. Like the "teaser," it should be tailored to the audience.

It is as much about personal chemistry as the opportunity. This is the chance to establish a rapport with investors as partners in the future success of the company. At this presentation other members of the management team should be prepared to answer questions. The entrepreneur should strengthen the oral presentation with the use of presentational aids such as prototype of products and Web sites.

Early arrival at the venue, allowing time for setup, is important. Survey the room and arrange it to suit the presentation. Start with personal introductions, exchange of business cards, and some general small-talk to relax the atmosphere. Ask how long the investors have for the meeting and tailor the presentation to allow for questions.

ACTIONS | An investor's presentation is a key event. It needs extensive preparation and rehearsal. Try to think of every difficult question you are likely to be asked and prepare answers for them beforehand.

Try to determine who the key decision influencer is in the group and make an extra effort to answer any questions or uncertainties this key person expresses. Don't get sidetracked by questions if they are to be dealt with later in the presentation, but answer relevant questions promptly and move on. If the answer is not readily at hand, don't bluff but indicate that an answer will be provided within, say, two days. If several persons are presenting, have one "director" of questions; avoid interrupting others on the team and do not disagree among yourselves.

An investor's presentation will follow the same general pattern of the "teaser" but will fill in many of the details. It should last no more than 20 minutes without questions, using about 12 to 16 slides covering the opportunity overview, customer value proposition, market, competition, products/services, business model, management, and financials. Table 12-1 shows eleven basic slides and their contents. The topics here are typical for an early stage company. However, the flow of information is similar for all stages of investment, loans, or an exit. Up to five more may be added for extra clarification. It is useful to anticipate probing questions and have "backup" slides that address these points. It impresses investors if they come up with a difficult question such as "Isn't Global Inc. a major competitive threat to this business?" The presenter can immediately show an analysis of Global Inc. and illustrate the new company's advantages over them. A well-prepared presentation of 12 to 16 slides may have as many again anticipated backup slides. All the comments made above regarding making an elevator pitch apply here too. In addition:

- Do not hand out copies of your presentation prior to the formal part of the meeting. Indicate that you will leave copies afterward for their reference. If you fail to engage all the participants you will be distracted by one or more reading forward from the handouts, and perhaps even participating in side conversations about points that you have not yet reached. You will have lost control of the situation.
- Do not read from the slides. Use the slides to raise points and add to the content with your presentation.
- Face the audience, not the screen.
- Do not overrun your time for the formal presentation. This may leave you no time for more personal engagement, and the opportunity will be lost.
- Fewer slides are better than too many.
- Design the presentation around a clearly articulated and visual roadmap.

Since prospective investors are often taking an unsecured position in the company, the presentation must include a financial plan that describes data to make an informed decision. Sophisticated investors will rigorously evaluate the abilities of the management team, the financial strength of the company, and the commercial viability of the business. Prior to the "real event," the entrepreneur should make the presentation before several people to get feedback and to make sure a compelling case is made for the new company.

PRESENTATION TIPS

- Goal is to offer a high-level, summarized view of the company.
- Presentation is not a business plan on screen.
- Have only one or two speakers, no more.

> ### PRESENTATION TIPS (cont.)
>
> - Limit material to 12 to 16 slides.
> - Slides should contain concise ideas, not sentences.
> - Use no more than five bullet points per page.
> - Choose Arial type face, 12-point font (simple non-curlicue font).
> - Dark background with white letters is an easier read on the screen.
> - Minimize the use of bullet points, check marks, boxes, and other non-information symbols.

Table 12-1   Template for an Investors' Presentation

Slides	Notes on Contents
SLIDE 1: OUTLINE - Market - Product or Service - Customers - Intellectual Property - Development Plan - Distribution Plan - Team - Competition - Financial Projections - Exit Strategy	This slide provides an overall guide to your presentation and a road map for the audience. You can title each slide to relate to this guide.

SLIDE 2: MARKET
- What market will your company serve with its _**first**_ product or service?
- How large is this market?
  – Is it existing or emerging?
  – Show third-party market research data: historical and forecasts
- Name entrenched or potential competitors.
- What market(s) might your company serve with potential future products or services?
	Starting with this topic will engage your audience and enable you to put your best foot forward. Describe who are you going to serve; how large is the market you are attacking; is it mature, developing, or must you create it? Show third-party research to support your claims. Name your first product or service and how you will add to this later.

SLIDE 3: PRODUCT OR SERVICE - What product/service will your company develop and sell _**first**_? - What competitive advantage does your _**first**_ product/service have over alternatives? - After the _**first**_ product/service gains traction in the market, what future offerings will you develop and sell?	Describe in detail your first product or service. 80 to 90 percent of your presentation should be based on this "market entry" offering as this is where you will spend your initial money. Show how you can build on this with later new products or services as a "roadmap" for expansion.

(Continued)

Table 12-1 *Continued*

Slides	Notes on Contents
SLIDE 4: CUSTOMERS ● Who are target customers for your **_first_** product/service? – Name at least two specific prospective customers and include contact information. ● Why will they buy from you, and how much do they say they will pay? – Describe your economic value proposition to these customers. ● What alternatives do your prospective customers have besides buying from you?	Name the customers showing interest in your product/service. Name the person you spoke to and what they said. Why are they going to buy from you, and how much are they willing to pay? Describe the value proposition of your product/service—how is the customer going to make and save money by buying from you rather than buying from someone else?
SLIDE 5: INTELLECTUAL PROPERTY ● State the form(s) of IP you will use (trade-marks, patents, copyright, trade secrets). ● Describe the competitive benefits they will provide. ● Describe how you plan to obtain, develop, expand, and protect your IP. ● If your company uses new technology, give a general overview, state the stage of development, and describe any risks remaining in its implementation.	Here is an opportunity to talk about your special attributes. Keep the discussion at a high level. How are you protecting your intellectual property? Have you filed patents, or are you planning on filing patents, trademarks, etc.? How long do you think your IP will protect you from competition?
SLIDE 6: DEVELOPMENT PLAN ● Outline the timetable under which your **_first_** product/service will be brought to market. ● Specify the resources required and when you need them defining milestones: – Personnel and materials – Capital equipment – Third-party products, services, or IP – Corporate partners	How long and how much is it going to cost to get your first product or service out and producing income? How many people is it going to take? Will you need to buy capital equipment? When do you need different amounts of funding? Are there third-party products/services or other partners needed for your success? Do you have a bootstrapping plan to minimize the amount of cash you will require?
SLIDE 7: DISTRIBUTION PLAN ● Describe the company's business model. ● Describe the company's sales model. – Direct, indirect, Web-based, IP licensing, franchising or other ● Describe any partnering plans with other companies.	How are you going to sell your product/service? How are you going to get it to your customers? Will you sell direct, through distribution, use licensing or franchising, etc.? Describe your business model and how that will provide you with healthy profits.
SLIDE 8: MANAGEMENT TEAM ● Describe team members. – Include founders, identified or committed follow-on hires, and the advisory board ● Describe the additional skills and key management personnel required to build a company and when you need to add them. – CEO, CFO or controller, VP Marketing, VP Sales, VP Engineering, etc.	Who are you? Who are the founders? Provide relevant background information on your team and their roles. Describe the ideal characteristics of the rest of the senior management team that you are going to have to fill as you build the company and/or get funding.

Table 12-1   **Continued**

Slides	Notes on Contents

SLIDE 9: COMPETITION
● Describe incumbent competitors.
  – Number, size, market shares, growth rates, IP, product/services positioning, likely roadmap
  – Can any of these competitors be turned into customers or partners?
● Describe emerging or potential competitors.
  – Stage, backing, technology, product positioning, likely roadmap
  – Why will you be the winning startup in your market?
	This is a very important slide. You are never unique. You will have competitors, and you must understand who they are, their strengths and weaknesses. Are they big or small companies, are they competitors you might be able to turn into a distribution partner, or customer, and why. What is your strategy to win against these competitors?

SLIDE 10: FINANCIAL PROJECTIONS
● Describe the amount and phasing of the capital you need to raise to reach exit.
  – Are Federal or State grants included?
● Show pro forma annual financials for 5 years.
  – Include gross margin forecasts
● Describe the potential enterprise value of the company you hope to build.
	State how big and how fast a company you can build. Give financials at a high level by year, showing revenues, expenses, and sources of capital, highlighting the breakeven point. Show use of federal or state grants supplementing bank or equity funding. It is important to state your expected gross margins after two or three years, how the value of your company will grow, and what it might be worth when you are ready to sell it.

SLIDE 11: EXIT STRATEGY
● Is your company an IPO candidate?
  – If so, explain why and show comparables
● Who are your likely acquirers?
  – How much might they pay, why, and when?
  – Have they completed similar acquisitions in the past?
  – What will compel them to buy you rather than see you bought by a feared competitor?
	Investors need to know not just how much money they need to put into a company but also when they are going to get it back out with a profit. This will occur when you sell or take your company public. What companies exist which are like yours and can serve as benchmarks either by looking at their public stock price or knowing how much an acquirer paid for them? Describe how, in four to six years, investors are going to earn a return on their investment.

A full investors' presentation based on the elevator pitch referred to earlier is available at www.wiley.com.college.kaplan. The presentation is accompanied by a commentary and the slide presentation.

AFTER THE PRESENTATION

The entrepreneur should contact the investors a few days after having completed the presentation to see if additional questions need to be answered.

Create Excitement Around the Investment

If investors have expressed any degree of interest, the entrepreneur should move interest into action and investment. He or she should set a realistic deadline for the investment and notify investors that the supply of available equity is rapidly dwindling. Once investors have put money into a company, the relationship isn't over, it's just beginning. To state the obvious, investors have a vested interest in seeing the business succeed. The company should always make a point of involving investors in the success of the business by keeping them updated on new business opportunities and sales and financial targets. Good communications are vital throughout the life of the investor–company relationship. This is particularly true when the company goes through some disappointments, as undoubtedly it will.

Learn the Investor Evaluation Process

During the evaluation period, investors analyze the business into four fundamental sections.

Management Team

Investors like to review the experience and previous successes of the management team and the entrepreneur. They like to know a team is in place to run the business. The entrepreneur does not have to hire an entire team immediately, but she should indicate the types of individuals the company will hire to operate the business. In cases where the entrepreneur has been involved in previous successful ventures, investor confidence in providing immediate funding is made easier. Also, other investors, advisors, or board members who have a stake in the business are reviewed.

Business Model

The business model, market size, and customers are examined along with the timing of the opportunity. It is important to emphasize that the company has sales or can obtain sales through a solid sales plan. The emphasis for investors is that the longer it takes to achieve sales, the longer it will take for investors to get their money back.

Context

Both internal and external factors that affect the business and includes customer reactions to the product, competitors, economic regulation, and the stage of technology are analyzed.

The Deal

The deal and the price structure relate to the valuation. Structure refers to the terms and timing of the deal, and price is the stock, cash, or debt that will complete the transaction. This can include a silent investor, active participation, or an advisor. A final valuation is generally made three to six months following the presentation, after the investors have conducted full due diligence along the lines explored in Chapter 6.

Dealing with Failure

The entrepreneur can view the experience of finding investments as a positive, even if the investment is rejected, owing to inadequate answers regarding the risks of the business. The entrepreneur should always inquire if the investor knows another interested party or under what conditions the investor would reconsider. Therefore, the entrepreneur should always ask the questions: Who else may be interested? Do you have a contact name? If we do not receive funding now, can we count on you for later financing? The entrepreneur must learn to turn negative experiences into positive opportunities.

The Financing Agreement

Once an offer is accepted, the entrepreneur will begin to negotiate the final financing agreement that includes ownership, control, and financial objectives. This is called a *term sheet* (see more on term sheets in Chapter 6), which sets out the initial investment and understanding between the issuer and investor. The ownership for investors can range from 10 percent (profitable companies) to 90 percent (financially troubled firms). Most investors, however, do not want to own more than 50 percent of a business. Voting control usually remains with the entrepreneur and his or her management team. However, the investors will generally ask for representation on the Board of Directors to have some say in important decisions. Therefore, the actual control exercisable by the entrepreneur is usually greatly curtailed after an equity investment.

The financial objectives of the investors are either a corporate acquisition or a public stock offering within three to five years of their initial investment. These objectives are discussed when long-term financial goals are negotiated with the investors. A major concern for the investor is in determining the valuation of the business and the returns, which will be dictated by the value of the business. Investors price a business on the potential capital return in the future. The share they expect to gain in return for their investment depends not only on the amount of money they contribute but also on their time and opportunity costs (investments in other businesses that they are missing). The entrepreneur wants the investor to value the company for what it will be worth in three to five years (i.e., a corporate acquisition or an initial public offering). This is important in order to determine how an investment today will be worth more tomorrow. Investors usually value a company at a lower price than the entrepreneur would. For example, an early-stage company has a great idea and a young management team but no sales. From the investors' viewpoint, ideas are cheap, and an inexperienced management team might not be able to execute or implement the plan. Investors are always interested in maximizing the return on their investments. See Chapter 6 for more on term sheets and deal structures and Chapter 11 for business valuations and the methods and procedures used.

SUMMARY

No idea or opportunity can create value unless the entrepreneur can communicate it effectively to all classes of potential stakeholders in the venture, including investors, lenders, customers, suppliers, agents, advisors, partners, and employees. Entrepreneurs must learn to lead others so that they can become as excited and driven by the opportunity as the founders themselves. Communicating, then, is vital.

Every communication medium must be tailored to fit the targeted audience. The entrepreneurs must become used to putting themselves in the role of recipient so that they can craft a message that will directly appeal to the individual needs and aspirations of the audience.

Entrepreneurs use oral, written, and presentation media to communicate. The concise forms of an elevator pitch, introductory letter and teaser, or executive summary require a surprising effort to make them lucid, concise, and engaging. It is often more difficult to express yourself in a limited time or space than in a full business plan or full-blown presentation. These shorter forms are used to create initial interest and must be followed up with a more detailed presentation, which highlights all the key points of a business plan. These skills need practice, and entrepreneurs should take every opportunity they have to present to an audience and to write brief summaries of their opportunity for different targeted stakeholders.

STUDY QUESTIONS

1. What are the various types of communications that an entrepreneur uses, and what is their main purpose?

2. What key points would you make in an investor's presentation to the following audiences? Bankers, angel investors, VC partners, suppliers, potential key employees.

3. What are the major content items in a teaser?

4. Name the 11 foundation slides for an investors' presentation.

5. Name five common mistakes made by entrepreneurs when making a presentation.

6. How does an entrepreneur handle the situation when an investor refuses to sign a confidentiality agreement?

EXERCISES

1. Read the SurfPark case study in Chapter 11. Prepare a teaser for this business targeted at one of the following audiences: a banker, a venture capitalist, a corporate partner. Identify the actual entity that you are targeting and the appropriate person by name and title to whom you wish to send the teaser. Write a one-page accompanying letter of introduction as if you were the CEO of SurfPark.

2. Read the SurfPark case study and prepare a 12 to 16 slide presentation for a group of angel investors.

3. Prepare five backup slides for difficult questions that you anticipate will be asked in the presentation.

4. View Ankit Patel's elevator pitch[5] on the book Web site. What three things do you like best about this, and why? How would you improve it?

5. View the investors' presentation by Ankit Patel for the same railroad opportunity. What are five key points that he makes? How would you improve the presentation, and why?

INTERACTIVE LEARNING ON THE WEB

Test your skill-builder knowledge of the chapter using the interactive Web site.

1. Self Assessment:
2. Multiple Choice:
3. Matching of Key Terms:
4. Demonstration:
5. Case:
6. Video:

NOTES

Chapter 1: The Entrepreneurial Process

1. Findings by the Entrepreneurial Research Consortium, a public and privately sponsored research effort directed by Dr. Paul Reynolds at Babson College, indicate that 7 million adults are trying to start businesses in the United States at any given time. The Global Entrepreneurship Monitor, a joint research initiative by Babson College and the London Business School and sponsored by the Kauffman Center for Entrepreneurial Leadership, was launched in September 1997 to analyze entrepreneurial activity, its impact on national growth, and those factors that affect levels of entrepreneurial activity.

2. See Dale Meyer, plenary address at USASHE on February 15, 2001, "Changes in Entrepreneurship Curriculum." Courses in entrepreneurship are now taught at nearly 1000 colleges and universities. Entrepreneurship education programs for youngsters in the K–12 age range now exist in more than 30 states. The YESS!/Mini-Society entrepreneurship curriculum has been accepted by the U.S. Department of Education's National Diffusion Network as being effective in both acquiring knowledge and improving attitudes toward school and learning.

3. See Alex F. DeNoble, Doug I. Jung, Sanford B. Ehrlich, and Mark Butler, A paper on Entrepreneurial Self Efficacy: The Development of a Set of Measures and a Preliminary Test of Their Properties, Entrepreneurship Management Center, College of Business Administration, San Diego State University, 1999. Paper submitted on September 23, 2001, at Babson Research Conference.

4. See Ray Smilor, *Daring Visionaries*, (Holbrook, MA: Adams Media Corporation, 2001), pp. xxiv–xxv. Smilor is the president of the Foundation for Enterprise Development and formally vice president of the Kauffman Center for Entrepreneurial Leadership.

5. See Smilor, p. xxvii.

6. U.S. Department of Commerce, *Statistical Abstract of the United States*, Bureau of the Census, Washington, DC, 1999.

7. Ibid.

8. Ibid.

9. See William B. Gartner, Barbara J. Bird, and Jennifer A. Starr, "Acting As If: Differentiating Entrepreneurial from Organizational Behavior," *Entrepreneurship Theory and Practice* (Spring 1992): 13–27.

10. See Rita McGrath and Ian MacMillan, *The Entrepreneurial Mindset* (Boston, MA: Harvard Business School Press, 2000), pp. 2–3.

11. Ibid., pp. 12–14.

12. See M. Kourilsky, "Entrepreneurship Education: Opportunity in Search of Curriculum," Kauffman Center for Entrepreneurial Leadership, 1995.

Chapter 2: The Art of Innovation—Developing Ideas and Business Opportunities

1. For a number of interesting anecdotes and insights illustrating how global trends are impacting the world of business, refer to Thomas L. Friedman, *The World Is Flat* (New York: Farrar, Straus and Giroux, 2005).

2. It is notoriously difficult to obtain reliable and verifiable data concerning the Internet and its usage. This is an estimate from the Internet Statistics Firm, Cyveillance, in July 2000. By the time this book reaches print and is read, any data reported here will surely be outdated. You can visit the referenced sites to get an idea about how rapidly the Internet is expanding.

3. These data are from www.zakon.org/robert/internet/timeline/.

4. See http://wcp/oclc.org.

5. Information on international trade can be found at the World Trade Organization's Web site, www.wto.org.

6. This data was taken from a *Wall Street Journal* article on currency flows, August 4, 2004.

7. See an article in *The Deal*, July 2004. Since then, a number of leading U.S.-based Venture Capital firms have launched initiatives for investments in India and China.

8. The observation made in 1965 by Gordon Moore, co-founder of Intel, that the number of transistors per square inch on integrated circuits had doubled every year since the integrated circuit was invented. The pace has slowed down a bit, but data density is still doubling approximately every 18 months. Most experts, including Moore himself, expect Moore's Law to hold for at least two more decades.

9. From a private conversation by one of the authors with Hans-Günther Hohmann, General Manager, HP Germany.

10. From a survey conducted by *Industry Week*, reported in January 2004, and an internal study by IBM also in 2004.

11. Innovation Models in the 21st Century, a project funded by the National Institute of Science and Technology, by G. Susman and A. C. Warren within the Smeal College of Business, Pennsylvania State University, published in 2005 and to be found at www.smeal.psu.fcfe/.

12. For more about how companies manage agility, see Pal and Panteleo (eds.), *The Agile Corporation* (New York: Springer Press, 2005).

13. See William J. Baumol, *The Free Market Innovation Machine* (Princeton, NJ: Princeton University Press, 2002). There is an excellent short white paper of Baumol's ideas entitled "David and Goliath," which can be found at http://www.econ.nyu.edu/user/baumolw/sfg.pdf.

14. See Alan Afuah, *Innovation Management: Strategies, Implementation and Profits* (New York: Oxford University Press, 1998).

15. The Blyth Candles Web site, www.blyth.com, is an interesting place to learn how the humble candle can be "innovated" into a major business.

16. Clayton Christensen has written extensively about "disruptive innovation" and the difficulties large companies have in dealing with these. See *The Innovator's Dilemma*, 1997 and *The Innovator's Solution*, 2003 (with Michael Raynor), both from Harvard Business School Press.

17. From the U.S. Small Business Administration Report, "The State of Small Business: A Report of the President" (Washington, DC: U.S. Government Printing Office, 1995), p. 114.

18. In 2000, Korea's LG Electronics, Inc., launched an Internet-enabled refrigerator, followed by an Internet-ready washing machine in what it expects will eventually be a family of Net-ready home appliances. The Internet LG Turbo Drum washing machine can connect to the Internet to download new programs to match new fabrics. In addition, according to Merloni, another appliance maker, "in the case of [our] washing machines, smart RFID tags on clothes will enable the appliances to select the washing program appropriate to the items in the load. If any incompatible fabrics end up in the drum, such as whites with colored items being washed for the first time, the display will tell the consumer which items to take out."

19. Learn more about how SmartPak started and grew at www.smartpakequine.com and the analogous human services at http://www.cardinal.com/pharmacies/hospital/index.asp.

20. You can experience first-hand how Ted Graef and Scott Johnson redirected their business after their first idea failed by visiting their original Web site at www.intuitivecontrols.com and then follow the link to www.alltrafficsolutions.com.

21. See Jack M. Kaplan, *Getting Started in Entrepreneurship*, 2nd ed. (New York: John Wiley & Sons, 2001), pp. 20–23.

22. See R. McGrath and I. Macmillan, *The Entrepreneurial Mindset* (Boston, MA: Harvard Business School Press, 2000), pp. 17–18.

23. See James Jiambalvo, *Managerial Accounting* (New York: John Wiley & Sons, 2001), p. 9.

24. Ibid., p. 23.

25. See Jack M. Kaplan, *Smart Cards: The Global Information Passport* (Boston, MA: International Thomson Computer Press, 1996), pp. 15–17.

26. See W. B. Walstad, *Entrepreneurship and Small Business in the United States: A Gallup Survey Report* (Princeton, NJ: National Center for Research

in Economic Education and the Gallup Organization, 1994).

27. See R. M. Kanter, "Supporting Innovation and Venture Development in Established Companies," *Journal of Business Venturing 1* (1985): 47–60.

28. See H. A. Simon, "What We Know about the Creative Process," in R. L. Kuhn (ed.), *Frontiers in Creative and Innovative Management* (Cambridge, MA: Ballinger Publishing, 1999), pp. 3–22.

29. See Jeffry A. Timmons, *New Venture Creation* (Boston, MA: Irwin McGraw Hill, 1999), pp. 119–121.

30. See H. Stevenson and D. Gumpert, "The Heart of Entrepreneurship," *Harvard Business Review* (March–April 1985).

31. Sample of Non-Disclosure Agreement provided by the Richards and O'Neil law firm, New York, 2001.

32. William T. Bovie is the inventor of the monopolar device.

33. Interview with Michael Treat, M.D., College of Physicians and Surgeons, Columbia University, May 2002.

34. *Standard & Poor*'s expects 2002 revenue growth to reach 8 percent, which is down from the growth of 10 percent in 2001.

35. *Standard & Poor*'s survey conducted in 2001 on medical products and services for companies.

36. Interview with Michael Treat, M.D., College of Physicians and Surgeons, Columbia University, May 2002.

37. Interview with Michael J. Cleare, Executive Director for Columbia Innovative Enterprise, Columbia University, May 2002.

38. See the Columbia Innovative Enterprise Web site at http://www.stv.columbia.edu, Columbia University Business School, New York, NY, February 2002.

39. Interview with Michael Treat, M.D., College of Physicians and Surgeons, Columbia University, June 2002.

Chapter 3: Analyzing the Market, Customers, and Competition

1. For additional reading on marketing, see P. Kotler, *Marketing Management Analysis Planning Implementation and Control*, 8th ed. (Englewood Cliffs, NJ: Prentice Hall, 1994).

2. For more on this topic, see C. Christiansen, *The Innovator's Dilemma, When New Techniques Cause Great Firms to Fail* (Boston, MA: Harvard Business School Press, 1997). His main thesis is that attending to the needs of good current customers can systematically inhibit a business from understanding the needs of new customers.

3. See R. C. Bidettberg and J. Deighton, "Interactive Marketing: Exploiting the Age of Addressability," *Sloan Management Review* 33, no. 1 (1991): 5–14.

4. See L. Fuld, *Competitive Intelligence* (New York: John Wiley & Sons, 1993), pp. 9–10.

5. J. Crew issues gift cards with purchases of specified amounts for specific promotions. Interview with Scott Rosenberg, J. Crew, New York, February 2002.

6. See Leo Jakobson, "Growing Pains," *Alley Cat News* (New York, May 2001): 76–78.

7. See B. Tedeschi, "Spy on Your Customers (They Want You to)," *Smart Business* (August 2001): 58–66.

8. See K. Coyne, "Sustainable Competitive Advantage: What It Is, What It Isn't," *Business Horizons* (January–February 2002): 27–34.

9. See P. Kottler, *Marketing Management,* 10th ed. (Upper Saddle River, NJ: Prentice Hall 2000). Kottler indicates that the firm should consider six factors in setting policies: (1) selecting the pricing objective; (2) determining demand; (3) estimating costs; (4) analyzing competitor's cost, prices, and offers; (5) selecting a pricing method; and (6) selecting the final price.

10. Ibid.

11. See P. Courtney and R. Mac Davis, *The Entrepreneur's Fast Track II Handbook* (Denver, Co: Entrepreneurial Education Foundation, 1997), pp. 109–112.

12. See Jack M. Kaplan, *Smart Cards: The Global Information Passport* (Boston, MA: International Thomson Computer Press, 1996), pp. 40–41.

Chapter 4: Setting Up the Company Objectives

1. See Amar V. Bhide, "The Questions Every Entrepreneur Must Answer," *Harvard Business School Review* (November 1, 1996): 8–9.

2. Interview with Roy Wetterstrom, Micro Model-ing/Plural Company, March 1999.

3. Interview with Robert Katz, Esq., Cooper & Dunham LLP, New York, May 15, 2002.

4. Sole proprietorships are very common for single owners and home businesses. See interview with Ann Chamberlain of Richards and O'Neil LLC law firm, New York, March 10, 2001.

5. For most companies that require financing, David Cohen, CPA, at J. M. Levy suggests a C Corporation.

6. "To increase business within a state, entrepreneurs should file for a Certificate of Incorporation in the state where they conduct business. The state of Delaware has attractive advantages for companies and should be investigated." Interview with Alan Brody, Esq., Buchanan Ingersoll Inc., Princeton, NJ, February 2001.

7. See S. Zellcke and K. Pick, "Unbalanced Boards," *Harvard Business Review* (February 2001): 1–2.

8. See Dwight B. Crane and Indra Reinberg, "Employee Stock Ownership Plans (ESOPs) and Phantom Stock Plans," *Harvard Business School* (November 8, 2000), pp. 5–6.

9. See Gordon B. Baty, *Entrepreneurship for the Nineties* (Englewood Cliffs, NJ: Prentice Hall, 1990), p. 219.

10. See Brian Hall, Carleen Madigan, and Norm Wassman, "Stock Options at Virtuanet.Com Case Study," Harvard Business School, 2000. This paper describes issues facing founders of a high-tech firm in negotiating equity and stock options.

11. Interview with David Cohen, CPA, J. M. Levy and Company, New York, June 2002.

12. Interview with Robert Katz, Esq., Cooper & Dunham LLP, New York, May 15, 2005.

13. Interview with Kurt Hoffman, consultant for Financial Services, Princeton, NJ, July 2004.

14. Ibid.

15. Interview with Ralph Subbiondo, partner, Ernst & Young LLP, New York, May 2002.

16. Ibid.

17. Interview with Kurt Hoffman, consultant for Financial Services, Princeton, NJ, August 2004.

18. Interview with David Cohen, CPA, J. M. Levy and Company, New York, June 2003.

19. See John L. Nesheim, *High Tech Start Up* (New York: The Free Press, 2000), pp. 59–60.

20. Ibid.

Chapter 5: Financing the Closely Held Company

1. Materials for this section were obtained from www.dyson.com together with a number of articles on James Dyson appearing in the popular press.

2. For a full review of bootstrapping techniques, see "Bootstrap Finance," by Dr. Lynn Neeley at *Coleman White Papers on Entrepreneurship*, http://www.colemanchairs.org/whitepaper.asp, December 2001.

3. See www.VentureEconomics.com for a wide range of information on global private data and trends. In addition, the site's daily news and statistics offer a snapshot of the U.S., European, and Asian private equity markets.

4. Interview with Liz Elting, President and CEO of Transperfect Translations, Inc., July 2002.

5. See Ellen Paris, "David vs. Goliath," *Entrepreneur Magazine*, November 1999.

6. "Microsoft loses Patent Suit," Associated Press Announcement, February 23, 1994.

7. "A Windshield Wiper Inventor Settles Suit against Ford," *New York Times*, November 15, 1990.

8. See Eric Rosenfeld, *Credit, Where Credit Is Due: Using Plastic to Finance.* [on-line cited, August 1, 1999]. Available at http://entreworld.org.

9. Interview with Rick Smith, an entrepreneur who received funding from his family when he started Smith and Solomon Training School, April 2002.

10. Interview with Mary Gelormino, Fleet Bank, New York, June 2002.

11. Interview with Lisa Abrams, entrepreneur, New York, 2001.

12. Interview with Mary Gelormino, Fleet Bank, New York, June 2002.

13. Small Business Administration, *Results on Small Business Borrowing Loans Study*, Washington, DC, 2001. The Small Business Administration's mission is to aid, counsel, and protect the small business community. There is a wealth of information at the agency's Web site, www.sba.gov.

14. Interview with Mary Gelormino, Fleet Bank, New York, June 2002.

15. Ibid.

16. Ibid.

17. Ibid.

18. Ibid.

19. See Rick Stephan Hayes and John Cotton Howell, *How to Finance Your Small Business with Government Money: SBA Loans* (New York: John Wiley & Sons, 1980), pp. 37–38.

20. For detailed information about the SBIR and STTR programs, visit http://www.sba.gov/sbir/. You can also find a complete guide of all federal funding programs for small companies for all government agencies, including topics of interest, available funds, and direct contact names, in the Federal Technology Funding Guide published annually by the nonprofit LARTA organization. The report can be downloaded from www.LARTA.org.

21. See www.dodsbir.net/deskreference/04.fast.asp.

22. To locate your local SBA office, go to http://www.sba.gov/regions/states.html.

Chapter 6: Equity Financing for High Growth

1. The Kauffman Foundation has studied angel investing and angel networks in detail. An excellent report on angel networks can found at http://www.kauffman.org/pdf/angel_guidebook.pdf.

2. See Carl Simmons, "Every Business Needs an Angel," *Inc. Magazine*, Summer 2002, p. 2.

3. *Inc. Magazine* publishes a list of angel investors annually.

4. There are two excellent sources of data for the Venture Capital sector: Venture Economics to be found at www.ventureeconomics.com and the National Venture Capital Association, www.nvca.org, which reports on the annual Money Tree Survey with PriceWaterhouseCoopers (PWC).

5. See Stephen C. Blowers, *The Ernst and Young Guide to the IPO Value Journal* (New York: John Wiley & Sons, 1999), pp. 97–99.

6. See Linda A. Cyr, "A Note on Pre-money and Post-money Valuation," *Harvard Business Review* (April 17, 2001): 2–5. This article provides a brief introduction to calculations inherent in pre-money and

post-money evaluations at multiple stages of financing.

7. See Tom Copeland, Tim Koller, and Jack Murrin, *Valuation, Measuring and Managing the Value of Companies* (New York: John Wiley & Sons, 2000), p. 64.

8. Ibid.

9. Ibid.

10. Ibid.

11. See Shannon P. Pratt, Robert F. Reilly, and Robert P. Schweihs, *Valuing a Business: The Analysis and Appraisal of Closely Held Companies,* 3rd ed. (Homewood, IL: Irwin Press, 1996), pp. 45–47.

12. Ibid.

13. Interview with Parviz Tayebati, June 2005.

14. Foster-Miller is an example of an R&D contract development company that in the past has derived a major part of its revenues from SBIR funding. See www.foster-miller.com.

15. This list was derived from one used by Adams Capital Management, a VC firm based in Pittsburgh.

16. This generic term-sheet was derived from one used by Adams Capital Management.

Chapter 7: Discovering the Value in Intellectual Property: The Competitive Edge

1. The Xerox Corporation originally enjoyed patent protection on this technology.

2. Other forms or types of marks include logos (such as the distinctive blue letters used by IBM) and slogans (such as Nike's "Just Do It"). Examples and application filing for a trademark provided by Eric Hirsch, June 2001, New York.

3. See Stephen Elias and Kate McGrath, *Trademark: Legal Care for Your Business,* 4th ed. (Berkeley, CA: Nolo Press, 1999), p. 297.

4. See Alan Gordon, *Introduction to the Real World of Intellectual Properties* (Boston, MA: Fish and Richardson, 1997), p. 2.

5. The USPTO keeps two lists of all trademarks that are registered: the principal register and the supplemental register. The lists specify the owner of mark, the date the mark was registered, and the type of mark.

6. All states maintain trademark registers, but they are considered unimportant to trademarks.

7. Litigation can get expensive, running into tens of thousands of dollars in legal fees.

8. In the United States, the first business to use a trademark owns it.

9. To avoid conflict, search state and federal trademark registers and the Thomas Registry at http://www.thomasregister.com. Explanations of and examples for the copyright symbols were provided by Eric Hirsch.

10. Copyright protects the expression of ideas rather than ideas or methods in and of themselves.

11. Copyright generally provides a weaker form of protection than patent law.

12. Copyright law has been interpreted to protect a range of software that includes applications, programs, and video games. See Alan Gordon, principal, Fish & Richardson, P.C., *Introduction to the Real World of Intellectual Properties* (Boston, MA: Fish and Richardson, 1997), pp. 27–28.

13. Ibid., p. 28

14. See Gordon, *Introduction to the Real World of Intellectual Properties,* p. 2.

15. Design patents must consist primarily of drawings, along with formal paperwork and filing fee.

16. Sample nondisclosure agreements can be found in Chapter 2, "The Art of Innovation—Developing Ideas and Business Opportunities," of this book.

17. There is a misconception that one must use a patent attorney. The law contains no requirement that one must have a patent attorney file a patent application. The sample U.S. patent was provided by Eric S. Smith, inventor of the Emergency Operating System for Piloting an Aircraft in a Smoke Filled Cockpit, June 2002.

18. See Jack M. Kaplan, *Getting Started in Entrepreneurship* (New York: John Wiley & Sons, 2001), pp. 242–243.

19. You cannot patent any process that can be performed mentally. The rule also applies to abstract ideas.

20. Also, there is no need to disclose details of the invention to the public, as you do with a patent.

21. Robert Katz, Esq., partner, Cooper and Dunham, New York, prepared this intellectual property case for class discussion.

Chapter 8: Business Models and the Power of Information

1. See *Direct from Dell*, by Michael Dell and Catherine Fredman, Rebound Press, 2000 and www.1.us.dell.com for this quote, a discussion of the Dell Business Model and more insights into how Michael Dell started and grew Dell Inc.

2. For an interesting discussion on business models, visit www.KMLab.com/4Gwarfare/.html.

3. IBM uses this definition for conveying the concept of business model innovation to its executives.

4. See for example, H. Chesbrough and R. S. Rosenbloom, "The Role of the Business Model in Capturing Value from Innovation," *(Industrial and Corporate Culture Change*, 11, no. 3): 529–555.

5. Visit DBI's Web site www.dbi.com, to see how the DeAngelo brothers have expanded their mowing services into a multitude of markets.

6. General Fasteners is part of the MNP group of companies. More can be learned by visiting www.mnp.com.

7. For a detailed licensing "how-to," see Richard Stim, *License Your Invention* (Berkeley, CA: Nolo Press, 1998). This book comes with a useful disc of all the necessary documents and forms needed for licensing. Also, the Licensing Executive Society provides useful contacts and further information on licensing at www.usa-canada.les.org.

8. See www.intertrust.com for a detailed description of the company's business. This site also links directly to the U.S. Patent and Trademark Office to see the 37 patents owned by Intertrust in the field of digital rights management.

9. See www.Amberwave.com for more details and what actions the company is taking to protect its intellectual property.

10. See the International Franchise Association and Horwath International, *Franchising in the Economy of 1990* (Evans City, PA: IFA Publications, 1991), pp. 22–23. Also visit www.franchise.org for information on franchising and to review over 1000 franchise opportunities.

11. A number of useful articles on franchising have appeared in *Entrepreneur Magazine*, including discussions on the UFOC. For a list of the best articles, go to www.entrepreneur.com/Your_Business/YB_Node/0,4507,308218,00.html.

12. Based on an interview with George Homan in June 2004. You can learn more about the services Chemstation provides at www.chemstation.com.

13. Some of the ideas in this section were first seen in an article from *Tyme Management*^{TM}, 2000, entitled "Knowing when to Outsource," an Internet monthly newsletter from Rutherford Press found at http://www.rpublish.com/tyme_management.html.

14. Marcia Robinson and Ravi Kalakota, *Offshore Outsourcing* (Alpharetta, GA: Mivar Press, 2004).

15. Visit www.Schoolwires.com to see how an ASP operates.

16. See *The Agile Enterprise*, Ed. Pal and Panteleo, Springer Press, 2005, p. 118.

Chapter 9: Managing the Money

1. See R. Breasley and S. Myers, *Principles of Corporate Finance* (New York: McGraw-Hill, 1996), pp. 224–250.

2. See investopedia.com for details on terms.

3. For an easier way to use financial analysis and a CD for exercises on ratios, see Clifford Schorer, "Grow," *Unpublished Work* (New York, 2001), pp. 20–21.

4. Ibid., p. 41.

5. For a more complete explanation, see Donald E. Vaughn, *Financial Planning for the Entrepreneur* (Upper Saddle River, NJ: Prentice Hall, 1997), pp. 12–15.

6. See Stephen C. Blowers, Peter H. Griffith, and Thomas L. Milan, *The Ernst & Young Guide to the IPO Value Journey,* (New York: John Wiley & Sons, 1999), pp. 97–99.

7. See Robert C. Higgins, *Analysis for Financial Management,* 3rd ed. (Burr Ridge, IL: Irwin Press, 1992), p. 346.

8. The original source for the financial documents of U.S. public corporations is the Securities and Exchange Commission's electronic data gathering, analysis, and retrieval system, also known as EDGAR, located on the Web at edgar.sec.gov. Other sites that have licensed EDGAR data include FreeEDGAR (www.freeedgar.com), EDGAR Online (www.edgar-online.com), and 10K Wizard (www.10kwizard.com).

9. For more detailed analysis, see Stephen C. Blowers, Peter H. Griffith, and Thomas L. Milan, *The Ernst & Young Guide to the IPO Value Journey* (New York: John Wiley & Sons, 1999), pp. 132–133.

10. Interview with David Cohen, CPA, J. M. Levy & Company, New York, June 2001.

Chapter 10: Scaling and Harvesting the Venture

1. Interview with David Carrithers, consultant and author of articles on employee culture and performance. He can be found at www.businesshive.com.

2. See N. Chaddha, "Established 80 Alliances," *Forbes,* May 21, 2001, p. 76.

3. See M. Roberts, "The Do's and Dont's of Strategic Alliances," *Journal of Business Strategy* (March–April 1992): 50–53.

4. Interview with David Carrithers.

5. Interview with Laurence Charney, partner, Ernst & Young, New York, May 2001.

6. Ibid.

7. Interview with Michael Bucheit, partner, Advanced Infrastructures Ventures, New York, June 2002.

8. See S. C. Blowers, *The Ernst & Young Guide to the IPO Value Journey* (New York: John Wiley & Sons, 1999), pp. 97–99.

9. See Jack M. Kaplan, *Getting Started in Entrepreneurship,* 2nd ed. (New York: John Wiley & Sons, 2001), p. 173.

10. Ibid.

11. Interview with Alan Trefler, founder of Pegasystems, New York, October 2000.

12. Blowers, The Ernst & Young guide, pp. 32–35.

13. Interview with Melissa Craig founder of General Telecom, April 2003.

14. Ibid., Kaplan, pp. 178–179.

15. See Ira A Greenstein, *Going Public Source Book* (New York: R. R. Donnelley Financial, 1999), pp. 5–7.

16. Interview with Laurence Charney, May 2001.

17. Ibid., Greenstein, pp. 5–7.

18. Ibid., Greenstein, p. 68.

19. Ibid., Kaplan, p. 180.

Chapter 11: Bringing It All Together—Writing the Winning Business Plan

1. See barbarak.com Web site for more details.

2. See Jack M. Kaplan, *Smart Cards: The Global Information Passport* (Boston, MA: International Thomson Computer Press, 1996), pp. 187–190.

3. See Eric Siegal, *The Ernst & Young Business Plan Guide* (New York: John Wiley & Sons, 1987), pp. 59–60.

4. See William A. Sahlman, "How to Write a Great Business Plan," *Harvard Business Review* (July 1, 1997): 2–5.

5. See Jack M. Kaplan, *Getting Started in Entrepreneurship* (New York: John Wiley & Sons, 2001), p. 95.

6. Ibid., p. 97.

7. Interview with Michael Bucheit, partner, Advanced Infrastructure Ventures, New York, May 2002.

8. See William A. Sahlman, "Some Thoughts on Business Plans," Harvard Business School, November 1996, pp. 3–5.

9. Interview with an angel investor, Eric Major, New York, June 2002.

10. Ibid.

Chapter 12: Communicating the Opportunity and Making a Presentation

1. For a short instructional guide on how to put an investors' presentation together, visit http://lucy.mrs.org/entrepreneur/instructions/. This demonstration is part of a "virtual business plan competition" hosted by the Materials Research Society.

2. *Pratt's Guide to Venture Capital Sources* by Stanley E. Pratt is published annually by Venture Economics in Wellesley, MA. For a list of libraries where you can find this complete guide, see www.worldcatlibraries.org.

3. From an interview with William A. Frezza, a partner in the Venture Capital firm, Adams Capital Management, www.acm.com in May 2004.

4. The authors thank a team of MBA students at Penn State for this example developed in the Opportunity Development Course in 2003.

5. We thank Ankit Patel, a member of an MBA class at Penn State in 2004, for his permission to use this material from a business plan competition based on concepts from Resco, Inc., in Kingston, Ontario.

ACCREDITED INVESTORS: Individual or institutional investors who meet the qualifying SEC criteria with respect to financial sophistication or financial assets.

ADVISORY BOARD: A group of individuals willing to serve in an advisory capacity in exchange for stock or other benefits.

ANGEL: A private investor who often has non-monetary motives for investing as well as the usual financial ones.

BOARD OF DIRECTORS: Individuals elected by stockholders of a corporation who are responsible to that group for overseeing the overall direction and policy of the firm.

BOARD VISITATION RIGHTS: The right to be present at board meetings as an observer but with no voting rights.

BOOK VALUE: The difference between the *tangible* assets of a company and its liabilities. For an early-stage company the book value is often negative. As the company grows and matures, the value may be many times the book value.

BOOTSTRAPPING: Accessing cash and noncash resources to build a company, avoiding the sale of stock.

BRAINSTORMING: A management technique used to foster ideas, solve problems, set goals, establish priorities, and determine who on the team will be responsible for following through with the various tasks needed to accomplish the goals and priorities established.

BREAKEVEN ANALYSIS: A means of determining the quantity that has to be sold at a given price so that revenues will equal cost.

BRIDGE FINANCING: Financing obtained by a company expecting to secure permanent financing (such as through an initial public offering) within a short time, such as two years.

BURN RATE: The cash needed on a month-to-month basis to sustain a company's operations (see **Runway**)

BUY–SELL AGREEMENTS: Contracts between associates that set the terms and conditions by which one or more of the associates can buy out one or more of the other associates.

BY-LAWS: Rules under which a corporation is governed. These rules can be amended as provided by state law and the by-laws. Rules and regulations under which a Board of Directors operates a corporation.

C-CORPORATION: The most common form of business ownership and the one preferred by investors. As a separate legal entity apart from its owners, it may engage in business, issue contracts, sue and be sued, and pay taxes directly.

CASH-OUT: (1) The time interval before a company no longer has any cash for operations, also known as **runway**; (2) investors are said to "cash-out" of a company at a **liquidity event.**

CHIEF FINANCIAL OFFICER (CFO): A member of a company's upper management who oversees all the financial aspects of the business.

CLOSING: (1) In accounting, when the books are summarized in financial statements for a specific time frame and no further entries are allowed for this period; (2) in real estate, when the buyer and seller (or their agents) meet to finalize the transaction. Sometimes called the settlement, this is the point at which the transfer of property and funds takes place. The term also applies generally to business transactions such as an investment, loan or company sales event.

COMFORT LETTER: A letter provided by a company's independent auditors detailing procedures performed at the request of the underwriters. The letter supplements the underwriter's due diligence review.

COMMERCIAL BANK: State or nationally chartered bank that accepts demand deposits, grants business loans, and provides a variety of other financial services. Typically used by the entrepreneur as an asset lender.

COMMON AND PREFERRED STOCK: Shares that represent the ownership interest in a corporation. Both common and preferred stock have ownership rights, but preferred stock normally has prior claim on dividends and assets (in the event of liquidation). Both common and preferred stockholders' claims are junior to claims of bondholders or other creditors of the company. Common stockholders assume the greater risk but have the voting power. They generally exercise the greater control but may gain the greater reward in the form of dividends and capital appreciation. The terms *common stock* and *capital stock* are often used interchangeably when the company has no preferred stock. Preferred stock may usually be converted into common stock upon a liquidity event.

CONVERTIBLE DEBENTURES: A form of investment whereby the investor loans the company funds carrying a "coupon" or interest, which usually accrues. Within a defined period, the investor may "convert" their loan and the accrued interest into stock at a pre-agreed price. This arrangement gives an investor greater flexibility in managing the investment.

COPYRIGHT: An exclusive right granted by the federal government to the processor to publish and sell literary, musical, or other artistic materials. A copyright is honored for 50 years after the death of the author.

COVENANTS: Restrictive terms in a loan or stock sale agreement that protect the lender or investor.

DEBT CAPITAL: Funds or assets acquired by borrowing.

DILUTION: The reduction of a stockholder's percentage of ownership in an enterprise, usually arising from selling more common stock to other parties, sometimes called "watering the stock." Investors may require "antidilution" protection so that their ownership position is protected in preference to the founders should certain milestones not be attained.

DISBURSEMENT: The act of paying out funds to satisfy a financial obligation.

D&O INSURANCE: An insurance policy that protects directors and officers of a company from lawsuits, particularly from shareholders. The cost of such insurance has escalated since the recent number of corporate fraud cases.

DUE DILIGENCE: The responsibility of those preparing and signing the registration statement to conduct an investigation in order to provide a reasonable basis for their belief that statements made in the registration statement are true and do not omit any material facts. Proper due diligence can help protect these parties from liability in the event they are sued for a faulty offering. The company, on the other hand, has strict liability for errors or omissions in the regulation statement. Due diligence is also undertaken by private investors and banks before reaching a final agreement on terms and releasing funds.

EARNINGS REPORT: A statement issued by a company reflecting its financial situation over a given period of time. This report lists revenue, expenses, and the net result.

EBITDA: The company's earnings before interest, taxes, depreciation, and amortization of long-term assets. It therefore reflects the inherent quality of the day-to-day operations of the firm.

ENTREPRENEUR: Derived from the French word "to undertake." Someone who is willing and eager to create a new venture in order to present a concept to the marketplace.

EQUITY: (1) Total assets minus total liabilities equals equity or net worth; (2) money invested in a company that is not intended to be repaid but represents an ownership interest.

ESCROW: Placing money in a special and separate account under the control of another party, usually a financial institution, to be held until the completion of conditions set forth in an agreement.

ESOP: Employees Stock Ownership Plan by which the employees can acquire ownership of a company over time. This transfer of ownership carries certain tax advantages and is one way in which founders and investors can create an exit strategy for themselves. This route is not favored by Venture Capitalists as the time frames are extended and the valuations usually low.

EXIT STRATEGY: (1) The way an entrepreneur gets his or her money out of the venture; (2) the vehicle for selling the enterprise; (3) what venture capitalists look for when funding new ventures—their way to realize the dollar profits from the investment. See **Liquidity Event.**

FACTOR: Financial institution that buys accounts receivables from a firm and bills customers directly, as opposed to a bank that only lends on accounts receivable.

FINANCIAL INSTITUTION: Any firm that deals with money and/or securities. Banks, savings and loans, insurance companies, hard-asset lenders, credit unions, stockbrokers, consumer financial companies and investment bankers, as well as a host of other highly specialized organizations are examples of the institutions that operate in the huge and highly complex world of finance.

FINANCIAL RATIOS: Measurements used to establish common standard figures that can be compared from year to year, company to company, or company to industry.

FINANCIAL STATEMENT: Periodic accounting reports of a company's activities, which usually include a balance sheet, an income statement, and a cash flow statement.

FINDER'S FEE: Commission paid to a person for furnishing to the payer a buyer or a property or for arranging an introduction that leads to a deal.

FORMS 10-K, 10-Q: The annual and quarterly report public companies file with the SEC. The reports are prepared by the independent accountants of the company.

FRANCHISE: A right conferred by a franchisor to a franchisee to operate a business using a defined brand, image, and stipulated business processes in exchange for a fee usually based on a percentage of sales.

GOING PUBLIC: The process by which a corporation offers its securities to the public.

GOODWILL: The difference between the market value of a firm and the market value of its net tangible assets.

HARVEST: Liquidating the accumulated assets and equity of a venture. Converting profitable investment into cash to realize a profit.

INCOME STATEMENT: A financial statement that shows the amount of income earned by a business over a specific accounting period. All costs (expenses) are subtracted from the gross revenues (sales) to determine net income, which outlines the profit-and-loss financial statement (P & L).

INCUBATOR: Accommodation for early-stage companies providing low rent and shared services.

INFORMATION RIGHTS: The rights of a lender or investor to receive certain defined information concerning the progress of the company on a periodic basis. This right is commonly sought by lenders who seek an early warning if the company is not meeting its projections.

INTRAPRENEUR: A term coined by Gifford Pinchot III to identify an "entrepreneur" working within the confines of a corporation while retaining some degree of independence. Often the term *corporate venturing* is used.

IPO: A privately held company that elects to sell a portion of its common shares of stock to the public. Also referred to as an initial public offering (IPO). Often used when a small company seeks outside equity financing for expansion.

INVESTMENT BANK: A company regulated by the Securities and Exchange Commission that acts as an agent for a company to sell stock to the public, private investors, or to another company. In the former case, they are said to act as an underwriter.

JOINT VENTURE: Usually refers to a short-lived partnership with each partner sharing in costs and rewards of the project; common in research, investment banking, and the health-care industry.

KEY-MAN INSURANCE: An insurance policy that protects investors or lenders from the death or disability of key employees upon which an early-stage company may depend.

LBO (LEVERAGED BUY OUT): A method by which a firm is purchased by a private investment company and a significant part of the financing is accomplished using debt. These transactions require that the company have a dependable and sufficient cash flow to service the debt. The LBO firm may install its own management team or retain the existing management structure.

LETTER OF INTENT: A preliminary nonbinding agreement between the company and the venture capital firm and/or investors specifying the terms of raising capital and the financial equity investment that will be contained in a formal agreement.

LICENSE: A right conferred on a licensee by a licensor to use intellectual property owned by the licensor under defined conditions in return for a license fee, usually in the form of a recurring royalty payment.

LIMITED LIABILITY CORPORATION (LLC): A separate legal entity like a corporation having "members" rather than stockholders. It is not subject to corporate tax and, therefore, tax liabilities or credits "flow through" to the members as in an **S-Corporation.**

LIMITED PARTNERSHIP: A form of partnership composed of both a general partner(s) and a limited partner(s); the limited partners have no control in the management of the company and are usually financially liable only to the extent of their investment in the partnership. The majority of VC firms are formed as a limited partnership.

LINE OF CREDIT: Short-term financing usually granted by a bank up to a predenominated limit; debtor borrows as needed up to the limit of credit without needing to renegotiate the loan.

LIQUIDATION: The requirement by order of a bankruptcy court, sometimes called compulsory liquidation, that a business dissolve operations and sell off or dispose of assets by converting assets into cash.

LIQUIDITY EVENT: An event that occurs when the stock of a private company has a market for sale usually either through an IPO or a sale to another company. The venture capitalists' objective is to reach a liquidity event when they can "cash out" their shares and receive a "return on investment."

M&A TRANSACTION: A merger or acquisition of one company with or by another. This term is commonly used to describe the liquidity event in which an entrepreneur's company is sold to another.

MARGIN: The amount the entrepreneur adds to a product's cost to obtain its selling price. This is also called markup.

MARKETING PLAN: A written formulation for achieving the marketing goals and strategies of the venture, usually on an annual basis. Business plans always contain a marketing plan section.

MBO (MANAGEMENT BUY-OUT): The purchase of a company by the management often financed by a private equity firm.

MEZZANINE FINANCING: Transitional money that helps entrepreneurial companies build to a level of growth that permits a public stock offering or a sale to another company providing an exit strategy for investors.

MULTIPLE: A firm's price-earnings ratio that is used for quick valuations of a firm. (For example, a firm that earns $5 million a year in an industry that generally values stock at 10 times earnings would be valued at $50,000,000.)

NET PRESENT VALUE (NPV): The current value of a future cash flow stream, discounted back at a defined discount or interest rate.

NEW VENTURE: A new business providing products/services to a particular market.

NONCOMPETE/NONDISCLOSURE AGREEMENT: Legal agreement(s) that stipulates that the signees must not disclose confidential information about the company and/or product. It also prevents the signee from joining or starting a similar venture.

OFFERING: The financial "package" presented by a new venture.

OPERATING BUDGET: A financial plan outlining how a company will use its resources over a specified period of time.

PARTNERSHIP: Business association of two or more people. There are two types of partnerships: the general and the limited partnership.

PATENT: Federal governmental grant to an inventor giving exclusive rights to an invention or process for 20 years from date of filing. A U.S. patent does not always grant rights in foreign countries.

POST-MONEY VALUATION: The valuation accorded a company after investment by venture capitalists or angels.

PRE-MONEY VALUATION: The value accorded a company prior to investment from venture capitalists or angels.

PRIVATE EQUITY: An umbrella term for investments that include venture capital and buyout funds. Sometimes used (especially in Europe) as a synonym for venture capital.

PRIVATE PLACEMENTS: A transaction involving the sale of stocks or bonds to wealthy individuals, pension funds, insurance companies, or other investors. It is done without a public offering or any oversight from the SEC.

PROPRIETARY: That which is owned, such as a patent, formula, brand name, or trademark associated with the product/service.

PROVISIONAL PATENT: A low-cost patent application filed with the USPTO, which establishes the date of an invention. This application is not published or reviewed by patent examiners and may be abandoned later, or it may be used as the basis of a full patent application.

PUBLIC OFFERING: The sale of a company's shares of stock to the public by the company or its major stockholders.

REGISTERED STOCK: Stock that has been registered with the SEC and thus can be sold publicly.

REGISTRATION RIGHTS: The right that a shareholder has to register her stock along with the founders at the time of an IPO.

RESTRICTED STOCK: Issued stock that cannot be traded until the restriction deadline has passed. Founders' stock is usually restricted for up to one year after a company has gone public as the new investors do not want to see the insiders selling too early and thereby devaluing the share price.

RETURN ON EQUITY (ROE): Measures the return on the owner's investment in the company and is perhaps the most important measure of a business's financial viability. The higher the ratio, the higher the rate of return on the owner's investment.

REVOLVERS: Another term for a bank line of credit, which enables companies to borrow and use funds as necessary, usually with a one- to two-year payback requirement.

RISK CAPITAL: Another term for equity investing, sometimes also referred to as investment capital or venture capital.

ROUNDS OF INVESTMENT: Investments made at different stages of a company's growth. These are referred to as "preseed" when the idea is embryonic, "seed" which is used to build a prototype before the company has any sales, and then a series of development rounds, entitled "A," "B," "C," and so on.

RUNWAY: The time until a company no longer has any cash on hand to continue its operations; also referred to as **cash-out**.

SALES PER EMPLOYEE: An important measure of your firm's overall productivity, its ability to manage the overhead associated with its workforce, and its long-term financial health. The higher the sales per employee, the more productive your employees.

SBA LOAN: A variety of loan programs that assist owners in obtaining financing (SBA does not provide direct loans to businesses). The most common source of SBA financing is the 7(a) loan guaranty, which is obtained through a lender and receives a guarantee of repayment from the SBA (the collateral holder).

S CORPORATION (SUB-CHAPTER S CORPORATION): A firm that has elected to be taxed as a partnership under the sub-chapters provision of the Internal Revenue Code.

SOLE PROPRIETORSHIP: A business firm owned by only one person and operated for his or her profit.

STAND-STILL AGREEMENT: An agreement between two parties that they will not enter into another agreement for a defined time. This allows parties to invest in due diligence processes without the concern that their efforts will be preempted.

STARTUP CAPITAL: Money needed to launch a new venture during the pre-startup and initial period of operation.

STARTUP STAGE: A stage of development a company may experience, characterized by a need for planning, people, and financial resources.

STATEMENT OF CASH FLOWS: A financial statement that reflects the increases and decreases in cash for a certain time period.

STOCK CERTIFICATE: A document issued to a stockholder by a corporation indicating the number of shares of stock owned by the stockholder.

STOCK DIVIDEND: A proportional distribution of securities to the company's stockholders.

STOCK OPTIONS: A right to buy a stated number of shares in a company at a defined price (the strike price) within a defined time period. Stock options are often used as part of the compensation for key persons in a company. The owner of the options can "exercise" them within the defined period and, if the stock price has appreciated, they will have a capital gain. If the share price has declined below the strike price, the options are "under water" and have little or no value.

STOCKHOLDER'S EQUITY: The portion of a business owned by the stockholders.

SYNDICATION: A means by which investors or bankers spread their risk by bringing in partners to share the transaction.

TOTAL AVAILABLE MARKET (TAM): The total annual sales that a company would derive if it were able to capture 100 percent of its targeted market.

TERM LOAN: A loan that must be fully paid back by an agreed date. If a lender does not meet the terms of the covenants of the loan, the lender may have the right to "call the loan" by shortening the term.

TERM SHEET: A summary of the principal conditions for a proposed investment by a venture capital firm or a lender.

TRADEMARK: A brand or part of a brand that is given legal protection because it is capable of exclusive appropriation.

VENTURE CAPITAL: Money from investment pools or firms that specialize in financing young companies' growth, usually in return for stock.

VENTURE CAPITALIST: An investor who provides early financing to new ventures—often technology based—with an innovative product and the prospect of rapid and profitable growth.

VESTING PERIOD: The time between the issuance of a benefit or right and the time it can be accessed. This often applies to stock options, which may not be exercised until the recipient has been with the company for a defined time.

WARRANT: An option to buy a certain amount of stock for a stipulated price that is transferable and can be traded.

WORKING CAPITAL: The amount of funds available to pay short-term expenses, such as unexpected or out-of-the-ordinary, one-time-only expenses. Working capital is determined by subtracting current liabilities from current assets.

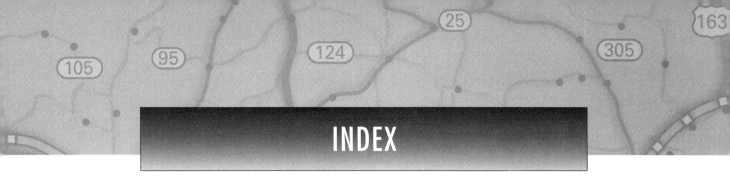

INDEX

A

B

Digital rights management (DRM), 267
Direct salesforce, 74
Discipline, 13
Disclosure document program (patents), 242
Discontinued operations footnotes, 292
Discounted cash flow valuation, 194–196
Discount rate, 195
Disraeli, Benjamin, 61
Disruptive innovation, 26–27
Distinguishing features of business, 42
Distribution channels:
    in business plan, 347
    in marketing analysis, 62
Diversification, IPOs and, 324
D-Marc Software, Inc., 115–124
    competition for, 121–122
    description and history of, 115–116
    E-Gift™ program, 119, 120
    electronic loyalty programs, 122
    products and services of, 117–119
    project life cycle at, 119
    success factors for, 120–121
Documentation of ideas, 241–242
Dog-and-pony show, 329
Dole, Robert, 57
Domain name, 107–108
DoubleClick, 37, 172–173
Dow Chemical, 200
Downes, Gile R., Jr., 47
DRM (digital rights management), 267
Due diligence, 178
    checklist for, 206–210
    in selling a business, 321
Dutter, Mike, 132
Dyson, James, 131–132, 135–136, 266
Dyson vacuum cleaners, 131–132

E

Early-stage financing, 8, 133–134, 184, 185
Earnings before interest expense, interest income, income taxes, depreciation, and amortization (EBITDA), 295
Earnings before interest or taxes, *see* EBIT
Earnings valuation, 191–193
eBay, 21, 263
EBIT (earnings before interest or taxes), 290, 294
EBITDA (earnings before interest expense, interest income, income taxes, depreciation, and amortization), 295
Economic impact of entrepreneurship, 3–4
EDGAR Online, 302
Edison, Thomas, 25–26, 235
Edison Venture Fund, 187
Egan, Michael, 182
E-Gift™ program, 119, 120
Ehrlich, Sanford B., 32
EIN (Employer Identification Number), 107

Elevator pitch, 381
Elting, Liz, 134, 313
Emerson, Ralph Waldo, 223
Employees:
    attracting/retaining, 109
    entrepreneurs vs., 9–10
Employee Stock Ownership Plan (ESOP), 109, 323
Employer Identification Number (EIN), 107
Employment agreements, 108
Empowerment (as cultural attribute), 275
End users, access to, 34
Engagement (as cultural attribute), 275
Entergy Arts Business Center, 166
Entrepreneurs:
    characteristics of, 13–14
    employees vs., 9–10
    serial, 10, 13
    types of, 10–11
The Entrepreneurial Mindset (Rita G. McGrath), 13, 36
Entrepreneurial process, 6–9
    acquiring funding, 8
    opportunity analysis, 6–7
    resource requirements determination, 8–9
    scaling and harvesting, 9
    setting up company, 7–8
Entrepreneurial Research Consortium, 10
Entrepreneur of the Year Institute, 10
Entrepreneurship:
    approaches to, 9–11
    defined, 4, 5
    economic impact of, 3–4
    motivations for, 11
    process of, *see* Entrepreneurial process
    reasons for, 9
    small business startups vs., 4
    subdisciplines of, 12
Equipment for company, 136
Equity financing, 130, 171–201
    angel investors, 181–183
    asset valuation, 193–194
    bridge financing, 178–180
    business valuation, 188–200
    classes of stock, 175–177
    discounted cash flow valuation, 194–196
    due diligence, 178
    earnings valuation, 191–193
    evaluating investment opportunities, 196–199
    initial public offerings, 172–173
    internal rate of return, 198–199
    net present value method, 196–198
    pre- and post-money valuation, 177–178
    preferences and covenants, 180–181
    private placements, 88
    private stock, 174
    for privately held companies, 174–175
    public stock, 173
    rounds of, 175